MATTHEW *and* EMPIRE

MATTHEW *and* EMPIRE

Initial Explorations

WARREN CARTER

TRINITY PRESS INTERNATIONAL

Trinity Press International, P.O. Box 1321, Harrisburg, PA 17105
Trinity Press International is a division of the Morehouse Group.

Cover art: People in town, street scene. Fresco from Pompeii. Museo Archeologico Nazionale, Naples, Italy. Erich Lessing/Art Resource, NY.

Cover design: Laurie Westhafer

Library of Congress Cataloging-in-Publication Data
Carter, Warren, 1955–
  Matthew and empire : initial explorations / Warren Carter.
      p. cm.
  Includes bibliographical references and index.
  ISBN 1-56338-342-X (alk. paper)
      1. Bible. N.T. Matthew – Criticism, interpretation, etc. 2. Rome in the Bible.
  I. Title.
  BS2575.6.R65 C37 2001
  226.2'06'7 – dc21
                                                              00–069091

Printed in the United States of America

01   02   03   04   05   06   10   9   8   7   6   5   4   3   2   1

Contents

Introduction

I N THIS STUDY I will explore the relationship between Matthew's Gospel and the Roman Empire. I will argue that Matthew's Gospel contests and resists the Roman Empire's claims to sovereignty over the world. It sustains an alternative community of disciples of Jesus in anticipation of the coming triumph of God's Empire over all things, including the destruction of Rome's empire.[1] That is to say, the Gospel resists Rome with a *social challenge* in offering a vastly different vision and experience of human community, and with a *theological challenge* in asserting that the world belongs to God not Rome, and that God's purposes run through Israel and Jesus, not Rome.

This approach to Matthew's Gospel is not the standard one,[2] and challenges the dominant paradigm or way of reading Matthew's Gospel. The conventional scholarly way of reading this Gospel over the last century has been in relation to a synagogue with which Matthew's community is having or has had a bitter dispute.[3] This work has provided much insight into the Gospel, and I do not intend to counter or dismiss the impact of this experience on interpreting the Gospel. While I do not think the conventional focus on synagogue relations is wrong, I do think it is too limited. It turns the Gospel into an exclusively religious work, concerned only with religious questions and personal matters.

Overlooked in this discussion, and almost completely absent from it, is the simple observation that the Gospel comes from and addresses a world dominated by the Roman Empire. It seems difficult to imagine that this world left no mark on the Gospel as most interpretations seem to suggest by their sheer inattention to this context. Moreover, in the Roman imperial world, religion was not an isolated personal matter. It was deeply interwoven with political claims, visions of social organization, economic structures, and ideological commitments. My goal is to explore the Gospel's interaction with this complex imperial world, and its critique of Rome's empire.

The book is divided into three parts. Part One comprises three chapters. Chapter 1 provides some description of aspects of the Roman imperial world. Chapter 2 outlines imperial theology that creates and legitimates the understanding of Rome as chosen by Jupiter and the gods to rule the world. Chapter 3 locates Matthew's Gospel in the city of Antioch-on-the-Orontes in the province of Syria in the 80s c.e., and describes something of the experience of Roman imperial power in the city.

Part Two comprises two chapters. Both chapters are thematic studies.

Chapter 4 explores Matthew's Christology in relation to Roman imperial theology. It argues that Matthew's presentation of Jesus challenges fundamental understandings about Rome and its emperors as agents of the gods' sovereignty, presence, will, and blessing. Chapter 5 examines Matthean soteriology or understanding of salvation. It argues that salvation comprises participation in the establishment of God's Empire over all things, including the destruction of Rome.

Part Three comprises four chapters. These chapters examine four passages in the Gospel, the evoking of Isa 7–9 in Matt 1:22–23 and 4:15–16, the call to take Jesus' "yoke" in Matt 11:28–30, the strange incident about the coin in the fish's mouth in Matt 17:24–27, and Jesus' appearance before the Roman governor Pilate in Matt 27:11–26. The four chapters develop the claim that the Gospel resists Roman imperialism and sustains an alternative community of disciples and their practices in anticipation of the coming triumph of God's Empire. These chapters provide examples of the sort of rereading that is necessary for the whole Gospel.

In the conclusion, I briefly explore some implications of this reading for contemporary faith communities.

The nine chapters engage significant topics in contemporary Matthean studies: Christology, soteriology, eschatology, continuity in salvation history (the place of Israel), the nature of discipleship/the Church, the function of the biblical or fulfillment citations, wisdom influence, the passion narrative, and, of course, the question of method. They also illustrate the Gospel's interaction with and critique of significant aspects of the Roman Empire: the domination structure of the imperial system, imperial theology, economic exploitation, military might, social hierarchy, dreadful urban and rural poverty and misery, illusions of power, taxation, provincial government and governors, justice.

In recent years I have been involved in an exciting process of rereading Matthew in relation to the Roman Empire. This book draws together some of that research as well as extends it. Several chapters utilize, in part, work previously published in scholarly journals, but none simply reproduces that earlier work. In an attempt to reach a wider audience, previous work has been significantly revised through abridgment and/or expansion. The earlier versions of material that constitute chapters 3, 4, 5 and 7 appeared as articles:

"Toward an Imperial-Critical Reading of Matthew's Gospel." *Society of Biblical Literature 1998 Seminar Papers: Part One*, 296–324. Society of Biblical Literature Seminar Papers 37. Atlanta: Scholars Press, 1998.

"Contested Claims: Roman Imperial Theology and Matthew's Gospel." *Biblical Theology Bulletin* 29 (1999): 56–67.

"Paying the Tax to Rome as Subversive Praxis: Matthew 17:24–27." *Journal for the Study of the New Testament* 76 (1999): 3–31.

"Evoking Isaiah: Matthean Soteriology and an Intertextual Reading of Isaiah 7–9 in Matthew 1:23 and 4:15–16." *Journal of Biblical Literature* 119 (2000): 503–20.

" 'To Save His People from Their Sins' (Matt 1:21): Rome's Empire and Matthew's Salvation as Sovereignty." *Society of Biblical Literature 2000 Seminar Papers,* 379–401. Society of Biblical Literature Seminar Papers 39. Atlanta: Scholars Press, 2000.

I am very grateful to the editor of *Biblical Theology Bulletin,* to the Society of Biblical Literature, and to Sheffield Academic Press Limited for permission to use the previously published material, albeit in significantly revised form. Chapters 6 and 8, along with the expanded forms of chapters 1 and 2 and the conclusion, comprise entirely new material.

I have also worked out this reading of Matthew in relation to the Roman Empire (as well as in relation to a synagogue) in a full-length commentary on the Gospel: *Matthew and the Margins: A Sociopolitical and Religious Reading.* The Bible and Liberation Series. Maryknoll, Orbis Books, 2000. The relationship between that book and this one is complementary. There I was able to develop the thesis across the whole Gospel, and as the references in the endnotes here indicate, it should be consulted for a fuller demonstration of the argument offered here. But while the commentary genre permits extensive engagement with a particular biblical book, publishing realities limit the depth of engagement with both the text and with the larger interpretive discussion. The different genre of this book allows me to engage the same thesis but in a different format. The thematic essays of Part 2 are simply not possible in a commentary. Nor are the sustained, in-depth examinations of the four passages in Part 3. While the positions taken in those chapters are essentially the same as in the relevant sections of *Matthew and the Margins,* I have been able to develop them in much more depth here, and in dialogue with other interpreters.

Overall the nine chapters form a coherent argument. Chapters 1 to 3 provide a contextual basis for the remaining six chapters. Those chapters, which assume chapters 1 to 3, can be read in any order. There is some overlap, of course, from chapter to chapter, even a little repetition. The repetition, consistent with Matthew's oft-noted predilection for redundancy,[4] may help communicate my argument.

SHOW ME A TEXT:
RECOGNIZING THE IMPACT OF CONTEXT

Responses to my previous efforts to explore Matthew's critique of the Roman Empire have been encouraging. One of the more frequent comments has been, "This makes a lot of sense, but show me a text. I need a text." My response has often been brief. "We are reading a story in which the main character is crucified, a distinctively Roman form of imperial control and execution used to remove troublesome members of the empire." But somehow that "text," the whole Gospel narrative, has not always satisfied some questioners. If pressed, I appeal to Herod in chapter 2, or Antipas in 14, or Vespasian's tax in 17, or Caesar in 22 or Pilate in 27 for some other obvious and immediate points of connection. Hopefully the studies presented here will provide further texts and indicate how pervasive is the Gospel's interaction with the Roman world.

But the question does raise an interesting point of method. My starting point for this anti-imperial reading is, in fact, that of historical context (to use conventional language) or, as I prefer, the audience's knowledge or experience that the Gospel text assumes. For quite some time now, I have been approaching Matthew through the eyes of the "authorial audience."[5] I understand the "authorial audience" to be the receptor or audience the author has "in mind" in writing the text. It is the author's image of the audience being addressed by the text, the image of the audience for whom the Gospel writer writes. This image approximates, though is not the same as, the actual audience.

In other terms, the "authorial audience" is a "contextualized implied reader" not so much present in the text as presupposed by the text. I reconstruct this audience partly from textual features (e.g., a Greek text attests they knew this language and at least someone could read it aloud) and from an examination of the interrelation between the text and the context in which the work was produced. This audience is understood to have the necessary linguistic competence and sociocultural knowledge to actualize the text (in diverse ways). In line with various "reader-response" or audience-oriented theorists,[6] I see this audience playing an active part in interpreting the text. I assume that it uses this knowledge, experience, and competence actively in making meaning of the text.

I have tried to identify some of this competence and knowledge in previous work. In sum it embraces at least

- knowledge of Greek,
- recognition of the Gospel's genre,
- knowledge about Jesus and of biblical traditions,
- a dispute within a synagogue community,
- the experience of belonging to a minority community,
- ability to interpret various narrative conventions.[7]

In this work I am adding to this list, and exploring, the role of the audience's experiences of Roman imperial power in the interpretive process. Throughout I will use various scholarly studies of aspects of the Roman world and quote from and refer to numerous writers in the ancient world. In doing so, I am not claiming that Matthew's audience has read these sources (a few of them weren't written by the end of the first century!). Rather I am claiming that they represent the sorts of ideas and mind-set that existed for centuries in various locations across the Empire and that were familiar to the Gospel's audience.

This "authorial audience" is of course my creation, constructed out of various historical, literary, and Gospel data. It is a historically and narratively informed interpretive strategy, but it overlaps a real audience. It is useful in that it identifies some specific factors and contexts that contribute to an interpretation. One could of course posit an audience from a very different time and place, and explore its interaction with the Gospel. Here I choose to utilize the authorial audience, an approximation of the Gospel's actual late-first-century audience. The use of the term "audience" rather than "reader" indicates that the Gospel was probably encountered in being read aloud.[8]

One of the main advantages of employing the strategy of the "authorial audience" is that it encourages interpreters to attend to and make explicit knowledge and experience assumed by the text but not made explicit in it. Matthew's Gospel does not seem to many contemporary readers to refer to the Roman Empire only because often we cannot supply the assumed imperial experience and knowledge. One of the purposes of this book is to make explicit some of the imperial realities that pervade this text. So, for example, the Gospel nowhere stops the action to explain that

- the term *basileia*, which is usually translated with the quaint English term "kingdom," commonly refers to empires like Rome's, just as the term *basileus*, usually translated "king," is used to denote emperors. To speak of, to pray for God's Empire (Matt 6:10) in the midst of Rome's empire is to indicate profound dissatisfaction with Rome's empire. To call Jesus "king" or "emperor" presents a challenge to the Roman emperor.

- religious leaders are not restricted to religious roles as in a modern understanding of the separation of "Church and state," but are members of, allies with, and representatives of the empire's ruling elite.

- the image of "yoke" is commonly one of imperial control, much more frequently than it is an image of wisdom or Torah.

- the image of "light" commonly denotes the emperor's presence.

- fish (along with animals and birds) are understood in imperial flattery to be subject to the emperor's sovereignty.

- disease results in part from the imperial economic (taxation) system that removes adequate nutrition and food supplies from much of the population.

There are lots of these examples that could be developed. But that's why nine chapters and a conclusion follow this introduction.

It remains for me to identify this book's authorial audience. I write for an eclectic readership that might comprise college and seminary students doing some work, either initial or advanced, in the Gospels, who will find here a distinctive and enlightening approach. I imagine also that pastors and interested lay people will find it accessible and hopefully useful in preaching and teaching. The contemporary Church's involvement in contemporary forms of empire is an issue that needs much discernment and appropriate action. I am also hopeful that scholars will engage the material and join the efforts to rethink Matthew in relation to the Roman imperial world. It is especially for this latter group that I have decided to retain fairly extensive endnotes to provide more technical discussion and to identify sources. Other readers can ignore these if they are of little interest, or use them to follow up specific points.

I especially wish to thank Dr. Bob Mowery for his insightful and careful reading of the manuscript, for keeping me honest across the years in numerous conversations as I have developed this approach, and for his gracious and collegial interaction. My student assistant, LeeAnn Ahern, has provided important and much-appreciated assistance. Henry Carrigan has been a skillful and patient editor.

– Part One –

THE ROMAN
IMPERIAL SYSTEM

– ONE –

Constructing the Roman
Imperial System

MATTHEW'S GOSPEL was written for an audience that probably lived in the city of Antioch in Syria, one of the provinces of the Roman Empire.[1] By the first century C.E., the time in which Matthew's Gospel is written, the term "Roman Empire" was understood to embrace two inter-related dimensions: (1) "the right of command within the Roman state," which was "affirmed by the gods" to a few representatives and officials of the people; and (2) a "concrete territorial sense" to denote the area or land, people and resources over which Rome extended control (Pliny the Elder,* *Nat.* 6.30.120; Tacitus,† *Germ.* 29.1; *Hist.* 1.16).[2] The two meanings are connected in that "the right of command" usually involved two spheres: legislation and jurisdiction, and warfare. Military action, or the threat of it, was "the context not only of the acquisition but also of the establishment of what became the Roman territorial empire."[3] This Roman imperialism, "the practice, the theory, and the attitudes of a dominating metropolitan center ruling a distant territory,"[4] constitutes the world from which the Gospel originates and in which its audience lives.

These two dimensions of the term "empire" point to several basic features of this Roman imperial world. The Roman imperial system was an "aristocratic empire."[5] That is, the "aristocracy," a very small group of perhaps 2 percent of the population, ruled vast areas of territory through a small bureaucracy in alliance with provincial elites. Basic to their exercise of power were their military resources. They did not rule by democratic consent but by the ability to enforce their will on most of the population. With control over the primary resource of land and its production, this group exercised great political control and acquired vast wealth for themselves through taxes, rents, and tributes. The economy of the Empire is, then, best

---

*Pliny the Elder: 23/24–79 C.E., killed by the Mt. Vesuvius eruption. Military and administrative career in various parts of the empire. Uncle of Pliny the Younger. Wrote the encyclopedic *Natural History* of thirty-one books dedicated to the emperor Titus. Includes wide-ranging knowledge about the universe, nature, agriculture, medicine, and the visual arts.

†Tacitus: Born 55 C.E.; date of death not known, but after 118. Notable Roman historian (see p. 14 below on *Annals* and *Histories*); orator; political career under emperors Vespasian, Titus, Domitian, and Trajan. Attacked Domitian for misrule in the biography of *Agricola*, governor of Britain and Tacitus's father-in-law. *Germania* describes German tribes and customs from a Roman perspective.

described as a "legionary economy." The threat of the military muscle of the legions ensured that most people complied with the payment of tribute and taxes. These economic measures, secured by military threat, dispossessed most of the population of any political or economic power, and coerced them into submissive cooperation.[6]

Plutarch,* a member of this ruling elite, writing a couple of decades after Matthew's Gospel, names three attributes necessary for a dominant role in this society. He observes deference to a person of "power or wealth or repute." People show respect not for "experience or virtue or age, but to wealth and repute" ("How to Tell a Flatterer," *Mor.* 58D; also 100D, 778A).

- Power derives from and is expressed through alliances, patronage, friendship, and kinship; through political debate and office; through control of land and peasants; and of course through military resources.

- Wealth is based in (often inherited) land ownership and production.

- Status or public repute derives from the recognition by others of one's dominant position expressed in various civic and patronal acts.

The empire's ruling elite values hierarchy, verticality, vast inequality, domination, exclusion, and coerced compliance.

When Matthew's Jesus says to his disciples, "You know that the rulers of the Gentiles lord it over them, and their great ones are tyrants over them," he is describing this system in which the elite values power, wealth, and status above all else. But Jesus also evaluates it and rejects it. "It will not be so among you." In its place he proposes an alternative: "but whoever wishes to be great among you must be your servant" (Matt 20:25–27). He calls the community of disciples to form an alternative society in which the quest for power and wealth as the goal of human existence and markers of a person's status is renounced. Instead, the only valued status is to be a marginal slave, an outsider, on the edge, at the bottom, one who lives to secure the well-being of others. He calls his followers to form a community that is antithetical to everything the Empire's ruling elite or aristocracy holds to be important.

Before elaborating Matthew's critique and alternative proposal in the subsequent chapters, it will be helpful to sketch the imperial structure a little further, even with rather broad brush strokes.

---

*Plutarch: 40s–120s C.E. Born in Greece. Widely traveled including to Rome. Philosopher; priest at Delphi. *Moralia* is a large collection of essays on various themes including religious topics. Often provides moral instruction with a "how to" approach ("Advice to a Bride and Groom"; "On Talkativeness"; "On Control of Anger"). Also wrote numerous biographies to illustrate virtues and vices.

THE RULING ELITE

At the top of the imperial structure, and at its center in Rome, was the emperor. He, and it was always a "he" in the first century, thereby ensuring that political power reinforced social gender inequality, exercised enormous power. Seneca* has the emperor Nero articulate the relationship he imagines he has with the gods and the nations (*Clem.* 1.2–3):[7]

> Have I of all mortals found favor with Heaven and been chosen to serve on earth as vicar of the gods? I am the arbiter of life and death for the nations; it rests in my power what each man's [*sic*] lot and state shall be: by my lips Fortune proclaims what gift she would bestow on each human being: from my utterance peoples and cities gather reasons for rejoicing; without my favor and grace no part of the whole world can prosper; all those many thousands of swords which my peace restrains will be drawn at my nod, what nation shall be utterly destroyed, which banished, which shall receive the gift of liberty, which have it taken from them, what kings shall become slave and whose head shall be crowned with royal honor, what cities shall rise and which shall fall—this is mine to decree.

The emperor shares the benefits and rewards of this power relationship with the small ruling elite. Those with inherited wealth, land, and social status, officials appointed by the emperor, bureaucrats, military leaders, and religious officials constitute this elite that comprises 1 to 2 percent of the population. In Rome the senate represents this group. In the provinces, provincial governors and their staffs, appointed either by the emperor or by the senate, exercised control through tours and assizes, administering justice, collecting taxes, and deploying troops.[8] They also formed alliances with local landowning elites, who exercised some political and economic power through city councils, as common beneficiaries of the empire's power structure.[9] Throughout the ruling class, influence and status were gained and exercised through networks of patron-client relationships, friendship, and kinship.[10]

Cooperation with the emperor leads to increased wealth, power, and status from his patronage, such as the granting of confiscated or conquered landed estates, or appointment to political office. Such prizes meant the governing class in Rome and the provinces also competed with the emperor and with one another for a maximum share of the taxes and services ren-

---

*Seneca: Born ca. 4 B.C.E. in Spain. Trained from early age in rhetoric and philosophy in Rome. Orator; very wealthy; prolific writer. Exiled by the emperor Claudius in 41. Returned to favor and Rome in 49 C.E. Tutor to Nero, and his political adviser and operative as emperor, though lost influence and increasingly withdrew from Nero's service after 60. Forced to commit suicide in 65 C.E. after being involved in Piso's conspiracy against Nero. "On Mercy" (Clem.), written to instruct the new emperor Nero in 55, is one of many moral and philosophical writings.

Roman Emperors from Augustus to Hadrian

Emperor	Dates of Reign	Some Christian History
Augustus	31 B.C.E.–14 C.E.	Birth of Jesus ca. 6–4 B.C.E.
Tiberius	14–37	Crucifixion of Jesus ca. 30 C.E.
Gaius Caligula	37–41	
Claudius	41–54	Paul's ministry 30s–50s
Nero	54–68	Jewish War 66–70
Galba, Otho, Vitellius	69 (civil war)	
Vespasian	69–79	Jerusalem and temple destroyed 70 C.E.
Titus	79–81	
Domitian	81–96	Writing of Matthew's Gospel ca. 80s
Nerva	96–98	
Trajan	98–117	
Hadrian	117–138	

dered by peasants and artisans. Claudius's attempts, for example, to ensure a regular grain supply for Rome provoke conflict with aristocratic groups.[11] Especially under Nero and Domitian, disputes over policies and the emperor's style of rule saw numerous members of the elite exiled or murdered if they were perceived to pose a threat to the emperor.[12] And emperors are not immune to danger. During the first century, at least four emperors are murdered: Gaius Caligula in 41, Claudius in 54, Vitellius in 69, Domitian in 96. A fifth, Nero, commits suicide in 68 after being declared a public enemy. An emperor controlled the military resources, though their maltreatment could and did mean a loss of allegiance. Troops also served as "an internal security agency throughout the empire," the *frumentarii,* charged with the emperor's security, and engaged in spying and gathering intelligence on any potential rebellion.[13] The struggle within the elite to gain, secure, or increase power is very understandable given that control of the state's organization was "the supreme prize" in ensuring "fabulous wealth and immense power...privilege, and prestige."[14]

How, then, does the elite maintain control and secure wealth? Essentially, two activities provide the basis for this "legionary economy": the powers to tax and to carry out war.[15] Both activities were sources of power, wealth, and status. Both activities were sanctioned by political offices and laws. That is, political institutions were a primary source of, and a means of protecting, political, economic, and social inequality and privilege.[16]

Military Might

Agrarian empires are, typically, conquest states whereby a group or area of land is forcibly subjugated. "Force is the foundation of political sovereignty."[17] The Roman army played a key role in coercing and maintaining submission. In addition to superior training, tactics, and weapons, the army's reputation functioned to intimidate and repress would-be opponents. Jose-phus* illustrates the impact of the "deterrent power" that derived from Rome's success and reputation. He explains that because the Gauls are "overawed at once by the power of Rome and by her fortune...they sub-mit to the orders of twelve hundred soldiers, they who have cities enough almost to outmatch that number" (*J.W.* 2.372–73).[18] Josephus justifies his own lengthy description of Roman military power by saying, "If I have dwelt at some length on this topic, my intention was...to deter others who may be tempted to revolt" (*J.W.* 3.108; cf. 3.70–107).

The army's reputation is sustained by values such as Rome's image of power and ruthless resolve, honor, security, revenge, fear, and deterrence by terror.[19] This commitment to be seen as invincible, as well as scorn for other peoples, is evident in the speech that Josephus has Titus, the emperor Ves-pasian's son and himself a future emperor (79–81 c.e.), give in addressing his cavalry before attacking the city of Tarichaea in Galilee.

> Romans—it is well at the outset of my address to remind you of the name of your race, that you may bear in mind who you are and whom we have to fight. Our hands to this hour no nation in the habitable world has succeeded in escaping.... [Y]ou will contend for a higher cause than the Jews; for, though they face war for liberty and country in jeopardy, what higher motive could there be for us than glory and the determination, after having dominated the world, not to let the Jews be regarded as a match for ourselves? (*J.W.* 3.472–73, 480).

Taxation

In addition to military might, "to rule in aristocratic empires is, above all, to tax."[20] The ruling elite acquired vast wealth by a "proprietary theory of the state" that sees the state as something to be used not for the maximal common good but for one's personal benefit and, in turn, for the good of one's heirs. Ownership of land provides wealth and status for landowners, as well as significant power over people's lives. Control of the land, those who work it, and its production is enacted not only through conquest, booty, seizure and confiscation, but also through local and imperial taxes, trib-utes, rents, and services.[21] The threat of military punishment and further loss of land and production by increased tribute and taxes coerces compli-ance, while laws and political offices and officials normalize the extractions. Taxes force peasants, who normally seek to supply only their own needs, to produce a "surplus" that the elite removes by means of taxes.

---

*Josephus: Born 37/38 c.e. Jewish priest and aristocrat. Led Jewish rebels in Galilee against Rome in the 66–70 c.e. war. Captured by Vespasian. Prophesied Vespasian would become emperor. Witnesses the fall of Jerusalem in 70 c.e. Wrote *Jewish War* on the 66–70 war with Rome. *Antiquities of the Jews* is a history of the Jewish people. He defends Jews against anti-semitic writings (*Against Apion*) and writes an autobiography (*Life*).

The nonpayment of taxes would mean the collapse of the lifestyle of the elite, both local and Roman. Nero hears of difficulties in collecting taxes and considers

> whether he ought not to decree the abolition of all indirect taxation and present the reform as the noblest of gifts to the human race. His impulse, however, after much preliminary praise of his magnanimity, was checked by his older advisers, who pointed out that the dissolution of the empire was certain if the revenues on which the state subsisted were to be curtailed (Tacitus, *Ann.* 13.50).

The immense economic power of the Roman elite and its devastating impact on the lives of most of population is reflected in Nero's actions to finance the expensive and extensive rebuilding of Rome after the fire of 64 C.E. Tacitus* comments: "Meanwhile Italy had been laid waste for contributions of money: the provinces, the federate communities, and the so-called free states, were ruined" (Tacitus, *Ann.* 15.45).

To ensure the elite's way of life, Roman conquest meant an infrastructure that would accomplish this systematic exploitation of the provinces. Aristides† notes Rome's achievement:

> You have measured out the whole earth, spanned rivers with bridges of different kinds, pierced through mountains to lay roads, established post stations in uninhabited areas and everywhere else introduced a cultivated and ordered way of life (*Roman Oration* 101).

By draining swamps, terracing mountains, irrigating waste lands, and clearing forests, Roman soldiers or local landowners, often using forced or slave labor, enhanced the productivity and profitability of their land. Bridges and roads served not only military purposes and raised income from tolls, but they also provided the very means whereby goods were moved from the provinces to Rome. Aristides, oblivious to the human cost, notes that the provinces supply Rome's aristocracy

> abundantly with whatever is in them. Produce is brought from every land and every sea, depending on what the season brings forth, and what is produced by all lands, rivers and lakes.... For what grows and is produced among individual peoples is necessarily always here, and here in

---

*Tacitus: Roman historian (see p. 9); wrote two big historical works. *Histories* dealt with the period from Nero's death (68 C.E.) to Domitian's death (96). Four and one-half of the twelve or fourteen books survive, covering the civil war and start of Vespasian's reign (68–70). *Annals* covered Augustus's death (14 C.E.) to Nero's death (68). Some of this is also lost. Discussion of years 14–29, 32–37, 47–66 survives.

†Aristides: Born in 117 C.E. in Asia Minor. Died 180s. Teacher of rhetoric; orator; prolific writer. Delivered *Roman Oration* in Rome in 144 C.E. Expresses the fawning and uncritical admiration of an elite provincial for Roman rule.

abundance (*Roman Oration* 11; cf. Pliny the Younger* *Pan.* 29; Tacitus, *Ann.* 3.53–54). All roads and cargo ships truly do lead to Rome.[22]

Several provincials offer some rare critique of Roman greed and exploitative power. In a saying attributed to Rabbi Simon (b. Shabbat 33b), the self-serving agenda of such developments is noted: "All that they have made, they made for themselves, they built market places, to set harlots in them; baths, to rejuvenate themselves, bridges, to levy tolls for them."

Calgacus, the British chief, agrees. Tacitus ascribes a speech to him in which Calgacus describes the Romans as

> robbers of the world... to plunder, butcher, steal, these things they misname empire; they make a desolation and they call it peace... our goods and chattels go for tribute; our lands and harvests in requisitions of grain; life and limb themselves are worn out in making roads through marsh and forest to the accompaniment of gibes and blows" (Tacitus *Agr.* 31.1–2).[23]

Taxes and tribute paid for "peace," "security," and "freedom" as the benefits of Roman sovereignty were euphemistically called.[24] Tacitus has the Roman general Cerialis inform the Treviri and Longones in Trier after suppressing their revolt:

> Although often provoked by you, the only use we have made of our rights as victors has been to impose on you the necessary costs of maintaining peace; you cannot secure tranquillity among nations without armies, nor maintain armies without pay, nor provide pay without taxes (*Hist.* 4.73–74; Cicero, *Quint. fratr.* 1.1.34).

According to the speech that Josephus attributes to King Agrippa, the Gauls provide Jews with an example of a people who "are yet content to be treated as a source of revenue to the Romans..." (*J.W.* 2.372).

Rome regarded the failure to pay tax and tribute as rebellion against Rome's sovereignty.[25] Discontent with tributes is a factor in several revolts. Gaul's rebellion against "continuous tributes, the grinding rates of interest, the cruelty and pride of the governors" is put down with military force (Tacitus, *Ann.* 3.40–41). The Frisians refuse a tribute of ox hides and then defeat the troops sent to punish and subdue them (Tacitus, *Ann.* 4.72–73). The Roman governor Vitellius sends troops from Syria to compel the Cietae's payment of tribute (Tacitus, *Ann.* 6.41). Josephus has Agrippa declare to the Jewish people in revolt against Florus in 66 C.E. that their nonpayment of

---

*__*Pliny the Younger:__ 61/62 C.E.–ca. 112. Distinguished career as orator, lawyer, imperial official including governor of Bithynia in 100–12 C.E. Nephew of Pliny the Elder (see page 9). Published books of letters that include those he sent to and received from the emperor Trajan while Pliny was governor. His work *Panegyricus* praises the emperor Trajan as Jupiter's agent, and denigrates Domitian.*

tribute is an "act of war." Paying the tribute would clear them of the "charge of insurrection" (*J.W.* 2.403–4).

Also imposed on the conquered as a means of effecting and maintaining control were "laws and Roman jurisdiction" (Tacitus, *Ann.* 15.6). Sales of favor (bribes), whether for beneficent action, legal decisions, or appointments to desirable positions, provided further income for the elite. Garnsey notes that the Roman legal system privileged the elite and worked against provincials and those of lower status.[26]

Elite Values and Social Display

The ruling class exercised its power through several interrelated roles "as warriors, as rulers, as administrators, as judges, and as priests." Certain values or ideology create, sustain, and interpret these elite roles.[27] Service and duty, maintaining one's honor, and acquiring glory are fundamental elite values that justify their exercise of power. Warfare provides an obvious arena in which to express those values,[28] but so also does the exercise of rule through taxation and acts of patronage and through civic beneficence such as financing a statue or fountain, or some form of entertainment, or a food handout.[29] Elite persons gain prestige and honor from being seen to do their civic duty in publicly beneficial acts.

Contempt for productive or manual labor is another elite value. The absence of such work separates the elite from peasants, and to a lesser degree from more prosperous merchants.[30] This contempt is expressed in and reinforced by collecting taxes as a primary source of wealth. Taxation secures and fosters another value. Wealth is not for investing or accumulating, since there is always a continual supply through the elite's exploitation of peasants. Wealth is for conspicuous consumption and display through buildings, clothing, jewelry, military acts, food, celebrations, entertainment, clients and servants, beneficent civic gestures. Such display maintains the distance between the aristocracy and peasants, and reminds the peasants of who they are and who they are not. For the ruling class, cities were commonly centers for the conspicuous display and consumption of wealth.[31]

This ability to subject and exploit creates and reinforces, in part, another value, the sense of the aristocracy's superiority.[32] This superiority can be asserted with claims of superior character, as well as in terms of a superior race. Titus appeals to Roman superiority as a race when prior to the attack on Jerusalem he essentially employs Cicero's century-old argument that Jews and Syrians were "born to be slaves" (*Prov. cons.* 10) to urge his troops to victory over "inferior" Jews who have "learned to be slaves" (Josephus, *J.W.* 6.37–42). Similar claims of racial superiority are evident in the passage cited above on p. 13 as Titus urges his cavalry to victory in Galilee (Josephus, *J.W.* 3.472–73, 480).

RETAINERS

The governing class creates a retainer class to assist it in governing. This group, perhaps 5 percent of the population, comprises "officials, professional soldiers, household servants, and personal retainers, all of whom served them in a variety of more or less specialized capacities."[33] Like the ruling class, retainers are usually based in cities. Retainers are the agents of the aristocracy, personalizing and representing its power among the lower orders, performing its wishes, enacting its decisions, and maintaining its hold over land and people. Their association with and deference to the aristocracy elevates them above most of the common folks, and enables them to share in the benefits of its rule, notably significant power, status, and wealth. Slaves in the imperial household, for example, could exercise great political power in determining access to the emperor. Helicon, the slave of the emperor Gaius Caligula and a source of great frustration to Philo* and his delegation from Alexandria, is one such example (Philo, *Legat.* 166–78).

Upper-level priests and religious leaders are retainers.[34] When Matthew's Gospel refers to the alliance of chief priests, Sadducees, leading Pharisees, and scribes, with whom Jesus is in conflict, it refers to Jewish officials who exercise religious roles yet are part of the ruling aristocracy in this retainer class with immense social and economic power. Josephus presents the chief priests as essentially the nation's leaders (*Ant.* 20.251). Often allied with "the most notable Pharisees," they are consistently pro-Roman in the events leading up to the 66 C.E. war (*J.W.* 2.320; 411).

THE REST: PEASANTS AND ARTISANS

The verticality and inequality of the empire is reflected in the large gap between the ruling class and the peasants and urban artisans. This group produces, rather than benefits from, the elite's wealth. Some merchants, those who gained enough commerce to elevate them above most of the population but not enough to join the aristocracy, occupy some middle ground. Merchants compete with the land-based aristocracy for control of the economic production, though taxation on commerce ensures further wealth for the elite and restraint on that gained by merchants.[35]

Peasants and artisans comprise most of the population. Given their illiteracy, they have left few records. They do not loom large in the materials written by the elite with their perspective "from above" and profound

---

*Philo: ca. 20/15 B.C.E.–ca. 50 C.E. Jewish philosopher; interpreter of biblical writings, especially the Pentateuch; leader of Jewish community in Alexandria. Two writings, (*Legatio ad Gaium; In Flaccum*) concern the delegation of Jewish leaders that he led to Rome to protest to the emperor Gaius Caligula against persecution of Jews in Alexandria by the governor Flaccus.

inattention to the quite different realities experienced by most "from below."[36]

Peasant and artisan labor produce the goods and services, rendered in taxes and rents (often paid in kind), that sustain the wealth and lifestyle of the ruling elite. Between 30 and 70 percent of their production was claimed through various taxes.[37] Forced labor or *corvée,* along with slaves, provide the elite with a ready supply of cheap labor for major building projects or schemes to improve the productivity and profitability of land. Accordingly "the great majority of peasants who lived in the various agrarian societies of the past apparently lived at, or close to, the subsistence level."[38] Akin to peasants, the smaller class of artisans, including dispossessed peasants and former slaves, sometimes linked to merchants and predominantly associated with urban contexts, employed varying degree of skills to produce goods and services predominantly for the elite.[39] Slaves existed at multiple levels and in numerous household and manual tasks.[40]

Peasant Resistance?

Given that resistance usually accompanies the assertion of power,[41] we might expect that peasants and artisans took some steps to resist their exploitation. Scholars, however, offer differing evaluations. Kautsky thinks there was little conflict.[42] While he recognizes some nonviolent actions on the part of peasants to defend their minimal livelihood, he does not think there was interclass struggle. The realities of peasant existence indicate few options or opportunities for resistance. To stop working is to starve. Peasants are peaceable by disposition, fear reprisal, know their place, are physically isolated from extensive networks, and lack organization, strategy, and leadership. Kautsky also argues that they lack imagination. Peasants cannot imagine a rebellion, different social structures, or themselves as agents of change. They are, to use one sociologist's concept, "organizationally outflanked" by the elite.[43]

Others, though, argue that while this view helpfully names some basic realities, the situation is a little more complicated. Lenski argues that peasants experienced a fundamental ambivalency. They were aware of the gap separating them from their social superiors, yet as survivors they sought to protect and maximize their own gains. Conflicts were inevitable as peasants tried to protect their livelihood by evading the various demands of taxes and services. Mostly these evasionary tactics were nonviolent: hiding produce or lying about production levels to tax collectors, working slowly, pilfering, sabotage. But at times, led by significant figures, violence, in the form of riots or attacks by Robin Hood-like bandit groups on aristocratic property and personnel, occurred.[44]

Scott also counters Kautsky's view. He warns against misinterpreting peasant passivity as a failure of imagination, or construing it as compliance. The lack of conflict does not mean lack of resistance. The apparent calm may derive from effective repression and may mask a "venerable popular culture of resistance." Nor should one trivialize the "weapons of the weak." They may not collapse the imperial system but they are significant as a means of limiting power, protecting interests, and expressing dissent from the dominant aristocratic agenda. They signal noncomplicity and indicate that the current demands are not just. They assert dignity, imagine an alternative, ensure survival. At times, they are surprisingly effective in making changes.[45]

Moreover, expressions of resistance indicate that there may not have been quite the shortage of imagination and abundance of complicity that Kautsky posits. For example, Tacitus narrates the scene quoted on p. 14 above in which Nero is aware that people (*populi*) are complaining about indirect taxes (*Ann.* 13.50). Even if fictive, the scene attests the emperor's awareness of and responsiveness to public opposition to taxes. Given that 90 percent of the population paying taxes were peasants or artisans, and given the enormous distance between emperor and people, one can only conclude that protests were widespread, vociferous, and effective enough to make the emperor aware that some people were exercising imagination about fewer and lower taxes. Likewise the attacks on debt-record buildings in Jerusalem and Antioch around 70 C.E. indicate that others are imagining a world without debt (Josephus, *J.W.* 2.426–27; 7.55, 61). Rome's puppet king Agrippa acknowledges that numerous Jews, very aware of "injustice" and "servitude," are fanning hopes of "independence" and "liberty" in seeking war against Rome (Josephus, *J.W.* 2.345–49). With the help of their leaders, Gallic "assemblies and conventicles" imagine a world without Rome's control (Tacitus, *Ann.* 3.40). Acts of imagination seem possible, and small gestures of protest are important and effective as indications of limits to the imperial system's hold on people's lives.

The very bottom layers of the social structure comprised the degraded and expendables. These groups consisted of those with no skills but only their bodies for labor, and those who performed little labor such as criminals, beggars, the physically deformed, and the sick. Estimates number this group between 5 and 10 percent.[46]

CONCLUSION

So far, I have outlined in quite general terms three "organized power networks" that enable the small ruling elite to control the vast Roman Empire and its legionary economy.[47] They exercise political, economic, and military power over 90 percent of the population. They define who belongs in the decision-making processes, they control production of wealth, and they have the power of coercion through military resources. In the next chapter, a fourth power network needs consideration. Theological claims and rituals also play a significant role in creating and reinforcing these relationships between the rulers and the ruled, and in securing the latter's compliance.

– T W O –

Roman Imperial Theology

IN CHAPTER I, I outlined the broad shape of Roman imperial control by sketching its political, socioeconomic, and military structures or networks of power. In this chapter I will outline the role that imperial theology played in creating and sustaining the relationships between the empire's ruling elite, especially the emperor, and its subjects.

It is crucial for twenty-first-century readers to realize that in the Roman world there was no separation between the religious and political spheres. Religion was not a private matter for individuals. Religion was a civic and public practice, visible to and observed by others. By underlining its public role, I am not making any judgment on the genuineness or integrity with which religious practices were undertaken. But I am highlighting a very significant difference between their society and ours. In our society, professions of religiosity by political figures *can* be viewed with suspicion, and representatives of the constitution, both elected politicians and appointees of the courts, exert great effort to maintain the separation of church and state.

But in the Roman world it was quite different. There was no separation of the political and the religious. Religious rituals and theological words were used by emperors and their officials, as well as by loyal supporters in Rome and in the provinces, to evoke "a picture of the relationship between the emperor and the gods" and "impose a definition of the world."[1] In these presentations, Rome and the emperor manifested the sovereignty, presence, will, and blessings of the gods among human beings. The gods sanctioned Roman rule. In this chapter I will describe in some detail some of these theological claims and practices. Since Matthew's Gospel is concerned with some similar theological claims, this discussion will provide an important foundation for the following chapters.

THE GODS WILL ROME TO RULE

Basic to imperial theology was the claim that Rome rules its empire because the gods have willed Rome to rule the world.[2] Consider these examples.

- A Roman governor, the representative of Rome's military and economic (taxation) power, announces to the leader of a German tribe that "all men had to bow to the commands of their betters; it had

20

been decreed by those gods whom they implored that with the Roman people should rest the decisions what to give and what to take away" (Tacitus, *Ann.* 13.51).

- Aristides surveys in wonder an empire in which "an individual rules over so many people and his officials and emissaries stand so far below him, yet far higher than those over whom they have control" and declares "all is well within the reign of Olympian Zeus." Rome's rule embodies Zeus's rule. In praising Rome, Aristides goes on to declare that "the gods beholding, seem to lend a friendly hand to your empire in its achievement and to confirm to you its possession." He invokes the gods' blessing that "this empire and this city flourish forever and never cease" (*Roman Oration* 89, 104–5, 109).

- In praising the emperor Trajan, Pliny the Younger calls the gods "the guardians and defenders of our empire" and prays to Jupiter for "the safety of our prince" since human "security and happiness depends on your safety" (*Pan.* 94).

- In writing of the imminent Jewish war, Josephus has Agrippa declare "that Fortune has transferred her favors" to Rome (*J.W.* 2.360; 4.622), and that "without God's aid so vast an empire could never have been built up" (*J.W.* 2.390–91). Josephus expresses similar attitudes in urging Jerusalem to surrender to Rome, arguing "that God was on the Roman side" (*J.W.* 5.368) and that "you are warring not against the Romans only but also against God" (*J.W.* 5.378; cf. 396, 412).

J. R. Fears argues that the Roman Empire espouses a worldview, "a myth of supernatural character . . . beyond military, economic and socio-political bases of power" that identifies and sanctions those who order, rule over, and benefit from the empire, and creates and confirms the subordinate roles and compliant responses of those who are ruled. Fears argues that for the empire this mythology

> was bound inextricably to the collective worship of the community. . . . [P]olitical ideology was formulated in theological terms and expressed through cult and ritual. . . . This aura of supernatural legitimation came to be enshrined in and expressed through the figure of the monarch . . . an image of the ruler as the visible embodiment of cosmic order, divinely ordained to ensure the prosperity of the human race.[3]

Such theological presentations of the relationship between the ruler and the gods, and hence of the ruler and his subjects, have a long tradition.[4] In the previous century, Virgil* has Jupiter appoint Romulus to found Rome

---

*Virgil: 70–19 B.C.E. Latin poet. The *Aeneid* is an epic poem in twelve books narrating Aeneas's flight from Troy, his wanderings, battles, and founding of Rome. Jupiter's will determines events.

and its empire for which, Jupiter declares, "I set neither bounds nor periods of empire; dominion without end have I bestowed." Jupiter ordains it that Romans will be "lords of the world" (*Aen.* 1.254, 278–79, 282). In outlining this imperial theology, we will focus on the last decades of the first century C.E., the likely time of the community addressed by Matthew's Gospel.

THE GODS DIRECT HISTORY

With Nero's death in 68 C.E., the Julio-Claudian line ended. Vespasian became the fifth emperor in two years in 69 after Nero's death, after the violent power struggle of the civil war and the short reigns of Galba, Otho, and Vitellius in 68–69. Vespasian ruled until his death in 79, and began the short-lived Flavian dynasty that consisted of his two sons Titus, emperor from 79 to 81, and Domitian, who ruled from 81 until his murder in 96. The senate appointed Nerva to succeed Domitian (see the table on page 12).[5]

Vespasian was initially proclaimed emperor by the legions in Egypt, supported by those in Judea and Syria. He defeated the current emperor Vitellius and his troops in 69 (Vitellius was publicly humiliated, tortured, and killed). Six months later, Vespasian's appointment was confirmed by the senate. Given this unrest and Vespasian's vulnerability in coming to power based on the legions rather than by dynastic succession or initial senatorial appointment, he sought to consolidate his power in numerous ways. His military prowess, an important deterrent to anyone who might challenge his rule, was displayed in a magnificent "triumph" in Rome that celebrated his military victory over Judea in 70 C.E.[6] He appointed his supporters to significant political offices. He, and his supporters, used speeches and coins to build links to previous emperors such as Augustus and Claudius, while distancing himself from and denigrating the excesses of Nero's reign.[7] His ability to provide a successor, his son Titus, was emphasized as protection against another civil war. He levied new taxes, one of which, a tax on Jews, will concern us in chapter 8's discussion of Matt 17:24–27.

Signs of Divine Sanction for the Emperor Vespasian (69–79 C.E.)

In addition to these measures, the Flavians and their supporters claimed divine sanction for Vespasian's reign and dynasty.[8] They appealed to various oracles, prophecies, dreams, omens, signs, and wonders as an indication of the gods' favor for Vespasian,[9] while associating signs of disfavor with predecessors and rivals. Suetonius,* for example, reports that some interpreted the death of a significant grove of trees and a lightning strike on the temple

---

*Suetonius: ca. 70–ca. 130 C.E. Imperial service with Pliny the Younger and in the reigns of Trajan and Hadrian. Many written works. Most famous are his biographies, including of Julius Caesar and the emperors from Augustus to Domitian. Evaluates the moral qualities of the rulers.

of the Caesars in which the heads fell off the statues and a scepter fell from Augustus's hand as signs of the withdrawal of favor from the Julio-Claudian line (*Galb.* 1).

Tacitus (*Hist.* 1.86) describes omens that some interpreted as signs of a similar fate for Vitellius:

> in the Capitol the reins of the chariot in which Victory stood had fallen from the goddess's hands, that a superhuman form had rushed out of Juno's chapel, that a statue of the deified Julius ... had turned from west to east [toward Vespasian] on a bright calm day" (cf. Suetonius, *Vesp.* 5.6).

Later, a flock of birds casts a dark shadow over Vitellius's troops, a bull about to be sacrificed escapes from the altar, and a "blood-coloured and black" moon appears (Tacitus *Hist.* 3.56; Dio Cassius* 64.11.1–2; 16.1). For Vespasian's supporters, these were clear signs of the loss of divine favor.

Numerous signs attested favor for Vespasian,[10] and encouraged him "to cherish the hope of imperial dignity" (Suetonius, *Vesp.* 5). These signs included, in addition to strange happenings with trees and submissive actions from animals, a prophecy from Vespasian's prisoner Josephus that Vespasian would become emperor (cf. Josephus *J.W.* 3. 399–408; 4.623; Dio Cassius 65.1.4), and a dream in which Nero was admonished "to take the sacred chariot of Jupiter Optimus Maximus from its shrine to the house of Vespasian," an action understood to show the transfer of Jupiter's favor from Nero to Vespasian and so Vespasian's legitimate succession as emperor (Suetonius, *Vesp.* 5.7; Dio Cassius 64.9.1; 65.1.2–4).

Tacitus and Dio regard Vespasian as both the recipient of divine favor in being ordained to rule, and the vehicle of divine blessing. In Alexandria, "many marvels occurred to mark the favour of the heaven and a certain partiality of the gods toward him" (Tacitus, *Hist.* 4.81). These marvels, through which "Heaven was thus magnifying him" (Dio Cassius 65.8.2) include (with the help of Serapis) healing a blind man, restoring a crippled hand (Tacitus, *Hist.* 4.81; Dio Cassius 65.8.1), healing a lame man (Suetonius, *Vesp.* 7), and the flooding of the Nile (Dio Cassius 65.8.1). Tacitus refers to a contested Jewish prophecy, used for Vespasian's advantage, that

> the East should grow strong and that men starting from Judea should possess the world. This mysterious prophecy had in reality pointed to Vespasian and Titus, but the common people, as is the way of human ambition, interpreted these great destinies in their own favor and could

---

*Dio Cassius: Born ca. 164 C.E. in Bithynia in Asia Minor of a leading family. Successful political career including provincial governor and consul (229 C.E.). Wrote lengthy history of Rome from its founding to his own day (not all of which has survived). Emphasizes divine direction of events.

not be turned to the truth even by adversity (*Hist.* 5.13; cf. Suetonius, *Vesp.* 4.5)

In addition to prophesying that Vespasian would become emperor, his supporter Josephus claims that God was responsible for Nero sending Vespasian to command the armies of Syria, thereby "shaping the destinies of empire" (*J.W.* 3.6–7). Josephus attributes to Vespasian thoughts that "divine providence had assisted him to grasp the empire and some just destiny had placed all sovereignty of the world within his hands," thoughts assisted by "many omens" (*J.W.* 4.622).

The Emperor Vespasian Mediates Divine Benefits to His Subjects

Vespasian's own propaganda, notably his coins, presents him as the agent of the gods who transmit their favor and benefits to the people through his rule. His coins celebrate certain conditions that are attributed to a particular god or goddess who is said to be working through Vespasian for the common good. Fears explains that these personified and deified qualities belong to a

> religious phenomenon common to the cult life of Greece and Rome: the deification of abstract ideas. A specific condition or quality, like peace, victory, martial prowess, or fidelity, is recognized as the operation of a characteristic and peculiar divine power, which in turn is designated by the condition or quality which it produces. Concordia [social harmony] is the godhead which establishes *concordia;* Pax [peace] is the godhead which establishes *pax.*[11]

After the civil war of 69 and the defeat of the Jews in 70, *Pax* and *Victoria*[12] are prominent on Vespasian's coins.[13] For example, *Victoria* or Victory stands on a ship's prow and on a globe signaling victory. She crowns Vespasian, carries shields marked by SPQR (The Senate and Roman People), and appears with spears and Jews who, defeated in 70 C.E., mourn and beg for mercy. She also gives Vespasian an eagle and the palladium, the symbol of Rome's eternal security. The divinity Roma[14] presents Victory to Vespasian.[15] The defeat of Rome's external and internal enemies "attested the manifestation of the godhead Victoria in the persons and achievements of the new emperor and his heir."[16] Epiphanies of supernatural power in his war activities benefit the Roman people.[17]

The frequent appearance of Pax ("peace") on Vespasian's coins claims epiphanies of this divinity in his reign in contrast to the violence of Nero and the civil war.[18] Pax is depicted with an olive branch, cornucopiae, an altar, and a torch to burn conquered arms. Pax also appears with the money bag of Mercury, god of trade, and the columns of Securitas (security). After defeating Judea, Vespasian erects a temple to Pax in Rome in 71–75 and restores a temple to Victory in Latium. Josephus mentions the building of the temple of Peace immediately after the lengthy description of Vespasian's triumph (*J.W.* 7.158). The sequence is most appropriate since without a doubt this "peace" rests on military supremacy. It is, to misuse Tacitus's words, "peace with bloodshed" (*Ann.* 1.10).[19]

Numerous other blessings, often connected with Augustus, are celebrated as Vespasian's gifts: good fortune (*Fortuna Redux*), hope (*Spes*), success (*Bonus Eventus*), prosperity (*Felicitas*), security for the Roman people (*Securitas Populi Romani*), guardian or protector (*Tutela*), grain and plenty (*Annona*), fidelity (*Fides*), welfare (*Salus*), honor (*Honos*) and courage in battle or virtue (*Virtus*).[20] Through Vespasian, commonly called κύριος (*kyrios*, Lord/Master) in the east,[21] these divine powers bless the empire's well-being. Syrian coins depict Vespasian with the aegis, a symbol of world empire linking him with Zeus and Tyche ("Fortune," to whom Antioch was dedicated), and with the eagle, symbolizing Jupiter/Zeus's blessings and sovereignty.[22] Even after his death in 79, also anticipated by signs and omens (Dio Cassius 66.1.1–3), the deified[23] Vespasian continues to bless. And the favor of the gods continues with his sons, the emperors Titus[24] and Domitian.[25] These claims of blessing seek to convince people that a system created to benefit a few at the expense of the many actually benefits all.[26] The claims disguise and hide the empire's overwhelming advantages for the elite by broadcasting spurious claims of benefits for all, and by invoking divine sanction.

Poets Praise Divine Benefits Mediated by the Emperor Domitian

The poets are certain that the world's well-being depends on the well-being of Domitian, Vespasian's son and emperor from 81 to 96 C.E. They are also sure that the gods secure Domitian's well-being.

For Statius,*[27] Domitian is the "Lord of the earth" (*Silvae* 3.4.20), "ruler of the nations and mighty sire of the conquered world, hope of men [*sic*] and care [beloved] of the gods" (*Silvae* 4.2.14–15). He sees everywhere and "knows the hearts of all his subjects" (5.1.79–80; cf. Martial,† *Epigrams* 9.28.8). While Pax is not prominent on the coins, the poets praise him as a peacemaker.[28] For Martial, Domitian is "the world's sure salvation" (*Epigrams* 2.91.1), its "blest protector and savior" (*Epigrams* 5.1.7), its "chief and only welfare" (*Epigrams* 8.66.6). Scott claims that Domitian executes people who committed *laesa maiestas*, words or acts against his sacred per-

---

*Statius: ca. 50 C.E.–ca. 96. Roman poet. The *Silvae* consists of 32 poems. They celebrate significant happenings in the lives of his circle of friends. Six poems flatter and effusively praise Domitian.

†Martial: Born ca. 40 C.E. in Spain; died ca. 101–4; lived in Rome 64–98. Latin poet. Wrote numerous epigrams, short poems with a twist in the ending. Often clever, witty and sexually crude. Strong supporter of Titus and Domitian.

son and therefore against the gods' agent who ensures the well-being of the state.[29]

Domitian's benefits attest that he is a *deus praesens,* "that present deity" as Statius calls him (*Silvae.* 5.2.170). His very being manifests divine presence[30] and bestows the gods' favor and blessings.[31] Domitian's numen, or divine power,[32] advances careers (*Silvae* 4.8.61–62) and prospers human endeavors (*Silvae* 5.2.154). Statius declares that those who work on Domitian's equestrian statue are invigorated by his power (*Silvae* 1.1.61–63). Curtius exalts in seeing Domitian's "immortal brightness" (*Silvae* 1.1.77). Even when Domitian "tempers the rays" and "veils the glory of his state . . . the splendour that he would fain conceal shone in his countenance" (*Silvae* 4.2.41–44). He outshines the constellations and the morning star and makes the temples more radiant, the altar flames burn brighter, winter becomes warmer, and people reflect his light (*Silvae* 4.1.3–4, 23–27). Statius invokes "the godhead of our mighty prince" as inspiration for his own work (*Silvae* 4. pref. 3).

Martial indicates that Domitian's numen (his will as representative of the gods) is so powerful that it causes animals to behave in unusual ways. Domitian's power, not human training, causes eagles and lions to show mercy to their prey (*Epigrams* 1.6; 1.4; 1.22; 1.104), causes leopards, stags, bears, boars, elephants, and bison to perform (*Epigrams* 1.104), enables parrots to greet him (*Epigrams* 14.73; cf. Statius, *Silvae* 2.4.29–30), prompts fish to "know their master and lick his hand" (*Epigrams* 4.30), and a goose to sacrifice itself to provide him a favorable omen in the Sarmatian war (*Epigrams* 9.31). It is Domitian's world. His power is celebrated and recognized to be that of the gods manifested through him. He is the agent of the gods for the benefit of his subjects.

THE EMPEROR IS JUPITER'S AGENT

While the emperors are representatives of the gods, particular gods are claimed to have special relationships with the emperors. Domitian, for example, is said to enjoy the protection of the warrior goddess Minerva, who particularly watches over soldiers in battle.[33] But especially prominent for the three Flavian emperors is their relationship with Jupiter.[34] After the growing use of Jupiter by Nero, and by the three emperors of 68–69, any imperial claimant had to secure Jupiter as the source of their power.[35] And the Flavians did so. This relationship recognized "the emperor as viceregent of Jupiter and Jupiter as protector of his viceregent."[36] The benefit of this relationship was in presenting "the emperor . . . [as] above human criticism because his power is rooted not in human institutions but in his election by the supreme god of the state."[37]

Several writers narrate Jupiter's election of Vespasian. Suetonius describes Nero's dream in which Nero takes the sacred chariot of Jupiter Optimus

Maximus to Vespasian's home (*Vesp.* 5.6; cf. Dio Cassius 65.1.3). This dream indicates Jupiter's choice of Vespasian to be emperor. Tacitus (*Hist.* 1.86) and Dio Cassius (64.8.2) describe Jupiter and other gods deserting Vitellius in 69 c.e. to join Vespasian. Vespasian and Titus portray themselves as bearers of Jupiter's blessing and power. As part of their triumph celebrating the military conquest of Jerusalem and Judea in 70 c.e., Vespasian and Titus offer sacrifices and prayers in the temple of Jupiter Capitolinus (Josephus, *J.W.* 7:153–55). They issue coins that depict Jupiter with a globe, representing Jupiter's bestowal of world rule on them and Jupiter Custos holds the scepter and protects the Flavians against plots and dangers.[38] Vespasian rebuilds the temple of Jupiter Capitolinus, "the home of Jupiter Optimus Maximus...pledge of empire," burned in 69.[39] It was financed by a new tax on the recently defeated Jews (Josephus, *J.W.* 7.218; Dio 65.7.2) that proclaimed the superiority of Jupiter, Rome, and the Flavians over the Jews and their God (see chapter 7 on Matt 17:24–27).

Official and unofficial materials claim that the supreme god Jupiter/Zeus has designated Domitian as his vice-regent or agent to rule humans on the earth. Jupiter protects Domitian as he carries out the task, manifesting Jupiter's presence, reign and blessing for the well-being of his subjects. Tacitus (*Hist* 3.74) and Suetonius (*Dom.* 1.2) observe that Domitian found safety during the civil war in the temple of Jupiter Capitolinus. Martial recognizes that Jupiter keeps Domitian (*Epigrams* 5.1.7–8; 7.60.1–2) and Silius Italicus* has Jupiter predict that "the burning of the Tarpeian temple cannot alarm thee; but in the midst of the impious flames thou shalt be saved, for the sake of mankind" (*Punica* 3.609–10).[40]

After the civil war, Domitian dedicated a temple to Jupiter the Preserver (*Conservator*). A relief of his escape on the altar acknowledged Jupiter's protection and election of him as vice-regent. Jupiter Conservator appears frequently on Domitian's coins, depicted variously with eagle, thunderbolt, spear, and scepter. Also on coins in 82 c.e. are the words CAPIT. RESTIT. with images of the temple of Jupiter Capitolinus, which Domitian restored after another fire in 80 (cf. Statius, *Silvae* 4.3.16; Silius Italicus, *Punica* 3.623–4; Suetonius, *Dom.* 5). A coin issued in 85 presents Domitian crowned by Victory, holding the thunderbolt as Jupiter's representative.[41] Jupiter Victor appears on coins in 88–89 with Victory and a scepter.[42] Tacitus notes that Domitian "dedicated a great temple to Jupiter the Guardian (*custos*) with his own effigy in the lap of the god" (*Hist.* 3.74; cf. Suetonius, *Dom.* 5; Martial, *Epigrams* 6.10). He rebuilds the temple of Jupiter Tonans, and in honor of Jupiter Capitolinus he establishes in 86 a quinquennial contest

---

*Silius Italicus: ca. 26/28–ca. 102/3 c.e. Political career serving Nero and Vespasian; proconsul of Asia (77). In retirement a Latin poet. *Punica* is a 17 book epic that deals with Rome's victory in the Second Punic War (218–201 b.c.e. against Carthage). Sees the gods actively shaping the outcome and the future. Very wealthy.

in music, riding, and gymnastics, over which Domitian presides wearing a golden crown that included a figure of Jupiter (Suetonius, *Dom.* 4.4).[43]

Scott observes that the link between Domitian and Jupiter/Zeus is also well attested in inscriptions and coins from the East. An inscription from Laodicea ad Lycum attests gates and a tower dedicated to Zeus "the greatest savior" and to Domitian, thereby associating the two. Another inscription identifies Domitian as Zeus Eleutherios. Syrian coins link the aegis with Domitian, portraying him as Jupiter on earth, the vice-regent of Jupiter in the heavens. Other signs of the cult of Jupiter also appear on coins and in the reorganization of the *sodales Flaviales* (a religious group and rituals devoted to Flavian emperors). Temples of Jupiter existed in various places including Antioch.[44]

Poets such as Martial, Statius, and Silius Italicus identify Domitian as Jupiter's vice-regent, "our Caesar" as Martial has Jupiter describe him (*Epigrams* 9.36.9), the one whom Jupiter protects (*Epigrams* 9.20.9–10). Jupiter reigns in the skies (*Epigrams* 9.24) while Domitian exercises Jupiter's rule on earth as the ruler, parent, or father of humankind and of Rome, just as Jupiter is ruler, parent, or father of the gods.[45] With the image of "father," imperial power and patriarchy coalesce. For Martial, Domitian is ruler of the world (*Epigrams* 5.3.3), of Rome (5.7.4), and of the human sphere (6.2.5; 8.80.5; 9.18.1), a task his child will inherit (6.3.4), and "parent of the world" (7.7.5; 9.6.1).

As ruler he handles, according to Statius, "all the powers and modes of empire," blessing the empire with adequate food supply and in warfare (*Silvae* 5.1.79–107). As Jupiter was victorious over the Giants and Typhoeus with Hercules' help, Domitian, who outdoes Hercules in serving Jupiter,[46] fights on earth against Rome's enemies as Jupiter's vice-regent for the benefit of Rome and humankind.[47] He employs Jupiter's thunderbolt against the Sarmatians (*Silvae* 4.7.49–52). His coins depict him after defeating the Chatti with spear and thunderbolt, crowned by Victory. The thunderbolt designates Jupiter's power to protect the cosmic order transferred to his servant Domitian. Domitian appears with the thunderbolt on the arch at Cumae.[48] In his epic poem *Punica*, Silius Italicus has Jupiter assure a worried Venus before the second Punic War of Rome's success (3.570–629). Jupiter previews the "future events" (3.630) that he has ordained, notably the military success of the Flavians, first Vespasian (3.593–602), then Titus (3.603–6), then Domitian (3.604–29) who will outdo them in conquests (3.612–17) and in oratory (3.618–21). At Jupiter's command Domitian rules "the happy [blessed] earth with paternal sway" (3.625–6). The three Flavians join Jupiter in the heavens (3.593–94, 601–2, 611, 626–29).

Jupiter provides other blessings through Domitian. Martial asks him to supply his house with water, the "rain of Jupiter" (9.18.8), and to give him money (6.10.1–4). For Statius, Domitian is "our Jupiter" who showers gifts on people just as heavenly Jupiter sends storms (*Silvae* 1.6.25–27). Domitian supplies so much food that he out-jupiters Jupiter, creating a golden age that exceeds antiquity in which "every class ... children, women, people, knights, and senators ... rich and poor" eat from the emperor's table. "Even Jupiter didst come and share our banquet" (*Silvae* 1.6.28–50). At a banquet with Domitian, Statius thinks "I recline with Jupiter in mid-heaven" receiving wine from Ganymede (*Silvae*. 4.2.10–11).

Domitian is a *deus praesens,* a θεὸς ἐπιφανής (*theos epiphanēs*), the vice-regent of Jupiter manifesting Jupiter's presence among humankind. Statius declares that it is Jupiter who commands Domitian to rule the world and thereby blesses the world (*Silvae*. 4.3.128–29, 139–40): a god is he, at Jupiter's command he rules for him the happy/blessed world. . . . Hail, ruler of men and parent of gods, foreseen by me and fore-ordained was thy godhead." He is "the god who holds the reins of earth, he who nearer than Jupiter directs the doings of humankind—he marks thee and beholds thy grief" (*Silvae* 5.1.37–39).

Domitian, though, does not seem to be worthy of Jupiter's election because he caused "terror and hatred." The gods, especially Jupiter, withdraw their favor. Strikes of lightning on the temples of Jupiter Capitolinus and of the Flavian family, Minerva's appearance in a dream to Domitian with weapons removed by Jupiter, and prophecies of his death are understood to indicate imminent disaster (Suetonius, *Dom.* 15–16; Dio Cassius 67.1.2; 67.16.1). Domitian is murdered in 96 C.E. and the senate chooses Nerva as emperor.[49]

RITUALS

Various media promote these theological claims, create and sustain the relationship of ruler and ruled, and solicit the submission of the empire's subjects to such an exalted and divinely legitimated emperor. Decorated gates, arches, columns, statutes, buildings, coins, images, and various inscriptions spread the message. Likewise, temples and altars, liturgical practices such as prayers, vows, and sacrifices, and festivals commemorating the emperor's birthday and accession, celebrated with different intensity and levels of significance in different parts of the empire, solicit submission and consent.[50]

- Aristides attests the practice of governors, none of whom can "remain immobile if he but hears the name of the ruler, but he rises, praises, and reveres him and says two prayers, one for the ruler to the gods and one to the ruler himself for his own well being" (*Roman Oration* 32).

- As governor of Bithynia and Pontus, Pliny the Younger informs Trajan of a ceremony for taking "our annual vows for your safety in which that of the State is included." In his response Trajan expresses gratitude that "you and the provincials have both paid and renewed your vows to the immortal Gods, for my health and safety (*Ep. Tra.* 10.35, 36).

- Pliny describes that on the day marking the emperor's accession, "we have sincerely implored the Gods to preserve you in health and prosperity as it is upon your welfare that the security and repose of humankind depend. I have administered the oath of allegiance to my fellow soldiers" (*Ep. Tra.* 10.52).

- Isidorus informs the emperor Gaius Caligula that "all people were offering sacrifices of thanksgiving for the emperor's preservation" except the Jews. Philo and his delegation protest that priests in the temple have offered sacrifices. Gaius agrees but grumbles that Jews offer sacrifices *for* but not *to* the emperor (Philo, *Legat.* 355–57).

- Such prayers and vows were part of numerous religious ceremonies. Apuleius* attests that in the ceremonies for initiates into the cult of Isis, the leader "read aloud from a book verbatim, first pronouncing prayers for the prosperity of the great Emperor, the Senate, the Knights and the entire Roman people" (*Metam.* 11.17.3).

- And Pliny requires Christians who come to his attention in his province to repeat "an invocation to the Gods and offer adoration, with wine and frankincense, to your [the emperor Trajan's] image" (*Ep. Tra.* 10.96).

One can imagine similar rituals in trade guilds and as part of public entertainments. All such acts secure the relationship of emperor and people.

PAX ROMANA: ROMAN PEACE?

In chapters 1 and 2 I have outlined four networks of power or key structures through which Rome ruled its empire: political, economic, military, and religious. A dominant way of summing up the experience of Roman rule in the first century is to speak of *Pax Romana,* or the establishment of Roman peace. Seneca uses the phrase essentially as a synonym for the empire, its structures, order, and benefits. These are secured by the emperor:

> For he is the bond by which the commonwealth is united, the breath
> of life which these many thousands draw, who in their own strength
> would only be a burden to themselves and the prey of others if the
> great mind of the empire should be withdrawn.
>
> > If safe be their king, one mind to all,
> > bereft of him, their trust must fall.[51]

---

*Apuleius: 125–ca. 170s. Writer, orator, philosopher. Active in Carthage in North Africa. *Metamorphoses* (also called *The Golden Ass*) is a long, witty, and surprising novel about Lucius. This man is changed into an ass by magic, has various adventures, and is changed back by the goddess Isis.

Such a calamity would be the destruction of the Roman peace, such a calamity would force the fortune of a mighty people to its downfall (*On Mercy* 1.4.1–2).

What constitutes this peace that is presented as being sanctioned by the gods?[52] Some have understood it to represent the absence of civil war. Certainly after the power struggles of the 30s B.C.E. and the battle of Actium in 31 B.C.E., Augustus could claim that he had brought peace and stability with the end of the civil wars.[53] And a century later, after similarly ending the civil wars of 68–69 C.E. and becoming emperor, Vespasian happily invoked the *Pax Augusta,* Augustan peace or the peace of Augustus established after the civil war, as his gift to the world, proclaiming it on coins (see above) and memorializing it in the Temple of Peace near the forum, just as Augustus had erected the Altar of Augustan Peace with its images of security and fertility in 13–9 B.C.E.[54] But the end of civil war is a somewhat narrow understanding of "peace."

Perhaps "peace" suggests the absence of war from the Empire as a whole? The empire's advocates certainly present Rome's rulers as peaceful, nonambitious, and reluctant in ruling the empire. Suetonius writes of Augustus:

He never made war on any nation without just and due cause, and he was so far from desiring to increase his dominion or his military glory at any cost that he forced the chiefs of certain barbarians to take oaths in the temple of Mars the Avenger that they would faithfully keep the peace for which they asked. (*Aug.* 21).

And Epictetus* observes (though somewhat critically in the context of pointing out that the emperor cannot bring inner peace that is independent of external circumstances): "Caesar seems to provide us with profound peace, there are no wars any longer, nor battles, no brigandage on a large scale, nor piracy, but at any hour we may travel by land, or sail from the rising sun to its setting (Epictetus, *Diatr.* 3.13.9)

But despite the rhetoric, neither Augustus nor Vespasian, nor any of the seven emperors in between, swore off waging war on opponents throughout the century and Empire who threatened their and Rome's interests, and on rebellious subjects who did not yield their own lives and production to Rome's control. Augustus's own record of military victories and his own writings (*Res Gestae* 24–35) indicate a quite different reality with territorial expansion and glorying in his military accomplishments. Even though

---

*Epictetus: ca. 55–135 C.E. Stoic philosopher. Born a slave of an official of both Nero and Domitian. Banished from Rome by Domitian with other philosophers in 89. Taught that inner peace does not depend on external circumstances. "Enduring" and "renouncing" are key life strategies.

subsequently the empire's boundaries at Augustus's[*] death were essentially not extended (cf. Tacitus, *Ann.* 1.11), emperors continued to fight wars. Claudius conquered Britain, Vespasian and Titus efficiently reduced Galilee and Judea to compliance, Domitian defeated Dacia. And Tacitus can support his claim that "peace was scarcely broken" (*Ann.* 4.32) only by downplaying military operations.[55] Nor did Roman rule end the violence of piracy and brigands as Epictetus claims. Both can be seen as violent expressions of resistance to and attempts to escape Rome's sovereignty.[56] If peace cannot be equated with "the absence of war," either civil or in the provinces, what does it attest?

Wengst observes that those who celebrate Rome's peace in poems, narratives, inscriptions, coins, and buildings are the ruling elite. They view its accomplishment "from above" as its beneficiaries and are keen to preserve it. Claims of "peace," then, are propaganda claims. Peace is a construct from the ruling elite that denotes the status quo, the way life is ordered under the empire for the elite's benefit. Peace is a convenient category that utilizes theological claims and religious activities to justify and celebrate the elite's military and economic power and activity, while ignoring its costly impact on the ruled, those "from below" who do not celebrate it.[57]

The cry of "peace" masks the strategies and structures of empire. It covers over the military basis for Rome's rule.[58] It disguises the fundamental inequities in the Roman system that exists for the economic benefit of the elite. It lays a veneer over the bloodshed and human misery experienced by the vast majority of the empire's subjects, those whose economic activity sustains the luxurious lifestyle of the elite. It claims divine origin and sanction for a way of life marked by domination and exploitation. Woolf argues that "Roman peace may be seen as simply a component of wider patterns of violence, a concomitant of other structures of domination."[59]

Peace, for the ruling elite, effectively means the absence of military challenges to Rome's power. It is built on military power and enforced compliance, carried out by economic exploitation (taxes and tributes), and sanctioned with religious claims. It signifies being pacified politically, militarily, and economically by Rome as the will of the gods. Josephus revealingly reports that in his Temple of Peace in Rome, Vespasian placed "the vessels of gold from the temple of the Jews on which he prided himself" (*J.W.* 7.161). The Temple of Peace displays the booty of a war of conquest and occupation. Such a temple is not only a religious building but also a political one with a propaganda function, witnessing to Roman military might and warning others of the likely price of resisting Rome's peace. This military power in the hands of the ruling elite is the basis for ensuring their control over

---

[*]**Augustus:** Emperor from 27 B.C.E. to 14 C.E. Left several documents to be read after his death. One of them, *Res Gestae*, celebrates his numerous accomplishments, including honors received, his financing of buildings and acts of civic patronage, and military victories and glory.

the economic resources in the provinces: land, people, and produce through the imposition of tax and tribute, conscription, billeting, requisitions, the administration of privileged justice.

The British chief Calgacus understands the economic implications of Roman "peace" in his address to his troops about to battle the invading Romans.[60] He describes the Roman economic motives that inspire them to war:

> Robbers of the world, now that earth fails their all-devastating hands, they probe even the sea; if their enemy have wealth, they have greed; if he be poor, they are ambitious; East nor West has glutted them; alone of humankind they covet with the same passion want as much as wealth. To plunder, butcher, steal, these things they misname empire; they make a desolation and they call it "peace." Children and kin are by the law of nature each man's dearest possessions; they are swept away from us by conscription to be slaves in other lands; our wives and sisters, even when they escape a soldier's lust, are debauched by self-styled friends and guests; our goods and chattels go for tribute; our lands and harvests in requisitions of grain... (Tacitus, *Agr.* 30.4–5).

Weinstock sums it up by saying "Pax [peace]...stood right from the beginning for Roman imperialism."[61] And Zampaglione observes that "almost all the Roman writers agreed that spreading peace...meant subjecting other peoples to Roman domination."[62] Such peace was political, martial, economic, and theological.

When Matthew's Jesus pronounces a blessing on the peacemakers in Matt 5:9, he does not speak God's approval on the Roman system and its "peace" based on military conquest. That system of domination, ruling over, and exploitation is not God's will as Jesus' strong rejection in 20:25–26 indicates: "You know that the rulers of the Gentiles lord it over them, and their great men exercise authority over them. It shall not be so among you" (RSV). Rather Jesus blesses those who work for a completely different world. In the biblical tradition peace is closely tied to the doing of justice, God's will, that ensures access to adequate resources and protection from the greedy and oppressive (Ps 72). The rest of Jesus' blessings in Matt 5:3–12 evoke these traditions and envision a different future.[63] They are subversive words that question the status quo, evoke visions of a different future, and mandate an existence of alternative practices in the present.

CONCLUSION

Imperial theology creates and reinforces in words and rituals an understanding of a relationship between the emperor and the gods. The emperor as ruler of the Roman Empire is the chosen agent of the gods, notably Jupiter's agent, with the tasks of manifesting the gods' rule, presence, will, and blessings among human beings. Thus in depicting a relationship between the emperor and the gods, imperial theology also creates and sustains a relationship between the emperor and his subjects. If he is the agent of the divine will, he is to be honored with submission and cooperation. If he represents the divine rule and will, the imperial system over which he rules (as outlined in the first part of this chapter) is presented as being sanctioned by the gods.

It is in this world of the Roman Empire that Matthew's Gospel comes into being. In the next chapter we will look at the ways in which Matthew's audience encounters these structures and claims in Antioch of Syria. In chapters 4 to 9 we will look at aspects of Matthew's critique of these claims.

THREE

Rome's Empire, Matthew's Gospel, and Antioch

IN CHAPTERS 1 AND 2, I have outlined the four networks of power—political, socioeconomic, military, and theological—that constitute fundamental structures and commitments of the Roman Empire. I am arguing that Matthew's Gospel assumes this experience of Roman imperial power on every page. Sometimes it refers explicitly to the imperial world, such as in the scenes involving Rome's allies (the Herods in chapters 2 and 14), or about paying taxes to Caesar (Matt 22:15–22), or in the crucifixion of Jesus (chapters 26 and 27). But often the imperial realities are not explicit. The Gospel expects that the audience will recognize these realities and understand the Gospel in relation to them. That is, of course, a fair expectation for a first-century audience in this imperial world. But for audiences in other periods of history like ourselves, whose experiences are very different, we have to learn to think our way carefully into each scene, being alert to the imperial dynamics.

For example, Jesus constantly comes into conflict with the "religious" leaders. It is easy for us who are not familiar with these imperial structures to think that this conflict is a religious matter involving only religious personnel. But from our discussion of imperial structures in chapter 1, we now know that the conflict cannot be limited to religious issues. First, religious leaders are members of the retainer class, part of the ruling elite committed to defending the current social order from which they benefit. Jesus and the religious leaders occupy very different places in the imperial world. The religious leaders are part of its power structure. They represent its interests. They like the way things are. Jesus has a very different set of values and social vision. And second, religious matters are not separate from social and political issues in the imperial world. No conflict is "just" or "simply" a religious one. The conflicts have social, political, and economic dimensions also. Knowing these two factors—that religious leaders are part of the ruling elite, and that religious matters are intertwined with social, political, and economic matters—casts the conflict between Jesus and the religious leaders in new light. Jesus conflicts with representatives of the ruling class, people who want to preserve the current social structure. They understand his attempts to change it as an attack on their power, wealth, and status.

In this chapter I will outline some of the ways in which the Gospel's audience, located in the city of Antioch in the province of Syria in the last few decades of the first century, experiences the imperial structures and theological claims described in the previous two chapters.[1] This is the experience, their lived daily reality, in relation to which they hear and make sense of Matthew's Gospel. The first step is to consider when, where, and for whom the Gospel was written.

WHEN AND WHERE
WAS MATTHEW'S GOSPEL WRITTEN?

While we do not know for sure, we can make some informed guesses about the time and place in which Matthew's Gospel was written, and the audience to which it was addressed. Various locations have been suggested. The two suggestions that have the most support among contemporary scholars are a location in Galilee such as Sepphoris or Tiberias, or a location in Syria, especially the city of Antioch. Though we cannot be certain, three factors make Antioch tenable or workable.

First, the earliest citations of Matthew's Gospel in other writings appear around the year 100 c.e. in works with strong links to Antioch and Syria. A work called the *Didache* quotes the version of the Lord's Prayer found in Matthew's Gospel (6:9–13), not the version found in Luke 11:1–4. And Ignatius, a leader of a church in Antioch at the beginning of the second century, writes a series of letters in which several times he refers to material that is unique to Matthew.[2]

Second, Peter plays a more prominent role in this Gospel than in Mark, one of Matthew's likely sources. Not only is Peter the first disciple to be called (4:18–22; 10:2), he acts as the group's spokesperson in confessing Jesus' identity as "the Christ the son of God" (16:16) and in the transfiguration (17:1–8), he imitates Jesus walking on the water (14:28–32) and receives the promise that he is the rock on which Jesus will build his church (16:16–18), scenes not in Mark. Why is Peter's role emphasized in the Gospel? We know from Paul that Peter played a prominent role in the church in Antioch in the first decades of its existence (cf. Gal 2:11–14). His prominence in the Gospel may reflect his previous significant role.

Third, there is a strange addition to one of the descriptions of Jesus' ministry. In Matt 4:23–25 Jesus goes about "all Galilee" teaching, preaching, and healing. His fame is said to spread in 4:24 "throughout all Syria." The reference to Syria is somewhat unusual since the emphasis has been on Galilee (4:12–23) and Jesus does not go to Syria. Moreover, this reference to Syria is missing from Mark 1:28, 39, the source for Matt 4:24. How do we account for it? Given these two other connections with Antioch and Syria, it looks like an attempt to write the author and audience's location into the story.

These three factors indicate Antioch as a likely origin for Matthew's Gospel. Though the case is not a strong one, no stronger case has been made for any other location. But two other factors need to be kept in mind. First, to locate its origin in Antioch does not deny that the Gospel came to be widely used by Christians in other places.[3] And second, even if this link with Antioch proves somehow to be incorrect, it would not undermine my basic thesis that Matthew's Gospel is affected by and addresses a world shaped by Roman imperial power. While the following discussion will demonstrate various ways in which imperial presence was evidenced in Antioch, this discussion is by no means unique to that city. Roman presence was experienced in similar ways in numerous cities all over the empire.

The Gospel's date is determined by several factors. On one hand the Gospel refers to, looks back on, and theologically interprets the destruction of Jerusalem in 70 C.E. by the Roman general Titus (Matt 22:7; 24:2). This event and reference will be important for several subsequent chapters in this book. Here its importance is that the Gospel has to be written after this event. Second, as I noted above, material found only in Matthew's Gospel is known by the *Didache* and Ignatius, works that originate around the year 100 C.E. This would indicate the Gospel was written before 100. Third, a little more "precision" (I use the term loosely) within this thirty-year span between 70 and 100 C.E. may be possible from the observation that Matthew's Gospel seems to rewrite Mark. Mark was written around 70 C.E. Matthew's rewriting often seems to take place in relation to a possible dispute with a synagogue community. For example, Matthew expands Mark's one reference to "their synagogues" to emphasize distance between Jesus and the synagogue, increases negative references to synagogues, omits Mark's favorable references to synagogues, maintains Mark's references to the "religious" leaders' roles in killing Jesus, restricts the use of *rabbi* to Judas, and heightens the negative presentation of scribes.[4] Given some time for Mark to circulate and to be read, and given some time for a dispute with a local Antiochene synagogue to develop after the crisis of 70 C.E., a date for Matthew in the 80s is likely.[5]

ROMAN IMPERIAL PRESENCE
IN ANTIOCH

While Rome is the supreme center of power for the Empire, other urban areas like Antioch extended Rome's political, economic, and cultural power throughout the Empire. Cities exercised control over the immediate area in which they were located.[6] Control over this surrounding area was crucial since control meant income from taxes, tributes, and rents, and goods for the city's inhabitants. Control over a larger area such as a province provided further security as well as access to even more resources. Gideon Sjoberg estimates no more than 10 percent of the empire's population lived in cities, but much of the services, products, trade, and commerce existed in order to supply the needs of the elite who usually lived in urban areas.[7]

According to Josephus (*J.W.* 3.29), Antioch in Syria "for extent and wealth unquestionably ranks third among the cities of the Roman world," presumably behind Rome and Alexandria. Population and size estimates are difficult, but more reliable estimates put the population around one hundred fifty thousand by the end of the first century.[8] Laid out in a conventional grid shape with its famous northeast-to-southwest, colonnaded main street paved with marble (a gift from Herod, so Josephus *J.W.* 1.425), the city's area was approximately two miles in length and one mile in width.[9] Rodney Stark has estimated an intense population density of about 117 per acre, though that figure increases to 205 per acre when the size of actual living space is reduced about 40 percent to account for the typical areas of an ancient city given over to public buildings and spaces.[10] That estimated population density is greater than the most intensely populated contemporary cities such as Bombay and Calcutta.

Provincial Governors

Antioch was the capital city of the Roman province of Syria and so was the base for the personnel needed for the province's government. The provincial government, headed by a governor or legate appointed by the emperor (Josephus, *Ant.* 18.1; *J.W.* 7.58–59), was based in Antioch. He was responsible for the four tasks of provincial governors: raising taxes, social order and defense, judicial matters, and supervision of the local government.[11] The first and last of these tasks were usually carried out in cooperation with local ruling elites. Antioch had a *boulē*, or council (Josephus, *J.W.* 7.107), whose *bouleterion* or meeting place burned in 23/24 C.E. and was probably rebuilt by Tiberius.[12] The *boulē* comprised perhaps between one hundred and five hundred members.[13] It exercised some power over civic matters in cooperation with the governor.

The governor and his staff rendered Roman control visible to Antioch's population. Each year he probably undertook a *conventus,* an annual assize or trip around a determined circuit to hear legal cases and petitions in towns throughout the province. He also inspected public buildings and roads to determine if they needed repair, oversaw building projects, inspected financial records of cities, and could intervene in local council affairs, especially in disputes.[14] A governor was assisted by a staff, both civic and military, of various advisers and scribes to assist in judicial and administrative matters: letter writing in response to petitions from provincials as well as in seeking the emperor's direction or approval for decisions,[15] record keeping, and financial administration. A fourth-century text presents an image of a provincial governor at work when it compares a religious opponent with a governor: "parading across the public squares, reading letters and answering them publicly as he went, surrounded by a large body-guard, some marching before him, some following behind."[16] The physical presence of the governor and his staff made Rome visible on a daily basis. The economic and judicial systems that they administered, reinforced by military power, ensured Roman control reached far into people's lives.

Emperors

Also evidencing Roman presence in Antioch were the visits of several emperors, or future emperors, to the city. Augustus and Tiberius visited in 20 B.C.E., and Caligula in 19 C.E. The future emperor Trajan visited in the 70s. His father was governor of Syria in the mid-70s.[17] Hadrian, governor of Syria, became emperor in 117 C.E. in Antioch. About a decade before Matthew's Gospel was written, Vespasian made several visits in 66–70 C.E., first in 66 as commander of the military forces that assembled in Antioch to attack Galilee and Judea. Three years later in 69, he returned as emperor to Antioch, where the oath of allegiance to him as emperor was administered to his troops and he addressed the enthusiastic city gathered in the theater before going to Rome (Josephus, *J.W.* 3.29; 4.630; Tacitus, *Hist.* 2.80). Titus, after his victory over Jerusalem and Judea in 70, received in ca. 71 a tumultuous welcome, if Josephus is to be believed. Enthusiastic crowds traveled some thirty *stadia,* or five miles out from the city to welcome him. Titus addressed the city in a rally in the theater, and upheld the rights of Jewish citizens of the city (*J.W.* 7.100–111). This welcome resembled aspects of an *adventus* or arrival ceremony (παρουσία; *parousia*) which welcomed emperors, generals, governors, or other significant imperial officials as they arrived in a city. It usually involved a procession into the city, welcoming crowds celebrating the arrival, hymnic acclamation, speeches from representatives of the local elite (for which rhetorical handbooks provided instruction on both the content and affect of the speech),[18] and a cultic act like sacrifice in a temple.[19]

Titus's visit is remembered for several other displays of Roman power in Antioch. It followed Rome's victory over Jerusalem and Judea. Josephus says that Titus "exhibited costly spectacles in all the cities of Syria through which he passed, making his Jewish captives serve to display their own destruction" (*J.W.* 7.96). Consistent with this parading of captured Jewish prisoners, the sixth-century chronicler* Malalas[20] says that Vespasian and/or Titus displayed in Antioch booty seized in the defeat of Jerusalem. Outside the city gate leading to Daphne, a suburb of Antioch, they set up bronze figures understood to be cherubim from the Jerusalem temple. And on the gate they placed symbols of the divinity Aeternitas to represent the claim that

---

*Malalas: ca. 480–570 C.E. Member of the educated governing elite in Antioch. Trained in rhetoric and law. Wrote an extensive, eighteen-book history of the world that provides much detailed information about Antioch.

Rome and the Flavians would last forever. Vespasian also constructed a theater after he "destroyed their synagogue, to insult them" (Malalas 10.45). It was inscribed, FROM THE SPOILS OF JUDEA, and had a statue of Vespasian in it.[21] Assuming Malalas is reliable, these acts, especially insulting to the city's Jewish population, display Rome's power and beneficence of peace, security, and material improvements, all at the expense of a conquered people. The warning not to mess with Rome is clear.

Four Legions of Roman Soldiers

Imperial officials and structures communicated Roman presence in and control over Antioch. So too did the twenty thousand or so soldiers from the four legions based in the city.[22] Located on the then-navigable Orontes river about seventeen miles inland from the Mediterranean coast and at the intersection of several significant north-south and east-west highways and trade routes, Antioch had obvious economic significance. But equally important was its strategic military role. The governor was charged with maintaining order on several fronts. To the south was the at-times troublesome province of Judea, prone to bandits and other unrest.[23] To the east was Parthia, with whom Rome had uneasy relations. The Syrian troops were "to guard against the kings and nations of the east" (Philo, *Legat.* 207), and all around the cities and land of Syria.

Governors and their troops played an active role in Judean crises through the century. The governor Petronius took two legions (Josephus, *Ant.* 18.262; Philo, *Legat.* 207) or three legions and auxiliaries (Josephus, *J.W.* 2.186) from Antioch to Ptolemais in 40 C.E. when Jews refused to allow Gaius Caligula to install his image in the temple. During Cumanus's governorship of Judea (48–52 C.E.), the Syrian governor Quadratus intervened in disputes between Galileans and Samaritans (Josephus, *J.W.* 2.232–44). In 66 C.E., the governor Cestius left Antioch with a legion, plus six thousand soldiers from the other three legions, along with cavalry, infantry, and auxiliaries to quell rebellion in Galilee (Josephus, *J.W.* 2.499–555). He advanced to Jerusalem but was forced to retreat hurriedly to Antioch. Josephus puts his casualties in the retreat at around six thousand, the equivalent of a legion or more (*J.W.* 2.555). In 67 C.E. Vespasian, appointed by the emperor Nero, used Antioch as a base to assemble his troops in order to march south to subdue Galilee and Jerusalem (Josephus, *J.W.* 3.8, 29). And Josephus records that "abundant supplies of corn and other necessaries from Syria" sustained Titus's army in its siege of Jerusalem in the 66–70 war (*J.W.* 5.520). These supplies, no doubt levied by taxes to the depletion of the local food supply, evidence the legionary economy at work to maintain Roman control on the basis of military power. Not surprisingly, these military and economic actions were connected to unrest between Syrians and Jews in Antioch and others towns in Syria.[24]

Scholars are not agreed about Rome's relationship with Parthia. The traditional view argues that the legions in Antioch were Rome's defense of its frontiers against the aggressor Parthia.[25] Benjamin Isaac is not convinced and sees Rome being much more militarily aggressive with unsuccessful military campaigns in 57–58 (invasion of Armenia), 61–62 (withdrawal) and 112–114 (annexing Armenia and then withdrawal).[26] The issue is, as Dio Cassius observes, a matter of Roman glory (68.17.1). The military actions of the Syrian governor Corbulo in 61–62, including the invasion of Armenia and defeat of Rome's troops there, ended in withdrawal and a negotiated diplomatic settlement, outcomes that needed redress. J. Brian Campbell places much more emphasis on diplomacy throughout the first century and denies that territorial and military expansion in Cappadocia and improved roads in Syria in the 70s were aimed at Parthia.[27] But, of course, they didn't hurt either, and they certainly weren't necessary for Antioch's defense, as Isaac notes.[28] The troops were available as and when diplomacy was no longer effective or useful.

Twenty thousand soldiers in a population of one hundred fifty thousand means a vast impact on the city of Antioch. In addition to the sheer visibility of Roman military control, one obvious consequence was a high tax bill for provisions and equipment. Such levies were often severe and difficult to control; "it is hard," says Isaac, "to distinguish between excessive taxation and plain robbery by soldiers." He cites John the Baptist's words against the actions of soldiers who rob with violence (Luke 3:14).[29] Such actions ensured that Antioch's residents experienced the empire's intimidation and violence on a personal level. The practice of *angareia,* the requisition of animals for transportation, of labor, and of lodging for soldiers (food and accommodation, including eviction from one's home) are further forms of taxation. The forced labor might involve carrying a solider's pack (Matt 5:41), or doing construction work on a road or bridge, often also financed by a local community.[30]

The widespread use, and abuse, of these practices is attested in a revealing letter that the emperor Domitian (81–96 C.E.) writes to the Syrian procurator Claudius Athenodorus.[31] In the letter, Domitian acknowledges that requisitions of animals and demands for labor and lodging have been burdensome to the provincials and need to be controlled: "for it is just to come to the aid of the exhausted provinces which with difficulty provide for their daily necessities." His plan for control, though, seems very inadequate. Domitian decrees that no such actions are to be taken without a written permit from him. But there are two ironies. The very reason Domitian gives for writing this letter and imposing this control is that his father, the emperor Vespasian, had previously issued a similar order but it had been ignored. Distance and limited access to the emperor or any imperial official combine to ensure that provincials supplied military demands whatever the benign wishes of the emperor miles away in Rome. And second, the true reason for Domitian's apparent concern for the "exhausted provinces" emerges:

"if the farmers are snatched away, the lands will remain uncultivated." Of course if that happens, there will be no agricultural products to extract by tax, no supplies for Antioch's elite, or for Roman soldiers, or for the city of Rome. Domitian's concern is not for the well-being of the provincials; it is to protect the imperial system that supplies the elite.

Tacitus attests how much at home soldiers were in Antioch. Masking the antagonistic role of occupiers and occupied, and maintaining the line that everyone wants to be part of Rome's empire, Tacitus writes, "For the provincials were accustomed to live with the soldiers and enjoyed association with them; in fact, many civilians were bound to the soldiers by ties of friendship and of marriage" (*Hist.* 2.80). The claim of marriage is interesting since soldiers were not allowed to marry. It may refer to those married before they were recruited, or it may refer, as Campbell discusses, to the custom of soldiers living with women as though they were their wives and raising families.[32] Tacitus's comment attests the high level of visibility for Rome's military in the city. What did Roman soldiers represent to those living in Antioch?

In part, of course, they saw and experienced members of an army "of conquest and occupation, as well as defense."[33] They encountered members of an army feared for its awesome power and effectiveness in enacting Rome's control and the gods' will. Each legion displayed the eagle, a "sacred emblem...the king and bravest of all the birds...the symbol of empire...and an omen of victory" (Josephus, *J.W.* 3.123). Klaus Wengst argues that the Roman legionary soldier was an instrument of both military conquest and of economic exploitation. A soldier's equipment included not only sword, javelin/spear, and shield for battle, but also "a saw, a basket, a pick/spade and axe, not to mention a leather strap, a bill-hook, a chain/handcuffs, and three days' rations..." (Josephus, *J.W.* 3.95).[34] Wengst draws attention to the order. The initial references (sword, javelin/spear, and shield) are to weapons of conquest. Then come instruments (saw, pick/ spade, axe) not only useful for establishing camp, but also for "the economic exploitation of conquered territory," for building roads, bridging rivers, draining swamps, clearing forests. The last-mentioned items, the chains or handcuffs, help to maintain control in the conquered area. No doubt troops were deployed to keep civic order in Antioch and consolidate Roman control, including in the civic strife between Jews and other citizens of Antioch around 70 C.E.

Isaac comments on the army's presence in Antioch:

The fact that [Antioch] became a centre of administration and, at times, a military command centre was the cause of great misery for its inhabitants. Occasional munificence was not enough to compensate for the rapaciousness of the soldiers and the greed of officials.[35]

Buildings

In addition to the presence of imperial personnel, various buildings attested Rome's "ubiquitous presence and the benefits it could bring."[36] Antioch possessed the usual public buildings of any ancient city: administrative, commercial (markets, shops, storehouses), cultural (library, theater, amphitheater), recreational (baths, circus, stadium, theater), hygienic (baths, latrine, water cisterns and fountains), and religious structures (temples, cult buildings).[37] In addition to the normal civilian buildings, there were also buildings specifically concerned with "the administration, security, and defense of the Empire."[38]

The governor's headquarters evidenced Roman presence,[39] as did buildings for the administration of justice and of financial matters such as taxes. Included in these were "the market square, the magistrates' quarters or government administrative offices, the record office and the law-courts and exchange" rebuilt after the fire of 66/67 (Josephus, *J.W.* 7.55).[40] Other emperors assisted in rebuilding parts of the city after natural disasters, Tiberius after fires in 23/24 C.E., Gaius Caligula (whose father Germanicus died in Antioch), and Claudius after earthquakes in 37 and in the 40s.[41] Augustus and Tiberius are associated with various building projects such as baths, aqueducts, a theater, hippodrome, fountains, and streets.[42] Vespasian extended the network of roads in Syria, and built a canal near Antioch.[43] Domitian built a public bathhouse that was named after him.[44] It is not clear how the legionary economy financed such building, perhaps by taxes in Syria, and/or funds from Rome raised by taxes and tributes elsewhere in the empire, and/or by public donation from leading wealthy citizens in Antioch.[45] Likely inscriptions on such rebuilt or new buildings attested Roman beneficence and proclaimed Roman presence and control.[46]

Statues and Gates

Statues advertised Roman sovereignty. Tiberius built a gate at the northeastern end of the main street on top of which was a statue of Romulus and Remus, Rome's legendary founders, being nursed by the she-wolf. To leave or enter the city meant literally to pass under this billboard that proclaimed Rome's sovereignty. Early in the second century Trajan built a similar arch in the middle of the street. Such statues functioned as billboards to advertise Roman rule. A statue of Tiberius, funded by Antioch's council and its elite members, and one of Vespasian performed similar roles, as did a cenotaph in honor of Germanicus, Tiberius's nephew and Caligula's father, who died in Antioch in 19 C.E.[47]

Coins

As I observed in chapter 1, coins had a similar "advertising" function. Along with the omnipresent taxes, they manifested Roman presence and claims in the midst of the economic transactions of daily life. They were, with their diverse images and minimal but significant words naming an imperial figure or office or imperial virtue, "organs of information," "a part of the imperial mentality..." that addressed

> an audience of countless thousands, all of whom in greater or lesser degree, looked to the *princeps* (emperor) as the apex of a political system on which depended the peace and stability of the civilized world; and it furnished world opinion with a miniature but strictly official commentary upon the man and his administration.[48]

Since Augustus and Tiberius, coins minted in Antioch bore the image of the emperor. Claudius and Nero increased the witness to Roman sovereignty by minting coins that not only bore the emperor's name and titulature in Latin, but which identified Antioch and the governor's name in Greek.[49]

Especially significant were coins, issued first by Vespasian and then by Titus, that contained the words JUDEA CAPTA ("Judea Captured") or JUDEA DEVICTA ("Judea Conquered"). These coins used various images to provide "the official commentary" on the war against Judea,[50] to celebrate Rome's victory in 70 C.E., and to warn anyone contemplating revolt of the likely consequences. One of the coins' common images is a bound female in various positions, who personifies the defeated province. Also common are piles of surrendered arms. Vespasian, both his bust and his full figure in battle dress, appears, as does Titus. The divinity Victory whose power and benefits are displayed in the defeat, is also depicted. Such coins were especially humiliating for Antioch's large Jewish population (Josephus, *J.W.* 7.43),[51] but were signs for all of Rome's great military power and warnings of the futility of revolt.

Taxes

I will discuss various types of taxes in chapter 8 below. Taxes were understood by the elite as a crucial means of paying for the costs of administering the empire. Payment was seen as an expression of submission to Rome. The failure to pay was regarded as an action of rebellion. Taxes and tribute reinforced the divide between the elite and the rest, and as instruments of the exploitation of the rest for the benefit of the elite, contributed significantly to the majority's endless poverty.

Especially humiliating for Jews in Antioch after 70 C.E. was a new tax that Vespasian levied on Jews after Jerusalem's defeat. This tax will be the focus of chapter 7 below since it is the subject of Peter and Jesus' discussion in Matt 17:24–27. It reminded Jews of their status as a defeated people, conquered by Rome's military might and at the will of Jupiter, against whom the Jewish God had not been able to defend the people. To add further insult, the tax was used to rebuild and maintain Jupiter's temple in Rome.

Coins of Vespasian and of Titus

Temples and Rituals

Temples and religious celebrations provide another means of manifesting Roman rule. Antioch contained temples dedicated to numerous gods. Included among these was the Temple of Jupiter, dedicated to the patron god of the Flavians. The emperor Tiberius renovated or rebuilt it, and perhaps set up an image of himself in it.[52] Statues could receive worship and some households linked the emperor with their household gods. It is not clear how widely observed or actively promoted was the emperor cult in Antioch, and it must be remembered that often ruling elites in the provinces took the initiative in establishing shrines or temples and encouraging sacrifices and prayers. Though there is little evidence, it would be most unlikely that there were not some sorts of prayers and vows offered to the emperor's likeness by at least Roman officials and troops, as well as by some of the local elite and residents, comparable to that described by Pliny (as noted in chapter 1). Likewise, it is inconceivable that festivals such as the emperor's birthday or day of accession or the founding of Rome were not celebrated in Antioch with much public display.[53] Provincial *koinon* games were held, which Downey claims were often associated with the imperial cult.[54]

Matthew's Gospel addresses an audience familiar with imperial presence and theology. To walk down the street in Antioch meant seeing Roman soldiers, perhaps glimpsing the governor or his staff, passing administrative buildings, temples, and statues, observing spoils from the Judean war, witnessing imperial festivals, paying taxes, and in one's pockets coins with imperial symbols. The "power of images"[55] ensured imperial theology was known in Antioch through the residency of the governor and his staff, visits of emperors, the large number of soldiers, buildings, coins including post-70 *Judaea Capta* coins, temples and rituals, statues, signs of military victories, festivals, and taxes, especially Vespasian's tax on Jews. These human and material billboards advertised Rome's sovereignty and will, destined by the gods to rule over all. They sought a response of compliance and submission.

LIFE IN ANTIOCH

There was another way in which residents of Antioch and its surrounding area experienced Roman rule. As was typical of the empire, many of the inhabitants of the city were artisans and those in the surrounding rural area were peasants. They experienced daily in their near-subsistence existence the impact of the imperial system that sustained itself through taxes, tribute rents, and tolls on their productivity and at their expense.

Antioch's economy was typical of the empire in that it was based in the agricultural production of the surrounding area, controlled by the elite, and structured for their benefit. The wealthy elite who lived in the city owned large amounts of land on the surrounding plain of Amuk and the lower

Orontes valley. They controlled the villages, land, yield, and lives of the peasants who worked the land. By rents for land use, taxes on production, tolls on transportation, and interest on loans, the landowners extracted a significant percentage of peasant production for their own benefit, and for profit in being sold to feed the rest of the city.

Philostratus* narrates the story of Apollonius arriving in the town of Aspendus to find almost nothing available in the market because "the rich had shut up all the grain and were holding it for export from the country" (*Vit. Apoll.*, 1.8). Galen† (6.749ff.) observes peasants in Asia Minor starving after the grain and bean harvests had been removed to the city because it was the normal practice of the city-dwellers "to collect and store enough grain for all the next year after the harvest." By such taxes and requisitions, the elite forced peasants to produce above their usual subsistence levels in order to meet the demands placed on them and to survive. Because the elite's wealth was concentrated in land, and land was considered a valuable asset at least to pass on to one's children, if not to be enlarged, little attention and resources were generally invested in trade or "manufacturing." There were of course exceptions; no city was totally self-supporting, and there is evidence for some trade and that some made considerable wealth from it, though this was not the usual focus of the elite.

Such a system was extremely difficult for peasants and small farmers. Not only did they have to meet the demands of the elite, they also had to supply their own household's needs through their own production and through barter or purchase, as well as ensure sufficient livestock and seed for the next year, while at the mercy of weather, soil quality, political events, the whims of the elite. If the yield could not sustain a household, some left to eke out a living in the city, perhaps as day laborers (especially during planting and harvest, as in Matt 20:1–16), or in some service or trade employment. The system meant that many peasants lived constantly close to famine and subsistence, with poor nutrition, poor health, endless hard work, and perpetual vulnerability.[56] There is no doubt that the imperial system was damaging to people's health.

Some scholars have seen the relationship between a city like Antioch and the surrounding countryside as symbiotic, with each area needing the other. They style the relationship as mutually dependent, with the country supplying necessary food to the city, and the elite-dominated city providing order and entertainment.[57] But while there is some truth in these claims of dependency, the sum is much larger than the parts. It is more accurate to describe

---

*Philostratus: 160s–240s c.e. Member of a leading family. Writer. Included in the circle of the wife of the emperor Septimius Severus. At her bidding, he wrote *Life of Apollonius of Tyana,* a biography of a first-century itinerant Pythagorean miracle worker, holy man, and philosopher.

†Galen: ca. 129–ca. 200 b.c.e. Court physician to the emperor Marcus Aurelius. Wrote on numerous topics. Extensive writings on various aspects of medicine.

cities, politely, as "consumer cities" or, less politely, as economically parasitic in relation to rural areas. The elite-dominated city exploited the peasants and consumed far more than the city itself produced or made available to rural dwellers.[58] The city, dominated by the non-working elite, was the center of the region and it drew to itself rural production. Corbier uses an appropriate image: "Cities could only live by siphoning off the resources of the country, and this did not only take the form of rents. They derived profit from the collection of taxes...[and] levies such as the requisition of grain."[59]

For the ruling class, cities were centers for the conspicuous display and consumption of their wealth, whether in luxurious houses, clothing, attendants and slaves, or in civic acts of patronage such as a building project, funding some entertainment, providing a food handout, or displaying largesse to some clients.[60] But while there was considerable comfort and plenty for the elite, it was a very different story for most occupants of a city. Apart from the elite, the rest of the city existed in part to provide necessary services for one another, but especially to furnish the expensive needs of the elite whether in clothing, housing, food, utensils, furnishings, entertainment, crafts and skills, transportation, or labor.

Rodney Stark provides a graphic description of the miseries of daily life for many of Antioch's inhabitants.[61] He chronicles "the extraordinary levels of urban disorder, social dislocation, filth, disease, misery, fear, and cultural chaos that existed." Stark notes the relatively small (compared to modern cities) but densely inhabited nature of ancient cities. Living space for most people consisted of "tiny cubicles in multistoried tenements" with no glass windows or chimneys for smoke from indoor cooking and heating. Streets were narrow, animals numerous, privacy scarce, sanitation (sewerage and garbage disposal) minimal, water from public cisterns unsanitary and not conveniently available. Incense and perfume abounded among those who could afford them to cover the stench. Public baths were not adequate for the population; "it is equally silly to think that everyone jogged off to the public latrines each time nature called." In sum, "tenement cubicles were smoky, dark, often damp, and always dirty. The smell of sweat, urine, feces, and decay permeated everything; dust, rubbish and filth accumulated; and finally bugs ran riot." So did disease, physical affliction, deformity, and of course death.

Beyond this, Antioch attracted newcomers, especially from land and villages no longer able to produce enough. Newcomers had fewer attachments to the social order, so crime, and the rivalries of numerous ethnic groups (by one count eighteen ethnic quarters in the city) meant competition, misunderstanding, conflict, and disorder. The first-century writer Plutarch attests fearful ethnic rivalries (as well as his own prejudices and xenophobia) in asking his reader to contemplate the ridiculous situation "that anybody feeling much troubled at the crowd of Greeks living in his city should fill up his city with Arab and Scythian immigrants ("Advice About Keeping Well," *Mor.*

134D). And Josephus describes much hostility toward Jews in the late 60s
C.E. in Antioch as the war against Judea was being waged (*J.W.* 7.46–62).[62]
In addition, Antioch is struck in the first century by numerous natural and
social disasters: fires, earthquakes, flooding, riots.

To this mix we have to add various other tensions. There is a well-attested
disdain for provincials on the part of citizens of Rome. Cicero* declares that
Jews and Syrians are people "born to be slaves" (*Prov. cons.* 10), an attitude
that Titus repeats over a century later in exhorting his troops to victory
in the Judean war over "inferior" Jews who have "learned to be slaves"
(Josephus, *J.W.* 6.37–42). Even allowing for the legal context of his writings
and Cicero's goal of discrediting witnesses, his sense of Roman superiority
emerges clearly. Cicero labels Africans, Spaniards, and Gauls "uncouth and
barbarous nations" (*Quint. fratr.* 1.1.27). In questioning the integrity and
motives of provincial witnesses, he declares that the most honorable native
of Gaul is not on the same level as the meanest citizen of Rome (*Font.* 27–
36; *Scaur.* 38–45). He tells a jury of senators and other members of the elite
that in hearing from the leading citizens of the province of Asia they must

> remember that when you hear Greek resolutions, you are not hearing
> evidence; you are hearing the wild decisions of a mob, the voice of
> every non-entity, the din of ignoramuses, an inflamed meeting of the
> most unstable nation. (Flac. 19).

Cicero also argues that provincials need Roman rule and troops to protect them (financed by taxation) because those who cannot rule themselves
are better off as slaves or subjects of Rome (*Resp.* 3.37–41; *Quint. fratr.*
1.1.34).[63]

Disparagement for provincials is evident in other ways. Tacitus reports
that Tiberius was having trouble recruiting people to take governorships
in unfashionable provinces like Syria (*Ann.* 6.27). The governor of Judea,
Pontius Pilate, also exhibits disrespect for provincial religious scruples, as
we will outline in chapter 8 below. Juvenal† refers to the regrettable influx
of provincials into Rome with their different customs by commenting that
Antioch's river "the Syrian Orontes has long since poured into the Tiber"
(*Sat.* 3.62). Such attitudes on the part of Roman officials and soldiers cannot
have helped social relationships in Antioch.

Equally well attested are similar attitudes of the wealthy toward the poor,
the elite toward the masses, the urban elite to the rustic peasants.[64] Mac-

---

*Cicero: 106–43 B.C.E. Outstanding and powerful orator, leading lawyer, active politically,
statesman. Governor of Cilicia, and consul in 63 B.C.E. Opposed Julius Caesar. Fifty-eight of his
legal speeches prosecuting or defending various figures have survived ("On Behalf of Flaccus";
"Against Verres"). Also numerous letters and writings on political theory and philosophy.

†Juvenal: Dates uncertain, perhaps 60s–130s C.E. Little is known of his life. Orator and
Roman satirist. Wrote 16 entertaining and biting *Satires*. Especially attacks the corruption of
the Roman elite: greed, the selfish rich, sexual perversity, patron-client relationships, social
upstarts, Roman women, the vanity of elite birth, prayer, the emperor Domitian.

Mullen compiles what he calls a "lexicon of snobbery" consisting of thirty terms of abuse and disdain that the literary elite use to describe the lower classes. Both Cicero and Apuleius use "rustic" as a term of derision for ignorant, uncultured, manual-working peasants.[65] Cicero disdains "craftsmen, shopkeepers and all the dregs of a city" (*Flac.* 18). Juvenal concludes that poverty "exposes people to ridicule" for their torn and dirty clothing (*Sat.* 3.147–54). Juvenal's wealthy Rubellius Blandus demonstrates the claim by referring to the poor as "dirt... the very scum of the populace... from the lowest rabble" (*Sat.* 8.44–48). Seneca observes "how much larger is the proportion of poor men" (*Helv.* 12.1) but thinks there is no point in helping the undeserving poor (*Vit. beat.* 24.1) and scorns the "common herd and the unthinking crowd" (*On the Shortness of Life* 1.1). That is not to say that there was no relief action, but as A. R. Hands demonstrates, it was understood within an honor and status mentality of conspicuous kindness that saw the action more in terms of its benefits for the giver's status and reputation than in alleviating the desperate needs of the poor.[66] The poor, then, who comprised most of the population, lacked not only material resources but also social honor or dignity. Despised or dishonored by the elite, they were excluded in an elitist, hierarchical society from most of the benefits of the empire and from the society that "really matters."

This glimpse of life in the Roman Empire as many peasants and urban dwellers experienced it reveals the challenge that confronts the imperial claims outlined in chapter 2. Claims that the gods have chosen Rome and the emperor to be the agent of the gods' will and blessing may play well among the provincial elite like Plutarch or Aristides who are guaranteed a share in the profits or, more euphemistically, the benefits of Roman rule. But the claims seem less persuasive in "back-street" Antioch amidst such poverty and conflict. It seems that Rome may well have had a hard time persuading much of the population that the imperial system actually benefited them.

A RESPONSE: MATTHEW'S GOSPEL

Numerous scholars have located the emergence of the early Christian movement and Matthew's Gospel in the stresses and ambiguities of life in the empire. Michael Mann, for example, argues that the empire's material and military successes created contradictions or tensions that it could not solve.[67] The empire claimed a universalism in bringing the world under Roman rule, yet it privileged a certain segment, the elite, whose exclusiveness "denied the notion of universal membership" in the empire. Or again, Roman expansion "generated notions of political participation and equality," yet the very hierarchical nature of the empire undermined that claim. Mann argues that the empire failed to provide an adequate social experience or sense of community, and failed to offer a plausible worldview. It could not solve the issue of social identity. It failed to "penetrate the everyday life of the mass of the people, urban or rural. It had failed to mobilize their commitments or praxis, or to give meaning and dignity to their lives." It could not organizationally answer the question "To what society do I belong?" Mann argues that Christians, ironically using existing networks or channels in the Roman world, offered an organizational solution to these contradictions in the formation of "universalistic, egalitarian, decentralized, civilizing" communities.

Luke Johnson also sees a fundamental dis-ease with the status quo as fundamental to the early Christian movement's growth. He describes various religious movements in the first-century world, with their oracles, prophecies, miracles, visions, teachings, communities, and ritual. These movements and practices express "the religious spirit of Hellenism in the early Roman Empire. That spirit is hungry for revelation, for transformation, and for a personal allegiance that would give a sense of identity in an alienating world."[68] The early Christian movement, sustained by written Gospels like Matthew's with its proclamation of the power of the risen Jesus and the experience of inclusive communities, addressed such yearnings.

Rodney Stark identifies another crucial element, the Christians' practical and merciful response to the imperial world's ills of hunger, homelessness, poverty, and social fragmentation. The early Christians provided the experience of a quite different social organization. They offered

> new norms and new kinds of social relationships.... To cities filled with the homeless and impoverished Christianity offered charity as well as hope. To cities filled with newcomers and strangers, Christianity offered an immediate basis for attachments. To cities filled with orphans and widows, Christianity offered a new and expanded sense of family. To cities torn by violent ethnic strife, Christianity offered a new basis for social solidarity. And to cities faced with epidemics, fires and earthquakes, Christianity offered effective nursing services.[69]

Significant in these three approaches is the recognition that Christianity provided an alternative communal experience and set of practices that were inclusive, egalitarian, merciful.[70] But while this emphasis on new social relationships and community is well placed, Christians were not the only movement to offer such possibilities. Numerous trade and funerary associations provided communal experience and organization, as did religious groups like the Isis cult. Along with a compelling alternative social experience, I would argue, Matthew's Gospel offers a plausible and persuasive worldview, or system of meaning, or theology, or way of looking at the world, that was expressed in and through the groups and their practices. The question "to what society do I belong?" has a corollary, "Who says?" or "To whom does the world belong?" Matthew offers a theological answer in asserting God's sovereignty.

This inclusive and egalitarian social experience and this theological worldview that asserts God's claim of sovereignty over the world and people's lives belong together. The combination is reflected in several passages in Matthew. In 4:17 Jesus announces the presence yet imminence of God's empire or reign. This claim of God's sovereignty over people's lives, God's empire, is immediately followed in 4:18–22 by a narrative in which Jesus forms a community by calling people to follow him as the one who manifests God's empire. Empires require and take form through people. God's empire constitutes and is expressed in this community. To it, Jesus gives the task of mission, of adding other people who encounter God's empire or rule and join the community (4:19). Theological claims and communal organization and experience go together.

In 10:8 Jesus again sends his disciples out in mission: "Cure the sick, raise the dead, cleanse the lepers, cast out demons." Such healings as extensions of Jesus' work offer people trapped in the daily miseries of Antioch numerous possibilities for transformed lives, new social relationships, and participation in an inclusive community. And at the end of the Gospel, the risen Jesus commands his disciples to "Go therefore and make disciples of all nations" (28:19a), again offering the experience of a different social reality. But each mission command is also accompanied by an instruction to preach or teach (10:7; 28:19–20). Each mission not only requires powerful actions and provides new social attachments, but also it provides an explanation, a proclamation of the significance of these actions in relation to God's purposes. Proclamation is not only about influencing people to live and act in certain ways; it is about influencing people to think and understand and perceive in certain ways.

And each command is accompanied by a claim of sovereignty. The command to do works of healing in 10:8 follows Jesus' instruction to proclaim God's empire in 10:7. The miracles are demonstrations of God's empire over the casualties of Roman imperial society (cf. 12:28). The notion of God's empire or God's rule is very political and "every day-ish." It is exactly the same language that describes political empires such as Rome's.[71] It centers on claims of who is in charge, who has the right to determine what human society and communities look like. It challenges Rome's claims and performance.

The mission command in 28:19 is similar. It follows Jesus' declaration in 28:18 that "all authority in heaven and on earth has been given to me." The passive construction ("has been given") expresses God's action. "Heaven and earth" is a way of describing all creation over which God is claimed to exercise sovereign rule with Jesus. But not yet is that empire established or acknowledged. Not yet is creation ordered according to God's purposes. That is why the world of Antioch is miserably unjust for most. Matthew's Gospel claims that Jesus' return will involve a reordering, a re-creating (19:28; 24:27–31), a new and different heaven and earth. Such a claim collides with Rome's claims that Jupiter rules the heavens and his agent, the emperor, rules the earth (see chapter 2). Matthew's worldview or theological claim disputes the assertions of imperial theology.

CONCLUSION

Running throughout the following chapters, then, is the argument that Matthew's Gospel challenges Rome's empire in two ways. The Gospel presents a *social* challenge in offering a different vision and experience of human interaction and community. Instead of a hierarchical, exploitative, exclusionary community based on "their great ones (being) tyrants over them" (20:25–26), it creates an inclusive, merciful, egalitarian community based on practical, merciful, loving service to others. But this social vision and organizational structure are rooted in and expressive of a theological traditional and worldview. The Gospel also presents a *theological* challenge. It contests the imperial theology or worldview that claims the world belongs to Jupiter and to Rome and the empire and emperor are Jupiter's chosen agents. It disputes the claims that the emperor is the gods' agent who mediates the gods' blessing to the world. The Gospel challenges the perception that Rome should rule the world. It refuses to accept Rome's claims to sovereignty, Rome's theological sanctions, and Rome's vision of social interaction that benefits a few and causes hardship to most. These claims do not seem plausible and the world does not have to be ordered this way. The Gospel sets Rome's claims within the context of God's greater purposes that declare different patterns for human interaction, different human allegiances and loyalties, and a different, yet-future reordering of the world. In so doing, it relativizes Rome's claims, demystifies them, reveals their shortcomings, and boldly dares to announce Rome's certain demise in the yet-future establishment of God's empire at the return of Jesus. God's empire reconfigures social relationships and will inevitably triumph over all other empires, especially Rome's.

Matthew's Gospel is, I am contending, a counternarrative, a work of resistance.[72] The following six chapters, chapters 4 to 9, will look at some of the ways in which this theological and social vision, enacted in local communities of followers of Jesus in Antioch in the very midst of the Roman Empire, is presented in Matthew's Gospel. In a concluding chapter we will need to think briefly about the plausibility of this vision in relation to contemporary discipleship.

- Part Two -

JESUS, AGENT OF GOD'S SALVIFIC PURPOSES

– F O U R –

Matthew's Presentation
of Jesus

I N THIS CHAPTER I want to draw attention to a remarkable but unnoticed similarity between claims made in Roman imperial theology about the emperor and empire and the presentation of Jesus in Matthew's Gospel. As we have seen in the previous three chapters, the emperor is presented as chosen by the gods to rule. He is regarded as the agent of their sovereignty, presence, and will on earth, and of their blessing that ensures society's well-being. Significantly, Jesus is also presented in Matthew's Gospel as an agent, chosen to manifest sovereignty, presence, divine will, and blessing for human well-being. But he is not the agent of Rome. He is God's agent. He asserts God's sovereignty, presence, will, and blessing among humans. In this chapter I will outline these claims and consider the implications of Matthew's Gospel presenting Jesus in a way that directly collides with and challenges the central claims that Rome makes about its empire and emperor.

I will proceed by comparing four overlapping motifs that are very significant for both imperial theology and Matthew's Christology: sovereignty, presence, agency, and societal well-being.[1] My concern is not to argue that imperial theology is *the* source for or origin of Matthew's presentation of Jesus.[2] While recognizing that imperial claims may well be one influence among others on the presentation of Jesus, I am more interested in examining the function or impact of this presentation in an imperial context. What happens when Matthew's story of Jesus is heard in a context in which an audience is familiar with imperial theology? How does this imperial theology affect the hearing of the Gospel?

My thesis is that the Gospel contests the claims of imperial theology that assert the empire and emperor to represent the gods' sovereignty, will, and blessing on earth. The Gospel's presentation of Jesus challenges imperial claims that the emperor embodies divine sovereignty and presence, and that the emperor, as the agent of the gods, ensures societal well-being. The Gospel's presentation of Jesus contributes to an alternative understanding of the world and life in it that subverts imperial theology and legitimates a community with an alternative worldview and lifestyle or set of practices. That is, this Christology, the presentation of Jesus as agent of God's sovereignty, is part of the Gospel's theological and social challenge to the empire.

A Distinctive Claim

The distinctive nature of this thesis can be seen by locating it in relation to previous scholarly discussions. First, discussions of New Testament Christology, of the significance of Jesus in the various presentations made of him in the New Testament documents, have generally focused on two issues: origin and development.[3] In terms of origin, scholars have examined various sources for the changing images of Jesus in the New Testament and in subsequent Christian writings and creeds: Jesus' self-understanding; various Jewish traditions (wisdom, apocalyptic); the role of various heavenly figures, especially angels; diverse Greco-Roman religious practices and understandings, and Christian experiences in teaching, mission, and worship. In terms of development, they have discussed the processes and circumstances through which these changes have come about. They have particularly tried to account for the development from more "functional" understandings of Jesus in the New Testament to the more ontological formulations (Jesus' divine and human natures) of the Councils of Nicea (325 C.E.) and Chalcedon (451 C.E.).[4] This discussion has been rich, insightful, and stimulating. But while some scholars like Adolf Deissmann have helpfully drawn attention to similarities in the *language* used for Jesus and for the emperor,[5] generally scholars have paid little attention to the larger shape and motifs of imperial theology, or to the impact of using imperially familiar terms in the Gospel's presentation of Jesus.

A second context of scholarly work highlights the distinctive approach I am offering in this chapter. Scholars who have discussed Matthew's presentation of Jesus have done so in two dominant ways. Much attention has been paid to the titles that are applied to Jesus: Christ, Son of God, Son of Man, Son of David, Lord.[6] Scholars have generally traced out the backgrounds of these terms in Jewish and Greco-Roman traditions, and/or have argued that one particular title is the most important one for the Gospel. J. D. Kingsbury's advocacy of "Son of God" as the "central Christological title" in Matthew has been especially prominent.

Others have been critical of this focus on the Gospel's titles for Jesus.[7] Scholars using different forms of narrative or audience-oriented criticism have argued that Jesus is not presented in the Gospel only by means of titles. And titles, whatever their historical backgrounds, derive meaning from the narrative contexts in which they appear. These scholars have tended to talk about Jesus as a character in the Gospel story who is the sum of various traits or characteristics that he exhibits throughout the Gospel. While titles may contribute to this picture, so do his actions, words, interactions with other characters, and sections of the Gospel in which no titles appear.

My focus on these four significant motifs of sovereignty, presence, agency, and societal well-being is an extension of this second approach in that it highlights aspects of Jesus' character that are not particularly shaped by titles (though titles will contribute to them as will be clear in the discussion of agency below). Yet the focus is distinctive in that neither approaches that have focused on titles nor narrative approaches have paid much attention to Roman imperial theology. Investigations of the title "Christ" or "Messiah," for example, have invariably discussed Jewish messianic expectations (or non-expectations). But in observing the term's basic meaning of "anointing" as an expression of being commissioned for a task, it has neglected the key "commissioned" figure who dominates late-first-century society, the Roman emperor who is commissioned to rule by the gods. Or to take a second example, David Kupp has completed a very informative study of the title "Emmanuel" and the theme of God's presence in Matthew's Gospel.[8] This is an important theme (1:23; 18:20; 28:20), but while Kupp presents a fine discussion of Jewish notions of God's presence, he does not consider the relevance of the imperial claim that kings and emperors are "Emmanuel," a *deus praesens*, a θεὸς ἐπιφανής (*theos epiphanēs*) who manifests the presence and will of the gods. One well-known claimant of this title was Antiochus IV Epiphanes, whose second-century B.C.E. attempts to dismantle faithful Jewish worship and observance are vividly described in the Maccabean literature, and whose defeat was celebrated in the first century by Jews in the festival of Hanukkah.[9] Similar claims to manifest the gods' presence are made about Roman emperors, as we observed in chapters 1 to 3. Surely it is most unlikely that Matthew's audience will encounter the presentation of Jesus' role as Emmanuel in the Gospel's opening chapter (1:23) without it colliding with this well-known imperial claim.

My focus in this chapter is, then, on what happens when these claims about the emperor as the agent of the gods' sovereignty, presence, and blessing collide with claims about Jesus as God's agent. Are we to understand the fact that the Gospel's presentation of Jesus utilizes four motifs that are so prominent in imperial theology merely as an accident of cultural influence? Is this intersection of imperial and Christian claims irrelevant? Or should we conclude that this religious text happens to use political motifs and language to make its own religious claims but they have nothing to do with imperial politics? But we have observed that in the imperial world, there is no such separation of the political and the religious. And it is rather hard to claim sovereignty without impinging on someone else's (claimed) territory. What happens, then, when these claims collide? I will argue that the collision of these claims about Jesus with claims about the Roman imperial system and the emperor functions to contest Roman imperial claims, to challenge and subvert their legitimacy, and to point to an alternative understanding, community, and set of practices for followers of Jesus.

WHOSE WORLD IS IT?
THE ISSUE OF SOVEREIGNTY

Jesus has little significance in Matthew's Gospel apart from God's perspective and actions. It is God who initiates his conception (1:18–25), who names him, and who commissions him for his life's work of saving people (1:21–23). It is God who declares Jesus' identity at his baptism and transfiguration, "my Son, the Beloved, with whom I am well pleased" (3:13–17; 17:5). Jesus makes it clear that he exists in intimate relationship with God (11:25–27) and that he is concerned with doing God's will (4:1–11; 26:42). Hence any discussion of Jesus in Matthew's Gospel should begin with God and God's purposes.

In fact, it is with God's purposes that the narrative begins. The opening seventeen verses of the Gospel display God's sovereign purposes at work in human history. The genealogy embraces a sweep of Israel's history from Abraham to King David (1:2–6a), to Babylonian exile (1:11–12), to the birth of the Christ (1:17). It views this history in a Christological perspective in that the coming of Jesus is the decisive event in a history that involves a whole host of characters beginning with Abraham. The genealogy demonstrates, among other things, that God supervises human history, that God's purposes especially run through Israel (not Rome), that God's purposes are not always faithfully embodied by humans but they are not thereby hindered (kings, exile), and that all sorts of humans (wicked and faithful, famous and obscure, firstborn and insignificant, male and female, Jew and Gentile) are caught up in those purposes.[10] The Gospel expands on these demonstrations. God's purposes span the whole period of history from the Creator's work at the beginning (13:35; 19:4, 8) to the end with the scenes of judgment (13:49–50, etc.), the establishment of God's empire (25:34), and new creation (5:18; 19:28; 24:35). God rules over all.[11]

Whenever Matthean scholars have attended to "the concept of history in Matthew," they have focused primarily either on Jesus' delayed return and the problem of continuing (salvation) history,[12] or on the timing of the dawning of the new age through Jesus.[13] But these opening verses in the genealogy and the context of imperial theology point to a much more basic issue, that of sovereignty.[14] Imperial theology proclaims, as I have indicated in chapters 1 to 3, that the gods have appointed Rome to rule an empire without limits (Virgil, *Aen.* 1.254, 278–79). Jupiter ordains the rule and military successes of Vespasian, Titus and Domitian (Silius Italicus, *Punica* 3.593–629). "At Jupiter's command [Domitian] rules for him the blessed world" (Statius, *Silvae* 5.1.37). It is because of the gods that Domitian is "Lord of the earth" (Statius, *Silvae* 3.4.20), "ruler of the nations" (*Silvae* 4.2.14–15), ruler of the world (Martial, *Epigrams* 5.3.3), "master of sea and land" (Philostratus *Vit. Apoll.* 7.3), and "ruler of lands and seas and nations" (Juvenal, *Sat.* 4.83–84). Rome rules human history, the world, its land, its seas, its events, its battles, its people. Rome exercises sovereignty at the will of the gods, especially Jupiter, who have chosen the Flavians as vice-regents to rule over human affairs.

The Gospel's assertions in the opening genealogy that God's purposes, not Rome's, are being worked out in human history, and that those purposes run through Israel not Rome collide with these imperial claims. The fundamental question is: "To whom does the sovereignty of the world belong?"[15] Whose world is it? Who or what directs human history and destiny? The Gospel's answer is clear. It is God's world. God created it (19:4), sustains it, rules it, and holds it accountable. The Gospel's scenes of final judgment depict God's "No" to Jupiter's claim of a Roman Empire that has dominion without end.[16]

In the present, Jesus manifests God's claim in his words and actions. The Gospel's central term for manifesting God's sovereignty is "the empire or reign of the heavens" with which Jesus opens his ministry in 4:17. The term is not a "stable concept" with fixed content but a "tensive symbol" that evokes various expressions of God acting on behalf of God's people or God's rule, and that gains definition and precision as the narrative progresses.[17] In the context of Matt 1:1–4:16, it refers to what God is doing through Jesus who is called "to save his people from their sins." This task involves, as I will discuss in the next chapter, the assertion of God's reign over the earth and nothing other than the eventual overthrow of Rome (24:27–31; 25:34). Only a world not ordered according to God's purposes, the world under Rome's domination, needs saving, needs the assertion of God's rule. Klaus Wengst rightly argues that Jesus' proclamation of God's empire

> amounts to a questioning of the Pax Romana: anyone who prays for the coming of the kingdom of God [Matt 6:10], expects it very soon, and has no faith in the imperial good tidings of a pacified world and human happiness in it.[18]

But it is more than a questioning, it is a challenge that subverts imperial claims and creates an alternative empire and way of life. In his actions and teachings, Jesus manifests God's sovereignty or empire in which he and God, not Rome, share "all authority in heaven and on earth" (28:18), an empire that prefers egalitarian structures rather than Rome's hierarchy (23:8–12; chs. 19–20),[19] an empire that emphasizes service not Rome's domination (20:24–28), that values inclusion not the elite's exclusion (9:9–13), mutuality not patriarchy (19:3–9; 23:9), healing not sickness (4:23–25), food and plenty not lack for the majority (12:1–8; 14:13–21; 15:32–39), the marginal not the center (19:13–15), inclusive love not privilege (5:45), mercy not intimidating violence (9:13; 26:52), God not Caesar (22:15–22). These actions and teaching negate any attempt to argue that God's empire is somehow "spiritual" or "individual" in its sovereignty, and poses no political threat.

The very language of "empire" or "reign" or "kingdom" (βασιλεία, *basileia*) underlines how great a threat the assertion of God's empire poses to empires like Rome's. The term "empire" or "kingdom" appears in a wide range of literature to name numerous empires: Nebuchadnezzar's Assyrian Empire (Dan 1:20; 4:31, 36; Jdt 1:1; 2:12); the Persian Empire of Artaxerxes (Esth 1:4, 19–22; 3:6), of Darius (Dan 6:4; cf. 11:4), and of Cyrus (1 Esd 2:2; Bel 1:1; Josephus, *C. Ap.* 1.150); the Empires of Alexander "the Great" (1 Macc 1:6; 11:1), of Babylon, the Medes, Persia, and the Greeks (Dan 2:37–45; 1 Macc 8:18), and of Antiochus Epiphanes (1 Macc 1:16, 41, 51; 2 Macc 4:7; Josephus, *J.W.* 1.40; 7.44). It also designates Rome's Empire (*Sib. Or.* 3.47; Josephus, *J.W.* 5.409; idem, *Ant.* 18.120 "from the kingdoms [βασιλειῶν] ruled by the Romans"; Hadrian's Roman Empire, Appian, *Bell. Civ.* 2.86; cf. 1 Pet 2:13, 17).

Empires require kings or emperors. The cognate noun βασιλεύς (*basileus;* "emperor"; "king") denotes Roman emperors in Josephus, *J.W.* 3.351; 4.596; 5.58 (Titus), 563 (see also 1 Tim 2:2; 1 Pet 2:13, 17).[20] Matthew's Gospel designates Jesus a βασιλεύς ("king," "emperor") from the outset when Jesus' birth is presented as threatening to Herod, Rome's puppet king in chapter 2. Both Herod and Jesus are presented as king (2:1–3, 9), a juxtaposition so frightening to Herod that he seeks to kill Jesus. Jesus is later hailed as a king or emperor in entering Jerusalem (21:5) and is crucified and mocked as king in chapter 27 (27:11, 29, 37, 42) in a scene that shows the supposed triumph of the will and soldiers of the Roman rulers.

The assertion of God's claim to rule and order the world according to God's just purposes and not according to Rome's system designed to benefit the elite at the expense of the rest threatens the imperial status quo. God's action in Jesus provokes the ruling powers to strike back with force and violence. The empire's violent intolerance for any opponents is depicted in several scenes. King Herod resorts to murderous violence to kill the newborn baby who is known as "king of the Jews" (ch. 2). Herod the Tetrach beheads John the Baptist who has been critical of Herod's personal morality and political alliances (14:1–12). Pilate, with whom the "religious" leaders are allied, readily executes Jesus, king of the Jews, a perceived leader of the resistance (27:11; see chapter 8 below).

Such actions by rulers are not new or unusual in the biblical tradition from which Matthew so frequently draws. These accounts recall that God's people have often lived in sociohistorical contexts of rival claimants to sovereignty. "Kings of the earth" (cf. 17:25; Ps 2:1–3) like Herod, and Pharaoh whom he resembles, always resist God's sovereignty, but God laughs them into oblivion (Ps 2:4). Jesus' proclamation and demonstration of God's imminent empire attest God's sovereignty and anticipate its final establishment over all.

The Gospel narrative makes a stunning claim about the sovereignty that Rome protects so violently. The narrative reveals that behind Rome's pretensions to sovereignty is another power, that of Satan. In the temptation scene (4:1–11), Satan offers Jesus control of "all the kingdoms/empires (βασιλεία, *basileia*) of the world" if Jesus will worship Satan (4:8–9). The offer is astounding. It expresses Satan's claim to control the world's empires, to have them at his disposal and under his rule. Rome's empire is viewed as devilish and diabolical, an expression of Satan's sovereignty. Further, Satan uses the same noun, "empire" or "kingdom" (βασιλεία, *basileia*), in making this offer in 4:8 as Jesus uses when he begins his public ministry a few verses later. In a programmatic statement, Jesus proclaims that "the empire of the heavens" is at hand in his ministry (4:17). Both Jesus and Satan claim sovereignty and their claims collide. Moreover, Satan's demand that Jesus "worship" Satan is expressed in language that has very explicit political and military dimensions. The verb for "worship" (προσκυνέω, *proskyneō*) echoes the political practice of *proskynesis*. This practice involved the act of prostration or bowing in submission before a ruler or emperor. It signified submission to Rome's military power.[21] But Jesus refuses any such recognition of Satan's/Rome's sovereignty. And Jesus exhibits power over Satan, resisting and dismissing him (4:10–11). Subsequently, Jesus casts out demons as a display of God's empire and sovereignty (12:28), claims that in the resurrection God has given him all authority in heaven and on earth (28:18), and promises that finally in the judgment and new creation he will overcome all Satan's resistance (13:39–42).

What happens, then, when these claims about God's sovereignty interact with Jupiter's/Rome's claims? One scene that shows this interaction is Jesus' response to the question about paying taxes (22:15–22). Taking a coin with the emperor's image on it, he says, "Give therefore to the emperor the things that are the emperor's and to God the things that are God's" (22:21). Whatever else this cryptic comment may mean,[22] it cannot in the Gospel's point of view[23] mean that God and Caesar are the same, or equal, or unrelated, or that God is subordinate to Caesar. In the Gospel's worldview, it asserts the priority of God's empire. It is God's, not the emperor's or Jupiter's, world, whatever the recent destruction of the Jerusalem temple in 70 C.E. and the tax imposed on Jews to restore the Temple of Jupiter Capitolinus in Rome may claim (see chapter 7 below and 17:24–27). Jesus' manifestation of God's empire is the assertion of God's prior claim on the allegiance of the world.

Throughout the Gospel Jesus asserts God's claim of sovereignty, often in language that expresses a polemic against imperial claims and practices. Jesus declares, for example, that God controls the sun and sends the rain (5:45), claims often associated with Jupiter.[24] He identifies God as "our Father... in Heaven" (6:9) and "Lord of heaven and on earth," (11:25), language frequently used by the imperial poets of Jupiter or his agent Domitian. The risen Jesus declares that he and God share "all authority in heaven and earth" not Jupiter or Rome or the emperor or the empire (28:18). The center of the divine purposes is not Rome but the community that acknowledges God's reign. This community and its claims exist within the very heart of the Roman Empire in an ambivalent relationship to it.[25] The emperor cannot be ignored, but he does not define ultimate reality. Caesar has power but God is sovereign.

How are we to assess the interaction of these claims? Do they simply coexist? Has God endorsed Rome's rule? Is God simply not concerned with Rome? None of these is a tenable option in the light of the previous discussion. Claims of God's sovereignty, taken up from Jewish traditions, contest and dispute Rome's claims to rule the world. The world belongs to God not Rome, despite all the evidence to the contrary whether military might, conquest, territory, or taxes and tribute. The Gospel's repeated assertion that God's empire will be established in full (chs. 13:36–43; 25:31–46) exposes the limits of Rome's power and declares its demise. Its demonstration in the present through Jesus' ministry, and continued through his disciples, critiques the structures and values of Rome's empire with the creation of an alternative community that anticipates the full and final display of God's sovereignty over all, including Rome.

A SECOND MOTIF:
MANIFESTING GOD'S PRESENCE

Matthean scholars have long noted the Gospel's focus on divine presence. But rarely have they brought this theme into dialogue with the claims of imperial theology that the emperor manifests the presence of the gods and of Jupiter/Zeus among their subjects. Philo reports the emperor Gaius Caligula's intent to convert the Jerusalem temple into a temple of his own to bear the name of Gaius, "the new Zeus made manifest" (*Legat.* 346). Domitian is "that present deity," *a deus praesens,* as Statius calls him (Silvae 5.2.170). As Jupiter's chosen vice-regent, he so manifests Jupiter's presence and is so identified with Jupiter as the agent of his will that Martial (*Epigrams* 4.8.8–9; 13.91.2) and Statius (*Silvae* 1.pref. 20) call him Jupiter. What happens when the Gospel's claims about Jesus collide with Roman imperial claims about the emperor and empire?

Three times the Gospel asserts it is Jesus (not the emperor) that manifests God's presence. The first instance occurs, prominently and influentially, at the beginning of the Gospel in 1:23 in a narrative interpretation of the angel's naming of the baby "Jesus." The name "Jesus," explained in 1:21 as meaning "he will save his people from their sins," now receives a further explanation from a second name for the baby, "they will name him Emmanuel." This (Hebrew) name, whose meaning is emphasized with an explanation in Greek ("which means, God is with us"), stands over the whole of the Gospel plot and places all of Jesus' ministry in its interpretive spotlight. Jesus' words and actions throughout the story, his teachings and miracles, his parables and conflicts, are to be understood as manifesting God's presence (cf. 12:28).

But the claim that he is Emmanuel has a polemical edge to it, partly in relation to post-70 Jewish debates,[26] but also in relation to imperial claims. The narrative explanation in 1:22–23 is one of Matthew's fulfillment citations and will be discussed in detail in chapter 5 below. The citation comes from Isa 7:14 and 8:8, 10. In these chapters God offers Judah, threatened by the imperial powers of Syria and Israel (and Assyria), a sign of hope and salvation in the form of a baby as an indication that God will resist and overthrow the imperialist aggressors. The use of the same text in Matt 1:23 in relation to another situation dominated by imperial power and to another baby portrays the baby Jesus similarly as a sign of resistance and hope for people under imperial control. In the midst of the Roman Empire, God has given Jesus the task of saving his people. Part of that task is to manifest God's presence and sovereignty. God's presence means liberation or salvation from imperial powers such as Egypt (Deut 31:23), Assyria (Isa 7–8), and Babylon (Isa 41:10; 43:5). Manifested in Jesus, God's presence will mean liberation from Rome's power.[27]

The second explicit statement of God's presence in Jesus comes in 18:20 in the context of the community of disciples gathered for prayer. In that gathering Jesus' presence is encountered. There is an implicit contrast with the empire in this scene. The verse claims that divine presence is not found in the dominating, excluding, hierarchical society formed by Rome's militaristic and economically exploitative elite, but in the inclusive community of disciples. Chapter 18 is commonly known as Jesus' "community discourse" because in this chapter Jesus teaches his disciples about their communal relationships and responsibilities that derive from God's empire/kingdom (18:1–4, 23). The communities of Jesus' followers are to be marked by service, mercy, reconciliation, and forgiveness. That is, the question concerning sovereignty over the world ("To whom does the sovereignty of the world belong?") has a corollary: "To what community, to what society, do I belong?"[28] The communities of followers of Jesus remain open for anyone to participate, emphasize inclusivity, provide practical mercy, and offer distinctively alternative structures and practices. In so doing the presence of Jesus is encountered.

Likewise, the third explicit statement about divine presence in 28:20 is addressed to the community of disciples. But this time, the risen Jesus commissions them to worldwide mission and promises, "I am with you always, to the ends of the age." In contrast to Rome's mission "to rule the nations with your power . . . to crown peace with law, to spare the humbled, and to tame in war the proud" (Virgil, *Aen.* 6.851–53, Anchises to Aeneas), this community knows God's presence through Jesus in a mission that announces God's empire, demonstrates it in acts of healing and mercy, and passes on Jesus' teaching as the basis for a different way of life (cf. 28:18–20; 10:7–8).

A Presence Threatening to Roman Imperial Power

Jesus' manifestation of God's presence disturbs and threatens the imperial status quo from the start of the Gospel story. After the initial statement of Jesus' mission to manifest God's presence in 1:23 and the evoking of the imperial context of Isa 7–8, Jesus enters the imperial world of Herod (2:1, 3), vassal king of the Romans, who acknowledges Rome as "masters of the world" (Josephus, *Ant.* 15.387). The narrative of chapter 2 depicts the way of God's presence (and sovereignty) in the imperial world.

The magi come from the east, the location of Rome's enemy Parthia. Not surprisingly, they do not support Rome's ally Herod in the narrative. Their inquiry in 2:2 into the birthplace of "who has been born king of the Jews" focuses on Jesus not Herod, even though Herod was known by this title (Josephus, *Ant.* 16.311). Their nondiplomatic question and reference ally the magi with Jesus against Herod and depict the magi in their conventional role of posing a threat to ruling powers.[29] The citing of Mic. 5 and 2 Sam 5 in 2:6 with its reference to Bethlehem (cf. 2:1) and threefold reference to rulers also points to Jesus not Herod. Another term, προσκυνέω (*proskyneō*) echoes the political practice of *proskynesis,* prostration or bowing before a ruler or emperor, as I observed above.[30] The term is used here three times in relation to Jesus (2:2, 8, 11), but not for Herod. The magi's worship of Jesus with gifts of gold, frankincense, and myrrh evokes traditions of Gentiles (nations and kings) making a pilgrimage to Zion with gifts (Ps 72:10–11; Isa 2:1–4). But the tradition is subverted because the travel destination is not the elite's powerful center Jerusalem, whose temple was destroyed in 70 C.E., but "insignificant" marginal Bethlehem. Jesus, the object of this worship, appears as a new temple. And in this scene King Herod does not journey to worship.

This conflict with and undermining of Herod continues in that Herod's initiatives to co-opt the magi (2:4, 7, 8) are turned aside by a dream and the uncooperative magi (2:12). His attempts to kill Jesus are thwarted by an angel and a dream (2:13, 19–20) and serve to further the divine will (2:15, 18). With irony the narrative refers three times to Herod's death (2:15, 19, 20), God's ultimate frustration of Herod's plan to put Jesus to death. Two systems clash, the imperial and God's. The imperial system actively opposes God's presence (and sovereignty). The narrative exposes it as ruthless and murderous, and deconstructs it. It is not ultimate.

Is this too much to make of chapter 2? I suggest not on at least four counts. First, scholars have noted numerous echoes of Moses and Pharaoh in chapter 2.[31] This is another story in which political power, representative of a theological worldview, conflicts with God's presence. The display of God's sovereign power and liberating presence in the exodus relativizes and overcomes Pharaoh's vicious power and resistance. Second, the reference to the exile in 2:17–18 (cf. 1:11–12, 17) evokes traditions of God's sovereignty and presence in liberating the people from Babylonian imperialism (Isa 41:10; 43:1–7). Third, the narrative recognizes the ongoing existence of imperial power. After the death of Herod, "Archelaus reigned over Judea in place of (ἀντί, *anti*) his father" (2:22). Though Herod dies, there is a successor whose reign causes an adjustment (2:22b–23a) but not the defeat of God's purposes (2:23b). Fourth, chapter 2 foreshadows Jesus' crucifixion by Pilate as the empire's agent.[32] The empire's ultimate effort to destroy Emmanuel is to crucify him. But the Gospel's conclusion will show the limits, not the triumph, of Rome's power. Jesus' resurrection indicates that while the imperial system has the power to inflict death, God's power and presence are not curtailed but overcome that death. The empire cannot accomplish its purpose of removing Jesus' presence because God thwarts it in raising him from the dead. The risen Jesus is thus present with his disciples "to the ends of the age" (28:20), when his presence will mean the destruction of Rome (24:27–31) and establishment of God's empire.

The Gospel's affirmation, then, that divine presence is manifested in Jesus and the community of disciples (1:23; 18:20; 28:20) challenges the imperial claim about Jupiter's presence with the emperor. It is the creator of the world, the God who overcomes death and who will yet complete God's purposes for the world in a new creation, that is encountered in Jesus. Inevitably there will be conflict and danger in the collision of rival claimants and systems (10:18; 16:24), but imperial claims are not ultimate.

A THIRD MOTIF: AGENCY

Imperial theology claims that the emperor and empire are the gods' agents chosen to manifest the divine will, presence, and blessing among humans. Jupiter ordains it that Romans will be "lords of the world" (Virgil, *Aen.* 1.281). Seneca has Nero say, "Have I of all mortals found favor with heaven and been chosen to serve on earth as vicar of the gods? I am the arbiter of life and death" (*Clem.* 1.1.2). "At Jupiter's command he [Domitian] rules for him the blessed world" (Statius, *Silvae* 4.3.128–29). As Jupiter's agent Domitian rules "the blessed earth with paternal sway" (Silius Italicus, *Punica* 3.625–26).

The Gospel disputes the claim that the emperor is the agent chosen to manifest the divine will. It contests the claim that the world as ruled and structured by Rome is ordered as it should be. Instead it asserts repeatedly that Jesus is God's agent chosen to manifest God's sovereignty, presence, will, and blessing.

Three Key Titles of Agency: Christ

The opening verse of the Gospel makes the claim that Jesus is God's agent. Jesus is called "Christ," the Greek term for the Hebrew word "Messiah" (1:1). The term literally means "dripped on" or "anointed." To be "anointed" means to be "commissioned" or recognized as the one who will carry out a particular task. But the term does not specify what the task or tasks will be. In the biblical traditions, numerous human figures are anointed or commissioned ("christed") to perform various tasks. These figures include kings (Ps 2:2), prophets (1 Kings 19:16), priests (Lev 4:3, 5), and a Gentile imperial ruler, Cyrus the Persian, who is anointed to set the people free from Babylonian rule (Isa 44:28; 45:1). Some but by no means all Jewish traditions expected various types of figures to be commissioned or "christed" in the near future to set the people free from Rome (Pss. Sol. 17; *4 Ezra* 12:32–34) or to have some other roles in establishing God's empire in full. For example in 1 Enoch 46–48 a heavenly figure called the Son of Man is "anointed" to judge "the kings of the earth and the mighty landowners" for their oppressive acts and exploitative quest for wealth. In Qumran a priestly messiah will teach God's will through interpreting the law (CD 7:18–21).[33]

Hence to call Jesus "Christ" in 1:1 is to recognize that God has commissioned him, not Rome, for a special purpose. But because of its diverse uses, the title does not specify what Jesus is commissioned or "christed" to do. So along with the affirmation that Jesus is the Christ or God's agent comes a question. What is Jesus commissioned to do? What task has God given him to do? The only way to answer this question is to read on in Matthew's narrative to find an answer.

The question is answered in part toward the end of chapter 1 in 1:21–23 in the names given to Jesus. The names elaborate his commissioning to save from sins (Jesus) and to manifest God's presence (Emmanuel). He is the agent of God's saving presence, a task that immediately sets him at odds with Rome's claims as I have outlined above. He will carry out this commission throughout the whole Gospel narrative in his words and actions.

King

A further answer comes in 2:2 as the magi refer to him as "king," a title that will figure prominently in his crucifixion (27:11, 29, 37, 42). Kings in the biblical traditions, ideally, represent God's reign. In Ps 72, the psalmist prays that God will give to the king "justice" and "righteousness" so that he will "judge your people with righteousness and your poor with justice" and "defend the cause of the poor . . . give deliverance to the needy and crush the oppressor" (Ps 72:1–4, 12–14; cf. Isa 32:1–8). The Psalmist also prays that the king will live a long time, that peace may abound, that the king will have "dominion from sea to sea" over his enemies, that he will receive tribute as the nations serve him, and that there will be abundant grain (Ps 72: 8–11, 16). Such a vision, though clearly impacted by imperial values, is in its concern with justice and the poor and needy very much at odds with Rome's empire with its exploitation of the poor for the benefit of the elite. Jesus is the agent of God's empire who is commissioned to enact these concerns in the present and to accomplish their full enactment in the final yet-future completion of God's purposes.

Son

A third designation for Jesus as "son" (2:15) also emphasizes he is God's agent (3:17; 17:5, "beloved son"). The language of being God's son is used in the Hebrew Bible traditions for kings (Ps 2:7), Israel (Hos 11:1), and the wise person (Wis 2). It expresses their special relationship to God as agents of God's will and as recipients of God's love (Deut 7:7–8; Ps 89:1–4; Hos 11:1). God's declaration at Jesus' baptism that Jesus is "my Son, the Beloved" expresses both these themes and articulates the "correct" evaluation of Jesus' identity and commission by which all other characters in the Gospel will be evaluated.[34] In confessing Jesus to be God's son, disciples recognize Jesus' agency in agreement with God's verdict on him (14:33; 16:16). Perhaps the most daring and subversive use of the term in the Gospel comes from the Roman soldiers who confess Jesus to be "son of God" at the cross in 27:54. The title "son of God" was particularly, though not exclusively, associated with the emperor Augustus. It was also used to refer to other emperors including Domitian,[35] whom Statius also describes as "beloved of the gods" (*Silvae* 4.2.14–15). This confession by soldiers of the empire that Jesus is God's son or agent agrees with God's designation of Jesus as "son of God." It discloses that in crucifying Jesus, the elite have killed God's agent, an indication of both the nature and intensity of their opposition. In using this title for Jesus, the soldiers transfer to Jesus a title that belongs to Augustus and other emperors. They express the recognition that Jesus, not the emperor, is God's agent, a recognition that the community of disciples makes.

Challenge and Conflict

As God's agent, Jesus' challenge to the imperial status quo is marked by conflict. He denies that the religious leaders, members of the retainer class (see chapter 1 above) and allies of Rome, are God's agent (15:13; 21:43–45). His rejection of the domination structures of the "rulers of the Gentiles" (20:25–26), his careful division of "the things of Caesar" from "the things of God" (22:21), and his prediction of Rome's demise at his future coming in glory (24:27–31) cast the same judgment on Rome. Jesus knows that empires always strikes back at those who confront them as evidenced by the fate of previous agents of God who challenged imperial power, Moses (Exod 14), Elijah (1 Kgs 19), Jeremiah (Jer 20:1–2), the suffering servant (Isa 52:13–53:12), John the Baptist (Matt 14:1–12). So he announces his own inevitable ("must") death at the hands of the religious leaders (16:21) and of the Gentiles (20:19). They are enemies of God's purposes and of God's agent. But his death is not their triumph and his defeat. It is a ransom, a means of liberation for others (20:28), because his resurrection exposes the limits of imperial power and demonstrates God's power over the ruling elite. Post 70, the Gospel looks back on the fall of Jerusalem in 70 which ended the priestly power with the temple's destruction, as God's judgment enacted through Roman power (21:43; 22:7; 24:3).[36] It looks forward in anticipation to Jesus' return and the triumphant establishment of God's purposes and empire.

Jesus commissions his disciples to continue his mission of manifesting God's empire through their words and actions (10:7–8; 28:18–20). The community of disciples will, like him, face opposition and conflict (10:16–18). But in faithfully undertaking its task, it continues the task given to Israel to be a "light to the nations" (5:14; cf. Isa 49:3, 6). The image is significant because Cicero uses it to describe Rome ("a light to the whole world," *Cat.* 4.11), and the imperial poets describe Domitian's presence as light shining in darkness (Martial *Epigrams* 8.21; Statius *Silvae* 4.1.3–4, 23–27). But for Matthew, Rome's empire is the darkness into which God's saving light shines in God's agent Jesus (cf. 4:15–16).

A FOURTH MOTIF: SOCIETAL WELL-BEING

Imperial theology boasts that the emperor and the empire, the agents of the gods' sovereignty and presence, bring well-being to a submissive world. The gods through the emperor have gifted peace, corn, harmony, well-being, safety, and protection to humans. This, of course, is the elite's view "from above,"[37] the view of the rulers and beneficiaries of empire whose well-being comes about at the social and economic expense of the subjugated and exploited population. But, as I will argue in the next chapter, it is Matthew's view that it is precisely *from* this imperial "well-being," from these sins of oppression, domination and economic greed, that the world needs to be saved. That is, the Gospel does not accept the imperial claims about the blessed state of the world, does not accept that Rome is a channel of blessing, and contends that only with the establishment of God's empire can such well-being and blessing be known. That empire is encountered in part now in Jesus and the community committed to him.

Matthew's Gospel views well-being in relation to God's sovereign presence. Various interconnected terms denote aspects of it—saving (1:21), the reign of God (4:17; 5:3, 10), good news (4:23), blessing (5:3–12) and righteousness or justice (5:10, 20; 6:33)—while numerous Gospel stories demonstrate its impact. Jesus declares in the Beatitudes that God's blessings are already being experienced among the poor in spirit, those who mourn the misrule of God's world, the powerless ("meek"), and those dissatisfied with exploitation and injustice (5:3–6).[38] The praying of Jesus' prayer asks God for the blessings that come from the hallowing of God's name, the coming of God's reign, the doing of God's will, namely God's gifts of bread, forgiveness, and deliverance from temptation and evil (6:9–13). Such petitions reject Rome's imperial order. They express a desire for God's transforming work to be completed.[39]

Among the first to encounter Jesus' manifestation of God's empire (4:17; 12:28) and the well-being it creates are the marginal, "the sick, those afflicted with various diseases and pains, demoniacs, epileptics, and paralytics" (4:23–24; chs 8–9; 10:8; 11:4–6). These people are of no account to imperial power. They are excluded from any social benefits by the elite. They are the poor in spirit, not the privileged and powerful, the victims and casualties of empire.[40] Jesus performs miracles to heal these sick people. But the significance of his actions in terms of the Gospel's verdict on imperial power cannot be missed. Jesus heals people who have been made sick by the imperial system. *Imperial power is bad for your health.* In chapter 3, I described something of the poverty, squalor, and misery that marked city life among the non-elite, and which was common among rural peasants. Poor nutrition, an inadequate food supply, excessive work, poor or nonexistent sanitation, overcrowded living conditions, and contaminated water were common. Disease was rife. But these conditions were common because of the imperial system's economic structures and practices. The elite extracted a significant percentage of peasant production in taxes and tribute, sold food at high profits, and secured their own wealth and comfort at the expense of the non-elite who could not afford improved housing or sanitation or leisure. In such conditions of poverty, people get sick with skin disease, blindness, poor bone development, weak immunity to germs, and so forth. Life expectancy is short for the non-elite.

Moreover, illness can express the impact of imperial power in another way. Even in modern times, we have witnessed in television reports the brutal impact of imperial power on people through trauma and rendering them speechless and paralyzed.[41] Further, sociopsychological approaches to demon possession observe the phenomena of trauma, speechlessness, and paralysis in situations of social tension, economic exploitation, and colonial domination.[42] Invading, alien forces (demons) are understood to take control and have to be "thrown out," the literal translation for the verb usually translated "cast out." One example is especially compelling. Jesus throws out demons into pigs who charge over a cliff to their watery doom (Matt 8:28–34). The pig was the mascot of Rome's Tenth Fretensis Legion that was stationed in Antioch and that played a prominent part in the destruction of Jerusalem in 70 C.E.[43] The exorcism represents, among other things, Jesus' victory over the demonic forces, the throwing out of Rome. Mental illness abounds in imperial situations. The oppressed are caught in a schizophrenic state between submitting (and so hastening their own demise) and resisting (thereby recognizing the superior power and risking being its victims).[44]

As far as the Gospel is concerned, the world under Rome's control is a sick place. This view conflicts with the quite different perspective expressed

in the propagandist writings of Aristides who, as one of the empire's beneficiaries, heaps accolades on Roman rule. This upper-class provincial crows
about Rome's wonderful benefits by observing that "the civilized world,
which had been sick from the beginning as it were, has been brought by
the right knowledge to a state of health" (*Roman Oration*, 97). And Josephus assumes the "health" of Rome's world in comparing Jewish revolts
against Rome's domination to "an inflammation [that] as in a sick man's
body, broke out in another quarter" (*J.W.* 2.264) and to a "contagion"
(*J.W.* 7.260). The burning of rebellious Jerusalem in 70 c.e. is, then, the
right medicine, "just what the doctor ordered" to destroy this sickness and
maintain good (Roman) health!

The numerous Gospel scenes that depict Jesus healing the sick name what
most people knew to be a reality of the imperial world. Many suffered from
numerous diseases whether from demons (see the *Testament of Solomon*) or
from poor economic conditions with limited resources, taxation burdens,
malnutrition, hunger, overwork, unhealthy living conditions, or from psy-
chosomatic illnesses in which the paralyzing and silencing impact of imperial
control is expressed in paralysis and muteness.[45] Matthew's inclusion of such
characters in the Gospel story reflects the realities of the imperial world. But
the scenes also show God's power of new creation at work in Jesus, bringing
healing and offering the possibility of new physical, social, and economic
life. In their healing is God's blessing and a new future (5:3–12). God's
reign and justice particularly, but not exclusively, work where there are no
options, no power, no resources, no hope. This display of God's merciful
blessing and power challenges the imperial and elitist system's discarding
of such people. Matthew's claim is that not only has Rome not healed a
sick world but it has sickened the world. Jesus, the agent of God's empire,
brings God's benefits to this world in healing it, in anticipation of the future
completion of God's purposes and establishment of God's empire in which
wholeness, health, and plentiful harvests abound at Rome's demise (cf. *2 Bar*
29:6–7; 73:1–2).

God's vision of societal well-being manifested in Jesus, then, looks very
different from Rome's. It takes form not only in Jesus' words and actions
but also in the community of disciples that rejects domination and hierarchy
(20:25–26; 23:8–12). Jesus contrasts this community with "the rulers of the
Gentiles [who] lord it over them, and their great men [who] are tyrants over
them" (20:25). Kenneth W. Clark denies that the verbs that depict Roman
rule, "lord it over" and "are tyrants over," denote "arrogance, oppression
and abuse of power" and argues that they simply designate the exercise of
power.[46] Clark, however, overlooks the context of the words. In the imperial
system the exercise of power, concentrated in the hands of a few, brings
well-being to those few at the oppressive expense of most.

Clark neglects another dimension. Both verbs are cognates of words used
for God and Jesus. At the heart of κατακυριεύω (*katakyrieuō*, "lord it over")

is the noun κύριος (*kyrios*) or "Lord." And the root of κατεξουσιάζω (*katexousiazō* "tyrants over") is ἐξουσία (*exousia*), the noun "authority." Why is the imperial system's use of power condemned and God's/Jesus' use of power approved? Again the question concerns who will lord it over, who will exercise authority, and to what end. An examination of κύριος (*kyrios*) or "Lord" and ἐξουσία (*exousia*) or "authority" suggests that how the power is used, to what end, what it accomplishes, makes the difference. In 8:5–13, the centurion's authority means obedience (8:9) and maintaining the empire's domination, whereas Jesus' authority means healing and life (8:8) and other benefits: the revelation of God's will (7:29), forgiveness and healing (9:6, 8; 10:1), an extension of God's authority over all things (21:23, 24, 27; 28:18). Likewise "Lord" denotes God's salvific will and authority over heaven and earth and over human existence (1:20, 22, 24; 2:13, 15, 19; 3:3; 4:7, 10; 5:33; 11:25; etc.). It denotes Jesus' life-giving authority over judgment (7:21–22), disease (8:2, 6, 8; 9:28; 15:22, 25), death (8:21), creation (8:25; 14:28, 30), and the believing community (10:24–25). It would seem that imperial rule and authority are condemned partly because they claim what rightly belongs to God/Jesus, and partly because they work against the well-being that God and Jesus' life-giving purposes accomplish.

This behavior of domination and the system it represents are not to be evident among disciples (20:26a). Disciples evidence God's well-being in an alternative social structure as a community of slaves that imitates Jesus who gives his life for others. In this community, well-being involves practices of indiscriminate mercy and social inclusion (5:43–48; 9:12), rejects violent resistance (5:38), alleviates economic misery (5:42; 6:1–4), and prays for the establishment of God's empire in full (6:10). This community of slaves (20:26–27) is marginal in the dominant culture but does not imitate its hierarchy, domination, and exploitation because it lacks a role for masters and fathers (23:8–12).[47] The existence of such a community, legitimated by God's will and presence, challenges the nature and extent of the well-being that imperial theology proclaims, and embodies an alternative understanding.

CONCLUSION

In this chapter I have outlined four motifs that are significant to both the Gospel and to Roman imperial theology: sovereignty, presence, agency, and societal well-being. I have argued that in the context of Rome's empire, the Gospel contests this pervasive imperial theology and offers a different perspective. Instead of acknowledging the emperor's sovereignty, it proclaims God as Lord of heaven and earth. Instead of claiming the emperor as the commissioned agent of the gods, it presents Jesus as God's anointed or agent. Instead of claiming the emperor manifests divine presence on earth, it proclaims Jesus as the one whom God has anointed to reveal God's saving presence and will. Instead of accepting that human and societal well-being are found in submission to Rome's emperor and a hierarchically structured, exploitative society, it claims well-being from God's merciful activity. It calls disciples of Jesus to live these claims as an alternative community. This story of Jesus presents both a social and theological challenge to Rome's empire.

"To Save His People from Their Sins" (Matt 1:21): Rome's Empire and Matthew's Salvation as Sovereignty

I OBSERVED IN CHAPTER 4 that Jesus is commissioned in Matt 1:21 to "save his people from their sins." This commissioning, the focus for this chapter, raises some interesting questions. From what sins do people need saving? Which people? How are they saved? Saved for what? What does their salvation look like?

Previous discussions of Matthew's understanding of salvation (soteriology) have typically taken three approaches. One approach has explored salvation as an individual's standing before God, and investigated the relationship of law and grace, mercy and judgment, faith and works, the indicative and the imperative.[1] A second approach, shaped by covenant/covenantal nomism,[2] or wisdom traditions,[3] has emphasized salvation's communal shape and wrestled, in part, with the relationship between the church and Israel in salvation history.[4] A third approach has highlighted the culmination of God's cosmic purposes in a new heaven and earth.[5]

Each approach highlights significant dimensions of Matthew's rich presentation of salvation. The diversity of the discussion points to the complexity of the issues. My goal in this chapter is not to assess the merits of each approach but to address an issue fundamental to all of them, namely, the scope or nature of Matthew's salvation. William D. Davies and Dale Allison summarize the typical scholarly view:

> The Messiah's first task is to save his people from their sins (1:21), not deliver them from political bondage. Jesus saves his people "from their sins." This underlies the religious and moral—as opposed to political—character of the messianic deliverance. Liberation removes the wall of sin between God and the human race; nothing is said about freedom from the oppression of governing powers (contrast Pss. Sol. 17).[6]

This view that Matthew's Gospel presents salvation as "religious and moral" and not political is rarely disputed. I will, however, attempt to show in this chapter that to understand the nature or scope of Matthew's salvation as individual, spiritualized, and moral is too restrictive. To contrast "forgiveness of sins" with "deliverance from political oppression" anachronistically and inappropriately assumes a divide between the religious and the political spheres. It falsely ascribes this contrast to both the Psalms of Solomon and to Matthew,[7] strangely asserts that oppression has nothing to do with sins, incorrectly posits a monolithic view of messianic expectations, and conveniently overlooks a very immediate form of "political oppression" in the Gospel's world, namely Roman imperialism.[8]

I will argue that Matthew's salvation does include "freedom from the oppression of governing powers" and deliverance from political bondage, notably from the sinful sociopolitical and economic structures of Roman imperialism that manifest Satan's rule. Matthean soteriology asserts God's sovereignty in ending all evil including Rome's empire, and in forming a new and just creation.

Method

I will address these issues by employing two methods previously neglected in the conversation about Matthean salvation. A narrative-critical or audience-oriented approach seems especially warranted.[9] Previous discussions tend to select pericopes according to predetermined theological schemes, focus on their redaction, and neglect their narrative location, sequence, form, and the audience's interpretive work.[10] An audience-oriented approach is interested in all of these dimensions of the interpretive act. An imperial-critical view counters the neglect of Roman imperialism in Matthean studies by asking what role the audience's experience of Roman imperial power might play in understanding Matthean soteriology.[11]

Verse 1:21c ("he will save his people from their sins") will be the focus verse. Located in the opening chapter, this birth and naming announcement, spoken to Joseph by an authoritative "angel of the Lord," commissions the yet-unborn Jesus to his life work. It defines the main character's name in salvific terms, and employs the verb "save" (σώζω, *sōzō*) for the first time. The verse, located in the Gospel's opening chapter, exercises a "primacy effect" whereby content located at the beginning of the Gospel shapes its audience's expectations, understandings, and questions throughout the whole work.[12] I will attend to the audience's political-historical experience of Roman imperialism (section 1), to 1:21's narrative context (sections 2 and 3), to its lexical items (sections 4 and 5), and to its intertextual connections (section 6), to argue that Matthean soteriology asserts God's sovereignty over the cosmos by ending all evil, including Rome's empire (sections 7 and 8).

I. MATTHEW'S GOSPEL AND
ROMAN IMPERIAL POWER

I have described in chapters 1 to 3 something of the imperial world that the Gospel assumes of its audience. Seven brief observations summarize points of connection between Matthew's Gospel and Roman imperial power.

- The Gospel's plot concerns the death of its main character by a distinctly Roman form of execution, crucifixion, and at the hands of a Roman governor.

- Jesus proclaims and enacts the empire (βασιλεία, *basileia*) of God, in a world dominated by Rome's empire (see section 4).

- Jesus conflicts with the "religious leaders," members of the ruling class allied with Rome (see section 4).

- The Gospel interprets Rome's destruction of Jerusalem in 70 C.E. as God's punishment of Israel's leaders for the rejection of Jesus (22:1–10; section 5).

- In chapters 2 and 14, the Gospel portrays two of Rome's murderous allies and puppet kings, and in chapter 27 Rome's provincial governor Pilate.

- Twice Jesus instructs about paying taxes (17:24–27; 22:15–22), a means by which Rome expresses and enforces its power.

- Roman imperial power pervades the Gospel audience's world as I have demonstrated in chapters 1 to 3, and throughout chapters 4 to 9.[13]

Klaus Wengst summarizes the military, political, and economic situation of most people who lived in a city like Antioch: "Internal conditions ordered by Rome, security from external enemies guaranteed by Rome, paid for by tribute, maintained by obedience."[14] And, I should add, legitimated by the gods as the divine will.

2. THE NARRATIVE CONTEXT OF 1:21:
THE GENEALOGY

The Gospel's opening genealogy provides the narrative context for 1:21 (1:1–17).[15] In this imperial context, the genealogy is much more than just a list of unpronounceable names. It has a polemical function.[16] A full discussion is not possible but four observations should be made.[17]

First, Rome is not mentioned in 1:1–17. How to interpret this silence? I would suggest that the silence denotes not the irrelevance of, but the assumption of and resistance to, Rome's imperial claims. The genealogy assumes knowledge of the dominant imperial claims about Rome's role in the world as the agent of the gods, and presents an alternative history. God's purposes run through Israel not Rome. The genealogy does not attest Rome's election by the gods, outline Rome's accomplishments, assert Rome's sovereignty, or proclaim the emperor's agency in manifesting the gods' blessings. Instead, it asserts *God's* sovereignty and identifies God's agents. God has elected Israel and Jesus to accomplish *God's* purposes. In so doing, it asserts that, despite all appearances to the contrary post-70, sovereignty belongs to God, not to Rome.

Second, the story of God and Israel that 1:1–17 summarizes attests that God's purposes triumph no matter the adversity. Like Abraham and David, most characters named in the genealogy exhibit faithfulness and unfaithfulness. In fact, the latter dominates. Of the thirteen kings after David in verses 6b–11, only four are evaluated in 1–2 Kings and 1–2 Chronicles as good kings. The repeated reference in 1:11–12 to exile (emphasized again by 1:17) highlights an event that the Deuteronomist, Chronicler, and Ezekiel, using the same noun, view as God's punishment of a sinful people.[18] The continuation of the genealogy after the exile (verses 12–17), that there is any story to tell at all, attests God's faithfulness in the midst of such unfaithfulness. It also emphasizes that both Babylonian imperial power and Israel's faithlessness are subordinate to God's purposes that continue in Jesus (1:16). For certain, Rome will not be able to resist those purposes.

Third, the repeated references to Abraham (1:1, 2, 17) recall God's promise that through Abraham God will bless all the peoples of the earth (Gen 12:1–3). This blessing (along with its opposite, the curse) is extensively developed in the covenant material in Deut 27–28 in terms of abundant fertility, ample provision, prosperity, health, and deliverance from other nations. Recalling the promise asserts that *God* blesses the earth, not gods like Jupiter. The promise's content contrasts God's will with the present state of life, marked by want and sickness, under Roman rule. As "child of Abraham" (1:1), Jesus is God's agent through whom God's blessing is encountered. Moreover, the beneficiaries of God's blessing are "all people," not just Jupiter's emperors and their privileged elite who exploit others for their own benefit.[19] The earth, including Israel's land (Lev 25:2, 23, 38), belongs to God (Ps 24:1), not to the occupying Romans. Jesus promises its restoration to a more equitable use (Matt 5:5; 19:28).[20]

Fourth, the references to David as "king" in 1:6 and his successors in 1:6–11 recall God's promise to David of descendants and an eternal kingdom (2 Sam 7:14; Ps 89:3–4). The phrase "by the wife of Uriah" in 1:6 recalls David's aberrations as king as he departs from the just kingship envisioned, for instance, by Ps 72. There, kingly reign embodies God's sovereignty over the earth, ensures justice for the poor, and does not exploit and oppress. This vision differs from usual oppressive kingly practices as Moses in Deut 17:14–17 and Samuel in 1 Sam 8:1–17 emphasize in their warnings.[21] This alternative vision of kingship contrasts with the injustices of Roman imperial practice and its emperors or kings. The contrast is highlighted by designating David as "king" (1:6), with the same Greek term as is frequently used to designate Rome's emperors.[22]

The Davidic reference prepares for King Jesus. He is identified as "son of David" in 1:1. The title is used subsequently predominantly by those who are marginal in the imperial world as they beg him for merciful healing

(9:27–31; 15:22; 20:29–34; 21:14–16). Jesus' healings enact God's empire and salvation.

3. THE NARRATIVE CONTEXT OF 1:21: JESUS' ORIGINS

Following the genealogy, the immediate narrative context of 1:21 concerns Jesus' origin (1:18 γένεσις, *genesis*). His conception occurs "before (Joseph and Mary) came together" and results "from the holy spirit." It is God's act and initiative. Conception by a god was typical of outstanding imperial figures like Alexander (Plutarch, *Alex.* 2.1–3.4), Rome's founder Romulus (Plutarch, *Rom.* 2.3–6) and the emperor Augustus (Suetonius, *Aug.* 94.4). It identifies them as agents chosen by the gods to do their will. Jesus is set in such elect and commissioned political company, but with the key difference: God elects him to accomplish God's saving purposes.

4. SAVING FROM SINS

The angel's explanation for the name "Jesus" ("for he will save his people from their sins," 1:21) prophesies future greatness. Such prophecies typically mark the births of future emperors like Vespasian and Titus, destined by the gods for political and imperial rule.[23] Jesus is to save "his people" (λαός, *laos*). Is this the church or Israel? If the pronoun is emphasized, "*his* people" suggests the church (ἐκκλησία, *ekklēsia*), those who follow Jesus (4:18–22; 16:18; 18:18; 28:16–20). But in the immediate context of God's covenant faithfulness to Israel outlined in 1:1–17, and the Scripture citation in 2:6 identifying Jesus "as a shepherd for my people Israel" (λαός, *laos*), an immediate reference to Israel seems more likely.[24] Jesus is to save Israel.

What sins?[25] The common view asserts that only "religious and moral" sins, "the wall of sin between God and the human race" are in view, but not oppressive political, social, or economic sins. The audience, though, knows from the genealogy's vast catalogue of human sinfulness that such a division is false. Elaborating the Abraham and David stories alone reveals "social" sins of deception, xenophobia, abuse of power, adultery, and murder (1:1).[26] The litany of failed kings and references to Babylonian exile attest further violation of social relationships and political structures (1:6–11). The kings are condemned in 1–2 Kings and 1–2 Chronicles, as well as by the prophets, for a range of wrongdoing, from failure to implement and maintain authentic worship to unjust and oppressive rule that greedily exploits the poor. All of this expresses a rejection of God's will. The sinfulness is simultaneously political, economic, social, religious, and moral.

Herod, Rome's vassal king, exhibits further dimensions of sin as he protects his political power with terror and viciousness (2:16). Chapter 2 exemplifies the sinfulness of imperial rule, the oppressive ways of "the kings of the earth" who resist God's just purposes (cf. Ps 2:2; Matt 17:24–27), and do murderous harm to the vulnerable Rachels of this world. Herod Antipas (14:1–12) and Pilate (27:11–26) will exhibit similar resistance to God's purposes in using their power to maintain their status quo.

The temptation scene in 4:1–11 reveals an important perspective on this sinful world of imperial power as we noted in chapter 3. In 4:8 Satan offers Jesus "all the kingdoms/empires (βασιλείας, *basileia*) of the world." The offer reveals Satan's control of the world and its political realms. If Satan controls the world's empires, it follows that the leading empire, Rome, is under the devil's control and is, in the Gospel's perspective, the devil's agent. Rome's rule manifests Satan's empire. The noun βασιλεία ("kingdom/ empire") in 4:8 recalls the use of βασιλεύς (*basileus*) for Rome's ally, King Herod, in 2:1, linking him to Satan, and reinforcing a contrast with King Jesus (2:2, βασιλεύς) and his God-given empire (4:17, βασιλεία).[27]

In this devilish, imperial world, Jesus as God's agent demonstrates the empire of God (4:17) and exposes and challenges imperial control as contrary to God's empire (20:25–28). The catalogue of diseases in 4:23–25 reflects in part the social, economic, and political hardships and inequities of the imperial world. One cause of disease, malnutrition, results from an inadequate food supply and land resources, from the poor's limited economic resources for land, seed, and animal improvement, from taxes and tributes, high food prices, overwork, and control of the market by elite merchants.[28] Healing resists such a world and anticipates God's transforming empire. Jesus' feeding stories (12:1–8; 14:13–21; 15:32–39) anticipate a time when all people enjoy abundant provision (cf. 2 *Bar.* 73:2–3; 74:1). Paralysis and demon possession (4:24) are frequently observed phenomena in contexts of political oppression, colonial dominance, and social conflict.[29] Jesus' exorcisms point to God's empire that overcomes the devil's sovereignty (12:28). Constantly Jesus challenges unjust social relations and the unequal distribution of and limited access to resources, and points to an alternative empire (5:3–12; 6:9–13).[30] He attacks the elite's fine houses and clothing (11:8), and markers of social prestige (23:5–7). He warns against amassing wealth and its power over human lives (6:19–34; 13:19). He advocates the sharing of resources (5:42) and almsgiving that is not self-regarding (6:1–4). The rich young man of 19:16–22 is guilty of much more than a little greed. He depicts the social elite whose excessive wealth is understood to result from an over-accumulation of a limited resource at the expense of the poor.[31] Jesus' instruction to him to divest his wealth, to redistribute it to the poor, and to follow him anticipates the dismantling of the imperial economic system of inequitable distribution. This imperial world is not structured according to God's will. In teaching about taxes, Jesus refuses to recognize the empire's ultimacy (17:24–27; 22:15–22).[32]

More Sins: Jesus and the *"Religious Leaders"*

As many have observed, Jesus' conflict with an alliance of "religious leaders" (Pharisees, Sadducees, chief priests, scribes) is central to Matthew's plot.[33] What has not often been observed, or accorded a central place in interpretive strategies, is the audience's understanding of religious leaders (not lower-level religious personnel) as members of the elite governing and retainer classes (see chapter 1 above).[34] The societal preeminence of religious leaders—chief priests,[35] Pharisees,[36] Sadducees,[37] scribes,[38]—derives from birth, wealth, political and social alliances, control of the cult, divine sanction, and education, and was typical of aristocratically dominated empires.[39] Their elite status and commitment to the current social structure are evident in their first appearance as allies of Rome's puppet king Herod (2:4–6). In their final appearance, they are allies of Rome's governor and soldiers against Jesus (27:62–66; 28:11–15).

Throughout, these leaders conflict with Jesus over specific issues. But as members of the imperial society's elite, they exercise not a restricted "religious" role, but social, economic, and political power and, in the Gospel's view, with detrimental effect. Jesus condemns them because they do not seek "justice and mercy and faith" (23:23). They resist Jesus' claims to be God's agent who offers God's benefits to all of society, especially to those on the margins (9:1–8, 9–13; 12:1–8, 9–14, 22–37; 21:14–16). He declares they are not Israel's leaders because as false shepherds they benefit themselves in a strictly hierarchical society (9:36; see Ezek 34). They acquire the temple's needs for various sacrifices and offerings through land holdings, tithes (virtual taxes), and direct taxes (cf. Josephus *J.W.* 6.335) that deprive the people of food, clothing, health, and security (21:13).[40] In defending the status quo and alliance with Rome, they hinder people from knowing God's empire (23:13), expose people to hardship and violence (21:12–13; 26:47–27:31), protect patriarchal structures (19:3–12), and practice injustice and deceit (27:62–66; 28:11–15). In rejecting Jesus' teaching and authority, they reject his prophetic attempts to form a different social order (a "domination-free" society), and defend their own privileged location in an inequitable society sanctioned by Rome ("the domination system").[41] Their conflict with Jesus reflects a collision of two different visions of society, and a struggle over who has the authority to shape society.

The narrative reveals them to be Satan's agents committed to resisting God's will.[42] Jesus announces that they are not God's agents (15:13–14), declares that the privileged societal structure with its inequities of power that they support does not belong to God's empire (20:24–28; 23:5–7, 8–12), and removes their role in God's purposes (21:43).[43] In response, they ally with Rome and Pilate to kill him.[44]

The world of sins from which the people are to be saved cannot, then, be understood to consist only of private, moral, and religious imperfections

(15:19; 19:18–19). The rejection of Jesus is part of a much larger, sinful world that consists of sinful imperial, social, economic, and religious structures and practices that benefit the elite, burden the rest, violate God's will and sovereignty, and resist God's empire and agent, Jesus. The Roman imperial world does not manifest the gift and blessing of the gods. It manifests Satan's reign. From this world people are to be saved.

5. ROME:
PUNISHING AND PUNISHED

What, then, does God do? To save Israel from its sins requires the defeat of Rome, the power that has punished Israel but which also rejects God's agent Jesus and the will of God that he manifests. The allegorical parable of 22:1–14, especially 22:7, concerning those who refuse the invitation to the king's son's wedding, provides some clarity of perspective on the present situation dominated by Rome. The king, angered by the elite's violent rejection of his repeated invitations to the wedding, "sent his troops, destroyed those murderers, and burned their city." Four factors suggest that this story interprets Rome's destruction of Jerusalem and of the temple (the center of the religious leaders' power) in 70 c.e. as God's punishment.[45]

- Verse 7, the burning of the city, looks to be an added verse. It disrupts the sequence between 22:6 and 8. It is an extreme response to the rejection of a wedding invitation. It also makes the rest of the story difficult. Are we to imagine that the wedding celebration was held in the smoking ruins of the city? And verse 7 is absent from the other version of the parable, a Q text, in Luke 14:15–24.
- The vocabulary of the story, especially king, wedding feast, son, and slaves, comprises frequently used images for God, the completion of God's purposes, Jesus, and the prophets.[46]
- Burning cities is a commonly used, punitive imperial tactic.[47]
- Josephus provides a graphic account of the burning of Jerusalem (*J.W.* 2.395–97; 6.249–408; cf. *2 Bar* 6–7).

These factors suggest we have in 22:7 a topical reference beyond the narrative world to Jerusalem's burning in 70 c.e. This event, the destruction of the city and temple in which the elite's power is centered, is interpreted in the parable as God's punishment of the elite and the people for not accepting God's invitation to participate in God's just purposes enacted by Jesus.[48] Typically, the people pay the price for the elite's self-centered choices and structures. But the parable makes it clear that for now Rome is God's agent in punishing Israel.

This interpretation of Jerusalem's destruction by Rome as God's punishment for sin utilizes the Deuteronomic view that God's blessings and curses take effect through historical events (Deut 27–28). God brings judgment on the leaders and people for covenant unfaithfulness. The Deuteronomist accounts for the sixth-century Babylonian destruction of Jerusalem and exile in these terms (Deut 28–30; 1 Kgs 9:1–9; 2 Kgs 17, 24–25; cf. Jer 25; 2 Bar 6–8). Just as imperial powers like Assyria (Isa 10:1–7), Babylon (Jer 25:1–11), Antiochus Epiphanes (2 Macc 6:12–17), and Rome in the first century B.C.E. (Pss. Sol. 2:1–15; 8:9–22) function as God's punitive agents, so Rome does in 70 C.E.[49] Ironically, the religious elite's ally carries out God's punitive will.

But while the sins have been punished, salvation has not yet been accomplished. The Gospel does not see this punishment as the end of God's covenant. Rome's act is not the final rejection of Israel (also Josephus, 4 Ezra, 2 Bar.). For Matthew, God's salvific purposes and faithfulness will continue through Jesus. Matthew 1:21c declares, post 70, that Jesus will save his people from the sins for which they have been punished in the fall of Jerusalem. The traditions that recognize imperial powers as God's punitive agents also affirm that these agents are themselves punished for not honoring God. So God uses, then judges and destroys, imperial powers: Assyria (Isa 10:12–34), Babylon (Jer 25:8–14; 27:5–22; Isa 44:28; 45:1), and Antiochus Epiphanes (2 Macc 7:32–36). Various traditions anticipate a similar fate for Rome (Pss. Sol. 2:16–25, 30–33; 17:21–34; Sib. Or. 3.46–53; 1QM 1; 2 Bar 1:4–5; 5:1–4; 8:1–5; 13:11–12). The end of Rome's punitive rule is certain. There is salvation from the oppression of governing powers and deliverance from political bondage.

6. ECHOES OF THREE OTHER RESCUES FROM NATIONAL DISASTER

In 1:21–23, there are echoes of three other texts that are concerned with God's saving of the people from imperial threats. These intertextual links reinforce the view that Jesus' saving from sin concerns not only moral and religious sins, but also the oppressively sinful political, social, economic, and religious structures and practices of Rome's imperial world.

Psalm 130

First, while commentators often suggest that 1:21c echoes Ps 130 (LXX 129):8,[50] few pursue the link. If the echo is understood metonymically, that is, if it is understood in the sense that citing a part of the Psalm actually evokes the whole Psalm,[51] all of Ps 130 is in view. The Psalm seeks God's deliverance from trouble. The opening two verses do not specify the trouble but the change of language in verses 3–4 from "trouble" to "iniquity" recognizes it as sin and punishment for which the Psalmist seeks "forgiveness" (v. 4). In verses 5–6 the Psalmist waits for the Lord (three times), and "hopes in" or relies on God. This "waiting" and the future orientation of both the waiting and the hope suggest that God's forgiveness will be experienced in changed circumstances.

After the personal expression of the opening six verses, the two final verses show the petition to be national. Twice Israel is named, exhorted to "hope" in God (the same verb ἐλπίζω, *elpizō*, appears in v. 6 and v. 7), assured of God's covenant faithfulness ("mercy/steadfast love") even in its unfaithfulness, and reminded of God's "great power to redeem." The final verse provides further reassurance with its confident declaration that God "will redeem Israel from all its iniquities." The use of the same word "iniquities" in verse 8 as in the initial, apparently individual section of the Psalm (ἀνομία, *anomia*, v. 3) indicates that the individual and the nation share the same trouble or iniquity. And the forgiveness sought in verse 4 has become redemption in verses 7–8. The verb "redeem" that is repeated in verses 7 and 8 recalls two specific previous situations of sin and divine redemption that are very prominent in Israel's traditions, redemption or salvation from Egypt and from Babylon.[52] God also "redeems" the people from Assyria (Sir 48:20) and from Antiochus Epiphanes (1 Macc 4:11).

The psalm's circumstances of trouble remain unspecified, as they so often do in the Psalms. But the generic language used to describe national trouble provides access for congregations in numerous similar situations. For post-70 worshippers such as the Matthean audience, Ps 130, evoked by Matt 1:21, recognizes Israel's present trouble of occupation by a foreign imperial power, solicits the worshippers' agreement that their iniquity brought about this situation, turns them to God, reassures them of God's covenant faithfulness even in the midst of unfaithfulness, exhorts them to hope in the Lord for redemption or liberation from Rome, and assures them that the promised salvation is at hand. God through Jesus will save the people from their sins punished by Rome in the fall of Jerusalem in 70 C.E.

Joshua and Jesus

A second intertext confirms this reading. The name "Jesus" is the Greek form of Joshua. As Moses' successor, Joshua was God's agent in completing God's redemption of the people from Egypt, and from the wilderness to which the sinful people were consigned for a generation (Deut 1). Joshua led their entry into the promised land, defeating the Canaanite kings and city-states and seizing their land. So Sir 46:1 comments that Joshua "became as his name implies, a great savior of God's elect, to take vengeance on the enemies that rose against them so that he might give Israel its inheritance."[53] This "salvation" exhibited God's faithfulness to the covenant, and required the people to maintain their covenant with God and location in the land by obeying Moses' teaching. But it was not a salvation in some restricted moral and religious sense. It was very political, socioeconomic, and military in execution.[54] The naming of the baby in Matt 1:21 "Jesus/Joshua" links the two situations. Jesus/Joshua is God's agent of salvation in another context of imperial control. The type of salvation remains the same, salvation from an enemy. What changes, at least in part, is that Jesus brings about this salvation by means other than military force.[55] I will return to this *how* question in sections 7 and 8.

Isaiah 7–9

A third intertext is evoked immediately after 1:21c in 1:22–23. Jesus is named Emmanuel, God with us. The verse applies to Jesus a common designation used for emperors and kings (*deus praesens/epiphanēs*) to claim that they manifest a god's presence and will. Its use for Jesus suggests some polemical function against such claims, and against one in particular.[56] Jesus, not Rome's emperor, manifests God's presence and will. But the citation from Isa 7:14 has further explanatory and encouraging functions. A metonymic understanding of the citation draws attention to Isa 7–9[57] where Judah is threatened by the imperial aspirations of Israel and Syria, who are in turn threatened by Assyria. God offers the worried king Ahaz a child called Emmanuel as a sign of God's presence.

Isaiah 7–9 provide three perspectives on imperial power. First, God opposes it in resisting Israel and Syria. Second, God uses it (Assyria) to punish sin. And third, imperial Assyria falls under God's judgment. For Matthew's post-70 audience living under a similar situation of Roman imperial control, the intertext provides perspectives on its present and future. Its present is punishment for sin as evidenced by the fall of Jerusalem in 70 C.E. Rome is God's agent. But there is hope in that God will save the people from Roman imperial control. The punishment and Rome's power will end as God's sovereignty is exhibited.

The three intertexts—Ps 130, Joshua, and Isa 7–9—identify situations in which God's sovereignty is asserted over political powers. Matthew's audience knows similar circumstances under Rome's rule, and is promised God's salvation through Jesus. There is no mandate to spiritualize the intertexts. But how will Jesus save from sins?

7. HOW DOES JESUS SAVE HIS PEOPLE FROM THEIR SINS?

Davies and Allison correctly recognize that 1:21 "is not very illuminating with regard to exactly *how* Jesus saves."[58] Some have observed ἁμαρτία (*hamartia*, sin) in 1:21c and 26:28 ("for the forgiveness of sins"), noted the link of the supper with the cross, and, by way of 20:28, concluded that Jesus saves through his death. But this is only a partial answer. From a narrative perspective, if Jesus saves only or primarily through the cross, there would be little point to the preceding twenty-five chapters of the Gospel narrative about Jesus' life, words, and actions. Chapter 9 is also problematic since nearly twenty chapters prior to the cross and without reference to it, Jesus announces God's forgiveness of a man's sins (9:2, 5, 6). Further, the language of saving (σώζω, *sōzō*), used in 1:21c, does not direct exclusive attention to the cross. The verb appears in the fourfold taunts about Jesus saving himself (27:40, 42 [2*x*], 49), but refers five times to eschatological rescue from distress (8:25; 10:22; 19:25; 24:13, 22), and three times to healing (9:21, 22 [2*x*]). Jesus' saving work includes healing and eschatological deliverance.

Nor can it be claimed that this verb signals the Gospel's only salvific moments.[59] Based on the "primacy effect" noted earlier, I would suggest that the commissioning of the newly conceived Jesus in 1:21c to "save his people from their sins" functions at the outset as a point-of-view statement.[60] It defines Jesus' whole ministry as the means of his saving work. His words call people to encounter God's empire (4:17) and to participate in an alternative community with structures and practices that nonviolently resist conventional cultural values and manifest God's reign (4:18–22; chs 5–7; 5:38–42). His actions, such as his healings, manifest God's empire in anticipation of the transformed new creation which displays God's purposes that include wholeness (Isa 35:5–6; 61:1–2; *2 Bar.* 73:2; 74:2). In anticipation of the same goal, he supplies food to those who are deprived (12:1–8; 14:13–21; 15:32–39; cf. *2 Bar.* 74:1). His exorcisms manifest God's empire that disrupts Satan's reign in anticipation of God's final victory (12:28). His meals display God's mercy or covenant faithfulness (9:13; 12:7). His death, a ransom for many (20:28), shows that the worst the religious and political elite can do cannot limit God's sovereignty since God raises Jesus from death. And Jesus speaks of his return in power to complete what is under way in his ministry, the establishment of God's empire and salvation.

Jesus' Return: Rome's Downfall and God's Salvation

Jesus' return, preceded by distress on the earth (24:3–26) and worldwide mission (24:14), is part of a multifaceted event for which the Gospel provides no timetable. Its main elements, though, are clear: Jesus' arrival, judgment (25:31–45), a new creation (19:28),[61] and the end of all unjust practices as God's sovereignty or empire is established in a heaven and earth marked by health, wholeness, and plenty (28:18).[62]

And Rome? The description of Jesus' return in 24:27–31 "with power and great glory" employs terms that echo imperial rule.[63] His return as Son of Man is a παρουσία (*parousia*, 24:27). While denoting God's presence (Josephus, *Ant.* 3.80, 202), the term especially signifies the approach of a king,[64] an emperor or future emperor,[65] a military commander,[66] or other officials or envoys[67] to a (subject) city (3 Macc 3:16–17; Josephus *J.W.* 4.345).[68] Jesus' παρουσία concerns not a representative of an imperial power like Rome, but of God's empire. His coming is public, visible, glorious, like flashes of lightning (ἀστραπή, *astrapē*, 24:27). Lightning is a polyvalent image that cleverly invokes competing sovereignties. It often designates manifestations of God's sovereignty and presence (Exod 19:16; Ezek 1:13; Dan 10:5; Wis 5:15–6:11, esp. 5:21). But lightning also commonly appears on coins to depict Jupiter/Zeus's sovereignty wielded by emperors like Domitian.[69] It symbolizes Jupiter's rule and world order, the "divine power exerted against the forces of barbarous hubris and on behalf of civilized existence."[70] The competing referents for the language point to the cosmic conflict. Here lightning images Jesus' coming and the assertion of God's sovereignty over all things, including Rome.

And his impact? "Wherever the corpse is, there the ἀετοί (*aetoi*) gather" (24:28). The noun is commonly translated as "vultures," though "eagles" is preferable.[71] The eagle can be a bird of prey that feeds on corpses (Job 9:26; 39:27–30; Martial *Epigrams* 6.62.4), but here the image is of "gathering" not feeding. Eagles also denote imperial powers like Babylon as agents of God's punishment on the people,[72] a role Rome performs in 70 C.E. (22:7; *4 Ezra* 11–12). Significantly, the eagle was a visual symbol of Roman imperial power (Suetonius, *Cal.* 14.3; Tacitus, *Ann.* 15.29; *4 Ezra* 13). It was "the symbol held in highest regard by the Romans" (Appian, *Bell. Civ.* 2.61). Roman legions carried this symbol into battle just as the eagle standards lead Titus's army on its march to Jerusalem (Josephus *J.W.* 5.48). Josephus calls these eagle-standards (*aquilae*) "sacred emblems," which "precede every legion, because it is the king and the bravest of all the birds; it is regarded by [Roman soldiers] as the symbol of empire, and whoever may be their adversaries, an omen of victory" (*J.W.* 3.123; *Ant.* 18:120–21).[73]

What then does it mean to describe the eagles gathered with the corpses at the coming of the Son of Man in 24:28? This scene does not present Rome as God's agent punishing Jerusalem. This scene concerns the return of the Son of Man. Nor do the eagles hover over or feed on the corpses. Corpses and eagles are gathered together (συναχθήσονται, *sunachthēsontai*). Rather, the scene depicts destroyed Roman troops ("the corpse") with fallen eagle standards scattered among them. The scene reflects apocalyptic battle scenes (see *The War Scroll* from Qumran, *4 Ezra* 11–13; *2 Bar.* 39–40) and is appropriate to other elements in the Gospel such as 16:18 that refer to the attacks of the forces of evil, as well as to 4:8 which allies Satan and Rome.[74] The *parousia* or coming or arrival of the Son of Man destroys Rome's power. The agent of God's punishment in 70 C.E. and agent of Satan (4:8) that resists God's ways is judged.[75] The final salvation of "his people from their sins" means the establishment of God's sovereignty or authority over heaven and earth (28:18).

This interpretation is supported by the image of the loss of light from the sun and moon in 24:29. It draws on scenes like Isa 13:10 and 34:4 that concern the destruction of imperial powers. The coins of Vespasian and Domitian use the sun and moon in association with the goddess Aeternitas

(Rome and the Flavian dynasty for ever).[76] But, ironically, Jesus' return is "lights out" time for Rome. The "sign" of verse 30 probably continues the military image with a reference to God's emblem in opposition to the eagle. The angels (24:30) are imaged in 26:53 as legions of heavenly warriors.

8. "FOR THE FORGIVENESS OF SINS": MATTHEW 26:28?

In Matt 26:28, Jesus identifies my cup as "the blood of the covenant, which is poured out for many for the forgiveness of sins." This verse is frequently understood in scholarly and worship contexts as indicating the forgiveness of personal sins and restoration to fellowship with God. Is the vision of cosmic salvation as I have described it at odds with these words in 26:28? I do not think it is, because the word translated "forgiveness" does not refer only or primarily to individual, personal sins and the restoration of personal fellowship with God. It refers also (primarily?) to the transformation of, or release from, social sins and to different patterns of social, economic, and political interaction.

Two factors support this claim. First, Jesus speaks in communal terms in 26:28. In 26:27 he addresses all disciples. The term "blood" recalls the liberation of the people from Egypt. The people had to smear blood from the lamb on the doorposts of their houses to be safe from God's action of judgment directed against the firstborn (Exod 12:1–13). The phrase "blood of the covenant" recalls God's covenant with the people at Sinai (Exod 24:8). The blood is poured out "for many" in anticipation of Jesus drinking it "with you" (plural) in the establishment of God's empire. Jesus is talking about the impact of his death not just on individuals but also on a people. That communal context includes relationships and social structures.

Second, the sort of "forgiveness" that is in view is clarified by attention to the word's use elsewhere. It appears, for example, at least fourteen times in Lev 25, often translated as "year of jubilee," or "a jubilee." Leviticus 25 envisions a social and economic restructuring and transformation every fifty years. It provides for rest from labor. Land and property are returned and redistributed. Slaves are freed, and households are reunited. In Deut 15:1–3, 9, the same noun refers to the forgiveness of debts every seven years. In Isa 58:6, it denotes the freeing of the oppressed, an act that "loosens the bonds of injustice and undoes the thongs of the yoke." How is this socioeconomic restructuring and transformation accomplished? By feeding the hungry, housing the homeless, clothing the naked, satisfying the needs of the afflicted. To accomplish these goals means nothing other than the dismantling of the economic oppression, social inequalities, and political exploitation that mark imperial societies. To accomplish these things means a world in which "The LORD will guide you continually, and satisfy your needs in parched places, and make your bones strong" (Isa 58:6–14). This is the world of plenty, health, and justice, the release from sins, that God's empire establishes.

Jesus' death, along with his life and return, effects this sort of "release from or forgiveness of sin." His death reveals the deep sinfulness of the imperial elite in rejecting God's will for the world (20:25–28). His resurrection reveals the limits of Rome's power. It also anticipates his return, which means Rome's overthrow, the ending of injustice and oppression, and the long-awaited establishment of God's empire in which all enjoy fellowship with God in a just world. This empire is known in part now through the actions of disciples with whom the risen Jesus, Emmanuel, dwells. Restoration to personal fellowship with God is part of the much larger cosmic transformation that Jesus proclaims and anticipates in 26:28.

9. A FINAL IRONY

I have argued for a very material and political, not spiritualized, understanding of Matthew's salvation. Matthew's vision of salvation reveals the world to be sinful, under imperial power and controlled by Satan. Jesus' words and actions create an alternative community and demonstrate God's empire that is yet to be fully established. The Gospel envisions salvation as the end of this sinful world, the defeat of Rome, and the establishment of a new heaven and earth under God's sovereignty.

But the irony must be noted. This bold vision of the completion of God's salvation and overthrow of Roman imperial power co-opts and imitates the very imperial worldview that it resists! For Rome and God, the goal is the supreme sovereignty of the most powerful. For both, the scope or extent of their sovereignty is the cosmos. Both appeal to the divine will for legitimation. Both understand the establishment of their sovereignty to be through a chosen agent and by means of the violent overthrow of all resistance.[77] Both offer totalizing perspectives. Both demand compliance. Both destroy enemies without room for the different or the noncompliant. Both recognize that those who welcome its sovereignty benefit from it. The Gospel depicts God's salvation, the triumph of God's empire over all things including Rome, with the language and symbols of imperial rule.

Is this imitation a good thing? In the sense that it means the end of all evil and establishment of God's good and just purposes, yes! But the violent imposition of God's will raises some troubling questions. The establishment of God's sovereignty means justice wrought on those who deserve nothing less. But the formulation reveals a revengeful character rather than, for instance, a reconciling stance (cf. Matt 5:43–48).[78] Or one could welcome this imperializing portrayal as a sign of an intense commitment to be free of domination. It is indeed, but at what price, and freedom for whom? Or one could differentiate the two systems by arguing that one sovereignty is imposed (Rome's) but God's is chosen in a covenantal context. That is true for the present, but not the future. Why does a Gospel that chooses the option not to dominate in the present (20:20–28) absolutize domination— its own—for the future? Or one could, as I think the Gospel finally does, attempt to bypass the ambiguity by appealing to God's otherness. God is benign, loving, faithful, and merciful to all (5:7, 45) which means the establishment of God's perfect sovereignty as God the creator intended from the beginning (19:4). The argument rests on the faithful and merciful nature of the covenant God who is fundamentally *not* like human beings. Such an empire is very welcome—until we recall that such a claim is classically imperialist at heart. Imperial rule typically presents itself as benign, especially for its immediate beneficiaries.[79] In the end, it seems, the Gospel cannot imagine a world without imperial power. It cannot find an alternative to this sovereignty model of power.

Such a conclusion is understandable. The imperial worldview is so prevalent that even this story of protest against imperial rule cannot escape its own cultural world. It has no other language to use. As much as it resists and exposes the injustice of Rome's rule, as much as it points to God's alternative community and order, as much as it glimpses something of the merciful inclusion of the non-elite in God's love and life-giving reign for all, as much as it offers alternative economic practices, renounces violence, and promotes more egalitarian household structures,[80] it cannot, finally, escape the imperial mindset. The alternative to Rome's rule is framed in imperial terms. Salvation comprises membership in a people that embodies and anticipates and celebrates the establishment of God's loving sovereignty, God's empire, over all, including the destruction of oppressive governing powers like imperial Rome. In the Conclusion, we will return to this issue.

- Part Three -

COUNTERNARRATIVES

SIX

Evoking Isaiah:
Why Summon Isaiah
in Matthew 1:23 and 4:15–16?

AFTER THE GOSPEL'S OPENING GENEALOGY (1:1–17) comes the narrative of Mary's pregnancy, Joseph's plans to divorce her, and the appearance of an angel in a dream to Joseph (1:18–25). The angel tells Joseph not to divorce Mary, that her baby is conceived by the Holy Spirit, and the baby's name is to be Jesus, "for he will save his people from their sins" (1:18–21).

As I have discussed in the previous two chapters, the angel's words in 1:21, spoken on behalf of God, commission Jesus for his life work. But a further significant thing happens. At this point the Gospel's action stops for two verses. In verses 22 and 23, the storyteller adds a comment that interprets the angel's announcement.

> All this took place to fulfill what had been spoken by the Lord through the prophet saying, "Look, the virgin shall conceive and bear a son, and they shall name him Emmanuel," which means "God is with us." (1:22–23)

This material does not belong to Joseph's dream. Though he does not wake from that dream until verse 24, verses 22–23 are not spoken by the angel, not located in Joseph's dream, and not even addressed to Joseph. The verses interpret for the Gospel's audience what has happened in verses 18–21. They provide a commentary on it. The happenings are in accord with God's will. Then the narrative moves on in 1:24–25.

But the interpretive comment in verses 22–23 raises two questions. First, it seems to be more than a general affirmation that "these happenings are in accord with God's will." The citation is precise, detailed, and specific. It refers to something God said through a particular prophet. It quotes the prophet, from Isa 7:14. And it even explains the meaning of the name Emmanuel in the citation to make sure the audience understands that it means "God with us." In this chapter I want to explore what happens when the Gospel's audience pauses over this citing of "the prophet." What happens when we elaborate this reference to Isa. 7–9? What is its contribution?

But there's a further question. In 4:14–16 a similar thing happens. Jesus has moved to Capernaum (4:13), and again the action stops because of an interpretive comment:

> so that what had been spoken through the prophet Isaiah might be fulfilled, saying; "Land of Zebulun, land of Naphtali on the road by the sea, across the Jordan, Galilee of the Gentiles—the people who sat in darkness have seen great light, and for those who sat in the region and shadow of death, light has dawned on them.

For the second time in the Gospel's opening section, Isaiah the prophet is quoted (Isa 8:23–9:1). And this citation comes from the same section of Isaiah as the citation in 1:23. What impact does it have that Isa. 7–9 is quoted twice at the outset of the Gospel? What contribution does this double citation make to the audience's understanding of the Gospel?

Matthew's Fulfillment Citations

It might be helpful to place these questions about the function of these two citations of Isaiah in the context of the larger scholarly discussion. Matthew's use of Scripture citations to provide interpretive commentary on the Gospel's plot is a distinctive feature of this Gospel that has been frequently noticed and studied.[1] Other instances are found in relationship to Jesus' infancy (2:5–6[?], 15, 17–18, 23), his healings (8:17), his ministry (12:17–21), his parables (13:35), his procuring the donkey for his entry into Jerusalem (21:4–5), and several aspects of the crucifixion story (26:54, 56[?]; 27:9–10).

Scholars, particularly redaction critics,[2] have focused considerable attention on Matthew's shaping of these fulfillment citations in the hope of identifying key aspects of the Gospel's origin, purpose, and pastoral-theological agenda. Numerous monographs,[3] articles,[4] and sections in monographs[5] attest extensive inquiry,[6] though for whatever reasons, scholarly interest may have declined somewhat recently.[7] Recent narrative or audience-oriented work has made what could fairly be called a minimal contribution.[8]

This scholarly work has concentrated on three issues:[9] (1) What text form did the Gospel's author use for these Scripture citations? Was it a Hebrew, Greek, or Aramaic version? Did the author use several different versions or make his own free translation?[10] (2) Did the Gospel author select his own texts for inclusion, or was he part of a group or "school" studying the Scriptures together? Did he use an existing collection or *testimonia* of such texts?[11] (3) And why did the author use them? Was he battling against certain opponents and critics or, as most think, was he instructing his community or audience?[12]

This scholarly debate about the form, origins, and authorial intent of the citations has concentrated on the author's work. It has attempted to reconstruct how the author worked with these texts and to what purpose. It has produced valuable insights. But in focusing on the Gospel author's work, it has ignored some other questions. Two will concern us in this chapter. (1) How do the quoted verses function in their new literary context as part of Matthew's Gospel? What do they contribute to the Gospel narrative? (2) Do the cited texts restrict focus only on the verse that is cited, or do they refer to the much larger narratives from which they are quoted? I will argue the latter view and demonstrate its impact in this chapter.

The Audience's Active Role

Basic to these questions is a shift in focus from the author to the role of an audience in making meaning of these texts.[13] Attention to the audience's role was anticipated in two 1980s articles that discussed the citations in relation to "the problem of communication." Lars Hartman suggested that an author quotes other authors to invoke their authority, to utilize their preferable words, or to point beyond the immediate citation to a larger bundle of ideas." Communication between author and audience occurs as both share a common tradition or cultural context in which the citation's authority and content are recognized.[14] Richard France develops Hartman's notion of "different levels of understanding" in arguing that the citations are capable of being understood at different levels of complexity by different audiences.[15]

Hartman's attention to the larger "bundle of ideas" or common cultural traditions counters what has been the dominant focus in much recent scholarship on the citations. Most work has maintained a myopic focus only on the cited verse and has treated the citation in an atomistic manner, disregarding the textual contexts from which the verse was taken and into which it was placed. This approach detaches the cited verse from any scriptural context and ignores the audience's knowledge of a larger common tradition whether at a general thematic level or a more detailed narrative level.

Hartman's encouragement to attend to the larger "bundle of ideas" or cultural traditions that a citation evokes receives support from the work of John Foley. Foley has studied narratives that are orally derived and performed, and has identified the importance of "traditional referentiality" in the performance of these narratives.[16] Foley's work is relevant because the audience for which Matthew's Gospel is written encounters the Gospel not by reading a written text, but by hearing it read aloud. In an oral culture, Foley argues, spoken texts frequently are metonymic. Metonyms are brief references that represent a larger whole. In abbreviated forms they reference a much larger entity. For example, the saying "I've got wheels" refers to a larger object, a whole car. Or "Lend me a hand" means I want a whole body, a person, to help me. Foley argues that spoken texts employ brief references—whether a phrase, themes, character traits, events, or narrative structures—that have much bigger, extratextual connotations.[17] It would be like, in our own time, a stand-up comic making a very brief reference to "Bill

Clinton" and allowing the audience to expand the reference by connecting
it to a larger body of unspoken, assumed information that the comic and
audience share in this culture. Foley argues that in "traditional referentiality" a brief textual reference assumes an audience knows the much larger
tradition that is being referred to, and can fill in the necessary information
from its own cultural knowledge. Audiences interact with these brief narrative references to supply the much larger traditions that the text does not
spell out, but assumes an audience will know. The audience elaborates the
brief reference to recall the larger character or event or narrative that is being evoked. The part summons the whole; the citation evokes a much larger
tradition.

Foley utilizes work done on audience interaction with a text (*Rezep-
tionsästhetik*) to articulate the audience's active role in constructing this
meaning from a brief citation.[18] An audience elaborates the gaps or in-
determinacies of a text, what a text briefly names but does not expand,
to build a consistent understanding. An audience does not supply whatever content it likes, but utilizes the tradition that it shares with the author
to elaborate the text. The common traditions or larger "bundle of ideas"
from a shared culture provide the audience with a frame of reference, the
"perceptual grid," for its interpretive work.

Much like the "Bill Clinton" example above, the Gospel's opening verse
and genealogy provide a good example of this work that an audience is expected to perform (Matt 1:1–17). The opening verse names Jesus as "son
of David" and "son of Abraham" without stopping to explain who these
characters are. The Gospel's audience is expected to know and to be able to
supply the content. Likewise, the genealogy's list of names (Abraham, Isaac,
Jacob, etc.) requires the audience's elaborative work by utilizing its knowledge of much more extensive and common traditions. In the last chapter,
I suggested that 1:21 functions in a similar way to recall Ps. 130 and the
narrative of Joshua's occupation of the promised land.

The dominant scholarly approach to the citations, which has focused on
the textual tradition and form that most influenced the cited verse, may not,
then, be the most helpful approach in determining a citation's meanings and
functions in its new Gospel context. The focus is too narrow (restricted to
one verse) and too centered on the origin of the verse to the exclusion of the
context from which it comes and its function in its present context. Rather, a
focus on the role of an audience's knowledge of the larger traditions or narratives evoked by the cited verse may be more productive.[19] This focus raises
further questions about the meaning-making process in which the audience
engages. How does knowledge from these larger narratives and traditions
(intertextual knowledge) relate to that derived from the immediate context
of the verse's new context in Matthew's Gospel, or from the audience's own
sociohistorical situation? How does an audience use citations in formulating
understandings of and questions about the ongoing narrative?

A full-length study could engage these and other questions about the audience's work with every one of Matthew's ten to twelve citations. This chapter will consider only the two citations highlighted in the introductory comments to this chapter. Two citations from Isa 7:14 and 8:23–9:1 appear in the Gospel's opening section (Matt 1:1–4:16)[20] in 1:23 and 4:15–16.[21] Specifically, following Foley's approach, what happens if an audience utilizes not just the isolated verses but the evoked common tradition, namely the larger context of Isa 7–9? Of what significance is it that Isa 7–9 is cited twice in the Gospel's opening section? What relevance does Isaiah have? Scholars have suggested that Isaiah is quoted twice because Isaiah is the only scroll available in the Matthean library[22] or Isaiah was a (rejected) proclaimer of God's salvation to Israel and to Gentiles.[23] But neither claim explains what meaning an audience makes out of these two Isaiah references in the opening section of Matthew's Gospel. And what contribution does this Isaiah intertext make to the presentation of Jesus' mission and ministry in the Gospel? That is, what happens if, in interpreting these two Isaiah citations, we attend to the audience-oriented concerns of progressive and retrospective movement in a text, of making explicit the knowledge or experience assumed of an audience, and of intertextuality or the connections between these texts that an audience creates?[24]

In this chapter, I will argue that the double citation from Isaiah in the Gospel's opening section contributes to a primacy effect[25] that impacts the hearing of the whole Gospel. Though it has commonly been overlooked by Matthean scholars, *the Isaiah texts address a situation of imperial threat, thereby establishing an analogy with the situation of the Gospel's authorial audience, also living under imperial power, that of Rome, and also promised God's salvation (1:21). The Isaiah texts provide perspectives on the imperial situation and give content to God's salvific promise.* But they also raise the questions of how people will respond and how God will deliver on the promise of salvation through Jesus.

THE CITATION OF ISAIAH 7:14
IN MATTHEW 1:22–23

At 1:22–23 an audience encounters the first fulfillment citation, from Isa 7:14. An audience can use the citation in several ways. It confirms and expands the understanding built up through verses 18–21 that Jesus' origin (γάνεσις, *genesis*, 1:18) is located in the purposes of God.[26] The citation also gives the child a new name that helps the audience clarify Jesus' significance. It knows from its cultural context that conception from the interaction of a human and the divine establishes the importance of a child.[27] It knows from 1:1, 16, 17, 18 that Jesus is the Christ, anointed by God to perform a special role on God's behalf.[28] The new name "Emmanuel," like "Jesus" in

1:21, denotes a life's work. The child is anointed to "save his people from their sins" and to manifest "God with us."[29]

Most of this is readily available to any audience. But Foley's emphasis on the metonymic function of oral-derived texts whereby a brief reference evokes a larger common tradition prompts further elaboration of the Isaiah reference. Several markers specifically invite the audience to pursue the citation's Isaianic context,[30] though much contemporary Matthean scholarship neglects this intertextuality. That scholarship is content to note briefly the woman's sexual experience and her and the child's possible identity, or quickly summarize Ahaz's situation, without integrating the material into an interpretation.[31] Audience-oriented work, though, seeks to make explicit the knowledge or experience that an audience supplies, including intertextual links.

The citation is introduced in 1:22 as "what had been spoken by the Lord through the prophet." The lack of the prophet's name is usually explained in terms of its irrelevance or the citation's divine legitimation or its christological content.[32] But one wonders if the presence of one name could be so distracting. The phrase "through the prophet" (διὰ τοῦ προφήτου, *dia tou prophētou*) indicates that the prophet's identity and agency do matter. It specifies a particular prophet and set of circumstances in which his word was spoken. That the prophet's name is absent suggests, rather, an audience very familiar with this part of the common tradition.[33]

Moreover, an audience has learned from the genealogy (1:1–17) that the Gospel's hearers are to supply information from the biblical tradition to expand cryptic textual references and to elaborate names. Sometimes in the genealogy, the elaboration is directed or restricted. The audience uses the occasional qualifiers—"and his brothers"; "by Tamar/Rahab/Ruth"; "David the king"; "by the wife of Uriah"; "at the time of the deportation to Babylon"—to focus on specific events within a larger story of the person's interactions with God. So by 1:22–23 an audience knows that the reference to "the prophet" requires elaboration, while citing a particular verse (Isa 7:14) restricts the elaboration to the circumstances in which the verse appears. The audience is to bring into play Isa 7–8 as it interprets 1:22–23. What happens when it does?[34]

Isaiah 7–9

Matthew 1:23 cites Isaiah 7:14 (essentially following the LXX). The prophet addresses King Ahaz of Judah (cf. Matt 1:9). King Ahaz is under threat from imperial aggression (Isa 7:1–2; cf. 2 Kgs 16).[35] The greater northern powers of Syria under King Rezin and Israel under King Pekah, who are themselves vulnerable to Assyria, threaten to take Jerusalem and overthrow the king (Isa 7:6). Ahaz and his people shake with fear (Isa 7:1–2). But God instructs Isaiah to assure Ahaz that the Syro-Ephraimite imperialism is doomed (Isa 7:3–9).

A second encounter follows (Isa 7:10–25). Through Isaiah, God invites Ahaz to request a sign to confirm God's word but he declines. Isaiah's harsh rebuke in 7:13 suggests that King Ahaz expresses not pious reluctance to test God (Deut 6:16; cf. Matt 4:6–7) but fear and distrust. Ahaz does not accept Isaiah's word, just as God had warned Isaiah in his call to be a prophet that people would reject his message (Isa 6:9–13). God, though, will provide Ahaz a sign anyway, the conception of a child to be named Emmanuel (Isa 7:14). The child signifies that the Davidic line will continue,[36] and that the Syro-Ephraimite imperialism will fail. The child expresses God's presence with the people ("will call him Emmanuel") and God's resistance to imperial aspirations. And God promises that during the baby's life, the land of the two imperial powers Syria and Israel will be laid waste (Isa 7:16).

So far, the news seems good for Judah and Ahaz, but then comes a dramatic turn. Isaiah declares that God's presence with Judah will mean not only salvation but destruction. God will bring Assyria to punish Judah for its unbelief (7:17–25). The sign of the child's birth that should express grace ("The Lord is with you") functions to express judgment ("The Lord is against you").

The ambivalence of this name matches that of another child, Isaiah's son Shearjashub, whose name means "A remnant shall return." His presence at the first meeting with Ahaz seemed to underline God's salvation (Isa 7:3). But in the context of Assyria's promised role, a reference to a remnant indicates punishment and destruction. Yet it also anticipates a future, offering the hope of new life since "a remnant shall return."

The emphasis on Emmanuel in Matt 1:23 suggests the audience continue into Isa 8 where the same name appears two more times (8:8, 10). Chapter 8 essentially parallels chapter 7. In 8:1–4 the birth of another child, a son for the prophet called Maher-shalal-hash-baz, which means "Spoil speeds, prey hastes," unambiguously attests the sure demise of Syria and Israel. A second encounter between God and Isaiah in 8:5–15 concerns God sending Assyria to punish unbelieving Judah.

So far I have elaborated Isa 7–9 on a narrative level to summarize the meetings between Isaiah and Ahaz, Isaiah and God, and the various meanings of the children's names. At a thematic level, the elaboration is more general. The cited verse (Isa 7:14) evokes a larger narrative that emphasizes themes of resistance to and the refusal to trust God's saving work, of imperial power as a means of divine punishment, and of God saving the people from imperial power.

Foley's metonymic approach, in which a small reference evokes larger traditions, enables us to recognize that these themes are not unique to Isa 7–9. They are part of a larger pattern of God's ways of working that the biblical writings present. Similar themes of imperial power as a means of punishment for disobedience and of God's salvation from powerful nations can be elaborated in relation to various big events in the biblical traditions.

God's deliverance of the people in the exodus from Egypt through the sea (Exod 14–15) is one such example.[37] Another comprises the interpretation of the sixth-century exile in Babylon. Prophets like Jeremiah and (Deutero-) Isaiah, as well as the Deuteronomists, interpret the fall of Jerusalem in 597– 587 B.C.E. as God's punishment for sin. God's agent in this punishment is the imperial power Babylon. The punishment is enacted in the defeat of Jerusalem and exiling of the leading citizens. But Babylon itself is punished. God subsequently saves or liberates the people through the Persian ruler Cyrus (called God's "anointed" or messiah in Isa 44:28; 45:1), who allows the people to return home.[38] In the second and first centuries B.C.E., the book of 2 Maccabees presents the Seleucid ruler Antiochus Epiphanes as the one who punishes the people in his imperialist actions. But 2 Maccabees is also sure that God will liberate the people from him (2 Macc 5:17–20; 6:12–17; 7:30–42). The Roman Pompey's violation of Jerusalem and temple in 63 B.C.E. is seen in similar terms. It is punishment for sins but God will save the people from their sins and punishment (Pss. Sol. 2; 17).

Our focus here, though, will be limited to Isa 7–9 since this is the particular text cited in Matt 1:23. How, then, does evoking and elaborating the Isaianic context contribute to the Gospel's audience's understanding? The presence of three children, whose names interpret the larger action, focuses attention on the child Jesus' name and mission as Emmanuel. His name is double-edged, promising salvation from imperial power but delivering judgment if God's action is rejected. This naming is part of the primacy effect, creating an expectation at the Gospel's outset that he will effect both salvation and judgment. The audience must continue on to find out who is saved and who is judged, who welcomes God's action and who resists it, and how it happens.[39]

Three Perspectives on Imperial Power

Evoking Isaiah elucidates the situation in which Jesus performs his saving/ judging work (cf. 1:21). Isaiah 7–9 addresses a context of pronounced imperial threat, from the Syro-Ephraimite alliance and from Assyria. While this context is usually acknowledged, commentators often proceed as though it is of no significance for Matt 1:21–23, preferring to spiritualize the promise of salvation in Matt 1:21.[40] But, I would contend, this situation of imperial threat is very relevant to the sociohistorical situation of the Matthean audience. Perhaps located in Antioch in Syria,[41] the administrative capital of the Roman province of Syria, this small marginal community knows daily the political, socioeconomic, legal, religious, and cultural reality of Roman imperial power and presence, as I have demonstrated in chapters 1 to 5 above.[42]

For this audience in its somewhat analogous situation, the Isaiah 7–9 passage provides three perspectives on imperial power. First, God opposes it. Syria and Israel will be rebuffed (Isa 7:19, 16; 8:1–4). Second, God uses the imperial power Assyria to punish God's sinful people (7:17–25; 8:5–15). Third, the punishment does not last forever. While the imperial power Assyria accomplishes God's purposes, it does not control its own destiny. It too falls under judgment. There is salvation for God's people. "A remnant shall return." The three perspectives exist in tension. While imperial powers accomplish God's purposes, God ultimately opposes them.

For the Gospel's audience living under Rome's power, the Isaiah material provides perspectives on its present and future. Its present life under Roman power is punishment for sin as Jerusalem's fall in 70 c.e. exhibited (cf. 22:7, and chapter 5 above),[43] but there is hope for its future. God will save God's people from Roman imperial control.[44] How they are to live in the empire in the present is not addressed in this passage (see 5:38–42; 17:24–27), but God's future plans do not suggest positive relations with the empire in the meantime.[45]

These claims of God's control of history and of the nations collide with a cultural value with which the audience is familiar. As I outlined in chapters 1 to 3, Roman imperial "theology,"[46] represented in Antioch by the military personnel of three or four legions, *Judaea capta* coins, statues, buildings, administrative officials, temples, festivals, displays of booty seized from the conquered Jerusalem temple, and a tax on Jews, asserts that Rome and the Flavians rule by Jupiter's will and accomplish the will of the gods (Statius, *Silvae* 4.3.128–40; 5.1.37–39; Silius Italicus, *Punica* 3.570–630). Rome's defeat of Jerusalem and the destruction of the temple in 70 c.e. seem to legitimate such claims. Tacitus captures the religious dimension of the Roman victory by reporting that as the Roman troops approached Jerusalem, the temple's doors burst open and a "superhuman voice cried: 'The gods are departing' " (*Hist.* 5.13; cf. Josephus, *J.W.* 6.299).

How, then, post–70, is God's presence known after Rome has devastated the temple and land? The text of Isa 7:14, forged in one situation threatened by imperial power, speaks to another time that knows the same danger. It provides assurance that despite all appearances to the contrary, Rome's empire does not hold sway, the empire is not sovereign, and God is not powerless. In these circumstances God's presence and saving purposes made known through God's designated agent, Jesus, are to be embraced as a challenge to Roman imperial claims.

As with Isaiah's Emmanuel, the child Jesus is a sign of resistance to imperial power. The name Emmanuel contests imperial claims that emperors like Gaius Caligula (Philo, *Legat.* 346) and Domitian manifest the gods' presence as a *deus praesens* (Statius, *Silvae* 5.2.170) or θεὸς ἐπιφανής (*theos epiphanēs*).[47] It confirms Jesus as the one who manifests God's will and blessings on earth. Through him God's purposes and reign will prevail.

Evoking Isaiah, then, destabilizes the status quo. To evoke a prophet is dangerous in an imperial context, since prophets point to different realities.[48] They contest the dominant reality, locating imperial claimants in the much larger context of God's purposes, reframing the present and future. They keep alive visions of a different order that challenge the claims made by powers like Syria-Israel, Assyria, and Rome. Just as the eighth-century prophet countered and relativized imperialist claims, so does his word for the Matthean audience. Matthew 2 will narrate the thwarting of the murderous plans of Herod, vassal king of the Romans, and like Ahaz, resistant to God's purposes being worked out in Jesus. This story along with its evoking of the Moses-Pharaoh struggle continues to affirm God's control of the nations.[49] And 24:27–31 will depict the return of Jesus in triumphant power, overcoming all including Rome to establish God's empire.

Pursuing the intertextual link with Isa 7–9 underlines this context of imperial threat, offers three perspectives on it, and asserts God's ultimately salvific intentions. In the conception of Jesus, God again promises salvation (1:21). In this context of Roman imperial power, how will Jesus save his people from their sins?

ISAIAH 7–9 AND MATTHEW 4:14–16

Isaiah 7–9 is evoked for a second time in 4:14–16 with a citation from Isa 8:23–9:1. As with 1:22–23, Matthean scholars have generally not given the Isaiah intertext any power,[50] but elaborating the Isaiah reference produces important understandings.

The section 4:12–16 closes the first narrative block and prepares for the beginning of Jesus' public ministry at 4:17.[51] Imperial power has been prominent in this section. In chapter 2 Jesus escapes from the Roman vassal and tyrant King Herod despite Herod's serious efforts to kill him. The baptism in chapter 3 asserts God's claim by restating Jesus' role in this imperial world. In God's purposes, Jesus is "my beloved son" or agent (3:17). This perspective on Jesus frames all his actions and words, and identifies the point of view by which all characters in the book are judged. After his baptism, Jesus is tempted by the devil (4:1–11). The temptation consists of the devil's threefold attempts to have Jesus do the devil's bidding. If Jesus carried out the devil's will and not God's, Jesus would be the devil's agent or son, not God's commissioned agent ("Christ") or son. In one of the temptations, the devil claims control of all the kingdoms or empires of the earth and offers them to Jesus (4:8). This very revealing claim identifies Rome, the world's leading empire, as the devil's possession. But Jesus does not do the devil's will and is not an ally of Rome and its empire. He announces and demonstrates God's empire that is opposed to Rome's empire. Jesus, hearing of the imprisonment of the prophet John the Baptist by another Roman vassal, Herod Antipas, withdraws[52] to settle in Capernaum in Roman-controlled Galilee (4:12–13).[53] John's criticism of the ruler's ways, a classic struggle of prophet against ruler, will cost him his life (14:1–12). Jesus' withdrawal does not mean a retreat to safety since Herod Antipas rules Galilee (cf. 14:1–12). His move, rather, continues the challenge to the Roman vassal's power by asserting there a different reign, God's empire (cf. 4:17).

Perhaps the naming of Capernaum utilizes the audience's knowledge. It was a small, insignificant, agricultural and fishing village (population around 1,000) on the northwestern shore of the Sea of Galilee. Or perhaps the audience has never heard of such an inconsequential place. But that's the point. Jesus does not move to the larger cities, Tiberias (built to honor and named after the emperor Tiberius) or Sepphoris, rebuilt by Agrippa. These centers of imperial political, economic, social, and cultural power in Galilee maintained the elite's interests and control over the surrounding villages through taxation and military force. As a Jew in Roman-dominated territory, Jesus is located among the marginal, with the rural peasants not the urban wealthy, with the ruled not the rulers, with the powerless and exploited not the powerful.[54] As is typical of the Gospel, the challenge to the imperial center comes from apparently inconsequential places like Capernaum (so Jerusalem and Bethlehem in 2:1–11[55]).

On Location

Several geographical qualifiers expand the reference to Capernaum. It is "by the sea," in the territory of Zebulun and Naphtali (4:13). The audience knows how important geographical markers are from previous fulfillment citations: Bethlehem in 2:5–6, Egypt in 2:15, Nazareth in 2:23. It is no surprise, then, that a fulfillment citation should follow Jesus' move to Capernaum. It learns that this move fulfills "what had been spoken through the prophet Isaiah" (4:14). Utilizing both "prophet" and "Isaiah," as well as the citation's metonymic function, the audience again contemplates what Isaiah the prophet said.

But immediately obvious is that Isaiah 7–9 does not mention Capernaum. Jesus' move to Capernaum *in and of itself* cannot be the focus of the citation. More is to be observed than that Jesus' living or ministering in the geographical environs of Capernaum was God's will.[56] Yet geography matters. Unusual is the inclusion of Zebulun when Capernaum is in Naphtali. Of course the double location Zebulun and Naphtali in 4:13 prepares for the Isaiah citation in 4:15.[57] But what is the significance of Naphtali *and* Zebulun? The Matthean form of the Isaiah citation emphasizes this double location. The initial placement of "land of Zebulun, land of Naphtali" results from omitting "In the former time he brought into contempt" (Isa 8:23/9:1a). In addition to this prominent placement, the repetition from 4:13 emphasizes these locations.

Zebulun and Naphtali

Their importance is elaborated by the Isaiah 7–9 narrative. The citation in Matt 4:15–16 from Isa 8:23–9:2, which does not exactly follow any textual tradition,[58] depicts the end of God's judgment announced in Isa 7–9 and evoked by Matt 1:22–23. Isaiah's word about disaster came to pass when the capital Samaria fell in 722 B.C.E. to Assyria, who exiled the leadership and seized and occupied the land (cf. 2 Kgs 15:29). Isaiah 8:16–9:1a narrates the terrible results for a (faithless) people subjected to imperial power. "Greatly distressed and hungry" because of appropriated resources, they know "distress and darkness, the gloom of anguish; and they will be thrust into thick darkness" (Isa 8:22). Isaiah 9:1a repeats the impact of Assyria's punishment, calling it "anguish" and "contempt." But "in the latter time," perhaps the coronation of Hezekiah in 716/715 (2 Kgs 18:13),[59] God will reverse these circumstances. Light shines in the darkness.

The names Zebulun and Naphtali underline the horror of Assyria's actions in seizing the land. The names Zebulun and Naphtali refer to tribal allocations of the land that God had sworn to Abraham, Isaac, and Jacob. These allocations are shown to Moses (Deut 34:1–4), and apportioned under Joshua (Josh 18:3; 19:10–16 [Zebulun in the Galilean highlands] and 19:32–39 [Naphtali, to the west and north of the Sea of Galilee]).[60]

Across the Jordan

These lands are "across the Jordan" (πέραν τοῦ Ἰορδάνου; *peran tou Iordanou*). This phrase recalls the exodus narrative, particularly the occupation of the land "across the Jordan" that God has given to the people.[61] Evoking these events (and so continuing the numerous exodus/occupation echoes throughout the Gospel's opening chapters) underlines how gravely Assyria has violated God's purposes by seizing the God-given land of Naphtali and Zebulun.

Again the Isaiah text evokes a context of imperial aggression that, as with 1:23, is analogous to the Gospel audience's situation under Roman rule. The Isaiah text connects one situation of imperial aggression to another. The audience knows that it is no longer Assyria but Rome that claims this territory. And it knows from its own experience what that means. Since 67 C.E., Vespasian and Titus claimed control of Galilee (Josephus, *J.W.* 7.216–17), redistributed land among loyal supporters, and ensured economic control of land and resources through taxation of the largely peasant economy.[62] Loyal local elites, who secured their own social and economic power through cooperation with Rome, assisted in maintaining control. The few and the powerful benefited at the expense of the many. This institutionalized injustice, sustained by the memory of the recent defeat and by the threat of military violence, and reinforced, for instance, by the presence of Vespasian's and Titus's images on coins,[63] was a far cry from the vision of the promised land. This tradition, evoked by the biblical names "Zebulun and Naphtali" and the phrase "across the Jordan," announces God's sovereignty and justice, and shows Rome's presence to be a violation.

Galilee under the Gentiles

This imperial context, emphasized by "Zebulun and Naphtali" and "across the Jordan," enables an audience to interpret a further puzzling geographical identifier. The "land of Zebulun, land of Naphtali,"a phrase consisting of names that evoke the sacred traditions of God's liberation and gift, is also "Galilee of the Gentiles" (4:15; cf. Isa 9:1). The term does not mean, as some have claimed, that Galilee was inhabited by non-Jews, or was particularly susceptible to Hellenization, or that Jewish ethnicity and piety had almost disappeared, or that Jesus was looking only for Gentiles (cf. 4:18–22, 23–25).[64] While some of these options are accurate, the term in relation to Isa 7–9 more likely designates Galilee's occupied status, a land under the power of, possessed by, belonging to, ruled or controlled by Gentile imperialists, Assyria and Rome (cf. 2 Kgs 17:24–27).[65] Jesus dwells in Capernaum in "Galilee under the Gentiles."

The nomenclature "land of Zebulun, land of Naphtali," "across the Jordan," and "Galilee under the Gentiles" locates Jesus not merely in Capernaum, but in the promised land that God gave to the people and over which God has sovereignty. The land is now occupied by Rome as it was occupied by Assyria in Isaiah's reference. The names Zebulun and Naphtali are, for those in the know, a daring reminder of God's sovereignty that contests and challenges Roman claims on Galilee, the presence of Roman client rulers like Herod, and an imperial "theology" that sees Jupiter's will being done. The terms challenge Roman claims by evoking another perspective. It is left to the audience to articulate the counternarrative that exposes and reframes Rome's claims within God's purposes.

Darkness and Light

The reality of Roman imperial presence is imaged in phraseology that describes "Galilee under the Gentiles" as a place of darkness and death into which light shines (4:16). The audience's knowledge of the symbolic associations of "darkness" enables it to elaborate the very nature of imperial aggression. While darkness symbolizes various realities,[66] it especially portrays that which is contrary to God's life-giving purposes: the chaos before God's creative light and life (Gen 1:2), the oppressive slavery in Egypt (Exod 10:21, 22; 14:20), exile in Babylon (Isa 42:7; 47:5; 49:9), and in Isa 8:22–9:2 Assyria's imperial rule. Darkness images the wicked who do injustice to the weak and needy (Ps 81:5; Job 24:2–17). By contrast the righteous, those who fear the Lord, who deal in justice, who are secure in the Lord, who give to the poor, are lights in the darkness (Ps 111:4). Darkness denotes not some spiritual condition,[67] but political, social, economic, and religious acts and structures (such as imperialism) contrary to God's purposes. Darkness is, for Isaiah 8–9, Assyria's empire that exercises its rule in Galilee. Darkness is, for Matt 4:14–16, Rome's empire that exercises its rule in Galilee. It is the rejection of God's call to a changed society, the call to repentance that John brings (3:2), for which he is arrested (4:12). To "sit in darkness" or "death" is to live in the midst of actions and structures—Rome's empire—contrary to God's will.

Yet such darkness is not the final word. Darkness in the biblical tradition is always subject to God's power (Isa 45:7). Light, an image of God's life and saving power (Ps 27:1), dawns and rescues people from darkness whether political oppression (Exod 10:21, 22; 14:20, Egypt; Isa 9:2, Assyria; 42:7; 47:5; 49:9, Babylon; *1 En.* 1:8–9) or personal misery (Ps 90:6; 106:10–16 LXX) such as hunger or affliction (Isa 58:10). Light means God's reign of justice, righteousness, and peace, which breaks the "rod of their oppressor" (Isa 11:4–7).

Significantly, the contemporary imperial poet Statius uses imagery of light to praise Domitian (the likely emperor when Matthew was written). Statius calls the emperor Domitian "that present deity" *(Silvae* 5.2.170) and describes his "immortal brightness" *(Silvae* 1.1.77) that shines even when he tries to dim it *(Silvae* 4.2.41–44). Domitian outshines constellations and the sun. People reflect his light *(Silvae* 4.1.3–4, 23–27). Another poet, Martial, greets Domitian's return to Rome as restoring light to the darkness *(Epigrams* 8.21).

But the light in 4:16 is not the presence of the Roman emperor who "rules" Galilee. Roman rule is part of the problem, the "darkness" and "shadow of death" under which "Galilee under the Gentiles" now suffers. The Gospel contests and counters such imperial claims. The light is Jesus' presence in Galilee, the one commissioned to manifest God's saving presence, to transform darkness with light. His public ministry is to commence (4:17).

Elaborating the Isaiah citation evokes both the reality of imperial power and the promise of God's salvation. Jesus' presence in Galilee promises liberation from Rome's rule. This is the mission of Jesus the Christ (1:1, 16, 17, 18) and son (2:15; 3:17) presented in the opening narrative section (1:1–4:16), to save his people from their sins and to manifest God's presence (1:21, 23). But the audience's evoking of Isa 7–9 not only makes explicit this harsh imperial reality and God's promised salvation, it also raises a question. How will Jesus carry out such a mission?

HOW WILL JESUS SAVE?

One approach to this question offers a "spiritual" answer. Davies and Allison are not alone, as I observed in the last chapter, in asserting his saving is "religious and moral—as opposed to political." They claim there is "a shift from literal destruction and political plight to moral and spiritual darkness."[68] While recognizing that the Matthean Jesus effects moral and religious transformation (e.g., 7:24–27), an approach that removes any sociopolitical component is inadequate in the light of the material from

Isa 7–9, the analogous situation of the Matthean audience under Roman imperialism, the force of the repeated Naphtali and Zebulun, the phrase "Galilee under the Gentiles," and the metaphors of light and darkness. Another unconvincing approach proposes a military solution in which Jesus leads violent rebellion against Rome.[69]

The only credible approach to this question is for the audience to continue on with the narrative. At 4:17 Jesus' public mission begins. In the "land of Zebulun, land of Naphtali," land given by God to the people, Jesus announces God's reign or empire or sovereignty and calls for repentance in recognition of that reign. In the land "beside the sea" (4:15, 18), he calls people to follow him, thereby forming an alternative community that acknowledges and anticipates God's reign. In Galilee "under the Gentiles," he proclaims the good news of God's empire, heals people of diseases, and casts out demons (4:23; cf. chs. 8–9). Miracles of healing and exorcisms of alien invading and controlling powers often reflect social conflicts. They express resistance to and liberation from imperial control,[70] as well as anticipate the full establishment of God's reign typically presented as a time of plenty and wholeness because God's justice is established (2 *Bar.* 73:1–2). Jesus goes "up a mountain" (5:1), a phrase that invokes both the liberation from Egyptian tyranny in the giving of torah to Moses and anticipates the establishment of God's reign at Zion.[71] He teaches an alternative way of life that embodies God's empire (5:3, 10); extends cherished teaching (5:17–48); urges just social relationships (5:21–26, 27–30, 33–37); encourages religious practices such as praying for daily bread and the fullness of God's purposes, reign, and will (6:7–13); emphasizes communal economic practices that offer an alternative to indebtedness (5:42; 6:2–4); advocates nonviolent resistance (5:38–48); warns of conflict and persecution since the empire always strikes back (5:10–12); and anticipates throughout the yet-future completion of God's purposes. He carries out his mission in his subversive teaching and actions, in his life and death, and in his resurrection and parousia, which ends all imperial claims (24:27–31). Along the way he creates a community with distinctive socioeconomic practices that recognizes and anticipates the full establishment of God's empire over all. Ironically, and regrettably, the Gospel ultimately envisages the replacement of one imperial ideology with another.

All of this could be developed at length. But a more modest goal has been in view in this chapter, notably to assess the contribution of evoking Isa 7–9 in Matt 1:22–23 and 4:14–16. The intertext recognizes the Gospel audience's experience of Roman imperial power, provides God's perspectives on that situation, explains the present, underlines the hope of change, warns of rejection, and raises the key question, at the end of the first narrative block and on the brink of the beginning of Jesus' ministry of how God will accomplish that salvation through Jesus.[72] These two citations require the audience to look back to elaborate the prophet Isaiah and forward to answer this question.[73]

– S E V E N –

Take My Yoke Not Rome's:
Matthew 11:28–30

T HE WORDS OF MATT 11:28–30 are often heard by modern congregations as words of comfort. These words speak to many in search of
peace of mind and spiritual refreshment in a competitive and materialistic
world marked by fretful stress, overcommitted schedules, and the drive to
increase profit margins.

> Come to me, all who labor and are heavy laden and I will give you
> rest. Take my yoke on you, and learn from me; for I am meek and
> lowly in heart, and you will find rest for your souls. For my yoke is
> kind/good and my burden is small.

Yet while contemporary congregations hear soothing and strengthening
words, it is by no means clear that Matthew's audience, inhabiting the unjust and inequitable world of Roman imperialism, did so. I will suggest that
they heard words of challenge and promise, words not intended so much to
help one survive in the status quo, but revolutionary words that proclaim
the overthrow of Rome's world and the establishment of God's empire.

CONTEMPORARY READINGS

Contemporary scholarly interest in Matthew 11:28–30 is vigorous,[1] with
extensive disagreement over Jesus' identity as its speaker, his addressees, the
nature of his call, and the nature of the promise or reward that they receive.[2]
It will be helpful to review some of this debate in order to surface issues that
need attention, identify some alternative readings of the verses, and locate
the distinctive contribution of this chapter.

The dominant view, argued forcibly by M. Jack Suggs in 1970[3] and emphasized more recently, for example, in a series of studies by Celia Deutsch,[4]
asserts that Jesus speaks as a sage and as personified Wisdom (Sophia) to
"would-be disciples" burdened by the teachings of other teachers, especially
followers of the Pharisees. Jesus calls them to take up his yoke, his revelation of Torah, the definitive teaching of God's will. Suggs claims that Sir
51:26–27 is crucial for understanding the passage, while Deutsch points to
a series of characteristics shared by Wisdom and Jesus.

This claim that Jesus speaks as Wisdom has been contested,[5] and various other identities for Jesus as the speaker of these words have been offered. Graham Stanton argues that while some wisdom themes are used in 11:28–30, "it is not at all clear that Matthew identifies Jesus as Sophia" or that the wisdom themes are "the key to the passage."[6] In support, he notes that verbal links with Sir 51 are slender, that Sir 51 offers no support for the Matthean phrases "all who toil and are heavy laden" and "meek and lowly in heart," and that the jump from "Son" in 11:27 to wisdom, often understood as a female figure, in 11:28 is difficult.[7] Instead, Stanton argues that the description of Jesus as "meek and lowly in heart" indicates Jesus speaks these words not as Wisdom but as the humble, healing servant (12:18–21; 8:17). Jesus the humble servant addresses disciples, calls them to the yoke of discipleship, and promises them his presence in their mission work.[8]

William D. Davies and Dale Allison recognize that the identification of Jesus with Wisdom is "implicit" in the scene, but argue that the "primary background...is to be found in Jewish traditions about Moses."[9] They point to Exod 33:12–13 where God and Moses share intimate and reciprocal knowledge, and to 33:14 where rest is promised. Jesus is described in Matt 11:29 as πραΰς ("meek") just as Moses is (Num 12:3), and Jesus reveals God's purposes and demands, God's Torah, just as Moses did. Jesus speaks, then, as Moses' "counterpart" or "eschatological complement," essentially as a new but "incomparably greater" Moses, to "all those who have not come to Jesus."[10] He offers these nondisciples his yoke, that is, himself, the one whose words and deeds reveal God's purposes and demands. He promises them eschatological rest, "the peace and contentment and fullness of life" associated with obedience and with his presence.[11]

Blaine Charette pursues a quite different line. He does not find a wisdom context necessary, but turns to prophetic and pentateuchal traditions to find "conceptual and terminological agreements" with this saying of Jesus, "especially in eschatological contexts which look forward to the promised restoration of the nation."[12] Charette emphasizes that "yoke" often refers in the prophetic traditions to foreign domination that God promises to lift in returning the people to enjoy "rest" in the land and to serve under God's yoke. Jesus speaks as the Messiah who announces, using metaphorical language, that this time of liberty for the captives has arrived. He calls the people of Israel to return to God's yoke or service, and to await the yet-future rest at the consummation of God's purposes.

Russell Pregeant tests the claims of a Wisdom Christology in 11:25–30 with a refreshingly different approach.[13] Instead of the usual history-of-religions and redaction methods, he employs a reader-response perspective. Taking the order of the finished form of the Gospel seriously, he reads 11:25–30 in the sequential context of the first eleven chapters, asking "how the text leads the reader to make specific confessions regarding the identity of Jesus and . . . whether and in what ways the wisdom passages participate in that process."[14] He argues that dominant in the opening ten chapters of the Gospel is the understanding that Jesus is Messiah/Son of God. Since in 11:27 "Jesus calls God Father and himself Son, the reader will be reminded of the crucial junctures at which Jesus has been directly and indirectly designated Son of God and will now associate that title with Jesus' revelatory function."[15] While it is not impossible to identify Jesus as personified Wisdom, nothing in the text solicits this confession. Without denying some wisdom influence especially on the presentation of the rejection of Jesus and of Israel, Pregeant argues that Jesus speaks in 11:28–30 as the Messiah/ Son of God who, in speaking for God, calls nondisciples (especially those suffering under Pharisaic teaching) to take up the yoke of his teaching. The reference to Wisdom in 11:19 does not emerge as "a key to Jesus' identity."[16]

Frances Taylor Gench, employing redaction criticism, also argues that Jesus speaks as Son of God.[17] While wisdom influence cannot be denied, Jesus does not speak as Wisdom. Rather Jesus speaks as "the Son of God, who mediates to humans God's revelation." The title "Son" in 11:27 invokes Matthew's preeminent "Son-of-God Christology." Jesus the "revealer-Son" addresses disciples in 11:28–30, renewing their call to discipleship because they "struggle with the costly nature of discipleship." To take his "yoke" is to learn from Jesus "who alone imparts an authentic understanding of the will of God" including the right interpretation of Torah, and to experience his enabling presence.[18]

Deirdre Good also emphasizes Jesus' identity as "son" but understands it in reference to Jesus as king.[19] Focusing on Jesus' claim to be "meek" in 11:29 ("gentle" is a common translation), she notes the same quality ascribed to Jesus as king in Matt 21:5. Meekness (or compassionate and humble service) is also a prime desirable quality in ideal Hellenistic kings. Moreover, the language of "yoke" designates service for a king (she quotes 1 Macc 8:31). Further, the use of "son" in 11:27, part of Matthew's extensive use of son language for Jesus, also points to Jesus as king since Israel's king was commonly referred to as son (Ps 2:7). Jesus the king calls people to the yoke of service.

Before evaluating these contributions, it may be helpful to summarize each scholar's analysis (see the table on the following page).

Evaluation

These contributions attest diverse methods and conclusions, and pose some interesting questions. Does Jesus speak in 11:28–30 as Wisdom, or as the humble servant, or as the counterpart of Moses, or as the Messiah, or as the Son of God, or as the meek king? What do we do with these multiple readings, especially when each reading is insightful, informed, and nuanced? One could, of course, identify various weaknesses and try to declare a win-

	Jesus' Identity as Speaker	Addressees	Nature of Call (Yoke Means?)	Promise/Reward (Rest Means?)
Suggs, *Deutsch*	Wisdom	Nondisciples burdened by other teachers	To receive his interpretation of Torah	Life; Jesus' presence
Stanton	Servant	Disciples	To ongoing mission	Jesus' presence
Davies *and* *Allison*	New/Greater Moses	Nondisciples	To obey Jesus	Peace/fullness of life/ contentment/Jesus' presence
Charette	Messiah	Israel	To God's service	Future completion of God's purposes
Pregeant	Messiah/ Son of God	Nondisciples suffering under other teachers	To Jesus' teaching as Torah	(?) Jesus' presence
Gench	Son of God	Disciples	Renewed call to Jesus' interpretation of God's will/Torah	Jesus' presence
Good	Son/King	?	Yoke of service	?
Carter	Jesus	All under imperial rule	To God's empire	Completion of God's purposes; overthrow of Rome

ner. Certainly not all the readings are equally persuasive at all points. For example, Stanton has raised questions that caution against a ready identification with Wisdom. But Stanton's own identification of Jesus as the humble servant itself falters in part because the key (redactional) phrase "meek and lowly in heart" (11:29) is absent from both of the "servant" passages to which he appeals (12:18–21; 8:17). And Davies and Allison's appeal to Exod 33:12–14, while insightful, is somewhat weakened by the absence of "yoke" from that passage, and of the language of "son" to denote Moses' relationship with God. Charette's work is strong in its use of various nonwisdom traditions, especially the prophets, to define the key terms of "yoke" and "rest." But Charette is vague when he appeals to "the 'captive' motif" in Matthew. He does not clearly identify what sort of captivity he thinks Jesus delivers from, especially when he asserts that "the notion of 'captivity' [is] no longer understood in a literal sense but as a metaphor."[20] And his emphasis on "freeing the captives" is suspect because, as Charette himself acknowledges, Matthew unlike Luke does not mention it. Pregeant's refreshing reader-response work is vulnerable precisely at the point where it could make a contribution. He allows only 11:27 and its sonship language to define the speaker of 11:28. But is the forward-moving (and backward-glancing?) reading process restricted so neatly only to the

immediately prior verse? Does the wisdom material of 11:19 have no contribution, or all of the Christology of chapters 1–11? And there are the larger
methodological issues of trying to sustain the claim that a particular reading is a "preferred" reading "in the eyes of the implied author,"[21] and that
the implied author should have such control over the interpretive process
anyway.

If we were looking for a winner, Pregeant and Gench may appear to have
an advantage since they can at least appeal to 11:27 as textual support for
their claim that Jesus speaks as son. But of course it is not that easy. Christological titles acquire content both from the larger narrative context and
from the traditions they assume and evoke. Jesus has been identified from
the outset as son of David, son of Abraham, son of man, and son of God, as
well as by numerous nontitular means. It is not immediately obvious why
"son of God" in particular should supply the content for the unqualified
"son" in 11:27.[22] Nor can it be overlooked that "son" is associated with
other christological designations such as wisdom in 11:19 (son of man), Emmanuel (1:21, 23; 2:15), or king (2:2, 15). And "son" is well at home in
various biblical traditions that the Gospel's audience is assumed to know,
such as those concerning kings (Ps 2:7), prophets (Ezekiel, *passim*) and, of
course, wisdom (Prov 5:1; 8:32; 10:1; Sir 4:11). Moreover, readers arrive at
11:28–30 knowing much about Jesus that is not associated with any particular title, such as his proclamation of the βασιλεία τῶν οὐρανῶν (*basileia
tōn ouranōn*; the empire of the heavens). The search for *the* monolithic,
all-encompassing title seems inevitably to lead to frustration.

Declaring a winner, then, seems both impossible and unnecessary given
the rich array of insight and the complexity of the verses' contexts. Recognizing the validity of numerous readings seems a more appropriate course.
Nor should adding to the polyvalency be ruled out. For instance, numerous
scholars have noted the citation of Jer 6:16 in Matt 11:29d ("you will find
rest for your souls"), in which the prophet is commanded to urge the people
to walk in God's covenant ways but the people refuse. Could we argue that
Jesus functions as a new Jeremiah? The use of "yoke" in Jer 6:16 to refer to
"the law of their God" may provide further support.[23] And, as I will demonstrate in this chapter, several intriguing insights exist in the scholarship
surveyed above that have not been adequately developed.

I will argue, building from some undeveloped insights especially in
Charette and Good, that 11:28–30 utilizes a series of terms (labor and heavy
laden; rest; yoke; meek) that are frequently associated with the exercise of
power, especially imperial and political rule. Jesus, the one who proclaims
and demonstrates God's reign or empire, issues an invitation to those who
are oppressed by Roman imperial power to encounter God's empire now
in his ministry in anticipation of the time when God destroys all empires
including Rome's.

ALL WHO LABOR AND ARE HEAVY LADEN

To whom does Jesus address these words? Who are "all who labor and are heavy laden"? Are they disciples or nondisciples? One view identifies them as disciples wrestling with the "costly nature of discipleship,"[24] especially the mission task of chapter 10.[25] Jesus renews their call. But this is not entirely persuasive, in part because the whole of chapter 10 is a call to mission and disciples do not go out in mission at the end of chapter 10. Moreover, as is commonly observed, the initial "Come to me" of 11:28 echoes Jesus' call of the first disciples from 4:18–22 where Jesus uses a similar phrase ("come after me"), the same language "come" (δεῦτε, *deute*, 11:28 and 4:19), and, in both texts, intensive, personal language[26] in calling people into relationship with himself. These similarities suggest that in 11:28 Jesus is calling those who are not disciples. He continues to make available to others the revelation that disciples already know (11:25–27).

What is the situation of these outsiders? One traditional approach identifies them as all people who are burdened by sin.[27] But while this suggestion may account for the "all" and perhaps "heavy laden" in the invitation, it does not make much sense of those "who labor" which is placed first in identifying the addressees. Another suggestion, by far the most popular among contemporary interpreters, is that Jesus addresses those burdened by Pharisaic demands for strict Torah observance. Interpreters distinguish "those who labor" from "the infants" or disciples of 11:27, and on the basis of a contrast between Jesus' "light" burden in 11:30 and his use of "heavy" to describe Pharisaic teaching in 23:4, conclude Jesus is calling Israel away from following the Pharisees' teaching.[28] But the tradition does not regard the law as a burden. It is "not too hard for you, nor is it too far away," and it offers life (Deut 30:6–14). The Pharisees have not been in view in chapter 11 and there is no obvious clue they should be summoned to mind. The dispute of 12:1–14 over the Sabbath cannot be understood as an example of Jesus' "light burden" since both he and the Pharisees exhibit a very "high" view of the Sabbath and Jesus' requirement of mercy as its legitimate observance is very demanding.[29] It is in fact typical of his interpretation, not abolition, of the law that demands more of people than do the scribes and Pharisees (5:17–20, 21–48).[30] And such a narrow restricting of the language to refer to a dispute with the Pharisees overlooks a weight of compelling evidence that points in some quite different directions.

A more obvious meaning for "those who labor" seems to have escaped Matthean scholars. Intent on religious and polemical matters, they have ignored the situation of most of the inhabitants of the first-century world. I suggest that Jesus' call is addressed to all those who labor desperately to keep themselves alive in the economically oppressive and destructive system of Roman imperialism, the daily reality of most people in the late first century.

As I have outlined in chapters 1 to 3, the late-first-century world of

Matthew's Antiochene audience was shaped by Roman imperialism. Such a world is one of profound "social inequality" whereby a minority elite—no more than 5 percent—exercises political, economic, and social control over the vast majority.[31] A proprietary mentality drives and is expressed through this vertical and hierarchical system in which the ruling elite secure wealth, status, and power (Plutarch, *Mor.* 58D, 100D) at the expense of the rest "through the collection of taxes, tribute money, rents, and services," through the exercise of public office and the sale of justice,[32] and always aware of the threat of punitive and harsh military action. "The burden of supporting the state and the privileged classes fell on the shoulders of the common people."[33] Lenski estimates that anything up to 70 percent of a peasant's production could be paid in various taxes to imperial and local masters.[34]

In describing Rome's exploitation of the provinces to sustain the elite's elegant way of life, Klaus Wengst cites Aristides' fawning comments in his *Roman Oration*. Aristides praises Rome's strategy whereby the provinces provide Rome

> abundantly with whatever is in them. Produce is brought from every land and every sea, depending on what the seasons bring forth, and what is produced by all lands, rivers and lakes and the arts of Greeks and barbarians.... For what grows and is produced among individual peoples is necessarily always here, and here in abundance. (*Roman Oration* 11)

For Aristides, Rome's port Ostia is "the common trading place for all people and the common market for the produce of the earth."[35] Aristides exults in, but does not question or expose, Rome's proprietary mentality enacted through taxes, tributes, forced labor, military threat, and a transportation system whereby all roads, and ships, truly do lead to Rome. The margins exist to supply the center. Nor does Aristides recognize that the lifestyle of the elite comes at enormous expense to 95 percent of the population. As we noted in chapter 3, Rodney Stark describes the desperate existence of many in cities like Antioch.[36] Most, whether rural or urban, lived around the poverty level, barely subsisting on a daily basis and lacking any surplus for either a safety margin or as a basis for improved production. For most, it is a world marked by desperate striving to meet the demands of empire.

This is the world of imperial power, injustice, and the wealthy's constant quest to sustain a life of conspicuous consumption and display.[37] Matthew's audience knows these realities on a daily basis. It knows Rome's recent assertion of its power in crushing insubordinate Jerusalem in 70 C.E. Jesus rejects it as contrary to God's way and proposes an alternative social organization. "You know that the rulers of the Gentiles lord it over them, and their great ones are tyrants over them. It will not be so among you..." (Matt 20:25–26). Jesus issues his call to "come to me," then, to "all who labor," to all members of this imperial society wearied by oppressive rule, under heavy taxation burdens. This is the particular form of "weary laboring" known to the Gospel's audience.

The Verb "Labor"

This view takes seriously the material realities of the world that shape the hearing of the Gospel. It is also supported by the previous appearance in the Gospel of the verb "labor" (κοπιάω; *kopiaō*). In 6:28 the lilies that do not labor are contrasted with king Solomon who has labored hard to gain great wealth.[38] The narratives about Solomon's reign elaborate the imperial context and oppressive means of Solomon's laboring to gain great wealth. In 1 Kgs 4–5 he exploits the people by forced labor (4:6; 5:29–32), tributes (5:27–28), reorganized tax districts (4:7–28), building projects (chs. 6–7), and military and trade alliances (chs. 10–11). This is precisely the sort of laboring that "the lilies of the field" do not have to undertake! "Labor" is intricately connected with the imperial system. While the lilies are sustained not by their own efforts but by trusting God's gracious gifts (cf. Josh 24:13; Wis 16:20), Solomon has unjustly increased weary laboring with harsh taxation and levies to expand his power and wealth at the expense of those he rules, and contrary to God's explicit instructions about how a king is to rule (so Moses in Deut 17:14–17; Samuel in 1 Sam 8:11–17). Solomon's labor causes much desperate labor among the people, labor that wearies and oppresses them. That is, the one previous use of "labor" in the Gospel evokes, by contrast, a situation of harsh oppressive rule that has cruel and exploitative impact on many people.

Septuagintal uses of the verb "labor" (κοπιάω, *kopiaō*) are frequently concerned with, shaped by and reflective of life under various imperial powers, whether Assyrian, Babylonian, Persian, or Hellenistic. These uses also recognize the connection between those with power and wealth, and the laboring of the poor. The laboring of the wealthy and the poor perpetuates unjust social structures and is always unsatisfying. According to Zophar, God ensures that the wicked wealthy cannot enjoy "the fruits of their laboring" in which they have "crushed and abandoned the poor, they have seized a house they did not build" (Job 20:15, 18–19). Sirach observes that laboring for more leaves one wanting more (Sir 11:11). The wealthy person who has "toiled to amass a fortune" can desist for a period of time but "the poor person toils to make a meager living, and if ever he rests he becomes needy" (Sir 31:3–4). Hence labor maintains the societal divisions of the powerful and the desperate.

Yet labor unites all humanity in weary, soul-destroying toil and striving. Sirach recognizes that "hard work was created for everyone" throughout their lifetime, whether "sitting on a throne" or "groveling in dust and ashes," whether "wearing purple and a crown" or "clothed in burlap." He bemoans the constant striving, anxiety, "anger, envy, trouble and unrest, fear of death, fury and strife" of the "heavy yoke laid on the children of Adam" (Sir 40:1, 3–5, 8). "To all creatures, human and animal, but to sinners seven times more, come death and bloodshed and strife and sword, calamities and famine and ruin and plague." The Lexica rightly recognize that the verb "labor" (κοπιάω) embraces a spectrum of hard work, weariness, and loss of heart.[39]

This weary labor pervades all forms of human social interaction. People and animals grow weary while engaged in the imperial activity of war[40] (Deut 25:17–18; 1 Sam 14:13; 2 Sam 17:2; 1 Macc 10:81).[41] People grow weary in sickness (Ps 6:7), from strife with personal enemies (Ps 69:3 [LXX 68:4]), even while imposing torture to force people to renounce their ancestral faith (4 Macc. 9:12). Weary laboring seems to be a feature of human existence in worlds dominated by imperial purposes. Weary laboring is not directed to God's purposes. It marks Israel who has grown tired of God and has abandoned life in covenant relation with God (Isa 43:22). And Israel cannot interpret its weariness as a warning to return to God (Isa 57:10). Weary laboring marks Moab engaged in false worship (Isa 16:12) and Egypt who, despite its efforts, cannot resist God's will (Isa 31:3). It marks Babylon who rebels against God in idolatrous worship (Isa 47:13, 15; Jer 51:58 [LXX 28:58]). It marks Judah being punished under the yoke of Babylonian imperialism (Lam 5:5).

Yet while weary laboring is a feature of human life not lived according to God's purposes, it is not so with God. God does not wearily labor (Isa 40:28). Nor do the works of God's order "hunger or wearily labor" (Sir 16:27). Those who are led by God do not wearily labor (Isa 63:13–14), nor do those who praise God (Sir 43:30) or are guided by Wisdom's instruction (Prov 4:12). In a world ordered according to God's purposes, there seems to be no desperate, weary laboring. But the world assumed by and addressed by Matthew's Gospel is not ordered according to God's purposes as Matt 4:8 and 20:25–28 make clear. Imperial Rome dominates. Its domination system is antithetical to God's purposes. "All who labor" do so in a desperate attempt to stay alive because of Rome's oppressive policies.

Heavy Laden or Burdened

The second verb "heavy laden" or "burdened" (πεφορτισμένοι, *pefortismenoi*) is uncommon but seems to have a general meaning of being "loaded down" either literally or metaphorically.[42] Most likely it is a synonym for those who "labor wearily" in which the Gospel's much-noticed repetition[43] emphasizes their burdensome situation of oppression. However, another possibility is that it specifies a particular burdensome aspect of the imperial world, the teaching of the "religious leaders" that supports the status quo. This connection with the Pharisees is suggested by Jesus' use of the cognate adjective form φορτίον (*fortion*) in 23:4 (also in 11:30) to condemn them for "binding (on people) heavy burdens hard to bear."

What are these burdens? We must be careful to analyze Matthew's presentation and not leap immediately to conclusions fed by unhelpful yet convenient stereotypes of dead, legalistic, rule-obsessed Pharisees that bear little relation to the Gospel presentation. Scholars readily equate the "heavy burdens" of 23:4 with the 613 commandments, but Jesus does not complain in chapter 23 about the *number* of commandments. He does, though, throughout the Gospel attack the content of their teaching. Jesus opposes their teaching and practices of excluding meal regulations (9:10–13), Sabbath requirements that ignore human need (14:1–12), and patriarchal divorce and marriage practices (19:3–9), but not on the basis that they are rule-obsessed or dead. Rather, these teachings and practices hinder doing mercy and good (9:13; 12:7, 12). Later in 23:23 Jesus identifies the issue that seems to underlie these conflicts, namely they are not concerned with God's will of "justice and mercy and faith." These are fundamental covenant values. Justice means fair judicial processes for the rich and poor (Lev 19:15; Deut 1:17), rescue for the oppressed, and advocacy and protection for the widow, orphaned, weak, and poor (Isa 1:17, 21–23; 3:13–15). Mercy, as exhibited by Jesus, has brought community by breaking down social hierarchy and including the excluded with food, healing, forgiveness, new life (Matt 9:13; 12:7). In both scenes the leaders have opposed Jesus' displays of mercy.

The conflict, then, seems to concern two different visions of society and the right to articulate such visions. They oppose him (9:34) and he opposes their teaching (16:12) and disqualifies their leadership of the people (21:45). They resist his claims to be God's agent who offers God's benefits to all of society, especially to those on the margins (9:1–8; 9–13; 12:1–8, 9–14, 22–37; 21:14–16), and so envisages a different social order. In defending the status quo, they hinder people from knowing God's empire (23:13) and practice injustice and deceit (27:62–66; 28:11–15).

Their role and condemnation are clarified by attention to two texts that Matthew evokes. In 9:36 Jesus laments that the people are like sheep without a shepherd. "Shepherd" is a common image for leaders, particularly kings, but including the ruling class (Ezek 34; Suetonius, *Tib.* 32; Dio 56.16.3). Of course there are leaders, but by asserting that the people are like "sheep without a shepherd," Jesus disqualifies the leadership of the ruling elite of Rome and Jerusalem. The shepherd image recalls the criticism of "false shepherds" in Ezek 34. They maintain a strictly differentiated society to ensure the elite has plenty at the expense of the rest. They feed themselves but exploit or burden the sheep/people by depriving them of food and clothing, by not strengthening the weak, healing the sick, binding up the injured, or looking for the lost and scattered (Ezek 34:3–6). They do not protect the people from the nations but let them be enslaved, plundered, frightened, starved, and insulted (34:27–29). The leaders are condemned because of their imperial style: "With force and harshness you have ruled them" (34:4). God promises a reversal with a Davidic prince and God's saving presence (34:23–24, 30–31). By evoking this passage, Jesus transfers its condemnation to the leaders.

A similar criticism is effected in Matt 21:13 when Jesus casts judgment on the temple by saying "you make it a den of robbers." The "you" refers to the chief priests who exercise control of the temple and its economy of tithes exacted from people and sacrifices for which people pay. Jesus quotes from Jer 7 in which the prophet condemns the worshippers for misplaced confidence. They appear to worship but do not act justly with one another, oppressing the alien, the orphan, and the widow, shedding innocent blood, and worshipping other gods (Jer 7:5–6, 9). Jeremiah, and now Jesus, charge the priests with being "robbers" or brigands" who steal from the people and threaten their survival. Such actions are judged by God in Babylon's defeat of Jerusalem in 597–587 B.C.E., and in Rome's defeat of Jerusalem in 70 C.E. (22:7).

As part of the Jerusalem leaders, the Pharisees in Matthew's story are allied with the ruling groups. They are introduced into the story as part of an alliance of religious leaders who are particularly associated with the ruling elite. In 2:4–6 the "chief priests and scribes" provide King Herod with the knowledge he requires. In 3:7 the Pharisees and Sadducees are introduced as representatives of the status quo in opposing John. Thereafter these four groups appear in various interchangeable combinations. Pharisees appear with scribes (5:20; 15:1) and chief priests (21:45) and, in their final appearance, with the Roman governor Pilate in 27:62. These alliances are exactly what we would expect from religious leaders in an aristocratic empire where as retainers they belong to the ruling class.[44] In extending its control, Rome turned local leadership into allies, since they had a shared common interest.[45] They upheld the status quo as allies with Rome and beneficiaries of the imperial system rather than create an alternative social order marked by "justice, mercy, and faith." In this sense those who "labor wearily" are also "the heavy laden" or "the burdened" who suffer under both Roman control and that of the religious leadership, Rome's allies.[46]

Jesus calls such people, then, to "come to me," and he promises them, "I will give you rest." "Take my yoke," he says, "and you will find rest [ἀνάπαυσις, *anapausis*][47] for your souls" (11:28–29). What does he promise to those who labor to stay alive and are "burdened" in a world of cruel Roman exploitation?

I WILL GIVE YOU REST

"Rest" has been understood in three sometimes overlapping ways. Numerous scholars notice the two appearances of the word in association with Wisdom in Sir 6:28 and 51:27 and conclude that Jesus assumes wisdom's role in offering "rest."[48] But this link is by no means obvious. In Sir 51:27

"rest" comes from "laboring little," hardly the situation of Matt 11:28. And these two references are a tiny percentage of the numerous uses of "rest" in the LXX. The remaining references do not refer to Wisdom. Moreover, even if the identification is made, it provides little specificity for the concept of rest. What precisely is it that Wisdom offers? Second, "rest" is associated with God's presence, for example in Exod 33:14 (also Ps 23[LXX 22]:2), certainly compatible with the Gospel's initial emphasis on Jesus as Emmanuel (1:23) and its closing promise in 28:20 in which his presence enables a life of discipleship.[49] But the question needs to be pressed. What does God's presence accomplish specifically for "all who labor" if they are not yet disciples? Third, others note eschatological associations. "Rest" comes with the establishment of God's purposes (Isa 25:10; 4 Ezra 7:36, 38; 8:52).[50] But again, there is little specificity for the term "rest." A review of the word's uses might provide some clarity.

The verb ἀναπαύω (*anapauō*), its cognate noun ἀνάπαυσις (*anapausis*), and its related verb καταπαύω (*katapauō*) are common in the Septuagint.[51] They designate a number of experiences, most commonly the rest of death,[52] rest from work,[53] or rest on the (literal) Sabbath.[54] None of these referents seems appropriate here. Until the full establishment of God's purposes and the provision of plenty, cessation from work would only mean starvation for most of Jesus' hearers in the context of Rome's world (cf. Sir 31:3–4; 4 Ezra 8:52). And Jesus will clarify his very active agenda for the Sabbath in 12:1–14. Presumably "rest" also means something more than "relief" from being overstuffed with food (Sir 31:21)!

In its most common usage, however, "rest" denotes a very political reality. The presence or absence of "rest" appears in contexts involving imperial powers and their political and military actions (war, oppression), or in passages that identify God's actions toward such powers (deliverance, judgment). Its absence often accompanies God's judgment enacted either through or against the people's enemies.[55] Its presence results from the presence or promise of God's salvation that triumphs over these enemies and liberates God's people to live according to God's ways.[56]

For instance, after the exodus, God gives "rest" when the Canaanites and their land have been subdued and occupied (Deut 3:20; 12:9–10; 25:19; Josh 1:3, 15; 11:23; 21:44; 22:4; 23:1).

> When you cross over the Jordan and live in the land that the LORD your God is allotting to you, and when he gives you rest from all your enemies all around so that you may live in safety.... (Deut 12:10)

The absence of war or threat from enemy nations means "rest" or divine favor subsequently for Solomon (1 Kgs 5:4; 8:56 "no adversary or misfortune"; cf. Sir 47:13; 1 Chr 22:9), David (1 Chr 22:18), and Asa (2 Chr 14:5–6; 15:15). In 2 Chr 20:29–30 for Jehoshaphat, "rest" follows his victory over the Moabites and Ammonites. It is God's salvation.

The fear of God came on all the kingdoms (βασιλείας) of the countries when they heard that the Lord had fought against the enemies of Israel. And the realm (βασιλεία) of Jehoshaphat was quiet, for his God gave him rest (κατέπαυσεν) all around. (2 Chr 20:29–30)

Likewise for Hezekiah, "rest" is salvation for Jerusalem in being delivered from the threat of King Sennacherib of Assyria.

So the LORD saved Hezekiah and the inhabitants of Jerusalem from the hand of King Sennacherib of Assyria and from the hand of all his enemies; he gave them rest on every side. (2 Chr 32:22)

If rest is associated with salvation from enemies, God's judgment means the absence of rest in the face of imminent war and "grievous destruction" (Mic 2:10). Moses warns that disobedience to the covenant and rebellion against God's yoke (Deut 28:47–48) will mean judgment through exile where there will be no rest (Deut 28:65; cf. Sidon in Isa 23:12). Faced by imminent Babylonian victory as God's judgment on the people, Baruch laments the absence of rest (Jer 45:3, 1–5; LXX 51:33). And the writer of Lamentations grieves that Judah has gone into exile with suffering and hard servitude; she lives now among the nations, and finds no resting place" (Lam 1:3).

But Habakkuk knows that Babylonian power will not remain unchallenged. God will save the people. So Habakkuk "rests quietly in the day of affliction," awaiting God's salvation (Hab 3:16–17). Daniel is assured that victory over Antiochus Epiphanes leads to the end of the age and rest in the resurrection (Dan 12:1–3; cf. 4 *Ezra* 7:36, 38). In 1 Macc 9:73, the victory of Jonathan and Simon over Bacchides, governor of the Syrian king Demetrius 1, means "rest" from warfare. Rest, then, is threatened or removed by imperial powers (as agents of God's judgment), and restored when that threat is resisted and God's salvation is encountered.

The term is common in Isaiah, partly in relation to the Assyrian crisis, but also in pronouncements of judgment on various nations and in visions of God's vindication of Israel over the nations.

But the LORD will have compassion on Jacob and will again choose Israel, and will *cause them to rest* (ἀναπαύσονται) in their own land. ...They will take captive those who were their captors, and rule over those who oppressed them. When the Lord has *given* you *rest* (ἀναπαύσει) from your pain and turmoil and slavery with which you were made to serve, you will take up this taunt against the king of Babylon: How the oppressor has *rested/ceased* (ἀναπέπαυται)! How his insolence has *rested/ceased* (ἀναπέπαυται)! The Lord has broken the yoke (ζυγόν) of the wicked, the yoke (ζυγόν) of rulers. Having smitten a nation in wrath...he *rested* (ανεπαύσατο). (Isa 14:1–7, selections; emphasis added)

In addition to this direct statement, "rest" or the absence of rest figures in longer passages as one of a number of images that describe a situation of defeat and judgment. So resting animals, or animals lying down, for example, can image the threat of Assyria, the agent of God's judgment (Isa 7:19), or God's promised destruction of and judgment on Babylon (Isa 13:20–21), Damascus (Isa 17:2), the enemy's city (27:10), Babylon (Ezek 17:23), and Israel's false kings (Ezek 34:14–15). Edom's destruction is such that wild animals live in her ruins and the storm god Lilith finds a place to rest (Isa 24:14, 17). The nonresting or tossing sea images the wicked whom God will judge while healing the humble (Isa 57:20, 15–21), or those in Damascus fearing judgment (Jer 49:23; lxx 30:23).

But "rest" also functions as one of numerous images denoting salvation. With the removal of Assyria's yoke (Isa 10:24–34) comes a righteous king on whom God's spirit rests (Isa 11:2) and from whom will come salvation from the nations (11:10–16). In this time of salvation and victory over the nations, God's presence rests with the people (Isa 25:9–10). The reign of justice and righteousness means "quiet resting places" for the people (Isa 32:16–18). Micah images this time of salvation when God reigns from Zion and all the nations have submitted to God's peaceful ways with the picture of people "resting" under vines and fig trees (fertility) and not being afraid (security; 4:4).

Rest, then, is closely associated with God's purposes for God's people and for the nations. The accomplishment of God's will means "rest" or salvation. To defy God's will is to encounter judgment, where there is either no rest, or a false sense of security that is about to be shattered (Isa 14:30; Philistia). But the experience of God's salvation from imperial powers like Egypt, Assyria, Babylon, and the Seleucids means "rest," the establishment of God's reign and ordering of the world according to God's purposes.

What, then, does Jesus promise? In promising "rest," Jesus again uses a political image, but one that expresses God's salvation. To "all who labor" in a world ruled by Roman imperial power, Jesus promises salvation. The absence of "rest" in the present situation suggests that this Roman imperial world is not ordered according to God's purposes and that God's judgment is under way. To know "rest" is to experience God's salvation from this imperial world with the establishment of God's reign over all, including Rome. Jesus promises judgment on and salvation from Rome, nothing other than Rome's annihilation, like other powers before it: the Canaanites, Assyria, Babylon, Antiochus Epiphanes. How and when will this happen?

TAKE MY YOKE

Jesus invites "all who labor" in and are "burdened" by this imperial world, those to whom he promises "rest" or God's salvation with its overthrow and establishment of God's empire, to "take my yoke upon you." In most discussions of 11:28–30, Jesus' "yoke" is commonly contrasted with Pharisaic teaching and identified as Torah and/or Wisdom as rightly interpreted and manifested in Jesus' teaching and action. This view draws on the use of "yoke" in Sir 51:26 for surrender to Wisdom's teaching, and its use in Jer 5:5 to image God's law.[57] These identifications are repeatedly asserted in the scholarly literature. They are, of course, quite possible readings of this text. But their weakness is the very slim textual base on which they depend, and a failure to investigate beyond these favorite texts. What does "yoke" image?

The investigation of ζυγός (*zugos*, "yoke") in the Septuagint shows that the identification of "yoke" with Torah and/or Wisdom is rare (only Jer 5:5; Sir 51:26). In fact, the data indicates that "yoke," more often than not, refers to quite different realities. Charette, almost a lone voice in resisting the common identifications, has highlighted the much-neglected use of the image in the Septuagint to denote ruling power, and especially, more often than not, imperial power.[58] But by spiritualizing the image he has failed to develop the implications of the data in relation to Matthew.

The noun "yoke" (ζυγός) appears sixty-three times in the Septuagint (including two readings from the Theodotian text of Daniel). Predominantly it has to do with control (forty-one of the sixty-three uses). Though its uses are diverse, they can be divided essentially into two groups.

First, twenty-one texts denote assessment or measurement,[59] and combine both literal and metaphorical uses. The literal references often instruct or warn about just and honest measures in daily business and trade (Lev 19:35, 36; Prov 11:1; 16:11; 20:23; Sir 42:4). The metaphorical uses frequently image the assessment of human circumstances (Ps 62:9; Job 6:2) including words (Sir 21:25; 28:25), and God's evaluation of (Job 31:6; Isa 40:15) and/or condemnation of the people's way of life (Hos 12:7; Amos 8:5; Mic 6:11; Ezek 45:10).

The second group of forty-one concerned with control can be divided into two unequal sections. One section of seven references embraces different types of control. This control may be the restraint of animals (Num 19:2; Deut 21:3; Job 39:10),[60] of domestic slaves (Sir 33:27), and of the tongue (Sir 28:19, 20). Sirach 51:26 invites individuals to "put your neck under [Wisdom's] yoke, and let your souls receive instruction."

The remaining thirty-four references, more than half the total of sixty-three uses of the term "yoke" (ζυγός; *zugos*), refer to political control, particularly the imposition of harsh imperial power. Seven of these references concern either the acknowledgment of or the absence of God's control. Three of these designate Israel's refusal to serve God (Isa 5:18; Jer 2:20; 5:5). In Ps 2:3 the kings of the nations rebel against the yoke or rule of the Lord and his anointed. In Pss. Sol. 7:9 Israel will serve under God's yoke, and in Pss. Sol. 17:30 God will ensure the nations do the same thing (also Zeph 3:9). That is, in these seven references to God's acknowledged or resisted control, the context is political in that it involves rule over Israel and the nations.

The most dominant use among this group of thirty-four concerns political rule, most commonly the imperial rule of nation over nation. For example:

Genesis 27:40—Edom will revolt against Israel's rule.

Leviticus 26:13—God has broken Egypt's rule over the Israelites.

Two Chronicles 10:4, 9, 10, 11, 14—Solomon's harsh rule is intensified by his son Rehoboam.

One Maccabees 8:18, 31—the heavy yoke of the Greeks (King Demetrius) rules over and enslaves Israel.

One Maccabees 13:41—the "yoke of the Gentiles" is lifted from Israel as the reign of Simon begins.

Three Macc 4:9—the literal yokes or bonds imposed on Jews represent Egyptian rule.

Isaiah 9:4; 10:27; 14:5, 25, 29—Assyrian/Babylonian imperial rule, allowed by God to punish the people, will end.

Isaiah 47:6—Babylon rules over Israel.

Jeremiah 27:8, 11 (LXX 34:8, 11); 28:2, 4, 11, 14 (LXX 35:2, 4, 11, 14); 30:8 (LXX 37:8)—Babylon rules but God will break its yoke.

Lamentations 3:27—the yoke is Babylonian imperialism.

Ezekiel 34:27—Israel is subject to imperial powers ("nations enslave them").

Daniel 8:25 (Theodotian)—Antiochus Epiphanes exercises harsh rule.[61]

The image of "yoke" designates in twenty-one occurrences the imperial power of the dominant players in the biblical traditions: Egypt, Assyria, Babylon, the "Greeks" (Seleucids). In a further six instances, it designates Israel's rule over Edom and Solomon's harsh rule built on alliances and pervasive taxes and levies of goods and labor.[62] If we add in the seven uses of "yoke" to refer to God's acknowledged or resisted rule over Israel and the nations, thirty-four of the sixty-three uses of the term "yoke" in the Septuagint designate rule over a people or nation of some description.

Predominantly, the references show that the term designates imperial rule imposed by a greater power over a lesser, against the latter's will and for the former's benefit. Moreover, the larger contexts of the references portray aspects of this imperial rule. Often this rule is oppressive and exploitative of resources and people. Often imperial rule is understood to be God's (unwitting) agent that punishes the people for their sins. Yet that empire is itself shown to be subject to God's power in that God frees the people from such rule and punishes the oppressor.

For example, the oracle against Assyria in Isa 10 acknowledges Assyria as God's agent, "the rod of my anger" (10:5). God sends them against the sinful people: "Against a godless nation I send him, and against the people of my wrath I command him" (10:6a). Exploitation and oppression follow: "to take spoil and seize plunder, and to tread them down like the mire of the streets" (10:6b). But the Lord "will punish the arrogant boasting of the king of Assyria and his haughty pride" (10:12). Though the Assyrians "beat you with a rod" and oppress the people "as the Egyptians did" (10:24; cf. Lev 26:13), the day will come when "his burden will be removed from your shoulder, and his yoke (ζυγός, *zugos*) will be destroyed from your neck" (10:27). God will free the people from Assyria's yoke or imperial rule.

In Isa 13–14, a similar situation occurs with Babylon. Its imperial rule is harsh and exploitative (Isa 14:6, 8, 17 "who made the world like a desert and overthrew its cities"). But God is stirring up the Medes against Babylon (Isa 13:17–19) and through them God will execute punishment: "The LORD has broken the staff of the wicked, the yoke (ζυγόν, *zugon*) of rulers" (14:5, 25). Through the Medes, God's people experience deliverance from Babylon's yoke.

Or again in Isa 47, Babylon is God's agent designated to punish the people for their sin by being subjected to and subjugated by Babylonian rule: "I was angry with my people, I profaned my heritage; I gave them into your hand, you showed them no mercy; on the aged you made your yoke (ζυγόν, *zugon*) exceedingly heavy" (Isa 47:6). But now "evil … disaster … ruin" will come upon Babylon, "there is no one to save you" (Isa 47:11, 15) as God removes Babylon's yoke from the people by defeating Babylon.

Jeremiah does not doubt that God has imposed the yoke of Babylon on the sinful people (Jer 21:1–10). "I have given all these lands into the hand of King Nebuchadnezzar of Babylon, my servant.…But if any nation or kingdom will not…put its neck under the yoke (ζυγόν, *zugon*) of the king of Babylon, then I will punish that nation…(Jer 27:6, 8, 11; LXX 34:6, 8, 11). Hananiah promises a quick breaking of this yoke "within two years" (Jer 28:2, 4, 11; LXX 35:2, 4, 11), a word that conflicts with Jeremiah's insistence that the punishment will last much longer (28:14; LXX 35:14; cf. 27:7). But after the time of "terror" and "distress" (Jer 30:5, 7; LXX 37:5, 7), God's saving action will be seen: "I will break his yoke (ζυγόν, *zugon*) from off your neck" (Jer 30:8; LXX 37:8) and restore the people to their land (30:10).[63]

This use of ζυγός (*zugos,* yoke) to identify God's power over the nations, expressed in God's use of them as agents of punishment and in God's ability to end their imperial power, is also evident in visions of the end of the nations' rebellion against God and their refusal to acknowledge God's "yoke" or control. "The kings of the earth[64] set themselves … against the LORD and his anointed, saying, 'Let us burst their bonds asunder, and cast their yoke (ζυγόν, *zugos*) from us' " (Ps 2:3). But finally the nations will, like Israel (Jer 2:20; 5:5; Pss. Sol. 7:9), come to serve under God's yoke (ζυγόν, *zugon*; Pss. Sol. 17:30; Zeph 3:9). That is, the image of the yoke to denote the rule of one nation over another also depicts God's rule or control over all nations.

This dominant political use of the term "yoke" (ζυγός, *zugos*) in the Septuagint is evident in texts outside the Septuagint. Josephus also refers to Solomon's/Rehoboam's harsh rule as a "yoke" (*Ant.* 8:213), and the *Sibylline Oracles* refer to the Medes' subjugation in that "you will place your neck under the yoke." In 1 Enoch 103:10–15 the "sinners and oppressors...have made their yoke heavy upon us" with toil, injustice and murder. Josephus refers to Roman imperial power as the "yoke" (ζυγός, *zugos*) of Rome (*J.W.* 5.365; 7.87). Similarly the *Sibylline Oracles* refer to Rome's control of Rhodes as "a terrible yoke" (*Sib. Or.* 3:448) and in *Sib. Or.* 3.537 Rome's "yoke of slavery will come upon all Greece." In 8.125–30 the end of Rome's rule comes when "No longer will Syrian, Greek or foreigner, or any other nation, place their neck under your yoke of slavery" (*Sib. Or.* 8:126–7).

Jesus' invitation to "take my yoke," then, is an invitation to experience God's rule or control. The dominant use of the image in the Septuagint and in other texts in relation to imperial power encourages us to look for a similar sense in relation to Matthew's Gospel.

Matthew 22:7 has interpreted Rome's destruction of Jerusalem in 70 C.E. as punishment on the people for their sins, supremely that of rejecting Jesus. Just as God was understood to have previously used Egypt, Assyria, Babylon, and Antiochus Epiphanes to punish the people, God has used the imperial power Rome to execute punishment. But as the biblical tradition attests, punishment is not the final word and imperial power is not supreme. God promises salvation through Jesus. "He will save his people from their sins" (1:21). The yoke of Roman rule will be broken. "Take my yoke upon you." The pronoun "my" and the use of this image of imperial power point to a collision of two empires in which God will be victorious. The ways of Rome, Satan's agent (4:8), are not God's ways (20:25–28). The assertion of God's empire at Jesus' return means judgment on Rome, the breaking of its yoke, and the setting free of those who labor wearily under and are burdened by imperial demands (24:27–31). God's salvation will again be displayed in a context of imperial power as God's people experience deliverance or liberation from this power.

MY YOKE IS KIND/GOOD AND ITS BURDEN IS SMALL

Appropriately, Jesus describes this "yoke," the establishment of God's empire, as "kind" or "good." The adjective χρηστός (*chrēstos*) appears nearly thirty times in the Septuagint, never with the meaning of "easy,"[65] but most commonly to describe God as "good" or "kind" (Pss 25:8, LXX 24.8; 34:8, LXX 33:9; 119:68, LXX 118:68; Neh 1:7; Pss. Sol. 2:36; 10:7). Other significant descriptive words and phrases are often associated with this word and elaborate dimensions of God's goodness/kindness. God is kind/good, but also strong, just, and merciful (2 Macc 1:24), ready to forgive and merciful (Ps 86:5; LXX 85:5), compassionate (Ps 145:9; LXX 144:9), true, patient, and ruling all things in mercy (Wis 15:1) and, most frequently, exhibits steadfast love/mercy that continues forever.[66] Likewise in three of its seven New Testament uses, the word refers to the goodness or kindness of God (Luke 6:35; Rom 2:4; 1 Pet 2:3).[67] So Jesus' "yoke," God's empire, is kind and good, displaying God's mercy, justice, and compassion in liberating those who wearily toil and are burdened by Rome's imperialism. It is fundamentally not like Rome's yoke, oppressive, exploitative, intimidating, cruel, unjust. The eschatological establishment of God's empire in a new heaven and earth (Matt 5:18; 19:28; 24:35) is life-giving and just (cf. 7:13–14), not sustained by oppressive taxes, tributes, and military threat, and not marked by domination or hierarchy. It restores access to land (5:5) in a new creation (19:28).

But God's empire, while manifested in Jesus in the present, is not yet established in full. This "not yet" dimension comprises the "burden" of Jesus' yoke in the present. But that burden is "small" (ἐλαφρόν, *elaphron;* Exod 18:26).[68] The anticipation of this eschatological goal relativizes the burdensome present under Roman control with the knowledge that the present situation will not last forever, that Rome's days are numbered. But the present has significance beyond anticipation. Jesus' instruction and presence (28:18–20) enable disciples to learn to live something of an alternative existence now in the midst of Roman power.

LEARN FROM ME

From the outset of his ministry, Jesus has manifested the empire or reign of God in his words (4:17–22), healings and exorcisms (4:23–24), actions and resurrection, as well as promising its establishment at his yet-to-happen return (24:27–31). Throughout his ministry, he has been about the task of forming a community of disciples centered on himself (4:17–22; 9:9; 10:1–4) with alternative commitments and social practices. This community is not to imitate the imperial society. It is marked by service to one another, not domination. "You know that the rulers of the Gentiles lord it over them, and their great men exercise authority over them. It shall not be so among you" (20:25–26). But such an alternative community is not natural for those conditioned by a hierarchical and dominating imperial society. They must be resocialized. They must "learn from me" (11:29). From Jesus' discourses (chs. 5–7, 10, 13, 18, 24–25), from his definitive teaching of God's will, and from his actions, disciples learn practices that challenge fundamental values and practices of the imperial society and begin to embody God's salvation even now in anticipation of the time when it will be established in full.

Jesus' Social and Theological Challenge to Rome

Four brief examples will indicate something of this alternative existence and community shaped by God's empire or yoke emerging in the present in anticipation of the completion of God's purposes.

Instead of domination there is service of one another (20:25–28) and new kinship patterns. The community is constituted not by wealth, gender, status, or ethnicity, but by becoming children of God, the heavenly father (5:9, 45). With God as father, there are new kinship patterns. Households are constituted in relation to God's will (12:46–50), not by patriarchal domination of a husband over a wife.[69] Husbands cannot divorce a wife for any reason (5:27–32; 19:3–9). Men do not have the power to expose women to such economic vulnerability. No male exercises fatherly power (23:9), but all disciples are children (19:13–15) and slaves (20:25–28).

It follows that there will be a different economic order.[70] Community members serve God, not wealth (6:24). The goal of their existence is not exploitative accumulation through oppressive taxes and tributes. It is not conspicuous consumption and display. Rather wealth is to be used to provide what people need to live. A wealthy man is to divest himself of his "great possessions," and give to the poor (19:21–22). Almsgiving is a vital practice marked not by reciprocity and calculated self-interest but the secret meeting of needs (6:1–4). The needs of beggars are to be met; lending to those who want to borrow circumvents increased wealth and indebtedness while making resources available (5:42). These practices begin to imagine a world that trusts God's control (6:24–34), where economic justice matters more than imperial exploitation.

This community also rejects violence, a mainstay of Rome's imperial mission to "rule the nations with your power" (Virgil, *Aen.* 6.851–53). The cycle of violence is broken not by matching violence with violence, nor by passivity, but by a third option.[71] Instead of fight or flight, Matthew's Jesus advocates nonviolent resistance to evil (5:38–42). The verb ἀντιστῆναι (*antistēnai*) in 5:39 does not mean "do not resist an evildoer," an impossible though regrettably common translation. Rather it denotes (with a negative) not using violence to resist evil. Jesus sets out in 5:38–42 four examples of what such resistance might look like in actions that refuse submission, assert human dignity, and challenge what is supposed to humiliate and destroy.

This community rejects the social divisions of the imperial world. Ramsay MacMullen has detailed the social snobbery of the empire, the intense tensions between the wealthy and the poor, Romans and provincials, free and slave, male and female, rural and urban.[72] Wealth and status exclude and demean. Juvenal comments that poverty "exposes people to ridicule" (*Sat.* 3.147–54). But it is especially among the marginals such as the sick and demon-possessed that Jesus ministers (4:23–25). He brings healing in anticipation of the health and wholeness that the fullness of God's purposes is expected to bring. He feeds the hungry in anticipation of future plenty (12:1–14; 14:13–21; 15:32–39). He eats with social outcasts even while being derided by the "religious leaders" (9:9–13). He instructs the community in a discourse about its relationships and values that they are not to despise the little ones (18:10). And he commits this mission to proclaim God's empire, to heal the sick, raise the dead, cleanse lepers, and cast out demons, free of charge, to his disciples as a missional community (10:7–8). The inclusion of such people within the community's care embodies God's indiscriminate and saving love for all people (5:43–48).

JESUS IS MEEK AND LOWLY IN HEART

This commitment to form an alternative community with distinctive practices requires much learning from Jesus. He lives what he teaches. "I am meek and lowly in heart" (11:29; my translation). To be "meek" and "lowly"[73] is, as Matt 5:5 indicates in its partial citation of Ps 37:11, 22, 29, to be among the powerless and humiliated. The wicked powerful exercise violence against them (Ps 37:14, 32), steal from them (37:21), and oppress them (37:35). But the meek are not to fret (37:1) or take revenge (37:6), but are to live righteously waiting for God (who seems so slow to act) to deliver on the promise that "you will live in the land, and enjoy security" (37:3; cf. Matt 5:5; 19:28). Jesus is among the suffering righteous, those who are crushed by oppressors and denied access to adequate resources, in solidarity with his followers, awaiting God's transformation of the world.

But to be meek is not to be passive. The same word occurs again in Matt 21:5 in describing Jesus as a "meek king." As Deirdre Good has pointed out, this image utilizes a tradition of the ideal king who acts compassionately in service to his people.[74] Jesus manifests such compassion (9:36) throughout his ministry, even in giving his life (20:25–28). His "meekness" of compassion and service contrasts with "the rulers" and the "great men of the Gentiles" who prefer rule and domination. His disciples are to imitate him.

The political contrast established in 20:25–28 is reinforced by the very next chapter in which Jesus enters Jerusalem. With the appearance of Jesus as a leader, a procession, celebrating crowds, hymnic acclamation, and a subsequent action in the temple, the scene employs some features that are common to entrance processions. Such processions comprised the arrival of an emperor or governor or military commander at a city (Josephus, *J.W.* 4.112–20, Titus), or the triumph in celebration of military victories in Rome (Josephus, *J.W.* 7.116–57, Vespasian and Titus).[75] These ceremonies displayed the imperial mindset. Brunt identifies the triumph as "the institutional expression of Rome's military ideal." Visser 'T Hooft argues that it displays an understanding of "human greatness in terms of power, acquired by military or political victory... [and the demand for] public recognition of such greatness."[76] Jesus' meekness consisting of compassion and service challenges such a power structure. His act of entering the city employs some features of the entrance processions and triumphs in order to contrast or reframe them, to parody them with a very different vision of human inter-action. Jesus rides a donkey, not an intimidating warhorse representative of strategies to dominate and exploit, an everyday common beast and one that was often a symbol used by Gentiles to deride and scorn Jews (Josephus, *C. Ap.* 2.80–88, 112–20; Tacitus, *Hist.* 5.3–4). He is not welcomed by the city's leadership with escort or speeches, only by his followers. And he is a very different sort of king, meek not triumphant, a compassionate servant not a powerful imperial official.

Moreover, the citation of Zech 9:9 in verse 5, which identifies Jesus as "meek," comes from Zech 9–14. These chapters celebrate God's defeat of Israel's enemies and the establishment of God's reign or yoke over all the nations. Its use here signals not only that Rome's empire will be overcome, but also that the defeat is already under way in the empire by means of the meek kingship of Jesus. His way of compassionate service even to death, his absorbing of imperial violence without resorting to a violent response, his prophetic challenge and rejection of powerful subjugation and exploitation will mean his death, but also his resurrection. Resurrection exposes the em-pire's limited power in not being able to keep him dead. His resurrection anticipates his return to establish God's empire of mercy and justice in full over Roman power (24:27–31).

It is from this one and in imitation of him that disciples are to learn an alternative way of being and doing in the world. The difficulty of this new learning cannot be underestimated. It is the way of the cross. The empire always strikes back.

THE IRONY

Such an idea is timelessly ironic. Jesus addresses these words to crowds suf-fering under the yoke of Roman oppression. He promises them rest, the experience of God's salvation from such rule. He calls them to take "my yoke," to experience the empire of God already encountered in part in his ministry, embodied in a missional community of alternative commitments and practices, and anticipated in full at his return when he crushes Roman rule and God's empire is established over all things. But we must not over-look that the language of labor, rest, and yoke is imperial language. In using yoke to denote God's empire or reign, the Gospel again employs imperial language to express the Gospel's rejection of Roman imperial rule. Yet, as happens so often in this Gospel, the language of "yoke" testifies to just how pervasive and deep-seated is the imperial paradigm. The Gospel has, regrettably, no other language with which to depict God's salvation.

EIGHT

Paying the Tax to Rome as Subversive Praxis: Matthew 17:24–27

IN THE DESCRIPTIONS of Roman imperial power in chapter 1, paying taxes figured prominently. The imposition of taxes provided the means by which the elite extracted the wealth that sustained their way of life. Rome regarded paying taxes as a sign of submission to its authority. For most of the population, living near subsistence levels, taxes were burdensome and oppressive. Since taxes were so central to the power dynamic that marked the Roman Empire, we would expect Matthew's Gospel, especially if it is a counternarrative that resists Roman claims, to address this central practice.

In Matthew 17:24–27, a strange incident occurs involving a double conversation about paying "the tax."

> When they entered Capernaum, those who collect the didrachma-tax approached Peter and said to him, "Does not your teacher pay the didrachma-tax?" He said, "Yes." And when Peter entered the house, Jesus spoke to him first and said, "What do you think, Simon? From whom do the kings of the earth collect tolls or tribute? From their own children or from others?" And he said, "From others." Jesus said to him, "Then free are the children, and so that we do not offend them, go to the sea, cast a hook, and take the first fish that comes up, and when you have opened its mouth, you will find a stater; take it and give it to them for me and for you." (my trans.)

Equally strange has been the way in which this scene has been interpreted. Even though the scene mentions different types of taxes four times, many interpreters do not think the account *as it now exists in Matthew's Gospel* has anything to do with taxes or politics. There is some agreement that in the ministry of Jesus it supported voluntary payment of the temple tax that helped to finance the temple's operations.[1] But after Rome's destruction of the Jerusalem temple in 70 C.E., so the argument goes, this tax was not collected. So *for the audience of Matthew's Gospel* written after the destruction of the temple in 70 C.E., it has no relevance as a temple-tax story since there is no temple! Instead, the scene takes on a different meaning.[2] Most think that it becomes an apolitical story that provides a theological object lesson for the Matthean community.[3] But what is that lesson if it now says nothing about taxes?[4] There is no shortage of suggestions: it instructs the community variously about God as a loving father,[5] about sonship (Jesus' and the disciples'),[6] about Peter,[7] about the rejection of Israel,[8] about freedom from the temple cult,[9] about giving as a voluntary action rather than as theocratic taxation,[10] and, especially, about exercising Christian freedom responsibly, either in relation to the state[11] or, more commonly, so as not to offend or cause a community member to stumble (so 18:1–14).[12]

In this chapter, I will argue that the scene is very much about paying a tax. It concerns the payment of a very significant post-70 Roman tax. I will structure the argument in eight sections. I will begin by showing that two current apolitical readings are not convincing and propose an alternative thesis (sections 1–2). In section 3 I will briefly describe some features of taxation in the Roman Empire. In sections 4–6, I will look at three parts of the passage, 17:24–25a, 17:25b–26, and 17:27. In section 7 I will address a somewhat similar passage, and in section 8 conclude by linking 17:24–27 with its literary context in chapters 17 and 18.

I. TWO UNCONVINCING "TAX-FREE" INTERPRETATIONS

Are these various interpretations that claim the passage has nothing to do with taxation but provides the Gospel's audience with theological object lessons convincing?[13] I will evaluate two of the most common interpretations briefly, though we will need to return to other dimensions later.

The last-named claim concerning not offending other disciples is probably the dominant reading. David Garland is typical in suggesting that 17:24–18:35 deals with not causing offense, 17:24–27 to outsiders and 18:1–35 to insiders.[14] But while 18:1–35 may demonstrate that disciples are not free from "the claims of love" toward each other, it is not clear that 17:24–27 exemplifies this behavior in relation to outsiders. If this is the temple tax and its collectors are agents of the religious leaders,[15] why is Jesus now suddenly concerned not to aggravate them?[16] He has scandalized them (cf. 13:57) since chapter 8,[17] and warned his disciples that they will do the same and pay a price for it (10:17–18). He knows that the leaders are "scandalized" at him (15:12), and intend to kill him (12:14–15), and he says so publicly (16:21–22). And he continues to offend them after 17:24–27.[18] In the clash of God's empire with Rome's, offense is inevitable.

The narrative context, then, destroys the claim that 17:24–27 exhorts disciples not to scandalize the religious leaders or their agents. Claiming that the narrative indicates some things to be worthy of conflict but not others does not solve the problem.[19] No such division is signaled. Moreover, if Jesus were teaching his disciples not to scandalize outsiders, we would have a clear example of "Do what I say but not what I do." Such a discrepancy in characterization is almost a generic impossibility in an ancient biography that conventionally demonstrates integrity between the central character's doing and teaching.[20] We will need to find some other link between 17:24–27 and chapter 18.[21]

The second most common interpretation of the story claims that it presents the rejection of Israel. This claim usually identifies the free sons who do not have to pay the tax as followers of Jesus the son, while those who do pay are not sons but unbelieving Jews, Israel rejected by God.[22] But this is unconvincing for several reasons, not the least of which is that the Gospel does not claim God has rejected Israel. Rather, it presents different responses within Israel to Jesus. While the leaders and urban elite reject him, some Jews follow (disciples) and others express interest (the crowds).[23] Mission continues to Israel (15:24; 28:19). In the mission commission of 28:19, the phrase πάντα τὰ ἔθνη (*panta ta ethnē*, "all the nations") is best understood linguistically[24] and in narrative context as including Israel.[25] In the parable of the tenants, the vineyard is not destroyed, though the tenants are changed and charged with producing fruits (21:33–43).[26] Jerusalem, the center of the urban elite, is condemned but the possibility remains that it will greet Jesus with words from the joyful and hopeful Ps 118, "Blessed is the one who comes in the name of the Lord" (23:37–39).[27]

These observations are sufficient to indicate that two of the dominant "tax-free" readings of Matt 17:24–27 concerned with not offending others and the rejection of Israel are not convincing. Formulating an interpretation that makes sense of the references to taxes is necessary.

2. MATTHEW 17:24–27 IN ITS IMPERIAL CONTEXT: A THESIS

Bruce Chilton rightly observes that "commentators [on Matt 17:24–27] have been historically reluctant to concede that any imperial aspect is at issue in the pericope."[28] Usually they dismiss the notion quickly and without argument. Chilton offers several factors that suggest an imperial reading of 17:24–27 but he does not offer such a reading.[29] I will argue that the pericope concerns the post-70 tax for the Temple of Jupiter Capitolinus levied by the Roman Emperor Vespasian and required of Jews, including Matthew's (largely) Christian-Jewish community.[30] The passage instructs the Gospel's audience that this tax is to be paid. I will also argue that payment is not a matter of pragmatic survival for a marginal community, nor an acknowledgment of or submission to Roman sovereignty, as paying imperial taxes usually denotes. Rather, paradoxical as it may seem, payment is presented as a defiant testimony to God's sovereignty. Payment expresses the community's allegiance to and anticipation of God's empire, subverting the claims of Roman rule.

David Garland offers several arguments against any link with this post-70 Roman tax. His first factor concerns uncertainty about who paid it: "all Jews" as Josephus (*J.W.* 7.218) and Suetonius claim (levied by Domitian "with the utmost rigour" whatever their observance, *Dom.* 12.2), or only those who "continued to observe their ancestral customs" as Dio Cassius later asserts (65.7.2)?[31] But for Garland these data are not especially relevant:

> The investigation of the history of the Roman appropriation of the temple dues makes it unwise to conclude that Jewish or Gentile Christians were liable from the beginning since the evidence indicates that those who were considered obligated to pay were *those who wished to continue to observe the customs of the fathers—to practice Judaism. This would not have included Christians.*[32] (my emphasis)

Garland's conclusion assumes a wide separation between Matthew's Christian group and Judaism, that Matthew's group does not practice Judaism, and that what concerned Jews does not concern Matthew's group. Each of these assumptions is very debatable. While Matthew's community, centered on Jesus the Messiah, has probably separated from the synagogue,[33] it is not at all clear that they consider themselves outside Judaism, nonpractitioners of Judaism, or unconcerned about Jewish matters. Daniel Harrington has rightly located the Gospel in the milieu of post-70 Jewish debates.[34] Anthony J. Saldarini has demonstrated that there is no rejection of Israel, no "new/true Israel," no fixed boundaries against Israel, no ending of mission to Israel. The community locates itself in the context of Israel's history (1:1–17) and Torah (5:17–48). It participates in post-70 debates about practices concerning sabbath, purity, taxes, divorce, oaths and vows, and circumcision, in which it asserts its view that love, justice, mercy, and faith have priority. It maintains Jewish practices such as almsgiving, prayer, fasting (6:1–18), tithing (23:23), and merciful acts (passim).[35] In this context, Matthew's (largely?) Jewish community is very interested in what happens to other Jews, including paying a tax that Rome uses to restore the Temple of Jupiter Capitolinus.

And second, Garland argues that 17:24–27 cannot refer to this tax because "no indications exist elsewhere in Matthew's Gospel that the Evangelist is particularly concerned about relations of Christians with the Roman government."[36] The Gospel's plot in which Rome executes the main character on a cross, in alliance with the local elite (the Jerusalem leaders), shows the inadequacy of this view. Nor should we overlook the fact that the Gospel originated in and addresses a world dominated by and familiar with Roman power and imperial theology, as I have argued throughout this book.

3. ROMAN POWER AND TAXES

I have outlined some basic features of Roman control in chapters 1–3. Roman control over provinces like Syria and cities like Antioch meant taxes, tolls, and levies of goods and labor. Though we do not know much about the Roman tax system and it was not standard across the empire,[37] some information is available from parts of the empire, and social-scientific models provide insight into their function within the imperial scheme of control.

"To rule in aristocratic empires," says Kautsky, "is, above all, to tax."[38] Taxes, both local and Roman, expressed "a proprietary theory of the state" that saw power as something to be used for the benefit of the ruling elite, not for the common good.[39] Taxes did not so much pay for public services as provide the necessary economic infrastructure for the elite's way of life.[40] The fundamental role of taxes in enacting and sustaining imperial society emerges in a reference to the emperor Nero. Tacitus writes that Nero, on hearing about protests against tax farmers collecting indirect taxes (customs and harbor dues),

> hesitated whether he ought not to decree the abolition of all indirect taxation and present the reform as the noblest of gifts to the human race. His impulse, however, after much preliminary praise of his magnanimity, was checked by his older advisers, who pointed out that the dissolution of the empire was certain if the revenues on which the state subsisted were to be curtailed (Tacitus, *Ann.* 13.50).

Taxes expressed various inequalities: between Italy, exempt from tribute, and the provinces; among cities some of which had tax immunity; between cities and the surrounding rural areas whose production was taxed for the urban elite's benefit.[41] Taxes enabled the elite to shun manual labor since they provided a source of income from the labor of the rest. And they provided a regular annual income that enabled the elite to display their wealth conspicuously and immediately, knowing more was coming next year.[42]

Taxes in provinces like Syria were usually calculated on the basis of a census and land surveys. They were collected for both Rome and local cities on various items such as a person's personal wealth (*tributum capitis*), land value and production (*tributum soli*), on the goods in transit (*portorium*), on the exchange of goods (sales tax), and on the use of public facilities.[43] Shaw notes that Egyptian papyri records seem to suggest taxes on everything. And Shaw offers this example of an exchange between the emperor Vespasian and his son (and future emperor) Titus to show how pervasive they were. There was no relief:

> To his son Titus who complained to him that he had even put a tax on urine [public conveniences], Vespasian put some money from the

first payment under Titus' nostrils, and asked him if the smell offended him. "No," said Titus. "That's odd," said Vespasian, "it comes from piss."[44] (Suetonius, *Vesp.* 23)

Wide-ranging taxes, not to mention tax collectors who doubtless collected as vigorously as possible, placed enormous burdens on peasants and their near-subsistence existence. Lenski estimates that up to two-thirds of peasant production was paid in rents, tolls and taxes. Oakman calculates that half to two-thirds of production was paid in taxes in first-century Palestine. Shaw estimates that while "official" rates were around 10 percent, in actuality peasants paid up to half of their production.[45] And of course peasants had no say in decisions about tax levels. When Vespasian increases "the amount of tribute paid by the provinces, in some cases actually doubling it" (Suetonius, *Vesp.* 26), the subsequent human misery has to be imagined. But the only response available to peasants was to comply. Justified as the price for maintaining peace,[46] taxes and tribute expressed sovereignty. The refusal to pay was regarded as rebellion against Rome.[47] This revenue from the provinces and their peasants and artisans paid for Rome's military presence, the elite's wealth, Rome's splendor and food supply, Antioch's building projects and infrastructure, and of course games and pacifying entertainment.

This imperial context, the observations that taxes were crucial to the very functioning of the empire, that taxes were a standard way of imposing the imperial will, that paying taxes was regarded as an act of submission to Rome and the ruling elite, and the passage's fourfold reference to taxes (17:24 [2x] τὰ δίδραχμα, *ta didrachma;* 17:25 τέλη ἤ κῆνσον, *telē ē kēnson*) should cause readers of 17:24–27 to have very good reason for claiming that the pericope does not concern taxes. The noun τέλος (*telos*) refers to various "taxes, customs duties and tribute money,"[48] while κῆνσον (*kēnson*) is a poll tax paid on the basis of a census.[49] The two terms embrace a broad spectrum of taxation.[50]

One Roman tax, τὰ δίδραχμα (*ta didrachma*) provides the initial focus of 17:24. Vespasian imposed this tax after the defeat of Judea and Jerusalem in 70 c.e. by Rome. Jews paid it annually to Rome post-70 and Rome used it to rebuild and maintain the Temple of Jupiter Capitolinus in Rome. The identification of the tax referred to in 17:24–27 with Vespasian's tax is clear from two sources. Both Josephus (*J.W.* 7.218) and Dio Cassius (65.7.2) refer to it by the same name that Matthew uses.[51] Pre-70, this was the "half-shekel" tax[52] collected from Jews even in the diaspora to sustain the Jerusalem temple.[53] After 70 and the destruction of the temple and defeat of the Jews, Rome created an imperial treasury, the *fiscus Judaicus,* under a procurator to administer the tax used now for a very different purpose.[54]

The tax, which for households of size was a burden, had punitive and propaganda value. Josephus refers to it in the context of Vespasian's seiz-

ing Jewish land and settling veterans (*J.W.* 2.216–7). Dio Cassius mentions
it after describing Jerusalem's fall (65.7.2). Its payment reminded Jews of
Rome's victory in 70 and of Roman political, economic, military, and religious sovereignty. It defined Jews as "a defeated race punished for [their]
nationality."[55] Smallwood observes some irony in the Roman co-option and
use of the tax. During the 66–70 war, the Jerusalem mint produced half-
shekels with inscriptions that asserted Judean freedom and national identity
as God's will.[56] Post-70, Rome reframed the significance of this coin to assert
Roman control and superiority as the will of Jupiter. That which had formerly proclaimed the Jewish God now provided a rebuilt temple in Rome
for the triumphant Jupiter, patron god of the Flavians.[57] Debates among
scholars as to whether the tax was political or religious thereby assume a
false divide.[58] It was both.

4. SHOULD MATTHEW'S AUDIENCE PAY THIS TAX TO ROME AND JUPITER? (MATT 17:24–25A)

Given this imperial and militaristic context, purpose, and use of the tax for
the Temple of Jupiter, and given the (predominantly) Jewish identity of the
Matthean audience, it is not surprising that there should be some discussion in Matthew about disciples of Jesus paying the tax. The presence of the
collectors of the tax in 17:24 dramatically embodies the immediacy of the
issue for the Gospel's audience. If the collectors' task was merely verification
that Jesus paid it, they could consult their records. But their task is to set
up a scene in which Jesus can instruct the Gospel's audience. Hence they
use the plural pronoun "your" (ὑμῶν, *humōn*, "your teacher") even though
the question is addressed to one person.[59] They question Peter who represents not only the disciples who entered Capernaum,[60] but also Jesus.[61] They
employ the verb τελέω (*teleō*) which concludes Jesus' teaching discourses,[62]
and they refer to Jesus as "teacher" (διδάσκαλος, *didaskalos*). This is an
appropriate address for nondisciples to use,[63] but one that, along with the
verb τελέω (*teleō*) indicates there is teaching for the Gospel's audience.[64]
Their question is formulated with οὐ (*ou*) rather than μή (*mē*) which, while
expecting a positive answer, momentarily raises the possibility of Jesus' resistance to the tax.[65] Peter's positive answer, though, confirms that Jesus
pays it (17:25a). The exchange establishes Jesus' practice. Disciples are of
course to imitate the practice of the teacher (10:24–25).

5. THE TAXING WAYS OF RULERS (MATT 17:25B–26)

If the scene were only about actions it could end at this point. But the
subsequent material suggests that more is at issue, the understanding that

shapes or interprets their practice. The scene is about praxis.[66] When Peter returns home (17:25b),[67] Jesus, who has not been present in 17:24, initiates conversation about tax paying. He wasn't present at Peter's conversation. Jesus has exhibited similar special knowledge previously (9:3–4; 12:14–15, 25) and will do so again in the next discussion about taxes (22:18). His mysterious knowledge not only helps the audience make narrative connections but enhances the authority of his characterization and so of his teaching.

Jesus asks Peter, called here Simon,[68] about the practices of "the kings of the earth." Commentators are usually content to observe that the phrase invokes God the king, that it refers to "all earthly rulers" (not just the Romans) and that the phrase has "pejorative connotations."[69] Its use in Ps 2:2 illustrates its pejorative sense.[70] "The kings of the earth...set themselves ...against the LORD and his anointed" to "burst their bonds asunder, and cast their cords from us" (2:1–3). The Psalm begins with a scenario that depicts "the kings of the earth" resisting God's reign, refusing to acknowledge God's sovereignty, and acting contrary to God's will. The Psalm then places the actions of these mighty and seemingly all-powerful kings in God's perspective. God "laughs" at their puny rebellion and holds them "in derision" (2:4)! God's speaking in wrath and fury "terrifies" them! God promises to "my son," Israel's anointed king, that the king will destroy these enemies. He will "break them" and "dash them in pieces" (2:9). The Psalm ends by warning the mighty kings to change their ways, calling them to "serve the LORD with fear" or face inevitable destruction (2:11). For the community that worships this God, the Psalm acknowledges that the ways of the kings are not God's ways. Moses (Deut 17:14–17) and Samuel (1 Sam 8:9–18) had previously warned of the oppressive and exploitative ways of kings who tax and requisition labor and property in order to wage war, expand power, and maintain military might.[71] But the Psalm also assures that "the kings of the earth" do not hold ultimate sway or determine human destiny. God's victorious ways are sovereign.[72]

The disclosure of the pretensions and limited power of "the kings of the earth" and affirmation of God's greater power and sovereignty over human destiny are recurring themes in the uses of this phrase in other Psalm references.[73] By disclosing and celebrating God's control and sovereignty, these Psalms recontextualize and so diminish the apparent power of "the kings of the earth," revealing to the worshippers the kings' rebellious ways, disclosing their futile actions despite all appearances to the contrary, strengthening the worshippers in their trust of God who controls the nations.[74]

Jesus' question to Peter about "the kings of the earth" invokes this tradition of kings who resist God. The phrase is generic but therein lies its power. Through the centuries, "the kings of the earth" take on particular identities whether Egyptian, Assyrian, Babylonian, Persian, Seleucid, or Roman.[75] The latter's emperors are commonly referred to by the same noun βασιλεύς (*basileus*).[76] From generation to generation and nation to nation, kings or emperors behave the same way, contrary to God's purposes, enslaving, exiling or oppressing God's people (cf. 1 Sam 8:1–19). And their fate is always, finally, the same. God laughs them into oblivion.

The Gospel has exemplified this divine point of view. Herod's attempt to kill Jesus is mocked by the narrative's references not only to God's protective intervention through angel and dream, but also to Herod's, not Jesus', death (2:15, 19, 20).[77] Solomon's exploitative practices are evoked and condemned in 6:29 in contrast to the trusting ways of the flowers.[78] But the ominous phrase "Archelaus ruled over Judea in the place of (ἀντί, *anti*) his father Herod" (2:22), and the grisly account of Herod the Tetrach's killing of John (14:1–12), remind the audience of the vicious ways that rulers employ to subjugate their subjects.

It is to the taxation demands of such kings that Jesus directs Peter's attention in 17:25 as the context for instruction about the τὰ δίδραχμα (*ta didrachma*). Jesus asks Peter who pays these "tolls (τέλος, *telos*) and tribute (κῆνσον, *kēnson*)" that "the kings of the earth" employ to control and subjugate "subjects" (so 1 Sam 8:11b–17). Do "the kings of the earth" levy them "from their sons (υἱῶν, *huiōn*) or from others (ἀλλοτρίων, *allotriōn*)?" (17:25). To whom is Jesus referring when he talks of "sons" and "others"? Are the "sons" the king's nation and "the others" foreign nations?[79] Or are the "sons" the king's household with everyone else being the "others?"[80] Or are the king's "sons" his immediate offspring and the "others" everyone else under the king's rule?[81] Support for identifying the nation and royal household as "sons" is lacking and neither enjoyed exemption from taxation. The "sons," then, are the ruler's immediate physical offspring,[82] the future, the apparently inevitable successors to and ominous continuation of the taxing ways of the kings of the earth.

Peter, then, answers correctly in verse 26 in identifying everyone else except the ruler's "sons" as those who typically pay taxes. Jesus confirms this answer by declaring that "the sons are free" of taxing demands. People like Peter and Jesus pay.

A Diversion: Allegorical Avoidances

But this is not the common reading of this passage. Interpreters who do not take the imperial context of Matthew's Gospel seriously and so cannot read 17:25–26 as a typical imperial situation have to treat the "sons" and the "others" as symbols of something else. They usually invoke specific religious referents.[83] They look for metaphor, for parables and "the implicit interpretation of the parable,"[84] for parallels and analogies,[85] for "comparisons" with what God does.[86] So they claim that the phrase "the kings of the earth" is a comparison with God who, like the kings, also does not tax God's children.[87] This link rules out the Roman tax as "an anachronism"[88] since God does not levy it. They also assume that "sons" does not refer only to literal offspring, but must have another referent. The most popular suggestion is God's people, either Christians or Israel.[89] As sons of God they, like the sons of the kings of the earth, are exempt from taxes levied in God's name (the temple tax).[90]

But in addition to neglecting the imperial context, several significant problems invalidate these moves. The first concerns the comparative purposes that interpreters find in invoking "the kings of the earth." They rightly observe that the traditions *contrast* "the kings of the earth" with God. But then, in actuality, most proceed to interpret 17:25b–26 in terms *not* of contrast but of similarity. The argument is typically expressed: "Kings are towards their sons *as* God is towards his sons.... The sons of earthly kings do not pay toll or tribute, and Jesus and his disciples are, as members of Israel, sons of God. They therefore should be exempt from any taxes levied in God's name" (my emphasis).[91]

But claims (1) of similarity between "the kings of the earth" and God as king, and (2) that the tax under discussion must be a tax "levied in effect by God"[92] run into the insuperable obstacle that in the traditions noted above "the kings of the earth" and God are not at all similar. The references to "the kings of the earth" do not indicate parallel behavior but contrasting actions. The kings are *not at all* like God. They resist and reject God. And instead of imitating them as the conventional reading of 17:24–27 posits, God punishes, thwarts, and condemns them.

In positing that the kings and God are similar in imposing taxes that their own children do not pay, interpreters face further dilemmas. One of course is that the reading allies God with those who resist God's will, the "kings of the earth"! God becomes an oppressive tyrant who like the kings of the earth imposes exploitative taxes, even though they are contrary to God's own will! A second is that interpreters, while quick to suggest referents for "the sons" as God's children, do not identify "the others" whom God does tax. The usual escape is into selectivity. Bauckham warns his readers that "with all parabolic interpretations, the application should not be pressed too far. Whether there are other people whom God does tax is not the point of the saying, and so we need not ask whom the 'strangers' represent."[93] But why not? Once one has arbitrarily identified one tax as the temple tax while overlooking the "tolls and tributes" of 17:25, linked the kings with God as king and the kings' sons with God's children while overlooking the contrast between God and the kings, why not complete the allegory? Perhaps the inability to find a satisfactory referent indicates that positing similarities (not contrast) between the kings and God, and assuming that the scene must involve a tax in God's name, are unsustainable moves.

The second step is also mistaken, namely seeking an external referent for the term "sons," whether Israel or disciples of Jesus. There is nothing in the phrase ἄρα γε ἐλεύθεροί εἰσιν οἱ υἱοί (*ara ge eleutheroi eisin hoi huioi,* "then free are the children/sons") that suggests it is to be allegorized.[94] The verb εἰσιν (*eisin*, "is") is a third-person form, not a first- ("then free are we . . .") or second- ("then free are you . . ."). First- or second-person pronouns are missing. The connective conjunction ἄρα γε (*ara ge*, "then") does not suggest a comparison or contrast with the preceding sentence. Rather it indicates a causal or temporal continuation here ("consequently"), as in 7:20.[95] The adjective ἐλεύθεροι (*eleutheroi*, "free") commonly refers to political or imperial freedom consistent with a scene involving kings.[96] The line is not introduced as a parabolic comparison, lacking a formula of comparison such as ὡμοιώθη (*hōmoiōthē*, 13:24) or ὁμοία ἐστίν (*homoia estin*, 13:31, 33, 44, 45, 47). Nor does the Gospel restrict the referents of υἱός (*huios*, "son/child") to Jesus, Israel, or disciples. Certainly it is used for Jesus as God's son (1:21, 23; 2:15; 3:17; 4:3, 6; 11:27; 14:33; 16:16; 17:5, etc.), and for disciples as children of God (5:45; 13:38 etc.), but by no means exclusively (10:37; 12:27; 13:38, 55; 17:15; 20:20–21, etc.).

I am suggesting, then, that there is no basis to sustain the allegorizing and spiritualizing of the exchange between Jesus and Peter. Rather we should read it as naming an everyday imperial situation well known to those who live with the taxing presence of empires. And rather than positing similarity between the "the kings of the earth" and God, we would do better to utilize the contrast between them that the tradition affirms. "The kings of the earth" refuse to recognize God's sovereignty and so do not rule in accord with God's will. That means they subjugate and oppress in different ways, including collecting a tax that reinforces the subjugated status of a conquered people. Jesus elicits from Peter the recognition that such taxes are not levied on the kings' children. Their privilege is contrasted with the "others" or "foreigners," those beyond the immediate family. Peter answers correctly. The "others," everyone except the sons, pay the taxes, including Jesus and Peter as Peter has already indicated (17:26a). Jesus confirms Peter's answer in asserting the obvious corollary, "then free are the sons" (17:26). The sons of the ruler are free of taxes, but the ruled pay. In an honor-shame culture, to not pay, then,[97] would be an offense that would "scandalize" the kings, the privileged sons, and their agents (17:27a).[98] That option was quickly rejected by Peter in verse 25 and confirmed by Jesus in verse 26. The audience knows all this as daily imperial reality. That's how things are with "the kings of the earth."

6. THERE'S SOMETHING FISHY HERE: PAYING TAXES AS A SUBVERSIVE ACT (MATT 17:27)

But where is the victory of God that the "kings of the earth" tradition proclaims? If "the kings of the earth" are opposed to God's will but ultimately thwarted by the sovereign God as the tradition says, how is paying this post-

70 tax to Rome anything other than a recognition of "the kings' " victory? And if this tax sustains the Temple of Jupiter Capitolinus, surely its payment by disciples of Jesus recognizes Jupiter's superior power in blessing Rome and securing its destiny over Israel's God. Does Jesus' teaching to pay the tax legitimate Rome's power? Where is any sign of God's thwarting and sovereign action? Where is the derisive and relativizing laugh that Ps 2:4 presents as God's response? For a community that professes encounter with, and recognizes the authority of, the empire or sovereignty of God manifested in Jesus, these are important issues.

The claim that disciples pay the tax in order to survive[99] does not adequately address this issue, even while it recognizes an important reality. Nor is it Jesus' approach in 17:27. Rather Jesus instructs Peter to cast a hook into the sea, catch the first fish, find in its mouth a στατήρ (*statēr*),[100] and pay the tax for both of them (17:27). Does Jesus procure the tax by miraculous means to emphasize his voluntary payment,[101] or to highlight God's provision?[102] The former option is not convincing since Jesus and the community of disciples are not among the free and must pay the Romans. The second option with its emphasis on God's provision offers a way ahead.

The fish provides an important clue. The Gospel's audience knows three previous stories about fish in the Gospel, two of which involve miracles. In 7:10 providing fish (not a harmful serpent) represents a parent's love, and pictures God's much greater (πόσῳ μᾶλλον, *posō mallon*) love and giving of "good things" to those who ask. In 14:13–21, fish figure twice (14:17, 19) as Jesus, with God's miraculous blessing, uses the boy's two fish and five loaves to feed over five thousand people. With gracious and sovereign power God supplies food. The point is repeated one chapter later, two chapters prior to 17:24–27. In 15:32–39 God overcomes impossible circumstances to demonstrate compassion and sovereign power, miraculously feeding more than four thousand people with fish (15:36). The audience links fish with God's compassionate and powerful actions in overcoming limiting circumstances, in supplying human need, and in displaying God's sovereignty.

Peter's procuring of the coin to pay the tax from the fish's mouth at Jesus' bidding emphasizes the same qualities. After 7:10, 14:13–21 and 15:32–39, the audience knows fish are subject to God's sovereignty. God ensures the catching of this fish. This affirmation of God's powerful sovereignty is profoundly significant in a world in which some believed the emperor's numen or genius (his will as representative of the gods) influenced not only people but also birds, animals and fish to recognize him as master and worship him. Martial (*Epigrams* 4.30.4–5) notes fish wishing to lick Domitian's hand, and Juvenal, in parody, describes a large fish given to Domitian, "the ruler of lands and seas and nations," because it "wished to be caught" (*capi voluit*).[103] The fisherman's motive for giving Domitian the fish attests Domitian's (oppressive) sovereignty.[104] So fine a fish was bound to be seized since, Juvenal says, "every rare and beautiful thing in the wide ocean ... belongs to the Imperial Treasury" (*Sat.* 4.51–55).[105] In Matthew's story, the fish is subject to God's sovereignty.

But a further implication is to be observed. The story not only emphasizes God's sovereignty over creation, but also over the tax. God not only ensures a fish is caught, but that the tax coin is in its mouth (17:27). The tax too falls within the sphere of God's sovereignty. The story does not promise to provide every disciple with the tax by this means (just as bread and fish will not miraculously appear every time a crowd is hungry). Rather, it reframes the significance of paying the tax, offering those who pay it a new context and perspective, that of God's sovereignty.

Rome imposes the tax to assert its supremacy and to subjugate, humiliate, and punish. The story of the fish, though, shows the tax to be subject to God's power and sovereignty. From the tradition of the kings of the earth and from the Gospel's point of view, the audience knows that God's sovereignty is supreme. Paying the tax, then, is no longer for disciples of Jesus an action defined by Rome, no longer an action that acknowledges the all-controlling power of the (Roman) kings of the earth and the oppressive sovereignty of the empire. Paying it also invokes, for those with eyes to see, God's sovereignty. That is to say, paying the tax becomes a subversive not a subjugating act, a defiant act that relativizes and undermines what the tax is supposed to reinforce: Rome's absolute power and control of its subject's reality.[106] The act of paying gives the empire what it demands but not on its terms. Fish and tax exist in God's greater sovereignty or reign. God laughs at "the kings of the earth" by refusing to let their claim of domination, signified by the tax, go uncontested. Rome imagines it rules, but for the community that knows this story, there is the reassurance, and in paying the tax a visible sign, that the destiny of the nations is in God's hands.[107]

7. OTHER SUBVERSIVE ACTIONS

Somewhat similar subversive actions have been presented previously in the Gospel. Walter Wink has argued that this is the nature of the strange actions in 5:38–42.[108] How do disciples respond to oppressive violence whether by master, rich creditor, or the empire's soldiers? The usual options of "violent fight or flight" are rejected in 5:39a as disciples are instructed to not use violence to resist evil. Rather disciples are to live a third way, of nonviolent, creative, subversive resistance.[109]

Wink argues that the three brief (and witty) scenarios in 5:39b–41 offer examples of disciples resisting oppressive power by reframing its ultimacy and exposing its limits and brutality. In these exemplary scenarios, the oppressed seize the initiative, secure dignity, confound the oppressing powers. Turning the other cheek is not doormat masochism, but a courageous act that seizes initiative in refusing to be cowed and subjugated. Giving one's cloak and coat means confounding the one who sues by offering everything. One's nakedness exposes among other things, the oppressor's greed and merciless power. Carrying the soldier's pack an extra mile contravenes the oppressor's rules of *angareia* by seizing the power of decision and placing the oppressor in a position vulnerable to accusations of abuse.

The payment of the tax, when viewed in relation to God's sovereignty, is a somewhat similar action. This story refuses to let the empire determine that the act of paying signifies subjugation to its control and power. But unlike the actions of 5:38–42, this action does not seek to shame or confound the oppressor since the external act of paying the tax remains the same. Here the focus is on the audience. Reframing the tax benefits the audience of disciples. The story strengthens their identity, reminding the Gospel's audience in Antioch that Roman power, which must be taken seriously as a daily reality, is not, though, the final or determinative reality. In Jesus' actions and teaching God's reign or sovereignty has been displayed. Disciples encounter and acknowledge that reign and sovereignty even in paying a tax that is supposed to emphasize Rome's control. Jesus' reframing of the tax by means of the fish undercuts and subverts Rome's claims for the present, and anticipates God's reign over all things, even the kings of the earth.

A frequently quoted, anonymous proverb sums up the basic perspective of the scene: "The emperor or the general or the landowner or the governor approaches, the peasant bows—and farts."

8. MATTHEW 17:24–27
AS PART OF CHAPTERS 17–18

And what does the audience do with such a story here in 17:24–27 located between 17:22–23 and chapter 18? It follows 17:22–23, in which Jesus announces for the second time that he must die.[110] The first passion announcement had specified the agents of this *suffering* as the religious leaders (16:21). This statement in 17:22–23 identifies the agents of his *death* more generally ("the hands of people," εἰς χεῖρας ανθρωπῶν, *eis cheiras anthrōpōn*). The subsequent narrative will clarify that these are the Romans in alliance with the Jerusalem leaders (20:18–19). The disciples are "greatly distressed" (17:22). It seems as though "the hands of people" hold sway.

The story about paying the Roman tax reassures them and the audience that it is not so, that God not Rome is sovereign (17:24–27). Chapter 18 follows as a natural consequence. The *theological* challenge to Rome's sovereignty that results from the story's affirmation of God's sovereignty is accompanied by the *social* challenge of the existence of an alternative community. To live as a marginal community in a threatening but uncertain imperial context, at variance with its fundamental claims, requires not only a resisting and subversive praxis that anticipates God's future victory and represents it in present actions (paying the tax), but also a strong communal life marked by vigilant support (18:1–14), discipline (18:15–20) and forgiveness for community members (18:21–35) that manifests God's kingdom or empire (18.1–4, 23).

NINE

Pilate and Jesus:
Roman Justice All Washed Up
(Matt 27:11–26)

PILATE CONDEMNS Jesus to die by crucifixion (27:11–26).[1] While one
might imagine that this scene would be widely recognized as attesting
a strained relationship between Matthew's Gospel and the Roman Empire,
it has not been so. Many interpreters deny or minimize any political and
Roman aspects of the scene, and focus almost exclusively on so-called religious and Jewish dimensions. That it should have to be argued, as I will do
in this chapter, that Pilate is not invisible or inconsequential to the scene, or
that Jesus' condemnation to crucifixion by a Roman provincial governor has
profound implications for interpreting this Gospel in relation to the Roman
Empire, or that religious and political matters cannot be separated, indicates
just how de-Pilatized and de-politicized is much contemporary scholarship
on this scene.

DISCUSSIONS OF PILATE

Some scholars have sought to reconstruct the historical Pilate, his character
and actions as prefect[2] of Judea between 26–36/37 C.E.[3] These attempted
reconstructions struggle with sources that are few in number, diverse in their
presentations, and partial in their coverage.[4] Only Philo, Josephus, and the
four Gospels present any substantive material about Pilate and, as recent
historical work has shown, each pursues its own particular cultural and
theological perspective in depicting Pilate.[5] Assessments of the man and his
rule[6] have ranged from very negative to quite positive. Influential has been
the negative verdict of E. Stauffer, who depicts a brutal, oppressive, anti-
Jewish governor influenced by the wicked anti-Semite, Sejanus.[7] But others
have seen him more positively, "neither a monster nor a saint...a typical Roman officer of his type"[8] caught up in serious conflict whether for
personal reasons[9] or circumstances beyond his control.[10] Scholars, always
influenced by their own circumstances and commitments, attempt to sift
through each of these six sources to identify particular slants of interpretation, and to build a historical picture of Pilate,[11] always with the risk that
where there were six Pilates, now there will be seven.

For this chapter, I am concerned with interpreting Matthew's presentation of Pilate as a character in his Gospel story, though these historical reconstructions will be by no means irrelevant to the discussion. I will be attentive to his character traits that appear in the scene that depicts his interaction with Jesus in order to elucidate Matthew's presentation and its implications.[12] However, in order to make sense of some of these character traits and in order to understand Pilate's role in the narrative *as a Roman provincial governor,* some historical knowledge of the larger sociopolitical world and the role of Roman governors as representatives of the Roman Empire is necessary.

The possibility exists that the Gospel ignores or is immune to these historical dynamics, but we have not found any evidence for such an approach in the previous chapters. Hence information about imperial ruling strategies, the tasks and roles of governors, alliances between Roman officials such as governors and local elites, the legal system's protection of elite privileges and bias against lower-status persons, and Roman attitudes toward provincials helps to illuminate the dynamics of this scene. When Matthew calls Pilate a governor in 27:2, for instance, he does not stop the narrative and elaborate some common understandings of this term: that a governor was appointed by Rome; came from the equestrian ranks; embodied tremendous privilege, had responsibilities for military, fiscal; and judicial control; was widely known for greedy self-serving practices; and was almost protected from any provincial protest by distance, expense, and the threat of retaliation. Rather the Gospel's author assumes his audience has some sort of picture or stereotype, perhaps even experience, of a Roman governor because they lived in a world where governors were somewhat familiar figures. Antioch was, after all, the residence of the governor of the province of Syria. However, because we do not live in that world, it will be helpful to elaborate some of this assumed knowledge. Living two thousand years later and in a different part of the world with a different government structure, we cannot be sure to reconstruct every aspect of this understanding but we can at least identify some contours of it.

The Conventional De-Pilatized, Depoliticized Reading

Scholars do not agree on how to interpret Matthew's scene of the interaction between Pilate and Jesus. By far the dominant view of Matthew's scene held by the majority of interpreters sees Matthew as exonerating Pilate by placing the blame for Jesus' death on the Jewish leaders and/or people who force "poor powerless Pilate" into condemning a man that Pilate knows to be innocent.[13] Pilate is weak, indecisive, without conscience, expedient, coerced. The scene culminates, so the argument goes, in the self-cursing of the Jewish people (27:25) as they reject God's Messiah and are rejected by God. Pilate is reluctantly or expediently or distantly complicit.[14] Such a view is seen to reflect the early Christian movement's attempts to differentiate itself from late-first-century Judaism after the destruction of Jerusalem, and to secure good relations for itself with Rome by assuring Rome that Jesus was no political threat.

Helen Bond's analysis of Matthew's Pilate-Jesus scene summarizes some features of the conventional reading that asserts the (essential) exoneration of Pilate, and sees him caught up in a religious dispute within Judaism that has little to do with Rome or politics. In arguing that Pilate is very much in the background of Matthew's theologically, not politically, focused scene, she claims that four particular Matthean concerns evident in the scene minimize Pilate's role.

The first theme to which she draws attention is the Jews' responsibility, not Rome's, for Jesus' death. Judas accepts responsibility (27:3–5), Pilate does not (27:24), and the "primary responsibility" is assumed by the people (27:25). Bond ascribes a profoundly pastoral motivation to the people's assumption of responsibility; they "reassure the Roman prefect that Jesus deserves to die" and "attempt to overcome Pilate's hesitation." For Bond, since Jesus is declared to be innocent by God, "the Jewish crowd must bear the consequences of its rejection of the Messiah."[15]

Second, Bond argues that Matthew has, when compared with his source Mark, increased the "anti-Jewish tone" of the scene in which Matthew condemns both the Jewish leaders and the people. The leaders plot his death (27:1); the crowd calls for Jesus' death, not Barabbas's (27:20–22), and assumes responsibility for it (27:25).

This choice between Jesus and Barabbas constitutes her third element. Barabbas is a notorious prisoner whose activity has been completely depoliticized by the vague term "prisoner" (27:16). And Jesus' religious identity has been emphasized by calling him the Messiah (27:17). The religious significance of rejecting Jesus is thus heightened.

Fourth, this title "Christ," not the political title "King of the Jews," dominates the depiction of Jesus (27:17, 22). Jesus' messiahship is on trial and the scene shows the Jews' rejection of it, for which God rejects them. Pilate becomes a "minor character" with the emphasis of the scene on the more urgent issue of relations not with Rome but with Judaism.

Some others, though by far a minority, do not think Matthew lets Pilate off the hook so easily or that the scene is not concerned with Rome. This minority view sees Pilate as representing and embodying Rome's ruthlessness and self-interest, and the scene exposing the injustice of Rome's touted justice.[16] My reading will develop this second view. In rejecting a rigid separation of political and theological concerns, I will argue that Pilate's responsibility is not minimalized, that the political nature of Jesus' death is not disguised, that the scene does not condemn or exclude Jewish people for rejecting Jesus, and that the scene is very interested in relations with Rome which it construes as dangerous and threatening but certainly not ultimate since they are subject to God's purposes.

PILATE: MEMBER OF THE RULING ELITE

Pilate first appears in 27:1–2. The alliance of Jewish leaders comprising the chief priests and elders[17] hands Jesus over (27:2)[18] to him. Legally this transfer is necessary because Pilate as governor has the judicial power of life and death (cf. Josephus, *J.W.* 2.117). But it would be inaccurate to think of Jesus being transferred from the hateful, vengeful religious officials to the weak, disinterested, secular power, Pilate, as a mere procedural step by which the religious leaders accomplish his execution. Such a view overlooks three crucial dynamics of how power operates in this imperial situation.

Priests and Political Power

First, as I have indicated in chapter 1, various scholars of aristocratic imperial societies have shown that "religious" officials are part of the retainer class within the ruling elite as those who maintain and advance the interests of the ruling elite.[19] Religious personnel do not have an exclusively "religious" agenda but uphold and impact the economic and societal structures of society. Their teaching and religious practices like tithing and taxes maintain the hierarchy and ensure their own wealth at the expense of the rest. They intervene in various local crises that threaten the status quo.[20] Josephus presents the chief priests as the essential rulers of Judea (*Ant.* 20.251) and consistently links the so-called "religious leaders" with the "notables" or "powerful ones/magnates" in advocating cooperation with and/or submission to Rome (*Ant.* 18.2–3, valuation of property; *Ant.* 20.178, with Felix; *J.W.* 2.237–40, Cumanus). The chief priests and the "most notable Pharisees," for example, assemble with "the powerful citizens" in 66 C.E. to discuss their opposition to the lower priests' provocative act of no longer offering the daily sacrifices "for Caesar and the Roman people" (*J.W.* 2.410–11; 197; cf. 2.321–23, 336, 342). This alliance of the elite sends delegations to the governor Florus and to Agrippa exonerating themselves from blame and expressing loyalty to Rome (*J.W.* 2.418). These actions attest a social and political alliance of the Jewish leaders and Rome's representatives that is assumed in this trial scene. The Jewish leaders and Pilate are allies as members of the ruling class.

This coalition of the Jewish leaders with the Roman officials and the intermingling of their religious and sociopolitical interests is established right at the beginning of the Gospel's plot in 2:4–6 where the "chief priests and scribes" are "assembled" and "questioned" by King Herod about the Messiah's birthplace. They supply knowledge that facilitates his violence against his subjects. At the end of the Gospel, the chief priests and Pharisees gather with Pilate to secure Jesus' tomb with Pilate's soldiers. After the resurrection, the chief priests and elders conspire with Pilate's soldiers to "satisfy" the governor (28:11–15).

Rome's Alliance with Local Elites and Legal Bias

Evident in these examples is a second factor. Part of Rome's strategy for so-cial control was to secure the cooperation of the local elite through alliances that emphasized their common interest in maintaining the status quo.[21] This does not mean that there were no conflicts among elites (Philo, *Flacc.* 105; Josephus, *J.W.* 2.308), but it does indicate a common commitment to the status quo. As one tactic among many in securing this alliance, Roman gov-ernors of Judea appointed chief priests and so controlled priestly loyalties. Josephus records that Pilate's predecessor, the governor Valerius Gratus, de-posed and appointed at least five high priests throughout his reign (*Ant.* 18.33–35).

In contrast, Caiaphas remained high priest from 18–36 c.e., throughout the whole of Pilate's administration, suggesting not only that he enjoyed Pilate's favor but also that he was adroit at keeping the governor "happy" (which meant furthering his interests). Vitellius, governor of Syria, deposes him after Pilate is removed, and appoints Jonathan high priest (*Ant.* 18.95). In a conciliatory gesture, Vitellius also returns the priestly garments to the priests and temple (Josephus, *Ant.* 18.90). Their previous control by Roman governors was another strategy to underline that chief priests, along with other religious leaders, were agents of the Roman governor's interests. Later in the century, as war seems imminent in the 60s, the chief priests dutifully exhort the people in Jerusalem to submit to the governor Florus and the cohorts he was bringing from Caesarea (*J.W.* 2.318–20). And they are hor-rified when in the late 60s, the "brigands," instead of having Rome appoint the high priest, elect by lot high priests who are "lowborn" and not from the usual, hereditary ruling families (*J.W.* 4.147–57). In Matt 27, this sort of al-liance between the Jewish leaders and Pilate is assumed as a normal imperial reality, just as is his alliance with them. Both parties need each other.

Third, another aspect of Roman strategy was to ensure elite interests were protected as much as possible in legal processes. Roman apologists often claimed that the establishment of Roman law and justice was part of Rome's divinely given mission and that the whole world benefited from such a marvelous gift. Virgil's Jupiter declares to Mercury that Rome is to "bring all the world beneath [its] law" (*Aen.* 4.231). Anchises tells Aeneas in the underworld that he is "to rule the nations with your power" and "to crown peace with law" (*Aen.* 6.851–53). Rome is "to impose on the conquered tributes, laws, and Roman jurisdiction" (Tacitus, *Ann.* 15.6).

But Peter Garnsey's study of Roman justice demonstrates on every page that there was a profound bias operating in every aspect of legal proceedings in favor of the elite and against those of lower status. The extent of this commitment to the elite's "legal privilege" is seen, for instance, in much more lenient penalties for higher-status offenders and far greater opportunity to appeal to the emperor.[22] In terms of these widely attested historical realities,

Matthew's Pilate is not going to resist the decision of the local leaders about Jesus, and they are going to make sure he understands that his interests are also being served in putting Jesus to death. This is not a level playing field, not an equal contest. Garnsey comments:

> In general it can be said that judges and juries [and Pilate is both in Matt 27:11–26] were suspicious of, if not resentful towards, low-status plaintiffs who attacked their "betters" in court, and were prepared to believe the worst of low-status defendants, while the pleas of high-status plaintiffs or defendants . . . were given more credance.[23]

Studies of the structure of aristocratic societies, of Roman imperial strategies, and of Roman legal practices illuminate the transfer of Jesus from the Jewish leaders to Pilate in 27:2. It is the transfer of a lower-status person (one of the *humiliores*)[24] from one part of the ruling elite (the *honestiores*) to another. It would be inappropriate to imagine that the scene plays the "wicked" Jewish leaders off against the "good guy" Pilate by contrasting the former's determination to kill Jesus with Pilate's reluctance. The scene, predictably, presents no such conflict or division. This is not a system in which checks and balances operate whereby the "secular" branch can protect against excesses by the "religious" branch, or even that the "religious" leaders have a burden of proof to demonstrate the "fairness" of their request to Pilate in order to execute Jesus. There are no such branches or checks and balances. Instead of burdens of proof, there are aristocratic alliances, "legal privilege," and bias against those of lower status, against which testimony about Jesus' righteousness (27:19), even knowledge of the leaders' envy (27:18), carry no weight.

This "handing over" was necessary in part because the governor, the representative of Roman justice with powers of life and death, could put Jesus to death. But the "handing over" has further significance. The narrative subtly exposes how "justice" works in the Roman world, whose interests are being served, and in so doing, evaluates it negatively because of its opposition to God's agent.

There are two initial clues, "nudge-nudge-wink-wink" signs, as to what is being exposed. First, in 27:1 the narrator reveals that the Jewish leaders "took counsel . . . to put him to death" (RSV). Their "taking counsel" is part of a series of previous meetings and strategies against Jesus (12:14; 22:15; cf. 28:12). Their goal to bring about his death is quite clear, but the construction of ὥστε (*hōste*) with an infinitive of result ("to put him to death") offers a particular view. This construction can indicate an intended result so that it functions essentially as a purpose clause. But it can convey more than intent. It can underline that the outcome is certain; ὥστε is appropriate "if an actual result is to be denoted."[25] Hence the construction indicates that when the leaders strategize to put Jesus to death through Pilate, it is as good as done. The outcome is inevitable.[26] Pilate's help is a given, not because he is weak and easily manipulated, but because they are aristocratic allies who control the system of justice as a means of furthering their own interests. Their interests are his, his are theirs.

This reading is strengthened by a further comment in 27:3 that the narrator also supplies. Judas, also the "hander-over" and so their ally (27:3), witnesses Jesus' binding and "handing over" to Pilate the governor. According to the narrator, Judas interprets this "handing over" to mean that Jesus "was condemned,"[27] a verb that in its previous use in 20:18 is associated with Jesus' death at the hands of the elite, both the Jewish leaders and "the Gentiles." That is, though the Jewish leaders as governed provincials do not have the power to put Jesus to death, their commitment to kill him and their handing him over to Pilate means, for Judas, that the deed is as good as done. Judas is so sure of it, so certain that Jesus' death is now utterly inevitable, that he returns the money and kills himself—before Pilate has even interrogated Jesus (27:3–10)! A provincial of lower status, no political power, and little wealth has no chance of any other outcome.

PILATE AMONG THE GOVERNORS

Pilate is introduced in 27:2 as "governor" (ἡγεμών, *hēgemōn*). This commonly used term for governors[28] attests the central significance of Roman presence to the scene and emphasizes Pilate's function within the ruling elite and the social, political, and legal structures outlined above. The importance of the term "governor" is highlighted by its sevenfold use through the scene:

27:11a	Now Jesus stood before the governor,
27:11b	and the governor asked him,
27:14	so that the governor was greatly amazed.
27:15	Now at the festival the governor was accustomed to release
27:21	The governor again said to them,
27:27	Then the soldiers of the governor.

For completeness 28:14 should also be noted: "If this comes to the governor's ears...."

The term "governor" commonly designates provincial governors appointed from Rome (Josephus, *Ant.* 18.170; 19.292), men often of the equestrian rank with, usually, some military experience and considerable status and wealth, though not of the highest senatorial order in the ruling elite.[29]

Josephus provides examples of the administrative, fiscal, military, and judicial tasks entrusted to governors.[30] Governors are seen settling disputes and keeping order especially among different ethnic groups (*J.W.* 2.487–93, Alexandria; *Ant.* 19.301; 20.125). They raise taxes (Albinus in Josephus, *J.W.* 2.273) and have responsibility for fiscal administration (Philo, *Flacc.*

Governors of Judea	(Approximate) Dates (C.E.)
Coponius	6–9
M. Ambivius	9–12
Annius Rufus	12–15
Valerius Gratus	15–26
Pontius Pilate	26–36
Marcellus	36–37
Marullus	37–41
Cuspius Fadus	44–46
Tiberius Julius Alexander	46–48
Ventidius Cumanus	48–52
M. Antonius Felix	52–60
Porcius Festus	60–62
Lucceius Albinus	62–64
Gessius Florus	64–66
Jewish Revolt	66–70

4). They engage in public works and building projects (Pilate's aqueduct: Josephus, *J.W.* 2.175; *Ant.* 18.60; also aqueducts, theater, gymnasium, public bath, etc.; Pliny the Younger, *Ep.* 10.37–44), and intervene in municipal financial affairs as necessary (Pliny the Younger, *Ep.* 10.38, 44). They command troops (Pilate in Josephus, *Ant.* 18.55; Philo, *Flacc.* 5), take military action to quell troublesome subjects (Cestius against Galilee and Judea; Josephus, *J.W.* 2.499–565), and engage in military action against bandits (Varro in Josephus, *J.W.* 1.398). Governors are responsible for justice, whether in its absence as with Festus (whom Josephus accuses of "overbearing and lawless actions" [ὑβρίζειν, *hubrizein*], *Ant.* 18.25) and with Flaccus (Philo, *Flacc.* 6–107), or in hearing cases brought to them (as with Paul before Felix and Festus in Acts 23:24–26:30; Philo, *Flacc.* 4),[31] or in traveling assizes such as those undertaken, for instance, by Cicero and Pliny.[32] Brent Kinman has suggested, not unreasonably, that Pilate is in Jerusalem because he is carrying out his assize or tour to designated prominent cities in his province, such as Jerusalem, to hear civic and criminal cases.[33] The Gospel's audience understands that Pilate encounters Jesus as one case among others that must be decided.

Josephus refers to governors (of senatorial provinces) who maintain control with the *fasces* (*J.W.* 2.365–66). The *fasces,* an axe and bundle of six rods, were often ceremonially paraded to represent the administration of Roman justice. They "constituted a portable kit for flogging and decapitation. Since they were so brutally functional, they not only served as ceremonial symbols of office but also carried the potential of violent repression and execution."[34] That is, they secured the perception of the life and death power embodied in and executed by Rome's justice. The first governor of Judea, "Coponius, a Roman of the equestrian order [was] entrusted by Augustus with full powers, including the infliction of capital punishment"

(Josephus, *J.W.* 2.117). Philo notes the governor Flaccus's power to crucify people (*Flacc.* 83–85).

The Quality and Style of Provincial Governors

It is hard to assess the quality of administration carried out by these governors. Clearly they represent a system that sustains the elite. They look out for the interests of the emperor, the empire, and the local elite in alliance with whom they exercise their rule. No doubt some governors did their best to fulfill a difficult role. Of course, Aristides would have us believe that governors ensure an almost paradisaical world with generous rule and meticulous attention to justice for all (*Roman Oration* 31–39). But Brunt rejects the view that governing improved and "abuses were infrequent and redress easy to secure" in the Principate, as some have claimed by pointing to greater prosperity and longer tenure of positions. Certainly Philo did not think things had improved. The abuses of Flaccus's predecessor in Egypt, initially repaired by the competent Flaccus (*Flacc.* 1–5, 7), pale into insignificance when compared with Flaccus's subsequent and deliberate excesses. And Philo can generalize:

> Some, indeed, of those who held governorships in the time of Tiberius and his father Caesar, had perverted their office of guardian and protector into domination and tyranny and had spread hopeless misery through their territories with their venality, robbery, unjust sentences, expulsion and banishment of quite innocent people, and execution of magnates without trial. (*Flacc.* 105)

Tacitus, no friend to Jews, does not present a picture of gradual improvement but seems to assume different intensities of abuse. Felix "practiced every kind of cruelty and lust, wielding the power of king with all the instincts of a slave.... Still the Jews' patience lasted until Gessius Florus became procurator; in his time war began" (Tacitus, *Hist.* 5.9–10).

In presenting various governors attending to their tasks, Josephus distinguishes varying levels of competency, but reserves his worst criticism for Albinus and Florus, governors of Judea in 62–64 and 64–66 C.E. "The administration of Albinus, who followed Festus, was of another order; there was no form of villainy which he omitted to practise" (*J.W.* 2.272). Josephus outlines those "villainies" as stealing property, imposing excessive taxation, freeing prisoners for a price, and stimulating social disorder by permitting attacks on the (wealthy) "peaceable citizens" to go unchecked and unpunished (*J.W.* 2.273–76). Clearly the governor benefited from stealing property and imposing extra taxes. Josephus continues, "Such was the character of Albinus, but his successor, Gessius Florus, made him appear by comparison a paragon of virtue" (*J.W.* 2.277).

Governors as Blood-Sucking Flies

In addition to these evaluations is a very significant passage, attributed to the emperor Tiberius no less, that seems to indict all governors as unjust, and to identify Albinus and Florus as different in degree, rather than in kind. Josephus, an ally of Vespasian, is commenting on Tiberius's tendency to leave governors in office for lengthy tenures. He reports Tiberius's rationale as being: "For it was in the law of nature that governors are prone to engage in extortion." He has Tiberius argue that short-term appointments were a great spur to engage quickly in as much exploitation for personal profit as possible. A new governor would repeat the process, making things continually bad for the subject people. A long tenure meant "those gorged by their robberies" would be sluggish to continue the exploitation thereby giving the people some reprieve (*Ant.* 18.172–73).

The emperor Tiberius then illustrates the point with a fable in which a wounded man requests a kind but apparently misguided passer-by not to shoo the flies away from his wounds because once they have had "their fill of blood" they do no more damage. But shooing them away and letting new flies near the wound with new appetites for blood would kill him. The fable is interpreted to show the demerits of short tenures for governors. "Their natural appetite for plunder would be reinforced by their expectation of being speedily deprived of that pleasure" (*Ant.* 18.174–76).

The fable, whether historical or not, is stunning for a number of reasons:

- its open use of a predatory image of flies sucking blood from an open wound to denote Roman provincial government;

- its recognition (in the mouth of an emperor!) that the relationship of governor and governed sucked the lifeblood out of the provinces;

- its comparison of governors with pesky and potentially fatal flies;

- its identification of the provinces with a wounded and bleeding man who is prone to death;

- its recognition that such predatory behavior is natural, inevitable, and uncontrollable;

- its request from the wounded man (the provinces!) for the passer-by not to intervene;

- the wounded man's inability to request any other help;

- the passer-by's inability to imagine any other intervention except to shoo flies away but certainly not to heal the man's wounded situation;

- the collective tolerance of controlled exploitation;

- its presence in a work authored by a Jew of priestly descent and loyal ally of the emperor Vespasian.

With this image Josephus lays bare the whole imperial system and the role of governors in it. But it is presented with a terrifying cynicism. In Josephus's narrative, the emperor Tiberius presents the image without any remorse for the damage that his system causes, or without any thought for its abolition. This is simply the way things are. In fact, he presents the status quo exploitation of provinces by governors as quite benign. Shorter tenures would make things a whole lot worse.

But such comments are not unusual. Juvenal advises that

> When you enter your long-expected province as its Governor, set a curb and limit to your passion, as also to your greed; have compassion on the impoverished provincials, whose very bones you see sucked dry of marrow (*Sat.* 8.87–90).

Plutarch comments on "the procuratorships and governorships of provinces from which many talents may be gained" (*Mor.* 814d), while Plutarch praises Brutus's good governorship in Gaul in contrast to "other provinces [that], owing to the insolence and rapacity of their governors, were plundered as though they had been conquered in war" (*Brut.* 6.10–12). The leader Civilis complains that "we are handed over to prefects and centurions; after one band is satisfied with murder and spoils, the troops are shifted, and new purses are looked for to be filled and various pretexts for plundering are sought" (Tacitus, *Hist.* 4.14). Suetonius criticizes Vespasian, emperor from 69 to 79, the time around which Matthew's Gospel was written, for using governors to further his "love of money" (*Vesp.* 16):

> He is even believed to have had the habit of designedly advancing the most rapacious of his procurators to higher posts, that they might be the richer when he later condemned them [and confiscated their wealth through fines]; in fact it was common talk that he used these men as sponges because he, so to speak, soaked them when they were dry and squeezed them when they were wet.

Yet as Klaus Wengst also notes, Rome had a vested interest in limiting the amount of plunder and keeping at least some semblance of law and order so as not to alienate the local elite, and aggravate the local people into revolt.[35]

Legal Action against Governors

While it might seem that in reality governors like Pilate had unbridled or unaccountable power, that was not the case, at least not in theory. P. Brunt discusses the legal provision of *repetundae*, established under the Republic and extended in the Principate, that prohibited various kinds of extortion involving force, intimidation, or fraud, undue extractions and illegal enrichment from the governed, and other oppressive acts of misgovernment.[36] Provincials did have the right of appeal for redress first, for Jews in Judea, to the governor of Syria, and to Rome.

But in practice, appeals against a governor who enjoyed the emperor's favor enough to be appointed in the first place had little chance of success. Philo cannot point to any governor removed from office in order to be tried for exploitative actions, though he knows of some punished after leaving office (*Flacc.* 105–7). And when the Jewish citizens in Alexandria try to appeal to Rome against Flaccus, they need Flaccus's permission to do so. He, predictably, omits to pass the petition on to Rome (*Flacc.* 97–101). Brunt catalogues numerous obstacles to such appeals: distance from Rome; the expense of an embassy both in travel and in accommodation awaiting a hearing; pressure from a governor's allies in the province not to pursue action; the need even for the governor's consent for such a petition (Philo, *Flacc.* 97–101; Josephus, *Ant.* 20.7, 193); the influence of a governor's supportive allies in Rome; the risk of reprisal; divisions and rivalries in the province.[37]

Examples of these obstacles are readily available. Philo's discussion of Flaccus has been mentioned. Garnsey notes that after the prosecution of Bassus, proconsul of Bithynia, the senate attempts to prosecute Theophanes, the leader of the provincial prosecutors.[38] Some Jews from Caesarea pursue a complaint against the governor Festus. Josephus comments that "he would undoubtedly have paid the penalty for his misdeeds against the Jews had not Nero yielded to the urgent entreaty of Felix's brother Pallas, whom he held in the highest honour." And in retaliation for bringing the complaint, Syrian leaders successfully intervene and persuade Nero's tutor to urge the emperor to annul the grant of equal civic rights to the Jews in Caesarea (*Ant.* 20.182). When Jews in Jerusalem seek an embassy to Nero against the governor Florus in 66 C.E., Agrippa tells them this action will only make matters worse. Flattery not irritation is the best approach; an embassy is an overreaction that "exaggerates minor errors"; it will lead to worse and open maltreatment; it will alienate the emperor who after all "cannot see in the west their officers in the east"; the best remedy is to wait "for the same procurator will not remain forever, and it is probable that the successors of this one will show greater moderation in taking office" (Josephus, *J.W.* 2.350–55). The latter argument is transparently false as the experience under Florus, Albinus's successor, had demonstrated. The Roman general Cerialis tells the Treviri and Lingones tribes in Gaul that they should endure "the extravagance or greed of your rulers" knowing that better ones will come, just as they endure "barren years [and] excessive rains" (Tacitus, *Hist.* 4.74).

Yet Pilate is the subject of such a complaint after attacking and killing a number of Samaritans. The Samaritans appealed to Vitellius, the governor of Syria, who ordered Pilate to "return to Rome to give the emperor his account of the matters," but Tiberius dies before he reaches Rome (Josephus, *Ant.* 18.88–89). This action effectively ends Pilate's governorship, but Josephus does not indicate whether any punitive action is taken against Pilate.

Matthew's reference to Pilate as governor in 27:2 evokes such realities. It establishes this context of Roman provincial administrative practice for the meeting of Pilate and Jesus. Given this context, it is hard to maintain the common view that Pilate is merely incidental to the trial scene or a secondary character in it. It would seem to be equally impossible to treat the scene as though this Roman presence is somehow peripheral to the scene's "real" attention on Jewish matters. Bond's claim that Pilate "retains his political neutrality in the affair" is very far from the mark given Pilate's role as governor to protect and advance Rome's interests in alliance with the local elite. And likewise, to suggest that "all hints of political pressure have been removed" from the trial scene simply ignores the whole imperial context that surrounds the scene and the imperial dynamics of power, elite alliances, and legal privilege that pervade it.[39] Rather the scene, informed by fundamental realities of imperial situations, introduces Pilate as a major player in the alliances that comprise the ruling elite. He represents and protects Rome's political, economic, military, and legal interests in an exploitative, oppressive, and largely unaccountable relationship with those he governs, and as the one who has the almost untouchable power to execute Jesus.

PILATE OR JESUS?

The term "governor" in 27:2 (ἡγεμών, *hēgemōn*) establishes Pilate's role and sociopolitical location among the ruling elite. It also clarifies the opposition and conflict that is at the heart of this scene. That is, the noun indicates a second reason why Jesus appears before Pilate (beyond the pragmatic factor of Pilate having the power of condemnation), namely as part of the conflict between God's empire that Jesus represents, and Rome's empire that Pilate represents.

The noun for "governor" has appeared twice previously in the Gospel, both in contexts of conflict. In chapter 10 Jesus commissions his disciples to mission in Israel (extended to the world in 28:18–20). They are to proclaim God's empire and demonstrate its presence in merciful acts that powerfully transform some of the misery of the imperial world and its numerous wounded people in Israel. They are to "heal the sick, raise the dead, cleanse lepers, cast out demons," thereby continuing Jesus' ministry.[40] Their ministry is necessary precisely because the imperial world is not justly ordered, and has not brought the "state of health" that Aristides falsely celebrates as one of its accomplishments (*Roman Oration* 97). After all, governors have sucked the provincials' bones "dry of marrow" (Juvenal, *Sat.* 8.87–90). The disciples' mission challenges the status quo with a different empire. Jesus warns them that the imperial world will not welcome their proclamation of this alternative empire, and its critique of the status quo. "Beware of them; for they will hand you over to councils and flog you in their synagogues, and you will be dragged before governors (ἡγεμών, *hēgemōn*) and kings because of me" (10:17–18).

These governors are included in the "wolves" among whom disciples are sent (10:16). "Wolves" is a common polemical image for opponents.[41] It is applied to Roman governors by Dio, who has the people of Dalmatia complain that they rebelled against Rome in 6 c.e. because "you send to your flocks as guardians not dogs or shepherds but wolves" (Dio 56.16.3). Tribulation is certain in the disciples' life of mission, and persecution is inevitable as the two empires collide. There is a fundamental antipathy of governors toward Jesus' followers. The sequence of conflict first with Jewish councils (10:17) and then with a governor (10:18), and the use of the same verb of "handing over" in 10:16 as in 27:2 indicates that the experience of disciples will be the same as Jesus' experience in chapter 27. There is a fundamental antipathy between the governor and Jesus.

Jesus the Governor/Ruler

But there is a dimension to this conflict between empires that disciples and Jesus do not have in common. Jesus is also designated a governor or leader. In 2:3–6 Herod responds to the magi's troubling question about the location of the one born king of the Jews by gathering the Jerusalem leaders to ask them about the birthplace of the Christ. They respond by citing, with some changes, Mic 5:1–3 and 2 Sam 5:2. The citation as it now exists in Matt 2:6 addresses and identifies Bethlehem: "You are by no means least among the rulers/governors (ἡγεμόσιν, *hēgemosin*) of Judah." This preeminence among the rulers/governors results from "a ruler (ἡγούμενος, *hēgoumenos*) [who] from you will come . . . who will rule/shepherd my people Israel." Bethlehem governs because a ruler comes from it, and of course the text refers to Jesus not to Herod! The first of the "ruling" verbs is the same term as in 10:18 and 27:2. The second is very close to it, and is perhaps chosen instead of the LXX form ἄρχοντα (*archonta*) precisely "because of its resemblance."[42] Jesus, the ruler/governor from Bethlehem, gives it prominence among the rulers in Judah.

A further reference to "ruling" expresses Jesus' task. He is to "shepherd/ rule (ποιμανεῖ, *poimanei*) my people Israel." The image of "shepherd" is commonly used for rulers (Jer 23:1–4; Ezek 34:5–6; Suetonius, *Tib.* 32; Dio Chrysostom *4 Regn.* 4.43–44; Dio 56.16). The image of shepherd appears in the Gospel in 9:36 where Jesus complains, in a critique of the ruling elite, that the people are "harassed and helpless . . . like sheep without a shepherd." The adjectives "harassed and helpless" indicate violent and repressive actions. The people are "beat up" and crushed by the leaders.[43] The critique, not limited to Israel's religious leaders since the ruling elite comprises both Roman and Jewish leaders, recalls other attacks against false shepherds. Suetonius has the emperor Tiberius respond to a governor who was advocating "burdensome taxes" for his province that "it was the part of a good shepherd to shear his flock, not skin it" (*Tib.* 32). Dio Chrysostom reminds Trajan that the emperor is a "shepherd of peoples" who is to "oversee, guard, and protect flocks, not ... to slaughter, butcher and skin them" (*4 Regn.* 43–44).

A similar picture, but in more detail, emerges in Ezek 34. The false shepherds maintain a strictly differentiated society to ensure the elite has plenty at the expense of the rest. They feed themselves but exploit or burden the sheep/people by depriving them of food and clothing, by not strengthening the weak, healing the sick, binding up the injured, or looking for the lost and scattered (Ezek 34:3–6). They do not protect the people from nations but let them be enslaved, plundered, frightened, starved, and insulted (34:27–29). The leaders are condemned because of their imperial style: "With force and harshness you have ruled them" (34:4). God promises a reversal with a Davidic prince and God's saving presence (34:23–24, 30–31). By invoking this passage, Jesus the son of David transfers its condemnation to the present ruling elite, both the Jerusalem leaders and Roman personnel like Pilate the governor, whose rule it describes most aptly. Nor is this the only time Jesus has attacked the leadership and system Pilate represents. In 20:25–26 he has rejected the domination style of "the rulers of the Gentiles" who "lord it over them" and called the community of disciples to be servants like himself.

Two Governors, Two Empires

The description of Pilate as a governor, and of Jesus as a governor/ruler throws the two together and reveals a fundamental contrast and conflict between the two. One is a representative of the Roman emperor and empire. The other proclaims and embodies God's empire (4:17–25). One represents a system that finds its legitimation in the claim that Jupiter has appointed it to rule the world. The other is anointed by Israel's God and attacks the imperial order as a representative of Satan's false claims (4:8). One embodies a domination system of "rule over" others. The other rejects this system as antithetical to God's will and requires the community of his followers to practice an alternative social order marked by service not domination (20:25–28). One promotes a system that benefits the few at the expense of the many. The other as son of David (1:1; 9:27; 15:22; 20:30–31) makes available to anyone, particularly those whom the empire decides are marginals, the benefits of God's inclusive mercy and transforming power. One incarnates a system that imposes diverse wounds on provincials. The other manifests God's empire among such provincials in acts of healing and restoration (4:23–25; 9:35).

Jesus the ruler appears before Pilate the governor as a continuation of the confrontation between two empires—Rome's and God's—that has been under way throughout the Gospel. The confrontation concerns issues of sovereignty and agency, and visions of well-being (see chapters 1–2 above). To whom does the sovereignty of the world belong? Who belongs to the world?

Throughout, Jesus has presented claims that not only differ profoundly from those of Rome, the dominant power, but claims that contest and challenge Rome's declarations.

The Name "Jesus"

This very political challenge continues in this scene through three names. The first of these is the name "Jesus." Eight times, as redaction critics have noticed, the narrative names him as "Jesus," in 27:1, 11 (2*x*), 17, 20, 22, 26, 27, whereas in Mark 15, the likely source for Matt 27, the name Jesus is used only three times (Mark 15:1, 5, 15). In four of these added instances, Matthew turns Mark's pronoun (he/him) into "Jesus,"[44] twice Matthew changes "King of the Jews" into "Jesus,"[45] and once he adds a reference to "Jesus" where Mark has nothing.[46] In 27:1, Matthew employs the name "Jesus" and not a pronoun for the first reference to emphasize the name.

To claim that the preference for the name "Jesus" depoliticizes and de-Romanizes the scene is without foundation. The prominent use of Jesus' name recalls 1:21 where the angel instructs Joseph not only on the newly conceived baby's name ("you are to name him Jesus"), but also on its meaning ("for he will save his people from their sins"). The meaning of the name is his mission. As God's agent, he is to save his people. As I argued in chapter 5 above, Jesus carries out this salvation in his life (teachings, actions), death, resurrection, and return. Salvation consists of saving his people Israel, post-70, from their sins' punishment in the fall of Jerusalem to Rome in 70 C.E. Rome, the agent of God's punishment, will be punished and defeated by God for rejecting God's purposes. Jesus accomplishes this deliverance finally at his return (24:27–31). The increased use of the name "Jesus" here in 27:11–26 points to this salvation. In this confrontation between Jesus and Pilate, God's purposes are being enacted, purposes that will lead to Rome's demise and the establishment of a new heaven and earth. Far from reducing the political significance of the scene as some charge, the numerous occurrences of the name "Jesus" in these verses greatly emphasizes the salvific significance of the events, and the inevitable destruction of Rome.

Jesus, King of the Jews

The second term used for Jesus appears in 27:11. Pilate asks him if he is "King of the Jews." Jesus seems to agree with the designation in replying, "You have said so." Further, the narrative emphasizes with a fourfold repetition that Jesus does not contest the title. In 27:12 Jesus "made no answer." Pilate questions his silence (27:13). The narrative records it (27:14; "he gave him no answer") and underlines it ("not even to a single charge"). If Roman law presumed that the lack of a defense meant guilty as charged,[47] Jesus has admitted his "guilt." He is King of the Jews.

But what is the significance of the title? What is Pilate asking Jesus and what does Jesus confess to with his answer and silence? This is the title that the magi use in looking for the newborn Jesus (2:2). The use of "king" for Jesus collides with the introduction of Herod in 2:1 as king, a puppet king of Rome.[48] The qualifier "of the Jews" resembles "Judea" in 2:1, the territory where Herod is supposed to reign, and anticipates 2:5 where Judea is the location of Bethlehem from whom will come a ruler. Bethlehem was of course the place in which David was anointed as king (1 Sam 16) so evoking Bethlehem points to a Davidic king. Herod seems to be very aware of these collisions and implications. He and the rest of Jerusalem's ruling elite are terrified (2:3) that there is a kingly challenger and are hell-bent on destroying anyone who could be a rival claimant. Herod's drastic response against Bethlehem's babies indicates how threatening to the status quo is this title as well as witnesses to the ends to which the elite will go to maintain its power.

This title "king" (βασιλεύς, *basileus*) was, after all, also the title used for Rome's rulers or emperors.[49] And Josephus evidences the seriousness with which Rome responds to others who exhibited royal pretensions in claiming a title not granted or sanctioned by Rome.[50] Simon is beheaded (Josephus, *Ant.* 17.273–76), Athronges is captured (*Ant.* 17.278–85), Menachem is killed (though not by Rome, *J.W.* 2.433–48), and Simon, leader of the longest and most successful of the revolts (*J.W.* 4.510), is ritually executed in Rome during Vespasian's triumph as a dramatic presentation of Rome's superiority and intolerance for challenge to its superiority (*J.W.* 7.153–55). Hence in asking Jesus if his title is "King of the Jews," Pilate asks Jesus, "Are you the head of the resistance?"[51] The title charges Jesus with sedition against the empire and Caesar. The title encapsulates challenge, threat, conflict.[52]

Moreover, the term highlights the vast differences between Jesus and Pilate over notions of empire that have appeared in Jesus' teaching and praxis. As a king, Jesus rejects imperial staples such as violence (5:38–42; 26:52) and domination (20:25–28). He rejects the exploitation and oppressive ways of kings (6:29)[53] and the hoarding of wealth (6:24–34). He rejects triumphant celebrations of domination through military subjugation (21:1–11).[54] Rather he prefers the way of meekness (21:5),[55] service (20:28), and prayer for God's alternative empire marked by bread and forgiveness of debt (6:9–13). The empire that his words and actions have attested, the βασιλεία τῶν οὐρανῶν (*basileia tōn ouranōn*, 4:17), differs significantly from Rome's in demonstrating inclusiveness not elite privilege, mercy not force, service not domination, wholeness not deprivation.

All of this could be elaborated at length. But it is sufficient to note that Pilate addresses Jesus with a term that denotes a clear alternative to Rome's political authority and its vision of social interaction enacted in its empire. Though this title appears only once in this scene with Pilate (also subsequently in 27:29, 37), it would be a mistake to argue, then, as Bond does, that this single appearance, and the elimination of two of Mark's uses of the title in favor of the name "Jesus," indicates a lessening of attention in Matthew's scene to political dimensions.[56] This title takes its place along with eight uses of the name Jesus. All nine instances point to God's salvation as central to what is happening. And God's salvation involves nothing other than the utter destruction of Rome as God's empire is established in full. The scene is very political and very Roman.

Pilate's response to Jesus' confession is described with a rare insight into a character's inner world (27:14). Pilate "wondered greatly." Pilate "wonders" not because he thinks Jesus is not guilty or not threatening, as some commentators assert. Jesus' responses in word and silence have removed all doubt. Pilate wonders because Jesus has brazenly not denied, both by his words and by silence, that he is a threat to Rome and that, strangely, he is not intimidated by imperial power into trying to save his life. But while Pilate wonders, the audience knows that Jesus is simply acting consistently with his own teaching. To try to save his life would be to lose it; but to lose it in crucifixion is to save it, because it opens the way for the Son of Man to return "in his empire" (16:25–28). Jesus denies Pilate and his imperial system the power to intimidate him into conformity and submission but maintains the challenge of his commission.

Jesus the Christ

The third title for Jesus in this scene rehearses similar material though with a slightly different accent. Twice Pilate refers to Jesus as "Christ" (27:17, 22). Bond claims that the use of "Christ" indicates that it is "the religious significance of Jesus which is at stake" in the trial.[57] But there is no clear religious/political distinction, and certainly not in the term "Christ" that signifies Jesus' commission to a role that is not good news for Rome.

More accurately, Pilate refers to Jesus as "Jesus the one called Christ." The qualifier has Pilate report the claim that the Gospel's audience knows from the beginning of the Gospel (1:1), that it has heard Jesus accept (11:2–6; 16:16) and declare to be revealed by God (16:17).[58] There was no monolithic or widespread expectation for a Messiah in first-century Judaism.[59] At root the term means "anointed" or commissioned. Numerous people were anointed or commissioned or recognized to perform various roles: prophets (1 Kgs 19:16), priests (Lev 4), kings (Ps 2:7), a Gentile ruler to deliver Israel from Babylonian control (Isa 44:28–45:1), a ruler to overcome Rome (Pss. Sol. 17; 4 *Ezra* 11–12). To call Jesus "Messiah" or "Christ" in 1:1 (again in 1:16, 17, 18) is, in part, to make a claim that God has commissioned or anointed or chosen Jesus. But it is also to pose a question, "What has God anointed or commissioned Jesus to do?" The only way of answering the question is to read the Gospel narrative and to observe it giving content to the term. Jesus is commissioned to save from sins (1:21), to manifest God's presence (1:23), to rule (2:6). Most recently, Jesus has talked of his identity as "Christ" in eschatological terms, as the elevated and returning Son of Man "seated at the right hand of Power, and coming on the clouds of heaven" (26:63–64). His coming means the final battle, the defeat of Rome, and the establishment of God's empire in full (24:27–31).

Here Pilate employs the title as a synonym for "King of the Jews" just as it is in 2:1–4.[60] For him it expresses Jesus' political threat of sedition, of claiming power without Rome's approval. And Pilate is right. He correctly understands that the term denotes opposition to Rome's rule and so Jesus must be resisted.

For the audience, the two uses of the term "Christ," like the eight uses of "Jesus" and one use of "King of the Jews," sum up Jesus' God-given mission of establishing God's empire over all, including Rome (24:27–31). Pilate, by designating Jesus "the one called Christ," signals he does not recognize these theological claims. He represents the empire's fundamental opposition to God's purposes, for which there can only be judgment. With these names, the audience is explicitly reminded eleven times in this scene that Pilate and Jesus stand in confrontational opposition to each other as representatives of vastly different systems of structuring human society.

PILATE A POWERLESS PUPPET?

In this judicial-political confrontation, Pilate the governor would seem to have an immense power advantage as representative of Rome's rule and as the one vested with the power of the death sentence. The scene presents him as the powerful figure who, on one level, controls the scene.[61]

1. Introduced as "governor" (27:2), he continues to be so identified in 27:11 (2x), 14, 15, 21. His name Pilate, associated with "governor" from the outset, appears four more times (27:13, 17, 22, 24; also 27:62, 65).

2. Pilate is also the center of the action. The religious leaders bring Jesus to him (27:2) and talk to him about Jesus in making their accusations (27:12). Jesus stands before him (27:11). Pilate initiates addresses to Jesus twice (27:11, 13). The Passover feast is mentioned in reference to the governor's customary action of releasing a prisoner (27:15). Four times the governor addresses the crowds (27:17, 21, 22, 23). His wife sends to him a report about the contents of her dream (27:19). He washes his hands (27:22), releases Barabbas, and hands Jesus over for crucifixion (27:26). Twice we are given rare insights into a character's inner world in being told Pilate's response to Jesus' silence ("the governor was greatly amazed" [27:14]) and his knowledge of the religious leaders' motivation of envy in handing Jesus over (27:18).

3. His power, disguised as benign patronage, is enhanced by the interaction with the subservient, dependent, and pleading crowd. He has

the power to release a prisoner (27:15). He invites the crowd to beg for someone (27:17, 20) that he can "release for you" (27:17, 21), as though he were doing them a personal favor.

4. His power to determine life or death is emphasized by bringing Jesus to him (27:2, 11–14), the reference to releasing a prisoner (27:15), the repeated questions about Barabbas or Jesus (27:17, 21), his sitting on the judgment bench (27:19), the leaders' urging of the people to ask Pilate to "destroy" Jesus (27:20, the same verb as 12:14!), the crowds' repeated demand to crucify Jesus (27:22, 23), and the handing of Jesus over "to be crucified" (27:26).

5. By contrast, both Jesus and Barabbas are presented as totally dependent on him. Both are nonactive characters in the scene, being done to, rather than doing.[62]

6. Pilate is very sure of his power. In offering the crowd an apparent choice to release Jesus or Barabbas,[63] he asks them, in essence, to choose freedom for one of two opponents of the Roman order.[64] He knows Jesus' threat as "King of the Jews," a title Jesus does not dispute (27:11). Barabbas is described as "a notorious prisoner," a description that removes Mark's details about Barabbas as a rebel involved in murder and insurrection (Mark 15:7). But while the details are gone, the association of Barabbas with criminal activity of whatever sort is not. Barabbas poses some unspecified threat to Roman order, just as Jesus does. Pilate invites the crowd to secure the release of one of them. Is he stupid in holding a referendum on preferred means of opposition? Whatever the outcome, Pilate seems confident that his power will not be threatened by whichever one is chosen.

PILATE'S LIMITLESS POWER?
(MATT 27:15–24)

Yet there are also indications that Pilate's power is not so secure and limitless. He has not been able to intimidate Jesus into lying, begging, or recanting in order to save his life, enough to make any true blue imperial official wonder (27:14). And even though he can get the crowd to beg, things seem to get almost out of hand as a shouting match (27:23) and then a riot begin to break out (27:24), just what the Jewish leaders sought to avoid (26:5).

Pilate's powerlessness, however, does not extend, as Weaver claims, to his powerlessness to act on his own convictions. She argues that Pilate knows Jesus is innocent: the leaders act out of "envy" (27:18), his wife says Jesus is innocent (27:19), and Pilate knows Jesus has done no evil (27:23). Yet he proceeds to execute Jesus anyway because of the power of the crowd.[65]

But this view misreads the scene's imperial dynamics and is based largely on a mistranslation of the term δικαίῳ (*dikaiō*) in 27:19 as "innocent." Pilate knows when Jesus does not contest the title "King of the Jews" that Jesus is guilty (27:11–14). He is not "innocent." He claims to be a king (not sanctioned by Rome), talks of an empire, and has promised to return with overwhelming power. The inclusion of Jesus in the referendum for release of a prisoner, a display of arrogant imperial patronage, is not a matter of determining guilt but of deciding the fate of two guilty men. The claim that Pilate knows the leaders to act out of envy says nothing about Jesus' guilt but about their motivation, and it doesn't sway Pilate's decision (27:18).

While Mrs. Pilate's message does not declare in 27:19 that Jesus is "innocent," it does declare Jesus to be "righteous" (δικαίῳ, *dikaiō*). Fundamental to this word is the notion of faithfulness, whether God's powerful and victorious faithfulness to the covenant and people (Ps 98:1–3; Isa 51:6, "salvation") or individuals acting faithfully to relational or societal obligations (Gen 18:19; Tamar in Gen 38:26, spoken by Judah). Her declaration that Jesus is righteous reminds the audience, as this death-sentence scene approaches its culmination, that Jesus is being faithful to his commission as "Jesus," "King of the Jews," and "Christ." He enacts God's justice (3:15), and is rejected because of his threat to the empire, in anticipation of his participation in God's final vindication (25:46). Faithfulness to God means guilt in the eyes of the Roman Empire. And Pilate knows how threatening such faithfulness might be; even his wife attests how troublesome Jesus is (27:19). The dream, prominent in chapter 2 as a means of resisting another tyrant, Herod, underlines for the audience that Pilate the Roman governor opposes God's anointed who is faithful to God's commission.

Why, then, if Pilate is convinced as early as 27:11–14 that Jesus is guilty, does Pilate ask the crowd in 27:23, "what evil has he done?" The usual scenario of "poor weak Pilate" who knows Jesus is innocent but is having his arm twisted by the crowd, manipulated by the nasty religious leaders is not sustainable, as we have seen. Instead, the question has to be interpreted through the central dynamic of the scene, the presentation of Pilate's power as governor. Pilate knows by 27:14 that Jesus is "King of the Jews" and by 27:17 that he is the Christ, guilty of rebellion and sedition. His fate is certain. What function, then, does the question perform?

As governor, Pilate does not know *how* dangerous Jesus is. What fallout will there be in executing him during Passover, the festival of freedom? What sort of following does he have? Who else should be crucified with him? He knows that the leaders are envious,[66] but that establishes only the intensity of Jesus' threat to them, not the extent of Jesus' popularity. So Pilate goes to work with his questions to find out.

The referendum on which prisoner to release offers Pilate the governor a way to assess the extent of Jesus' popularity and threat. The question-and-answer scene in 27:17–23 depicts Pilate *not* trying to decide on Jesus' guilt (already determined), but Pilate assessing the strength of Jesus' support and possible repercussions from crucifying him. The first answer, a call to release Barabbas (27:21), indicates Jesus is not the crowd's preferred option. Jesus does not have great support. The second question in 27:22 ("What should I do with Jesus?") concerns Jesus' destiny. The crowd's call for Jesus' crucifixion is not discouraging to a "weak" governor intent on releasing Jesus as it is usually interpreted. Rather it is most encouraging for Pilate. It again suggests little support for Jesus. Pilate can crucify Jesus as an opponent, exhibit him as a deterrent, and not be concerned about social unrest. His third question in verse 23 ("What evil has he done?") seeks to confirm this conclusion. It does so, not by eliciting any list of Jesus' evil, but with a repeated and stronger cry for crucifixion.[67] This third response confirms the crowd's first two responses but adds nothing new. Pilate is gaining no further information. "When Pilate saw that he was benefiting nothing" (οὐδὲν ὠφελεῖ *ouden ōphelei*, 27:24a),[68] his questioning stops.

Such a reading is supported by three factors. This sense of "benefit" is most appropriate for the verb ὠφελέω (*ōpheleō*) as is attested by its two previous appearances in Matthew at 15:5 and 16:26. Pilate is astutely assessing and controlling the situation for his own advantage. Second, this reading clearly identifies the progression of the scene. In verses 11–14, Pilate establishes Jesus' guilt as a threat to Roman interests. In verses 15–23, Pilate is presented as ruthless, efficient, but somewhat politically astute in doing his job as governor, just as his allies, the Jewish leaders, cunningly do their job in manipulating the people. He knows by verse 14 that Jesus should die. In verses 15–23 he honors the festival tradition and assesses how much damage control will be needed in executing Jesus. And third, it explains why none of Jesus' followers is crucified. Pilate decides that Jesus, while dangerous, does not have extensive support.

Why does he then wash his hands and declare himself to be innocent of Jesus' blood (27:24)? This act does not declare that he thinks *Jesus* is innocent. He knows that Jesus is guilty as charged and worthy of death by verse 14. Rather his action allows the narrative to expose further the self-serving nature of the governor's administration of Roman justice. Having heard the crowd shout twice for Jesus' crucifixion, Pilate in this action now *places the responsibility for what he as governor in alliance with the Jewish leaders is doing onto the people.* His hand washing pretends that Jesus' crucifixion comes about because of their demands, not because of the actions of the ruling elite. It foregrounds the people's demand for Jesus' execution and backgrounds the elite's involvement. His hand washing is a disguise that seeks to mask the elite's actions under the crowd's demands.

But the narrative of the hand washing exposes the cynicism of Roman justice, its self-serving nature that masquerades behind claims of maintaining *public* order. Public order, the public good, is shown to mean maintaining the elite's privilege and benefit. Twice Pilate offers to release a prisoner "for you" (27:17, 21; ὑμῖν, *humin*). But though disguised as an act of benefit to the people, it is nothing of the sort. A prisoner's release is an act of the elite's control masked under claims of benefit for and responsiveness to the ruled. It maintains the deception that Roman rule is responsive to their wishes and that they benefit from Roman rule only because it continues to misrepresent the oppressive imperial relationship as one of public benefit. The hand washing and pronouncement of his own innocence are part of the same deception.

The narrative reveals the lies of Pilate's action and words, and of the claim of the "for you" nature of Roman justice. By focusing on Pilate's power in alliance with the religious leaders, the narrative makes it impossible for Pilate to rid himself of the responsibility of participating in and maintaining a violent system that destroys those who resist its claims. The scene exposes Roman justice to be administered by the elite for the elite's benefit. There is no doubt that by Rome's rules Jesus deserves to die. But this scene, in the context of the Gospel story, raises profound questions about the nature of those rules, and in the hand-washing scene delivers the verdict that Roman justice is all washed up.

The final tragedy of the scene comes in 27:25 as the people accept the responsibility that Pilate dumps on them.[69] Such is the extent of the ruling elite's control over the people in this imperial situation. They are puppets prompted by, and in this instance permitted by, their masters to declare themselves masters of this situation. And it is precisely such co-opting that this scene exposes. Jesus is crucified not because the people call for it. Jesus is crucified because the elite engineer it. The scene displays the how,[70] the who (the local leaders and the governor), the why (Jesus' challenge), and the outcome.

But it also casts its judgment. Rome thinks it has the ultimate power in coercing compliance, the taking of life.[71] But the scene reveals its limits, its pretense to have life and death power. Rome cannot keep Jesus dead. In the subsequent resurrection narrative in chapter 28, the worst that the empire can do, as bad as that is, is shown to be unable to thwart God's purposes. Even soldiers and stones (27:62–66), lies, imperial propaganda, and bribe money—a veritable catalogue of elite manipulative strategies—cannot do it (28:11–15). Pilate's power enacts death but it is not the final word, even though so often it seems to be. Ironically, the death that Pilate brings about will be the death of him and his imperial system. The risen Jesus who shares "all authority in heaven and earth" (28:18), not with Rome but with God, will return and Rome's empire will end as God's empire is established in full (24:27–31).[72] Indeed his death that leads to this return is a "ransom" or means of liberation for many from imperial power (20:28).[73] That will be the final exposure of the powerlessness of Pilate, the powerful Roman governor.

In the meantime, Jesus' followers live in this imperial world that crucified him. They cannot underestimate its danger and power. But this account of Jesus' confrontation with Pilate urges them not to overestimate them either. They are to live faithfully, performing the acts and practices that embody God's empire, sustained by the community of disciples, anticipating Jesus' coming. They must not be intimidated by Rome's power, even though they too walk the way of the cross in which to give one's life is a real option.

Conclusion

I N PART 3 I have looked at four counternarratives in the Gospel, four examples of the Gospel's pervasive stance toward the Roman Empire. In
this conclusion I will summarize the argument of the previous chapters and
suggest some ways in which contemporary readers of Matthew and followers of Jesus might be affected by this material. Three brief but significant
conclusions can be drawn from the previous chapters.

MATTHEW AND THE ROMAN EMPIRE

In the Introduction I observed that scholars of Matthew's Gospel have
throughout much of the last century read Matthew as a predominantly religious text and concentrated on the interaction between this Gospel and its
Jewish environment. To the fore has been a debate about its relationship to
a synagogue.[1] Is Matthew's community part of a synagogue community or
has it separated from it? If it has separated from it, why did this parting of
the ways come about? Did it withdraw or was it expelled? Once separated,
does it consider itself still to be part of Judaism or a new religion? I indicated
appreciation for the fine work that has been done on these issues.

But I have also proposed that there is a further aspect of the ancient world
from which Matthew's Gospel originated that has been much neglected by
Matthean scholars and that requires exploration. How does the Gospel interact with the world of Roman imperialism? I proposed in this book to
explore aspects of this imperial context and of the Gospel's presentation of
Jesus to see what connections between the two might exist. In chapters 1–3,
I sketched—with very large brush strokes—something of the structures and
commitments of the imperial world.

I have argued throughout that attention to this imperial context opens
up crucial dimensions of the Gospel's content. It shows the Gospel to be
resistant to Roman imperial structures, practices, and claims by offering a
social and theological challenge. There is, for example, a startling similarity between key aspects of the Gospel's presentation of Jesus and imperial
theology's understanding of the role of the emperor (chapter 4). Issues of
sovereignty, agency, presence, and societal well-being are important to both.
The Gospel's claims about Jesus are exclusive and suggest that both sets of
claims are in competition. They are not equally accepted and do not eas-

ily coexist. *Matthew's Gospel presents a theological challenge to Rome's imperial propaganda.*

The discussion of Jesus' saving mission in chapter 5 highlighted the antithetical relationship between the two. The world of imperial rule needs transformation. Rome's defeat of Judea and Galilee and destruction of Jerusalem and its temple in 70 C.E. mark Jews as a defeated people who, in the eyes of a number of late-first-century writers including Matthew, were being punished for their sins. But Matthew's good news is that Jesus saves his people from their sins (1:21). In his actions and words, life, death, and resurrection, Jesus has demonstrated the alternative and transformative nature of God's empire. At his return in power, he will overthrow Rome and establish a new creation, a new heaven and earth under God's reign. This is God's empire, for which Matthew's audience is to pray (6:10).

Chapters 6 and 7 confirm the argument by observing the Gospel's concern with imperial power in its citations of Scripture (chapter 6) and in the metaphorical language that presents Jesus' challenge and alternative existence ("Take my yoke," chapter 7). I argued in chapter 6 that the citing of Isaiah 7–9 twice in the opening section of the Gospel (Matt 1:22–23; 4:15–16) invokes a situation of imperial threat from the eighth century B.C.E. somewhat analogous to the first-century B.C.E. situation of the Matthean audience under Rome. The Isaiah material provides three crucial perspectives on imperial power: God opposes it. God uses it to punish sin. God brings salvation from it. In chapter 7, the antithesis between Jesus' mission and the Roman Empire is demonstrated in his invitation to those suffering under imperial demands to accept his yoke, not Rome's, and so live for God's salvation or "rest" from that rule. The acceptance of Jesus' yoke means learning to live a different set of practices in an alternative community.

In these chapters the future nature of God's salvation is evident. It is at Jesus' return in power and glory that "the eagles will be gathered together with the corpse" (24:27–31; my trans.). What does Jesus offer in the meantime? What form does salvation take in the present, if any? In chapters 4–7, I have briefly referred to signs of God's empire that are evident in the present, especially through the formation of an alternative community. This community of disciples of Jesus is marked by its commitment to him and by an alternative set of practices and lifestyles that challenge practices and values of the imperial world. These practices include the continuation of Jesus' healing ministry, the inclusion of those marginalized and of little value to the empire, and an alternative social experience based on service not domination. It is the thesis of various writers such as Rodney Stark and Michael Mann (see chapters 2–3) that the existence and practices of this alternative inclusive, more egalitarian community were key aspects in the appeal of the early Christian movement's resistance to the empire. In addition to its theological challenge, *Matthew's Gospel thus also presents a social challenge to the empire.*

One issue of immediate concern to Matthew's audience is that of paying taxes. Chapter 8 looked at the strange incident in Matt 17:24–27 involving a coin found in a fish's mouth. I argued that this incident concerns paying the tax imposed on Jews by Vespasian after Jerusalem's defeat in 70 C.E. Jesus instructs his followers to pay the tax, but there is a twist. The coin from the fish's mouth portrays God's sovereignty over the tax. The tax is a reminder that God's sovereignty will be established over the earth. Until the final establishment of God's empire, followers of Jesus live in this "in-between," this "in-both" or marginal lifestyle. In the midst of Rome's empire, and in anticipation of its downfall, they live in tension with it, embodying some alternative perspectives and practices.

Chapter 9 underlines the antithetical nature of the two empires in its discussion of Jesus' appearance before Pilate in Matt 27:11–26. Jesus' vision of an alternative social order is quite unacceptable to the ruling elite. The empire strikes back. Pilate performs Roman justice and the narrative displays how washed up it is. Such dangers threaten faithful disciples in their present situation.

I have argued throughout that Matthew's Gospel resists Roman imperialism, and sustains an alternative community of disciples and their practices in anticipation of the coming triumph of God's empire over all things, including the destruction of Rome's empire. I have argued that the Gospel presents a *social* challenge in offering a vastly different vision and experience of human community, and a *theological* challenge in asserting that the world belongs to God, not Rome, and that God's saving purposes and blessings are encountered in Israel and Jesus, not Rome.

AN IRONY: IMPERIAL IMITATION

In exploring this critical interaction between Matthew's Gospel and Rome's empire, I have on several occasions indicated a significant irony that pervades the Gospel (chapters 5 and 7). As much as the Gospel resists and exposes the injustice of Rome's rule, as much as it points to God's alternative community and order, as much as it glimpses something of the merciful inclusion of the non-elite in God's love and life-giving reign for all, as much as it offers alternative economic practices, renounces violence, and promotes more egalitarian household structures, it cannot, finally, escape the imperial mindset. The alternative to Rome's rule is framed in imperial terms. Salvation comprises membership in a people that embodies, anticipates, and celebrates the violent and forcible establishment of God's loving sovereignty, God's empire, over all, including the destruction of oppressive governing powers like imperial Rome. The Gospel depicts God's salvation, the triumph of God's empire over all things including Rome, with the language and symbols of imperial rule.

MATTHEW AND TODAY'S FOLLOWERS OF JESUS

At this point our discussion could end. I have demonstrated a close and vital interaction between Matthew's Gospel and the Roman imperial world. Argument supported. Case closed.

But for many contemporary readers, Matthew's Gospel is not only, or even primarily, a first-century document shaped by its imperial world. It is a text that belongs to a faith community, a text that shapes the lives of contemporary followers of Jesus. Hence the Gospel's advocacy of God's empire and its imitative use of an imperial framework to image the completion of God's purposes needs some evaluation. Is this a good and helpful image for contemporary believers?

The evaluation of the text's concern with imperialism is made more pressing by the observation that imperialism is not a past occurrence. Imperialism—the effort to exert control over others, whether their land, resources, or lives, whether national, ethnic, political, militaristic, economic, social, cultural, religious, personal—has not disappeared from the human community. In the contemporary world there is one superpower that is not shy about exerting and protecting, with military force if necessary, its own interests around the world. The global village with a global economy, contested resources and markets, mass communications, international and ethnic strife, and instant access to many parts of the village by pushing a few buttons or making a few computer strokes is both conducive and vulnerable to such control. And capitalist societies with their constant attention to the bottom line, the making of profit, know very well the imperialist urge of "more for us" at the expense of the rest. Hand in hand with economic expansion goes cultural influence that so often respects no local culture and exports its own values and commitments. And over the centuries, the church, through various mission emphases and political alliances, has been a willing partner in numerous imperialist and colonizing efforts, with disastrous impact on local populations and resources. The Gospel's concern would seem, then, to be both relevant and urgent.

We can compare values in Roman imperial society that are criticized in the Gospel—domination, hierarchy, exploitation, greed for wealth, conquering others—with values celebrated in contemporary entertainment. As I write this, cultural entertainment in this society is dominated by several top-rated television shows that glamorize fundamental acquisitive capitalist values (*Who Wants to Be a Millionaire?* and *Greed*). All are interested in constituting an elite based on wealth. All present the individual gaining of wealth as the definition of human success. All reinforce these values by turning them into games. A third show, *Survivor,* models a society in which each person lives for his or her own advantage, and the "weakest" is eliminated by being expelled. The most productive and most influential dominate the weaker and rule by dismissing them. So much for Matthew's Gospel vision of a society that is inclusive, protective of the weak, merciful, and structured for the good of all!

So what implications does this study of Matthew have for readers who live in this imperialist age, either as its perpetrators or its target, and/or as those who seek to resist it? I will mention two implications briefly though readers of this book will identify others.

Christians and Ruling Powers

Attention to this Gospel's interaction with the Roman imperial world, and reading Matthew as a work of resistance to Rome's empire, *trains contemporary readers to be suspicious of the structures and actions of all ruling powers whether national, ethnic, political, economic, social, cultural, or religious.* By "suspicious" I mean "discerning" or "critical" in evaluating their policies, structures, and actions. By "ruling powers" I mean not only governments but any political, economic, cultural, or religious organization that seeks to impact others in some way. The Gospel is suspicious of ruling powers like kings and rulers and of all religious power (including the community of disciples in chapter 23). It is clear that Rome's empire is not God's. Rome will be destroyed. The Gospel refuses to identify the two, unlike some contemporary Christians who readily identify ruling structures and actions with God's reign and will.

Some will immediately react with disclaimers. "But our world is not Rome's world. We are not a tyranny or oligarchy or aristocratic empire. We are a democracy with liberty and justice for all. Capitalism offers any one who wants them opportunities for wealth." And of course it is right to note the obvious and important differences between our world and the first century. But it is precisely this sort of instant response that Matthew's Gospel cautions us against. To most folks living in the Roman world, the empire and its structures were as natural and normal as our political institutions appear to be for us. One of the functions of Matthew's Gospel is to help its audience evaluate its world and discern the nature and impact of their societal structures and the exercise of power. For example, it claims Rome's empire is controlled by Satan (4:8), and its dominating ways are opposed to God's purposes (20:25–26). These broad-sweeping perspectives were not self-evident. They were not obvious to most people living in the empire. They certainly were not the views of the ruling elite as we have seen. The Gospel trains its readers across the centuries to engage in the same evaluation of and insight into the ruling powers that impact their lives and the lives of others in the world.

The Gospel offers a key criterion for doing this discerning or critical work. Shaped by the biblical tradition's obsession with God's will, especially the prophets, it wrestles with the questions: What impact does the empire have? Who benefits? Who gets harmed? Scene after scene—Herod's murderous rage, resistant religious leaders, healings and exorcisms, warnings against wealth, instructions to take care of one another, the crucifixion of Jesus—expose the empire's self-serving and harmful ways. The poor are harmed, at least 90 percent of the population. The few benefit at their expense. It is a profoundly unjust system. Contrasting practices—wholeness instead of sickness, service instead of domination, providing instead of hoarding, love instead of self-serving reciprocity, equality instead of hierarchy, inclusion instead of exclusion—highlight Jesus' alternative community and empire. For contemporary readers who live in worlds marked by democracy and capitalism, or any other system, the same questions of impact, benefit, and harm must be asked and answered. Do these systems deliver on their claims to benefit all? In a world of aggressive economic imperialism and global markets and strategies, who (and what) is harmed? How do such ruling powers impact people and resources? Do they provide benefits for all or only to a few? Are they empires by another name?

What to Do?

The Gospel does not offer strategies for reforming the Roman Empire. There is no sense of access to the ruling elite or of the possibility of influencing it through a political action committee, petition, or any form of social action. Nor is there any advocacy of armed violent struggle; the disastrous outcome of that approach is very recent with the fall of Jerusalem in 70 C.E. Nor does it propose a defeatist passivity of compliance ("Can't beat it, may as well join it") or advocate complete physical or cultural withdrawal from society in the form attempted, for example, by the Qumran community.

Instead, the Gospel offers its audience, as I have argued throughout, a resistant stance, a marginal existence, an "in-between" or "in-both" way of life, an alternative social or communal experience. This lifestyle consists of a critical perspective, a hopeful anticipation of God's transformative intervention, and a community of alternative practices that seeks to redress the impact of some injustices and enact different patterns of social interaction.[2]

This strategy is available to and embraced by contemporary Christians in numerous locations around the world, especially in times of crisis and threat when a ruling power refuses any accountability or commitment to justice, and tries to eliminate any opponents.[3] But it is not the only available strategy. In a very helpful discussion of church-state relations, Walter Pilgrim, using the work of Thomas Strieter, offers a threefold paradigm of responses that can guide interaction with governments.[4] I will employ it here but extend its application to any "ruling power" including multinational corporations, cultural agencies, religious groups, and so forth.

The first option in their threefold paradigm names the situation of Matthew's Gospel; options two and three name further options that are perhaps more common among contemporary followers of Jesus in this society.

1. A critical-resistive stance is appropriate when the powers are responsible for demonic injustice or idolatry and refuse to be responsible to change.

2. A critical-transformative stance is appropriate when authority errs, but can be realistically moved to salutary change.

3. A critical-constructive stance is appropriate when the powers that be are attempting to achieve justice.

Basic to the Pilgrim-Strieter paradigm is the practice of discernment or being critical. Discerning the power's commitment to a just society, discerning its concern with who benefits and who is harmed, and discerning whether it is "bent on serious mischief or self-assertion"[5] determines the appropriate response. The "critical-constructive stance" sees a partnership between ruling powers and communities of faith for the common good or just treatment of all. It is essentially a subordinationist approach in which faith communities recognize governments as doing the will of God.[6]

The "critical-transformative stance" involves more "critical distancing." Within a basic recognition of a ruling power's commitment to the common good, communities of faith claim allegiance to their own prophetic traditions and distinctive perspectives and commitments to be a watchdog. This critical stance means that particular issues become points at which a power's actions or policies (or inaction and lack of policies) are opposed and an alternative advocated by various peaceful though forceful means. The relationship is one of "constant tension and uneasy peace."[7] The "critical-resistive stance" is more conflictive, recognizing a fundamental difference in commitments. It is not persuaded that the state is committed to a just society. Being an alternative community is crucial to this strategy.

Whichever response seems an appropriate strategy for particular times and circumstances, I would suggest on the basis of our reading of Matthew that it must incorporate both theological engagement and social embodiment. The theological discernment brings a commitment to God's justice to bear on the situation. The social embodiment recognizes that communities of faith must with integrity live their commitment to God's justice.

Visions of God's Future

A second implication concerns how we envision God's future and purposes. I have noted above the irony that pervades Matthew's Gospel. The Gospel opposes Roman imperial power but adopts and imitates the same imperial language, metaphors, and dominating worldview to envision the coming triumph of God's empire over all things at Jesus' return, including Rome's violent defeat. This formulation is understandably shaped by its first-century world. And there is no denying how empowering the vision of the coming establishment of God's just world was, and still is, for many Christians. The removal of all evil, the end of political tyrants, the absence of pain, suffering, and tears, the just redistribution of and access to resources, the acknowledgment of God's life-giving reign are fundamental and good dimensions of the new creation under God's authority that Christians hope for, live for, and anticipate.

But we cannot be blind to the irony in Matthew's presentation of this eschatological hope. It seems clear that in depicting the future violent and forceful imposition of God's empire (13:41–42; 24:27–31), the Gospel has not lived up to its own critique. The Gospel has presented God's empire at work in the present world in terms of mercy not violence (4:23–25), service not domination (20:25–28). In the present, God's authority is exercised on behalf of the weak (chapters 8–9), by servants (Jesus and disciples, 20:24–28) who seek the good of others. Yet in presenting the final triumph of God's reign, the Gospel resorts to the age-old imperial methods of domination and violence! This irony reminds me of several bumper stickers I have seen: I'D RATHER BE SMASHING IMPERIALISM and PEACE CONQUERS ALL. The sentiments are noble but the violent language betrays the dominant paradigm.

So what are contemporary Christians in a multireligious world and global village to do with the Gospel's formulation of Jesus' ministry and God's purposes? *Is there a way that contemporary readers can be faithful to the Gospel's vision of the establishment of God's triumphant empire and to its critique of imperialist scenarios?*

One option is not possible. To collapse the tension between the vision and the critique, to settle for one of the aspects and to ignore the other, is to distort the Gospel message. For example, to be faithful to the Gospel's vision of the future and sure establishment of God's empire might mean, for example, the vigorous proclamation of God's coming triumph. At Jesus' return, God will destroy all those not committed to Jesus. But such a proclamation comes at an enormous price in the present. Part of that price is intolerance of all and any difference. A narrow Christian imperialism dominates all others. Part of the price is also a serious distortion of fundamental aspects of the Gospel's own assertions. The God of mercy who graciously provides life to all including God's enemies (5:43–48) becomes an oppressive tyrant, like Herod and Pilate, ready to smash to pieces all who do not comply. God's authority, manifested in the present among and for the poor and weak, becomes oppressive in dominating all others. The Gospel's vision of an inclusive community of disciples open to all becomes an exclusive community, the elite who maintain their self-interest at the expense of others. That is, the price of such one-sided proclamation is to betray the Gospel's critique of imperialism.

But to collapse the tension in the other direction would be to maintain the Gospel's critique of imperialism and abandon the vision of the establishment of God's just world.

This option would mean eternalizing the struggle against imperialist injustice because it no longer sees God's powerful and final intervention to end oppression and exploitation. In the absence of the establishment of God's reign, there is little hope that the powers will give up their privileges, control, and wealth voluntarily. But the expectation of God's action against unjust rulers and all injustice withers into futile rhetorical assertions that lack substance. Human history becomes hopeless without accountability to God, without the anticipation of any real socioeconomic and political reversal, and shut off from God's determinative intervention. There is no end, no goal, only eternal struggle toward something that will never be accomplished.

To emphasize either dimension, then, at the expense of the other is very problematic. The challenge becomes: How is it possible to be faithful to the vision of God's just world and to its critique of imperialism without resorting to an imperial formulation? Or to rephrase it, *how can Christian readers bring the Gospel's critique of imperialism into play against the Gospel's, and against our own, imperialist hopes for God's triumph?*

While any solution is difficult, and a lengthy discussion is not possible here, I would suggest that one possible solution lies in the direction I will now briefly sketch. At least four problematic elements in this classic Christian imperialist vision need to be reframed. In the interest of brevity I will assert the four problems rather than argue them, suggest an alternative, and develop only the last aspect a little.

One problem in the scenario of the triumph of God's empire is to imagine that it is known now only among followers of Jesus. It is impossible to claim that only communities of Jesus are concerned with a just world. Recognizing a solidarity with numerous communities involved in a quest for justice removes a false totalizing vision.

A second problem concerns *how* we might understand God to be at work. It has been conventional for some to assert that God "has no hands but ours." But while human agency, indeed partnership, in God's work can never be denied, nor is it sustainable to assert that God is bound to human hands and agents. Creatures cannot so limit the Creator.

A third problem concerns language. By far the dominant way of talking about God's purposes in Matthew is "the reign/kingdom of the heavens." As I have explained, the language denotes "reign" and "empire." It designates structures of domination, control, violence, hierarchy, patriarchy, elitism. Some have sought alternative expressions that shift the image from the imperial world to that of households and relationships. One option is "kin-dom."[8] This term helpfully highlights alternative communities and relationships, but it fails to express the larger cosmic dimensions of God's purposes.

A fourth problem with the scenario of God's coming triumph concerns the violent means by which God's empire is imposed. This violent imposition is at odds with the way in which the Gospel conceives the empire to be at work in the present in communities of service, inclusion, healing, relieving need, mercy. Of course violence and conflict are part of the present also in the collisions between the imperial system and the alternative communities. But is violence to be the final word in imposing God's empire? That would make God nothing other than a copy of any emperor.

Is there a way ahead? Perhaps we can take hold of these hints from the Gospel about God's present actions and reconceive God's future action in a way that the Gospel itself does not do, not in terms of violence and imposed and dominant power, but in terms of life-giving service and merciful action.[9] Perhaps in faithful acts of imagination and in the embodied actions of alternative communities of resistance we can extend those Gospel hints to see cosmic consequences from God's merciful and life-giving work in making the sun to shine and the rain to fall on the just and unjust. Perhaps we can conceive of God's work as persuasively and mercifully dismantling divisions rather than maintaining them. Rather than destroying opponents in battle, perhaps God's life-giving and merciful work causes them to shrink their military budgets, reduce their military personnel, lay down their arms, and dismantle their missiles, warheads, and silos. Rather than hoarding and exploiting material assets, perhaps God's merciful work will mean that the rich will cancel debts and redistribute wealth. Rather than being driven by opinion polls and spin, perhaps governments will, because of God's life-giving and merciful work, become steadfast in a commitment to the poor, those denied resources and without options. Perhaps because of God's life-giving and merciful action the powerful will abandon the way of domination and embrace that of service. And perhaps, instead of the final violent imposition of God's will and empire, we can imagine God's action as continuing to be such that eventually all embrace and are embraced by God's life and mercy, justice and goodness. Nonimperial terms such as "reconciliation" and "transformation" in the establishment of "God's just world" seem more consistent with the Gospel's vision of God's work in the present.

Some might say that all of that is just a fantasy. Perhaps it is. I would suggest, though, that, it is preferable to a fantasy of violence and domination. Fantasies—of justice, reconciliation, transformation, inclusion—can be very powerful and truly threatening as any totalitarian regime knows. How we conceive of the world affects how we act. How we envision the future shapes our present actions and decisions. Perhaps a vision of God's future in which God acts in ways continuous with how Matthew's Gospel sees God acting in the present, a future shaped by God's life-giving and reconciling mercy (5:43–45), may motivate God's people to "greater righteousness," to consistent acts of justice that embody God's alternative order and challenge and question the "conventional norms" of exploitation and acquisition.

And stranger things have happened. A tax collector, an ardent supporter of and an active beneficiary of the imperial system, one who actively participates in sucking the lifeblood out of provincials in order to sustain the elite, decides to follow Jesus (Matt 9:9). Whoever would have thought that could happen? Tax collectors are primary agents of imperial control. Without them, there can be no imperial system. And amazingly, some soldiers, active agents of Rome's militaristic power that subjugates and intimidates, the very basis of empire, recognize Jesus, not the emperor, as God's agent (27:54). Without soldiers there can be no large-scale acts of aggression against other peoples. Without an imperial mindset there can be reconciliation and transformation.

And God, despite everything else, has not run out of patience, and continues to send sun and rain mercifully and indiscriminately on all (5:45).

Notes

Introduction

1. For the relation of Paul to the empire, Richard A. Horsley, ed., *Paul and Empire*; John White, *Apostle of God*.

2. It is novel but not quite unique; for some analyses heading in a somewhat similar direction, Klaus Wengst, *Pax Romana*, 55–72; Walter E. Pilgrim, *Uneasy Neighbors*, 37–80, 98–124; Norman A. Beck, *Anti-Roman Cryptograms*, 93–117; for a more general discussion with a primary interest in Paul, David W. J. Gill, "Roman Empire."

3. For example, Graham Stanton, *Gospel*; Anthony J. Saldarini, *Matthew's Christian-Jewish Community*; Warren Carter, *Matthew: Storyteller*, 80–96, and the literature cited there.

4. Janice C. Anderson, *Matthew's Narrative Web*.

5. Peter J. Rabinowitz, "Whirl without End," 85; idem, *Before Reading*, 15–46; idem, "Truth in Fiction"; Warren Carter and John Paul Heil, *Matthew's Parables*, 9–17; Carter, *Matthew: Storyteller*, 1–115.

6. Wolfgang Iser, *Implied Reader*; idem, *Act of Reading*; Hans R. Jauss, *Toward an Aesthetic of Reception*.

7. I have just summarized the main sections of *Matthew: Storyteller*, Part One: Before Reading. I recognize that differences in gender and social status would have an impact on the realization of the text, hence my parenthetical reference above to "in diverse ways." But methodologically I am not persuaded that we know enough detailed information about these aspects of the Matthean community to formulate some sense of how they might affect an authorial audience's interaction with the text.

8. Stanton, *Gospel*, 73–76.

1. Constructing the Roman Imperial System

1. I sustain this claim in ch. 3.

2. J. S. Richardson, "*Imperium Romanum*," 1, 5.

3. Richardson, "*Imperium Romanum*," 8.

4. Edward W. Said, *Culture and Imperialism*, 9.

5. John H. Kautsky, *Politics*; see also Gerhard E. Lenski, *Power*, 189–296; Peter Garnsey and Richard Saller, *Roman Empire*; Richard Alston, *Aspects*, 208–318.

6. Michael Mann, "Roman Territorial Empire," *Sources of Social Power*, 250–300, esp. 250, 260.

7. J. Rufus Fears, "Nero"; Alston, *Aspects*, 248–52; Fergus Millar, ed., *Roman Empire*, 33–51.

8. Peter A. Brunt, *Roman Imperial Themes*, 53–95, 163–87, 215–54; Austin and N. Rankov, *Exploratio*, 123–25, 142–84; G. P. Burton, "Proconsuls."

9. See V. Nutton, "Beneficial Ideology"; Peter Garnsey, "Rome's African Empire"; Martin Goodman, *Ruling Class;* Brunt, *Roman Imperial Themes,* 267–81; 282–87.

10. K. C. Hanson and Douglas E. Oakman, *Palestine,* 19–99; Richard P. Saller, *Personal Patronage;* Garnsey and Saller, *Roman Empire,* 148–59; Alston, *Aspects,* 217–26.

11. Kautsky, *Politics,* 235–38; for Claudius, Thomas F. Carney, *Shape of the Past,* 285–304.

12. Alston, *Aspects,* 129–36, 181–84.

13. Austin and Rankov, *Exploratio,* 136–37.

14. Lenski, *Power,* 210–212.

15. Kautsky, *Politics,* 6, 144–55.

16. Lenski, *Power,* 210; Alston, *Aspects,* 227–45; 265–88.

17. Lenski, *Power,* 51, 195; Said, *Culture and Imperialism,* xii–xiii, 78.

18. Tessa Rajak, "Friends, Romans," 131; Edward N. Luttwak (*Grand Strategy,* 4) illustrates the role of "coercive diplomacy" whereby the *possibility* of Roman military action compels and maintains submission by discussing the attack on Masada. For further discussion, John Rich and Graham Shipley, *War and Society.*

19. Mattern, *Rome and the Enemy.*

20. Kautsky, *Politics,* 150.

21. Lenski, *Power,* 58, 200, 214, 217–19.

22. Richard Bauckham, "Economic Critique"; Carney, *Shape of the Past,* 285–304.

23. D. J. Mosley, "Calgacus."

24. Klaus Wengst, *Pax Romana,* 19–26; Geraldo Zampaglione, *Idea of Peace,* 155–69.

25. Stephen Dyson, "Native Revolts."

26. Peter Garnsey, *Social Status;* Wengst, *Pax Romana,* 37–40.

27. Kautsky, *Politics,* 161, 169–229.

28. Brunt, *Roman Imperial Themes,* 291–300, 440–46, 468–77.

29. Saller, *Personal Patronage;* Hanson and Oakman, *Palestine,* 70–86.

30. Lenski, *Power,* 250–56.

31. Wengst, *Pax Romana,* 40–44.

32. MacMullen, *Roman Social Relations,* 58–63, 138–41, for example.

33. Lenski, *Power,* 243–48.

34. Saldarini, *Pharisees,* 35–49; Lenski, *Power,* 256–66.

35. Lenski, *Power,* 250–56; MacMullen, *Roman Social Relations,* 88–120; Carney, *Models of the Past,* 98–101; Brunt, "Labor."

36. Wengst, *Pax Romana,* 7–11; Peter Garnsey, "Peasants."

37. Lenski, *Power,* 267; Douglas E. Oakman, *Jesus and the Economic Questions,* 72.

38. Lenski, *Power,* 271.

39. Lenski, *Power,* 278–80.

40. Thomas Wiedemann, *Greek and Roman Slavery.*

41. J. M. Barbalet, "Power and Resistance."

42. Kautsky, *Politics,* 49–75, 230–46, 273–319.

43. Michael Mann, *Sources of Social Power,* 7; Stewart Clegg, *Frameworks,* 218–23.

44. Lenski, *Power,* 273–78; Brent D. Shaw, "Bandits"; Richard A. Horsley and John S. Hanson, *Bandits, Prophets;* Hanson and Oakman, *Palestine,* 86–91.

45. James C. Scott, *Weapons of the Weak,* 28–47.

46. Lenski, *Power,* 280–284.

47. Mann, *Sources of Social Power,* 1–33, 250–300.

2. Roman Imperial Theology

1. Simon R. Price, *Rituals and Power,* 247–48.

2. Klaus Wengst, *Pax Romana,* 46–51.

3. J. Rufus Fears, "Cult of Jupiter," 7–9.

4. Lilly R. Taylor (*Divinity,* 1–34, 239–46) traces Persian, Egyptian, and Hellenistic (especially Alexander) practices that Julius Caesar and Augustus imitate, preparing for the imperial cult of subsequent emperors. Fears (*Princeps*) discusses Oriental, Hellenic, early, republican and imperial Roman understandings. See also Dominique Cuss, *Imperial Cult,* 23–35.

5. Richard Alston, *Aspects,* 145–90; Brian W. Jones, *Emperor Titus;* Jones, *Emperor Domitian.*

6. For a description, See Josephus, *J.W.* 7.120–57.

7. Edwin S. Ramage, "Denigration," 209–14. For Vespasian and Augustus, Kenneth Scott, *Imperial Cult* 25–32; Jean Gagé, "La théologie," 11–13.

8. Fears (*Princeps,* 10–12, 189–205) rightly distinguishes official (documents, coins, works of art) and nonofficial expressions of this ideology. My quest is not for the historical Vespasian or Domitian, but for a widespread cluster of understandings (divine favor, election, presence, protection, and agency) that recognizes divine sanction for the emperor's role in ensuring the well-being of the ruled. For discussion, Scott, *Imperial Cult;* Gagé, "La théologie."

9. Scott, *Imperial Cult,* 1–19.

10. Key scenes include Tacitus, *Hist.* 1.10; 2.1, 78; Suetonius, *Vesp.* 5; Dio Cassius 64.8.1–2; 65.1.1–4.

11. Fears, "Cult of Virtues," 828; Harold L. Axtell, *Deification of Abstract Ideas;* Cicero, *De Natura Deorum* 2.60–62.

12. Fears, "Theology of Victory"; Gagé, "La théologie."

13. Larry J. Kreitzer, *Striking New Images,* 139–40.

14. Ronald Mellor ("Goddess Roma," 995–96) notes that Vespasian rarely employs *Roma.*

15. Scott, *Imperial Cult,* 28–31.

16. Fears, "Cult of Virtues," 2.899.

17. Fears, "Theology of Victory," 2.737–49. Cicero (*Pro Leg. Man.,* 47–49) recognizes divine favor (*felicitas*) in granting military success. Fears ("Theology," 2.797–801) claims Cicero's work is a "primary source for the role and imagery of the theology of victory in Hellenistic panegyric."

18. Scott, *Imperial Cult,* 25–28, 32; Fears, "Theology of Victory," 2.813; Ramage, "Denigration," 211–13.

19. Wengst, *Pax Romana,* 7–26, misquoted because Tacitus refers to the deaths

of Roman soldiers, not of those conquered by Rome as part of Rome's military strategy.

20. For catalogues, Fears, "Cult of Virtues," 2.899–900; Fears, "Theology of Victory," 2.813. For explanation of each deity, Axtell, *Deification of Abstract Ideas*.

21. Cuss, *Imperial Cult*, 61; Paul Bureth, *Les Titulatures*, 38.

22. Scott, *Imperial Cult*, 32–33; Fears, *Princeps*, 115.

23. Price ("Gods and Emperors," 79, 83, 94) argues that *divus* "applies only to dead emperors"; θεός is not functionally equivalent, but designates the living emperor "in an ambivalent position, higher than mortals but not fully the equal of the gods." Fears (*Princeps*, 98) notes Cicero's *functional* use of *divinus* and *deus* to emphasize the ruler's displays of power, which benefit individuals and the state. For discussion of apotheosis, Kreitzer, *Striking New Images*, 69–98.

24. Fears, "Virtue," 2.901; Scott, *Imperial Cult*, 51–52, 55–60, 61–72, 119–22. For Martial's treatment of the Flavians, especially Titus, and his "hierarchical vision of imperial society as it should be," J. P. Sullivan, *Martial, passim*, esp. 115–45.

25. Scott, *Imperial Cult*, 91–96; Fears, "Cult of Virtues," 901–902.

26. This is not to deny that there is some evidence for improved living conditions throughout the first century for some of "the masses." Michael Mann (*Sources*, 265–67) points to improved crop yields and agricultural techniques, trade, levels of material artifacts, population figures. But "improvement" within an exploitative legionary economy in which 90 percent of the population continued near subsistence level to sustain the much higher living standard of the elite is quite relative.

27. Scott, "Statius' Adulation"; Alex Hardie, *Statius and the Silvae*.

28. Scott, *Imperial Cult*, 94–95. Silius Italicus, *Punica* 14.684–85; Martial, *Epigrams* 9.70.7–8; 101.21; 14.34; Statius, *Silvae* 4.3.134.

29. Scott, *Imperial Cult*, 126–32; Jones, *Emperor Domitian*, 119–24, 180–92; Frederick H. Cramer, "Expulsion," 41–46. Contrast Dio Cassius (66.19.1) concerning Titus's refusal to do so, and Nerva's release of those awaiting trial or exiled (68.1.1).

30. Does Domitian depart "from the *moderatio* of Augustus, Tiberius, Claudius, Vespasian, and return to the ways of Caligula and to some extent of Nero..." and demand, contrary to the Senate's concerns, to be worshipped as a god, as Scott (*Imperial Cult*, 89) claims? Certainly a number of writers make such claims.

Martial (*Epigrams* 1.70.6) and Suetonius (*Dom.* 13.2) note images in front of his palace. Reports indicate him demanding to be addressed as "our Master/Lord and God" (*Dominus et deus noster*) in letters, conversation, and public gatherings (Suetonius, *Dom.* 13; Statius, *Silvae* 1.6.81–84; Dio, 67.5.7; δεσπότης καλούμενος καὶ θεός, cf. 67.13.4). Whatever Domitian's *actual* attitude, others use this language when referring to him. Martial calls him *dominus* and/or *deus* (*Epigrams* 5.5.2–4; 5.8.1–2; 7.2.1–6; 7.5.1–6; 9.66.3, etc.), and prays to him as a god (*Epigrams* 7.60.9). Inscriptions and coins from the east identify Domitian (as well as Vespasian and Titus) as θεός, υἱὸς θεοῦ, σωτήρ, εὐεργέτης, and κύριος. See Scott, *Imperial Cult*, 96–98, 109; Cuss, *Imperial Cult*, 61 n. 2, for references to Nero, Vespasian and Domitian as κύριος; as θεός, Michael McCrum and Arthur G. Woodhead, *Select Documents*, nos. 136, 137. Also Adolf Deissmann, *Light*, 353–61; Caligula (Philo, *Legat.* 4.1), Vespasian (Josephus, *J.W.* 3.459; 7.71) and Titus (Josephus, *J.W.* 4.112–13) are called σωτήρ καὶ εὐεργέτης; for inscriptions, Deissmann, *Light*, 368–69; for υἱός θεοῦ, Cuss,

Imperial Cult, 71–74; Bureth, *Les Titulatures,* 38–45. But there are two correctives. Martin P. Charlesworth (*Documents,* 3–5) cites a letter to Alexandria; the (added) introduction calls Claudius τοῦ θεοῦ ἡμῶν Καισαρος even though Claudius declines such honors in the letter (also Charlesworth, " 'Deus Noster Caesar' "). Suetonius's claims are widely doubted for polemical reasons; see Fears, *Princeps,* 190–91; Jones, *Emperor Domitian,* 108–9.

31. Scott, "Statius' Adulation," 250–51, 255.

32. Scott, *Imperial Cult,* 113–25.

33. Scott, *Imperial Cult,* 166–88; Leslaw Morawiecki, "Symbolism of Minerva."

34. Fears, "Cult of Jupiter"; for the relationship of Jupiter with previous emperors, especially Augustus, Gaius Caligula, and Nero, its presentation by poets (Virgil, Manilius, Ovid and Horace) and in material forms; Fears, "Jupiter," 56–74. A. M. Taisne ("Le thème," 486) notes that the triumphant emperor as "un représentant de Jupiter en personne" is a standard theme in imperial flattery "de Virgile à Stace, d'Auguste à Domitien." Kreitzer (*Striking New Images,* 77–79) discusses carved cameos that present *divus* Augustus as Jupiter, carrying a *lituus,* "the instrument whereby the will of the god was communicated to his earthly representative," and Tiberius as Jupiter, being watched over by *divus* Augustus on the likely occasion of the triumph of Tiberius's son, Germanicus. A *sestertius* issued in 21–22 C.E. by Tiberius depicts *divus* Augustus in "Jupiter-like pose" (idem, 141); see Scott, *Imperial Cult,* 91–92, 133–38, especially for Domitian and Jupiter.

35. Fears, "Jupiter," 75–76.

36. Fears, "Jupiter," 69–74, esp. 71.

37. Fears, "Jupiter," 81.

38. Fears, "Jupiter," 76–7; Scott, *Imperial Cult,* 92.

39. Tacitus, *Hist.* 3.71–72; 4.53. Tacitus notes the restoration begins with prayers to "Jupiter, Juno, Minerva, and the gods who protect the empire" (*Hist.* 4.53). He claims (*Hist.* 4.54) that rebellions in the Gallic and German provinces were encouraged by interpreting the fire as divine disfavor, "a proof from heaven of the divine wrath" that indicated "the passage of the sovereignty of the world to the peoples beyond the Alps."

40. William McDermott and Anne Orentzel, "Silius Italicus and Domitian."

41. Fears, *Princeps,* 222–26; Ian Carradice, *Coinage and Finances,* 17, 19–20, 24, 112–14, 120, 130, 131.

42. Scott, *Imperial Cult,* 91, nn. 2–3, 5; 92, nn. 5–6; 175, n. 5; Fears, "Jupiter," 78–79; Suetonius, *Dom.* 5.

43. Jones, *Emperor Domitian,* 92; Fears, "Jupiter," 78.

44. Scott, *Imperial Cult,* 139–40; Fears, "Jupiter," 78; Glanville Downey, *History of Antioch,* 100, 103, 179 (rebuilt by Tiberius).

45. Fears, *Princeps,* 134–35; Scott, *Imperial Cult,* 133–38; on the emperor as *Pater Patriae,* "father of the fatherland," Augustus, *Res Gestae* 35.1; for Vespasian, Suetonius, *Vesp.* 12.

46. Martial, *Epigrams* 9.101; Domitian like Hercules will be rewarded by joining the heavenly court (*Epigrams* 5.65.15–16; 13.4). For comparison with "wandering Hercules," Scott, *Imperial Cult,* 141–46.

47. He fights "his first war for Jupiter" (Martial, *Epigrams* 9.101.14) and "wins the wars of Jove and the battles of the Rhine" (Statius, *Silvae* 1.1.79).

48. Fears, "Jupiter," 79–80; Fears, *Princeps,* 222–26.

49. Pliny the Younger (*Pan.* 1.3–6; 5.1–6; 8.1–5; 67.5–8; 72.1–5; 80.4–5; 94.1–5) celebrates Jupiter's choice of Trajan to serve as vice-regent through good government.

50. Price, *Rituals and Power;* P. Zanker, *Power of Images.*

51. In these two lines he quotes from Virgil, *Georg.* 4.212, on the devotion of bees to their king.

52. For two helpful discussions, Tim Cornell, "End of Roman Imperial Expansion"; Woolf, "Roman Peace." While my assessment is largely negative, it cannot be denied that Roman presence brought some benefits to some provincials. Keith Branigan, "Images—or Mirages—of Empire."

53. Woolf, "Roman Peace," 177, 186.

54. For Augustus's altar, Augustus, *Res Gestae* 12; for Vespasian's temple, Suetonius, *Vesp.* 9; Josephus, *J.W.* 7.158–62; Dio Cassius 66.15.

55. Cornell, "End of Roman Imperial Expansion," 152–53; Woolf, "Roman Peace," 181–82.

56. David Braund, "Piracy under the Principate"; Brent D. Shaw, "Bandits."

57. Wengst, *Pax Romana,* 7–11. In a very helpful discussion, he then elaborates, with a good selection of ancient texts, the military basis (11–19), the political claims (19–26), the economic benefits and costs (26–37), the legal privileges and injustices (37–40), the cultural expressions (40–46), and the religious sanctions (46–51) of this peace.

58. For some opposition to Roman militarism, see the discussion of Musonius Rufus, Epictetus, and Dio of Prussa in Harry Sidebottom, "Philosophers' Attitudes to Warfare."

59. Woolf, "Roman Peace," 171, 185–89, for a description of "peace in the provinces."

60. D. J. Mosley, "Calgacus."

61. Stefan Weinstock, "Pax," 45.

62. Geraldo Zampaglione, *Idea of Peace,* 135.

63. Warren Carter, *Matthew and the Margins,* 130–37, on 5:3–12.

3. Rome's Empire, Matthew's Gospel, and Antioch

1. In my book *Matthew: Storyteller,* 15–115, I outline some other aspects of the audience's experience and knowledge, including their familiarity with the Gospel's literary genre, traditions about Jesus, social and religious experiences such as belonging to a minority and marginal community, a recent conflict with and separation from a synagogue, their involvement in creating an alternative community, and their competency to recognize and utilize various narrative conventions employed in telling the story. Their experience of Roman imperial power belongs with these assumed experiences.

2. Ignatius, "To Smyrna" 1:1; "To the Philippians" 3:1; "To the Ephesians" 19:1–3; "Polycarp" 2:2.

3. Richard Bauckham, ed. *The Gospels for All Christians.*

4. For details, see Warren Carter, *Matthew: Storyteller,* 80–88.

5. For more sustained discussion of its author, date, and place of composition, Carter, *Matthew: Storyteller,* 15–34, 35–54, 80–88.

6. Gerhard E. Lenski, *Power,* 200; Thomas F. Carney, *Shape of the Past,* 83–136; Wayne Meeks, *First Urban Christians.*

7. Gideon Sjoberg, *Preindustrial City,* 110–16; Lenski, *Power,* 204–6. For discussion of preindustrial cities, see also John Stambaugh, *Ancient Roman City;* Richard Rohrbaugh, "Pre-industrial City in Luke-Acts"; John Rich and Andrew Wallace-Hadrill, eds., *City and Country;* Rodney Stark, "Urban Chaos and Crisis."

8. Tertius Chandler and Gerald Fox, *Three Thousand Years,* 81, 303.

9. Jean Lassus, "Antioch on the Orontes," 62. The paved and colonnaded main street was, according to Josephus, twenty *stadia* (translated "furlong" in the LCL) in length. Sixty *stadia* measures 10.8 kilometers (so Marvin A. Powell, "Weights and Measures," *ABD,* 6.901). The street, then, was about three and a half kilometers, or just under two and a quarter miles.

10. Stark, "Urban Chaos and Crisis," 149–50.

11. Peter A. Brunt, "Laus Imperii," in *Roman Imperial Themes,* 303–5. For further discussion of provincial governors, see chapter 9 below on Pilate in Matt 27.

12. Glanville Downey, *History of Antioch,* 175, 621–22.

13. Since no figure is available for Antioch, this figure is a guess based on the nine examples that Thomas R. Broughton ("Asia Minor," 814) gives for Asia Minor. The 9 examples span 30 to 650 in number, with 5 being under 100. Since Antioch was larger and a provincial capitol, perhaps the *boulē* was larger.

14. Anthony J. Marshall, "Governors on the Move," 231–46; G. P. Burton, "Proconsuls, Assizes," 104–5. Burton focuses on senatorial provinces because of better evidence, but asserts no "fundamental differences" with imperial provinces (92, n. 2). Fergus Millar, ed., *Roman Empire,* 161–69; Richard Alston, *Aspects,* 256–59. See also ch. 9 below on Pilate and Matt 27:11–26.

15. See the letters between Trajan and Pliny in Pliny the Younger, *Ep.* 10.

16. Eusebius, *Hist. eccl.* 7.30.8–9, cited in Millar, *Roman Empire,* 60.

17. Glen W. Bowersock, "Syria under Vespasian."

18. Donald P. Russell and Nigel G. Wilson, *Menander Rhetor,* 94–103. Menander says that in welcoming the official, the speech must be joyful, praise the emperor, and celebrate the dignitary's virtues and notable actions.

19. Marshall, "Governors on the Move," 231–46; Brent Kinman, "Pilate's Assize."

20. Malalas 10.45–51, or 260–66. On Malalas, Elizabeth Jeffreys, Brian Croke and Roger Scott, eds., *Studies.*

21. Downey, *History of Antioch,* 206–7, with possible archeological support. Malalas, 10.45 or 261.

22. Denis van Berchem ("Une inscription flavienne") discusses an inscription that indicates four legions in the mid-70s.

23. Benjamin Isaac, *Limits of Empire,* 77–83; Brent D. Shaw, "Bandits"; Richard A. Horsley and John S. Hanson, *Bandits.*

24. John M. G. Barclay, *Jews,* 249–58.

25. Edward N. Luttwak, *Grand Strategy,* 57–58.

26. Isaac, *Limits of Empire,* 19–53, and 436–38, for Antioch's role in campaigns against Parthia over the next five centuries.

27. J. Brian Campbell, "War and Diplomacy."

28. Isaac, *Limits of Empire,* 51.

29. Isaac, *Limits of Empire,* 282–91, though much of the discussion focuses on the third century.

30. Isaac, *Limits of Empire,* 291–304, though much of the discussion draws on material later than the first century.

31. For what follows, Naphtali Lewis, "Domitian's Order."

32. Campbell, "Marriage of Soldiers," 154, 159.

33. Isaac, *Limits of Empire,* 2.

34. Klaus Wengst, *Pax Romana,* 27.

35. Isaac, *Limits of Empire,* 276.

36. Stephen Mitchell, "Imperial Buildings," 356.

37. William L. MacDonald, *Architecture of the Roman Empire,* 2.111–42.

38. Mitchell, "Imperial Buildings," 336.

39. N. J. Austin and N. Rankov (*Exploratio,* 163–167) provide plans of several such buildings from various cities throughout the empire.

40. Downey, *History of Antioch,* 204–5.

41. Downey, *History of Antioch,* 175, 190–92, 196.

42. Downey, *History of Antioch,* 169–89.

43. Isaac, *Limits of Empire,* 34–36.

44. Downey, *History of Antioch,* 208; Malalas 10.50, or 263.

45. Mitchell, "Imperial Buildings," 343–57.

46. V. Nutton ("Beneficial Ideology," 209–21) notes material gifts to cities and persons as one of the benefits that elite provincial writers like Aristides and Plutarch celebrate about Roman rule (along with peace, freedom, laws, and a common fatherland).

47. Downey, *History of Antioch,* 181–82, 183, 186–88, 206, 215.

48. C. H. V. Sutherland, "Intelligibility," 54–55.

49. Downey, *History of Antioch,* 166–67, 198, 200.

50. H. St. J. Hart, "Judea and Rome."

51. Larry J. Kreitzer, *Striking New Images,* 136–39; Douglas R. Edwards, "Religion, Power and Politics," 301–6.

52. Downey, *History of Antioch,* 179.

53. For Asia Minor, Simon R. Price, *Rituals and Power;* Alston, *Aspects,* 309–12.

54. Downey, *History of Antioch,* 209, n. 36.

55. P. Zanker, *Power of Images.*

56. Galen observes peasants starving, eating very poor quality diets, and becoming sick. Peter Garnsey, *Famine and Food Supply,* 26, 29.

57. Ramsay MacMullen, *Roman Social Relations,* 49.

58. Carney, *Shape of the Past,* 101–2; Alston, *Aspects,* 227–38.

59. Mireille Corbier, "City, Territory, and Taxation," 234.

60. Wengst, *Pax Romana,* 40–44.

61. I will summarize Stark, "Urban Chaos and Crisis," 147–62.

62. See the discussion of Jew-Syrian relations in Barclay, *Jews,* 249–58.

63. I am following Brunt, "Laus Imperii," in *Roman Imperial Themes,* 316–22.

64. The best discussion is MacMullen, *Roman Social Relations.*

65. MacMullen, *Roman Social Relations,* 30.

66. A. R. Hands, *Charities and Social Aid.*
67. For what follows, Michael Mann, *Sources,* 301–40, esp.306–310, 323–28.
68. Luke T. Johnson, *Writings,* 29.
69. Stark, "Urban Chaos and Crisis," 161.
70. For similarities between these Christian groups and voluntary associations or *collegia,* see John Kloppenborg and Stephen Wilson, eds., *Voluntary Associations,* including Wendy J. Cotter, "Collegia and Roman Law."
71. The term is βασιλεία, *basileia.* It names Rome's empire in Josephus, *J.W.* 5.409. See also Dan 2:37–45, the Babylonian, Median, Persian, and Greek empires; 1 Macc 1:6, Alexander's empire; 1 Macc 1:16, 41, 51, and Josephus, *J.W.* 1.40; 7.40, for Antiochus Epiphanes and the Seleucid empire.
72. Carter, *Matthew and the Margins,* 1, *passim.*

4. Matthew's Presentation of Jesus

1. While I will discuss the four themes separately for the sake of clarity, they are clearly interconnected.
2. I am not arguing the issue of origin here, but the possibility that imperial theology is *one* of numerous sources affecting NT reflection should not be dismissed.
3. Oscar Cullmann, *Christology;* Reginald Fuller, *Foundations;* Ferdinand Hahn, *Titles;* Larry W. Hurtado, *One God, One Lord;* James D. G. Dunn, *Christology;* Arland J. Hultgren, *Christ and His Benefits;* Frank J. Matera, *New Testament Christology.*
4. Richard Bauckham, ed., (*God Crucified*) finds appeals to heavenly intermediary figures unconvincing, and proposes that the starting point for NT Christology is Jewish monotheism. He argues that Jesus is seen to be within the unique identity of God.
5. Adolf Deissmann, *Light From the Ancient East,* 342–84.
6. For an overview, Jack Dean Kingsbury, *Matthew: Structure,* 40–127.
7. Leander Keck, "Toward the Renewal"; Kingsbury, *Matthew as Story;* idem, "The Figure of Jesus"; Matera, *New Testament Christology;* Warren Carter, *Matthew: Storyteller,* 189–228, and literature cited there.
8. David Kupp, *Matthew's Emmanuel.*
9. That Antioch is the likely provenance of 4 Maccabees suggests interest in the struggle with Antiochus ἐπιφανής (*epiphanēs)* among some first-century Antiochene Jews. See Dominique Cuss, *Imperial Cult,* 133–34.
10. For discussion, Carter, *Matthew and the Margins,* 53–66.
11. Bauckham (*God Crucified,* 10–22) emphasizes that the assertion of God as "the sole Ruler of all things" is the characteristic that, along with God's creative activity, constitutes God's unique identity in Second Temple Jewish literature. Bauckham does not discuss the challenge that Roman imperial theology makes to such an affirmation. Matthew affirms this quality in a context that contests it.
12. Georg Strecker, "The Concept of History."
13. John P. Meier, "Salvation-History in Matthew"; Andries G. van Arde, "Matthew 27:45–53 and the Turning of the Tide."
14. In each of the four sections devoted to the four themes, I will provide only a few, brief examples of the theme in imperial theology and in Matthew. A more

extensive discussion can be found in chapter 1 and Carter, *Matthew and the Margins*, 53–66.

15. Ernst Käsemann, "On the Subject," 135. David Sim (*Apocalyptic Eschatology*, 54–69, 204–221, 246–47) locates Matthew's apocalyptic eschatology in local Antiochene crises (synagogue dispute; ethnic disturbances; ecclesial issues) but sees no direct link with Roman imperial power, though see pp. 103–8.

16. On 24:27–31 see the discussion in chapter 5 below.

17. Norman Perrin, *Jesus and the Language*, 16–34; Wendell Willis, ed., *Kingdom of God*; Bruce Chilton, ed., *Kingdom of God*; Chilton, "REGNUM DEI DEUS EST"; Warren Carter and John Paul Heil, *Matthew's Parables*, 36–63; Carter, "Narrative/Literary Approaches," 14–27.

18. Klaus Wengst, *Pax Romana*, 55.

19. Carter, *Households and Discipleship*.

20. The verb βασιλεύω (*basileuō*, I rule) denotes Nero's rule in *J.W.* 4.491. In *Ant.* 18.46, Josephus refers to the "two greatest empires" (ἡγεμονίαι, *hēgemoniai*), Rome and Parthia. Note also the generic use of βασιλεία (*basileia*) meaning "empire" or "kingship" in Letter of Aristeas 15, 20, 24, 36, 37, 45, 125, 187, 245, 267, 271, 286, 291, and T. Job 34:4.

21. For examples, before the emperors Gaius Caligula (Philo, *Legat.* 116–17; Suetonius, *Vit.* 2.5), and Nero (Pliny the Elder, *Nat.* 30.6.16–17; Dio Cassius 62.23.3). For the use of the term in Josephus to assert submission to Rome, and often to Rome's military power, Josephus, *J.W.* 2.359–60, 366, 380; 6.331.

22. Walter E. Pilgrim, *Uneasy Neighbors*, 64–72.

23. Carter, *Matthew: Storyteller*, 119–48, and the literature cited there.

24. God's provision of sun and rain draws on liturgical, sapiential, and prophetic material; for sun: Gen 1:14–19; Ps 19:4–6; rain: Gen 2:5; Job 28:26; Amos 4:7. Hans Dieter Betz, *The Sermon on the Mount*, 316–18.

25. Carter, "Matthew 4:18–22."

26. Daniel J. Harrington, *Gospel of Matthew*, 10–19; Kupp (*Matthew's Emmanuel*, 134–37, 220–24) pays minimal attention to this dimension.

27. Kupp, *Matthew's Emmanuel*, 109–56; 234–40.

28. Michael Mann, *Sources*, 306–10, 323–28, underlines this quest for meaningful (inclusive, egalitarian) community and for meaning and dignity in lives.

29. Philo identifies the diviner Balaam as a *magus*. He refuses to curse the Israelites but blesses them instead and predicts they will defeat Moab, contrary to the wishes of Balak king of Moab (Philo, *Mos.* 1.276; Num 22–24). Note also the rebellion of Gaumata, a *magus*, against King Cambyses. P. Henning, "Murder of the Magi"; Samuel K. Eddy, *The King is Dead*, 65–72.

30. For examples, see n. 21 above.

31. Dale Allison, *The New Moses*, 140–65.

32. Cf. Jerusalem (2:1, 3; 26–27); "king of the Jews": (2:2; 27:11, 29, 37, 42); "assembling" of Jesus' enemies (συνάγω, *synagō*, 2:4; 26:3, 57; 27:17, 27, 62); "the people" (2:4; 27:1, 25); "Messiah" (1:16, 17, 18; 2:4; 26:63); "destroy" (2:13; 27:20); "deceived/mocked" (2:16; 27:29, 31, 41).

33. See the fine article by Marinus de Jonge, "Messiah," *ABD* 4.777–88.

34. See Carter, *Matthew: Storyteller*, 119–48, 189–228.

35. See the data in Tae Hun Kim, "Anarthrous," 235–237, n. 36.

36. See the appropriate sections in Carter, *Matthew and the Margins*.

37. Wengst, *Pax Romana*; Alistair Kee, "Imperial Cult."

38. Carter, *Matthew and the Margins*, 130–37.

39. Carter, *Matthew and the Margins*, 163–70.

40. Mark Allan Powell, "Matthew's Beatitudes," 463–65; Carter, "Narrative/ Literary Approaches," 23–25.

41. Deborah Amos, "The Littlest Victims," *ABC News*, April 13, 1999, reporting on Kosovar children so traumatized by Serbian aggression and war that they could not speak or move.

42. Paul Hollenbach, "Jesus, Demoniacs," 573; John Dominic Crossan, *Historical Jesus*, 317.

43. Carter, *Matthew and the Margins*, 211–14.

44. Hollenbach, "Jesus, Demoniacs," 575; Crossan, *Historical Jesus*, 317; Carter, *Matthew and the Margins*, 123–25.

45. Carter, *Matthew and the Margins*, 123–25, and the literature cited there; also chapter 5 below.

46. Kenneth W. Clark, "Meaning of [Kata]kyrieyein," 207–8.

47. Carter, *Households and Discipleship*, 161–92; on marginality, Carter, *Matthew and the Margins*, "Introduction," 24–27, 43–49.

5. "To Save His People from Their Sins" (Matt 1:21): Rome's Empire and Matthew's Salvation as Sovereignty

1. These relationships are variously depicted. Some (often operating with an inadequate view of first-century Judaism that emphasized human effort and legalism) saw works as paramount; so Hans Windisch, *Der Sinn der Bergpredigt*, 9–11; 46–51, 69, 89–91; Benjamin W. Bacon, *Studies in Matthew*, 47, 88–89; Siegfried Schulz, *Die Stunde der Botschaft*, 157–97; Willi Marxsen, *New Testament Foundations*, 231–48. Others emphasized the priority of God's grace: Gerhard Barth, "Matthew's Understanding," in G. Bornkamm et al., *Tradition and Interpretation*, 82–85, 105–12, 131–37; Edward P. Blair, *Jesus in the Gospel*, 132–37; William D. Davies, *Setting*, 96–99; Jack Dean Kingsbury, "Theology of St. Matthew's Gospel," 348; Ulrich Luz, *Theology*, 150–51, "the primacy of grace" though compare the discussions on 42–61, 146–53; Frank J. Matera, *New Testament Ethics*, 59–63, quoting Roger Mohrlang, *Matthew and Paul*, 80, "the fulfillment of the imperative is a prerequisite for the ultimate full and final expression of the indicative"; Petri Luomanen, *Entering the Kingdom*, 284–86. Yet others have seen works and grace woven together without either having priority: Georg Strecker, *Der Weg*, 166–75; Daniel Marguerat, *Le Jugement*, 215–19. With some modifications, I am following the survey of Luomanen, *Entering*, 7–23.

2. Wolfgang Trilling, *Das Wahre Israel*, 187–198, 212–14; Hubert Frankemölle, *Jahwebund und Kirche Christi*; Blaine Charette, *Theme of Recompense*, 21–62, 165–66; Benno Przybylski, *Righteousness in Matthew*, 105–107; Mohrlang, *Matthew and Paul*, 17–19, 78–81; Kari Syreeni, *Making of the Sermon*; David Seeley, *Deconstructing*, 21–52; Luomanen, *Entering*, 23–32, 42–48, 278–84.

3. Felix Christ, *Jesus Sophia*; M. Jack Suggs, *Wisdom*; Fred W. Burnett, *Testament of Jesus-Sophia*; Pregeant, "Wisdom Passages," Deutsch, *Lady Wisdom*;

Gench, *Wisdom,* passim, 1–33; Luomanen (*Entering*) mysteriously omits wisdom perspectives.

4. Various schemes have been proposed. Strecker, *Der Weg,* Israel, Jesus, Church; Kingsbury, *Matthew: Structure,* 25–39, Israel, Jesus and the church. Some analyses mistakenly advocate supercessionist readings, with the church replacing Israel (e.g., Trilling, *Das Wahre Israel;* Arland J. Hultgren, *Christ and His Benefits,* 69–76, esp. 75–76) and the inauguration of a "new" covenant (Charette, *Theme of Recompense,* 77–78, 162–68; Mohrlang, *Matthew and Paul,* 78–80).

5. Bornkamm, "End Expectation and Church," in Bornkamm et al., *Tradition and Interpretation,* 15–51; Lamar Cope, " 'To the Close of the Age' "; Marguerat, *Le Jugement;* Donald Hagner, "Matthew's Eschatology"; David Sim, *Apocalyptic Eschatology.*

6. William D. Davies and Dale Allison, *Matthew,* 1.174, 210. Robert H. Gundry (*Matthew,* 23–24) says that Jesus the Davidic king "must *act* like a king by saving his people from oppression" but goes on to separate saving from sins from "deliverance from political oppression," and to elevate the former. Charette (*Theme of Recompense,* 87) also spiritualizes the verse. Jesus saves "his own (from a) spiritual rather than physical" exile. Hagner (*Matthew 1–13,* 19) makes the interesting comment that "The natural expectation regarding the significance of σώσει [*sōsei*] 'will save,' would be that it refers to a national-political salvation, involving in particular deliverance from the Roman occupation." Hagner goes on, though, to assert that the situation after 70 c.e. and the phrase "from their sins" renders this an impossible view. "The deliverance from sins is in a much more profound, moral sense and depends finally upon the pouring out of Jesus' blood (26:28)." Wolfgang Wiefel (*Das Evangelium,* 33) and Walter Grundmann (*Das Evangelium,* 69) contrast traditional Jewish endtime expectations for a Messiah who redeems from foreign domination, with Jesus' quite different task that does not involving redeeming people from political enemies but from sins.

7. This contrast with Ps. Sol. 17 and elevation of Matt 1:21 also appears in David Hill, *Gospel of Matthew,* 79; Gundry, *Matthew,* 24; Joachim Gnilka, *Das Matthäusevangelium,* 1.19. A contextual examination of the twenty-three uses of ἁμαρτία in the Psalms of Solomon (including its four uses in Ps. Sol. 17) shows that the Psalms of Solomon are concerned with much more than "deliverance from the oppression of governing powers" (though they are very concerned with that), and are very concerned with sin between people and God, as well as among people. That is, the Psalms do not sustain the posited separation of forgiveness of sins and deliverance from political oppression, but include both in God's saving work, as does Matthew. Pierre Bonnard (*L'Évangile selon Saint Matthieu,* 21) is almost a lone voice in protesting this typical (mis)use of Ps. Sol. 17, calling it "une mauvaise habitude." On diverse messianic expectations, James H. Charlesworth, ed., *Messiah.*

8. Eschatological approaches pay minimal or no attention to Rome: David Sim, *Apocalyptic Eschatology,* 102–109; Marguerat, *Le Jugement,* 503–6; Bornkamm, "End-Expectation"; Hagner, "Matthew's Eschatology."

9. For the "authorial audience," see the Introduction. Also Peter J. Rabinowitz, "Whirl without End"; idem, *Before Reading,* 15–46; Warren Carter, *Matthew: Storyteller,* 15–115; Warren Carter and John Paul Heil, *Matthew's Parables,* 8–17; Carter, "Narrative/Literary Approaches."

10. Examples abound. Luomanen (*Entering*, 51–58) superficially dismisses "the modern literary approach" (52; note the misleading singular!) and begins with 5:17–20 as the first reference to "entering the reign." But surely Matt 1–5:16 including particular sections (1:21 "save" and 4:18–22 "follow") contribute something.

11. On an audience's assumed knowledge, Powell, "Expected and Unexpected Readings"; Carter, *Matthew: Storyteller*, 1–115, though regrettably I omit the experience of Roman imperialism. See chapters 1 and 2 above for this experience.

12. Menakhem Perry, "Literary Dynamics." Studies of the Gospel's plot attribute a prime role to 1:21 and 1:18–25. Powell, "The Plot and Subplots," 195–99; Carter, *Matthew: Storyteller*, 149–75.

13. To recall chapters 1 and 2 might be helpful at this point.

14. Klaus Wengst, *Pax Romana*, 21.

15. David R. Bauer, "Literary and Theological Function."

16. Recall my thesis that Matthew's Gospel is in part a work that inspires religiously based, nonviolent opposition to the empire through an alternative commitment to God's empire manifested by Jesus, and in a community with a corresponding set of practices. Carter, *Matthew and the Margins*, "Introduction." See also Ramsey MacMullen, *Enemies of the Roman Order*, 95–162; Arnaldo Momigliano, "Preliminary Remarks"; Glen W. Bowersock, "Mechanics of Subversion"; Edward W. Said, *Culture and Imperialism*, 191–281.

17. Carter, *Matthew and the Margins*, 53–66, and the literature cited there.

18. Carter, " 'Solomon in all his glory,' " 11, and nn. 27–28.

19. God's purposes involve significant figures like Abraham and David, as well as nobodies who leave no trace in the traditions (1:3b–4, 13–15). On the elite's exploitation of the rest, Wengst, *Pax Romana*, 19–45; Carter, *Matthew and the Margins*, "Introduction."

20. See n. 61 below. "The main battle in imperialism is over land, of course" (Said, *Culture and Imperialism*, xii–xiii, 78).

21. Carter, " 'Solomon,' " 16–24.

22. Josephus designates Roman emperors as βασιλεῖς (kings) in *J.W.* 3.351; 4.596; 5.563; Titus the βασοιλεύς, *J.W.* 5.58.

23. Suetonius, *Vesp.* 5; *Tit.* 2; note also Romulus in Plutarch, *Rom.* 2.4; Cyrus in Herodotus, *Hist.* 1.107–8; Alexander in Cicero, *Div.* 1.23.47; Augustus in Suetonius, *Aug.* 94; Tiberius in Suetonius, *Tib.* 14; Moses in Josephus, *Ant.* 2.215–16. Note the portents of disaster in Suetonius, *Vit.* 3.2.

24. Gnilka, *Das Matthäusevangelium*, 1.19; Alexander Sand, *Das Evangelium*, 47–48. Combining the two readings highlights the faithfulness but incompleteness of God's purposes.

25. An investigation of ἁμαρτία (*hamartia*) clarifies little. In its six appearances (Matt 3:6; 9:2, 5, 6; 12:31; 26:28), the contexts lack specificity.

26. On Hagar, Phyllis Trible, *Texts of Terror*, 9–35. On Abraham's shabby treatment of Sarah, Gen 12:12–13; 20:13; his xenophobia, Gen 12:10–20; 20:8–18. Sarah claims to be wronged by Abraham (Gen 16:6), and Abimelech protests his wrong actions (Gen 20:9).

27. For βασιλεία as "empire," Dan 2:37–45 (Babylonian, Median, Persian, Greek empires), 1 Macc 1:6 (Alexander), 1 Macc 1:16, 41, 51; Josephus, *J.W.* 1.40; 7:40 (Antiochus Epiphanes/Seleucids); Josephus, *J.W.* 5.409 (Rome and Vespasian);

Appian, *Bell. Civ.* 2.86 (Hadrian). As noted, Josephus designates Roman emperors as βασιλεῖς (kings) in *J.W.* 3.351; 4.596; 5.563; Titus the βασιλεύς, *J.W.* 5.58.

28. In Philostratus, *Vit. Apoll.* 1.15, civil conflict and famine result from manipulation and hoarding. One of Trimalchio's guests comments that with high prices and shortages, the "jaws of the upper classes" do well while "the little people come off badly" (Petronius, *Satyricon,* 44). Peter Garnsey, *Famine and Food Supply.*

29. Paul Hollenbach, "Jesus, Demoniacs"; John P. Brown, "Techniques of Imperial Control"; Gerd Theissen, *Miracle Stories,* 231–64; Walter Wink, *Unmasking the Powers,* 43–52.

30. Jesus resists amassing wealth (6:19–34; 11:8; 13:19; 23:5–7) and urges redistribution of resources in non-repayable loans (5:42) and almsgiving without patron-client reciprocity (6:2–4). Carter, *Matthew and the Margins;* Sharon Ringe (*Jesus, Liberation,* 33–90) links these practices to Jesus' Jubilee vision; Michael Crosby, *House of Disciples,* 147–70.

31. Bruce J. Malina, "Wealth and Property."

32. See chapter 7 below on 17:24–27.

33. Sjef van Tilborg, *Jewish Leaders,* 1–6; Kingsbury, "Developing Conflict"; Carter, *Matthew: Storyteller,* 229–31. It has often been noted that the Gospel overlooks differences among these groups to ally them against Jesus.

34. One exception is Anthony J. Saldarini, *Pharisees.* Utilizing the work of Lenski, Kautsky, and Eisenstadt, Saldarini correctly locates the religious leaders among the governing and retainer classes (*Pharisees,* 35–49, esp. 40–41, and 157–73 for Matthew).

35. Josephus notes that "the high priests were entrusted with the leadership of the nation" (*Ant.* 20.251). He is horrified when in the late 60s, the "brigands" elect high priests who are not from the hereditary, traditional families (*J.W.* 4.147–57). The pro-Roman stance of the "chief priests and notables" is evident in 66 C.E. when the chief priests urge the people's submission to Florus after he had sacked part of Jerusalem and killed over three thousand (Josephus, *J.W.* 2.320), and when they oppose the lower priests for abandoning "the customary offering for their rulers" and urge them to offer them "for Caesar and the Roman people" (*J.W.* 2.197). Josephus sees here "the foundation" for the war with Rome (*J.W.* 2.410), a view he ascribes to the "powerful ones/notables" and chief priests (*J.W.* 2.414).

36. Josephus notes that in 66, "the powerful ones" (δυνατοί, "the principal citizens") assemble with the chief priests and "the most notable Pharisees" to discuss the (lower) priests' refusal to offer sacrifices (*J.W.* 2.411). This alliance sends delegations to the Roman governor Florus and to Agrippa to express loyalty and to distance themselves from the priests' actions. Josephus links himself with the "chief priests" and "leading Pharisees" in *Life,* 20–23; Saldarini, *Pharisees,* 79–198, 277–97. For pre-66–70 Pharisaic political involvement, Josephus, *J.W.* 1.110–12, 571.

37. Josephus links the Sadducees with political power and the wealthy in *Ant.* 13.297, and with high status people in *Ant.* 18.17. At least one high priest was a Sadducee (*Ant.* 20.199). Gary Porton ("Sadducees," 894) notes Josephus's pro-Pharisee stance. Saldarini, *Pharisees,* 298–308.

38. In interpreting sacred texts and representing authoritative traditions, scribes typically exercise a role that conserves the status quo. John Kautsky, *Aristocratic*

Empires, 326–327; Sjoberg, *Preindustrial City*, 230; Saldarini, *Pharisees*, 41–42, 241–76.

39. Lenski, *Power and Privilege*, 256–66; Kautsky, *Aristocratic Empires*, 81–83, 161–66 ("an aristocratic occupation"); Saldarini, *Pharisees*, 35–49.

40. The shepherd image, a common one for leaders (Matt 2:6; Isa 44:28), especially evokes the condemnation of false leaders in Ezek 34 for these offences. Their condemnation is summarized in 34:4: "With force and harshness you have ruled them." The citing of Jer 7:11 in Matt 21:13 functions to condemn them in a similar way. On the function of priests in the temple economy and its political and socioeconomic impact, K. C. Hanson and Douglas E. Oakman, *Palestine*, 131–59. See also ch. 9, sec. 4 below.

41. Wink, "Jesus and the Domination System"; idem, *Engaging the Powers*, 13–137. While Wink's terminology helpfully highlights the conflict of social visions, I have some reservations as the final section of this chapter will indicate.

42. They are "evil" like Satan (6:13 and 12:23; 16:4), and "tempt" Jesus like Satan (4:1, 3 and 16:1; 19:3; 22:18).

43. Carter, "Matthew 21:33–46," in Carter and Heil, *Matthew's Parables*, 159–68.

44. On Pilate see ch. 9 below.

45. So most commentators. For dissenting views, K. H. Rengstorf, "Die Stadt der Mörder (Mt 22:7)"; Gundry, *Matthew*, 436–37.

46. Davies and Allison, *Matthew* 3.197–208.

47. Antiochus Epiphanes, 1 Macc 1:19, 29–32; Pompey, Pss. Sol. 2:1–6; 8:1–5, 19–21; Cestius, the Roman governor of Syria in 66 C.E., Josephus, *J.W.* 2.504–5, 508, 530. See also Adam Ziolkowski, "*Urbs direpta* or How the Romans Sacked Cities."

48. Also 21:12–13, 18–19, 41–43; 23:37–39; 27:25. See the relevant sections in Carter, *Matthew and the Margins*. For Jerusalem's fall in 70 C.E. as God's punishment (though not for rejecting Jesus) enacted through Rome, see *4 Ezra* 3:24–36; 4:22–25; 5:21–30; *2 Bar.* 1:1–5; 4:1; 6:9; 32:2–3; Josephus, *J.W.* 4.386–88; 5.559; 6.40–41, 96–110; 7.323–36, 358–60; N. R. M. de Lange, "Jewish Attitudes to the Roman Empire"; Philip F. Esler, "God's Honour and Rome's Triumph"; Jacob Neusner, "Judaism in a Time of Crisis."

49. Compare Josephus, "God indeed long since had sentenced (the temple) to the flames" (*J.W.* 6.250; cf. 2.539; 6.110); P. Bilde, "Causes."

50. For example, Davies and Allison, *Matthew*, 1.209; Hagner, *Matthew*, 1.19; Gundry, *Matthew*, 23; Sand, *Das Evangelium*, 48.

51. John M. Foley (*Immanent Art*, 1–60) identifies the metonymic function of citations as part of the "traditional referentiality" of oral/aural texts. See the discussion of Matt 1:23 and 4:15–16 in the next chapter for elaboration.

52. About one-third of the approximately one hundred uses of the verb λυτρόω (*lutroō*) in the Septuagint designate redemption from Egypt and Babylon. Many of the uses in the Psalms (about one-fifth of the verb's appearances) designate contextually unspecified, personal or national redemptions. The other significant group of references comes in Leviticus to denote cultic redemption of people and property.

53. Note also Philo (*Mut.* 12.121); "Jesus is interpreted salvation of the Lord, a name for the best possible state."

54. Norman Gottwald, *The Tribes of Yahweh*. Without any explanation, Douglas R. A. Hare (*Matthew*, 11) asserts a *contrast* between Joshua who "saved Israel from their Gentile enemies" and Jesus who "will save his people from their sins."

55. Jesus rejects violent resistance in Matt 5:38–42. Wink, "Neither Passivity nor Violence"; idem, *Engaging the Powers*, 175–257. But his return is another story (sec. VII-VIII).

56. Dominique Cuss, *Imperial Cult*, 134–40, and 139 for Domitian. Antiochus Epiphanes is probably the best known (see 1 Macc 1). For another example, see Philo, *Legat.*, 346, for the emperor Gaius Caligula's claim that he is "Zeus made manifest."

57. See ch. 6 below for a developed discussion.

58. Davies and Allison, *Matthew*, 1.210.

59. Neither σωτήρ nor σωτηρία (*sōtēria*, salvation) appears in Matthew. σωτήρ (*sōtēr*, savior) commonly designates emperors: Josephus, *J.W.* 3.459; 7.71; Adolf Deissmann, *Light From the Ancient East*, 368–69. The verb σώζω (*sōzō*, save) designates Rome's favor experienced in not being destroyed and by submitting to Roman rule (Josephus, *J.W.* 1.27; 1.391; 2.421; 5.360–61, 373).

60. Carter, *Matthew: Storyteller*, 119–48.

61. Sim, "Meaning of παλιγγενεσία," and Gnilka, *Matthäusevangelium*, 2.172. For heaven and earth passing away, 5:18; 24:35. The beatitude (5:5, inheriting land) promises a new earth not dominated by Rome (Carter, *Matthew and the Margins*, 5:3–12). For the renewal of heaven and earth in Jewish apocalyptic texts, Sim, *Apocalyptic Eschatology*, 50, 111–14 (*4 Ezra, 2 Bar.*, 1 Enoch 72, 91:16; 45:4–5). There is no textual reason to spiritualize 5:5 (contra Charette, *Theme of Recompense*, 84–91). "The main battle in imperialism is over land, of course" (Said, *Culture and Imperialism*, xii–xiii, 78).

62. For discussion of each aspect, Sim, *Apocalyptic Eschatology*.

63. Davies and Allison list eight interpretations of 24:27–31 (*Matthew*, 3.355–56); none includes judgment on Rome. Larry J. Kreitzer (*Striking New Images*, 30–68) proposes influence of the "Roman legionary *aquilae*" (68) but seems to think Rome's destruction of Jerusalem is in view (61).

64. See Polybius, *Hist.* 18.48.4; Josephus, *Ant.* 19.339.

65. Titus, in Josephus, *J.W.* 5.410.

66. See Josephus *J.W.* 2.617; *Life* 90–91, 273.

67. See Josephus, *Ant.* 12.86.

68. See the further references in BAGD (W. Bauer, W. F. Arndt, F. W. Gingrich, and F. W. Danker, *Greek English Lexicon of the New Testament* [Chicago: University of Chicago Press, 1979]), 629–30; for inscriptions and coins, especially the *adventus* coins of Nero and Hadrian, see Deissmann, *Light*, 372–78; Albrecht Oepke, "παρουσία" *Theological Dictionary of the New Testament* 5.858–61; Kreitzer, *Striking New Images*, 146–86, 212–19; for later Christian uses, Sabine MacCormack, "Change and Continuity."

69. Kreitzer, *Striking New Images*, 66–67, provides examples including an aureus with an eagle clasping a lightning bolt in its claw.

70. J. Rufus Fears, "Theology of Victory," 817. Also idem, "Jupiter and Roman Imperial Ideology," 79.

71. The first meaning in BAGD, 19; Kreitzer, *Striking New Images*, 62–63.

72. Deut 28:47–53, esp. 49; Jer 4:13; Lam 4:19; Ezek 17:1–21; Hab 1:8; Dan 7:4.

73. Ovid laments the shameful capture of eagle standards by the Parthians in 53 B.C.E. Augustus procured their return in 20 B.C.E.(*Fasti,* 585–90). In 66 C.E. Jewish fighters "routed" the Roman governor of Syria and "took one of his eagles" (Suetonius, *Vesp.* 4.5). Herod, Rome's puppet, displays an eagle on the temple gate (Josephus, *J.W.* 1.650–653; *Ant.* 17.151–63). Kreitzer, *Striking New Images,* 31–57.

74. Sim, *Apocalyptic Eschatology,* 103–4; Joel Marcus, "Gates of Hades."

75. Is there any hope for Rome? Apparently for only a few individuals (the centurions, 8:5–13; 27:54).

76. Harold L. Axtell, *Deification of Abstract Ideas,* 33–34.

77. Sim (*Apocalyptic Eschatology,* 227–241) notes violence and "scare tactics" in the eschatological scenes.

78. For revenge in Roman imperial strategy, Susan Mattern, *Rome and the Enemy,* 171–94.

79. See, variously, Seneca, *Clem.* 1.4.1–2; Tacitus, *Agr.* 21; Aristides, passim; the nineteenth-century Englishman, John Ruskin, cited in Said, *Culture and Imperialism,* 101–2.

80. The Gospel is suspicious of human patriarchy, both domestic (19:13–15; Carter, *Households and Discipleship,* 90–114) and political (the empire is an imperial patriarchy; the emperor is the *pater patriae,* "father of the fatherland"; Augustus, *Res Gestae* 35.1; Suetonius, *Aug.* 58; *Vesp.* 12), yet it images God, albeit benignly (5:45–48), as the father whose will must be obeyed (12:46–50). The same irony is evident in kingship language. For some aspects of Matthew's references to God as "Father," R. L. Mowery, "God, Lord and Father"; idem, "From Lord to Father."

6. Evoking Isaiah: Why Summon Isaiah in Matthew 1:23 and 4:15–16?

1. My references to Matthew's use of the Scripture are only to the fulfillment citation. I am not including a whole host of other explicit and implicit connections.

2. For an explanation of redaction and narrative approaches, Warren Carter, *Matthew: Storyteller,* 273–81, and the literature cited there.

3. For example, Krister Stendahl, "School of St. Matthew"; Robert H. Gundry, "Use of the Old Testament"; Wilhelm Rothfuchs, *Die Erfüllungszitate;* Richard S. McConnell, "Law and Prophecy"; George Soares Prabhu, *Formula Quotations;* Lamar Cope, *Matthew.*

4. Rudolf Pesch, "Der Gottessohn"; Franz van Segbroeck, "Les citations d'accomplissement"; Michael Oberweis, "Beobachtungen zum AT-Gebrauch"; Graham Stanton, "Matthew's Use of the Old Testament," in *Gospel.*

5. For example, Georg Strecker, *Der Weg,* 21–30, 49–85, esp. 55–57, 63–66; Alexander Sand, *Das Gesetz und die Propheten,* 151–56; Ulrich Luz, *Matthew 1–7,* 156–64; William D. Davies and Dale Allison, *Matthew,* 3.573–77.

6. For instance, for work on Jeremiah (more extensive than the fulfillment citations attributed in 2:17–18 and 27:9–10), see Michael Knowles, *Jeremiah;* Ron Witherup, "Jeremiah and the Gospel of Matthew"; for the passion narrative, Donald Senior, "The Lure of the Formula Quotations."

7. Notice the absence of any contribution focused explicitly on the fulfillment texts from two excellent, recent English-language collections of twenty-two essays on Matthew spanning the mid-1980s to early 1990s: David L. Balch, ed., *Social History;* David Bauer and Mark Allen Powell, eds., *Treasures New and Old.* This collection contains twelve studies from the Matthew Group of the Society of Biblical Literature.

8. Narrative work has seen the citations as "commentary" on the action of the plot. So Jack Dean Kingsbury, *Matthew as Story,* 33, "narrative commentary"; David B. Howell, *Matthew's Inclusive Story,* 179, "direct commentary"; Janice C. Anderson, *Matthew's Narrative Web,* 52–53, 59–61, "explicit commentary"; In *Matthew: Storyteller,* 136, I follow Howell and include a brief reference in a discussion of "Maintaining God's Point of View."

9. I am following the excellent (introductory) discussion in Senior, *What Are They Saying About Matthew?* 51–61, esp. 52. See also Davies and Allison, *Matthew,* 3.573–77.

10. There seems to be significant support for the position that the text forms are mixed, deriving from various Greek (LXX and non-LXX), Aramaic, and Hebrew (MT) traditions. Claims of targumic influence (Anton Baumstark, "Die Zitate") have generally not convinced, except in support of the notion that "Matthew was his own targumist" (Gundry, *Use of the Old Testament,* 172–74; Davies and Allison, *Matthew,* 3.575).

11. Stendahl's argument *(School of St. Matthew)* of a school using pesher interpretation has generally not persuaded. Nor has Strecker's argument for collections of *testimonia (Der Weg,* 49–51, 65–66, 82–85). Luz *(Matthew 1–7,* 159–61) has revived George D. Kilpatrick's thesis *(Origins,* 56–58) of oral tradition. But if the author is using traditional material, there would be no need to draw attention to the citation. And greater conformity with the LXX would be likely if the author were not conforming material to his narrative. These factors suggest the author is responsible for the citations he did not receive from Mark or Q. Emphasis on the author's role is evident, to varying degrees, for instance in Gundry, *Use of the Old Testament* (who sees considerable continuity from Jesus); Rothfuchs, *Erfüllungszitate;* McConnell, "Law and Prophecy"; Raymond Brown *(Birth,* 101–4), and Davies and Allison, *Matthew,* 3.575–77.

12. While some have emphasized an apologetic intent, especially in relation to the synagogue (Barnabas Lindars, *New Testament Apologetic,* 13–31, 251–65), most see a didactic intent to sustain the christological claims of followers (Brown, *Birth,* 96–99; Davies and Allison, *Matthew,* 3.576–77).

13. For the notion of authorial audience, see the Introduction; also Peter J. Rabinowitz, "Whirl without End," 85; idem, *Before Reading,* 15–46; idem, "Truth in Fiction"; Carter and Heil, *Matthew's Parables,* 9–17. For a focus on actual audiences, Fernando Segovia, " 'And they began to speak' "; idem, "Cultural Studies and Contemporary Biblical Criticism."

14. Lars Hartman, "Scriptural Exegesis."

15. Richard France, "Formula-Quotations." On a communication model, Mark Allen Powell, "What is 'Literary' About Literary Aspects?" 40–48; Anderson, *Matthew's Narrative Web,* 34–44.

16. John M. Foley, *Immanent Art,* 1–60. Foley works especially with Homer

and with Serbo-Croatian epic narratives. Studies of orality in relation to the Gospels have often focused on Mark.

17. See the discussion in Dale Allison, *New Moses*, 1–23, esp. 19–20. My focus, though, concerns what an audience does rather than what the elusive author intends.

18. Foley, *Immanent Art*, 38–60; Wolfgang Iser, *Implied Reader;* Hans R. Jauss, *Toward an Aesthetic of Reception;* Rabinowitz, "Whirl without End"; idem, *Before Reading.*

19. For a somewhat similar approach, Wim Weren, "Jesus' Entry."

20. It is widely recognized that 4:17 introduces a major development; Ernst Lohmeyer, *Das Evangelium*, 64, 264; Edgar Krentz, "Extent," 409–14; Kingsbury, *Matthew: Structure*, 7–17; Sand, *Das Evangelium;* 83; Gundry, *Matthew*, 61; Joachim Gnilka, *Matthäusevangelium*, 1.99–100; Carter, "Kernels and Narrative Blocks." I omit the Isaiah citation from 3:3 because it is used in relation to John, is not a fulfillment citation, and does not come from Isa 7–9. It should be noted, though, that by citing Isa 40:3 it invokes another imperial context, that of Babylonian control.

21. Isaiah is named six times (3:3; 4:14; 8:17; 12:17; 13:14; 15:7). Four of Matthew's texts relate to Assyrian imperialism (1:23; 4:14; 13:14; 15:7–9), and three to Babylonian imperialism (3:3; 8:17; 12:17). I set aside the possible use of Isa 4:2 in Matt 2:23, and of Isa 62:11 in Matt 21:5.

22. Luz, *Matthew 1–7*, 157–8, disputed by Davies and Allison, *Matthew*, 3.576.

23. Rothfuchs, *Die Erfüllungszitate*, 40–44; 103; van Segbroeck, "Les citations," 126–28; Sand, *Das Gesetz*, 156; Davies and Allison, *Matthew* 1.292–93.

24. In addition to Rabinowitz cited above, see Iser, *Act of Reading*, and Susan Suleiman and Inge Crosman, eds., *The Reader in the Text;* Sipke Draisma, ed., *Intertextuality;* Richard Hays, *Echoes of Scripture*, 14–19; Dana N. Fewell, ed., *Reading between Texts.*

25. Menakhem Perry, "Literary Dynamics," 53–58.

26. The term "virgin" restates the information that Joseph and Mary have not yet "come together" (1:18) either for sexual intercourse or residence. It emphasizes the double reference to God's work through the Holy Spirit in conceiving the child (ἐκ πνεύματος ἁγίου, *ek pneumatos hagiou*, 1:18, 20).The audience can judge the Gospel's narrator to be reliable, as is God who acts consistently to accomplish God's will revealed previously in the Scriptures. It can judge Joseph's proposed action of a quiet divorce (1:19) to be inappropriate despite its conformity with cultural practices (cf. Deut 24:1).

27. See, for example, Charles Talbert, "Prophecies of Future Greatness."

28. Compare Ps 2:2, the king; Lev 4:3, 5, 16, a priest; 1 Kgs 19:16, Elisha the prophet; Is 44:28, 45:1, Cyrus the Persian.

29. Gnilka, *Das Matthäusevangelium*, 1.21.

30. The focus in this discussion on Isa 7–9 does not preclude an audience invoking other intertexts (cf. Deut 20:1). See van Unnik, " 'Dominus Vobiscum.' "

31. For example, Pierre Bonnard, *L'Évangile*, 21–22; Walter Grundmann, *Das Evangelium*, 70; Sand, *Das Gesetz*, 151–56; Gnilka, *Matthäusevangelium*, 1.20–21; Daniel J. Harrington, *Gospel of Matthew*, 35–36, 39; Ulrich Luck, *Das Evangelium nach Matthäus*, 21–23; Hubert Frankemölle, *Matthäus: Kommentar 1*, 148–59,

191–95. M. J. Lagrange *(Évangile selon Saint Matthieu,* 16) sees no reference to Isaiah's time in Isa 7:14.

32. W. C. Van Unnik, " 'Dominus Vobiscum,' " 287; Pesch, "Gottessohn," 403–11; Gundry, *Matthew,* 24; Sand, *Das Gesetz,* 153–56.

33. Rothfuchs's claim *(Die Erfüllungszitate,* 40–44) that Matthew omits the name "Isaiah" in 1:22 because he wishes to associate Isaiah's name with Jesus' saving work in Israel (so 4:14; 8:17) makes little sense given that 1:22 follows the commission of 1:21.

34. I have justified elaborating Isa 7–9 on the basis of the metonymic function of 1:23, the phrase "through the prophet," and the audience's experience of 1:1–17. Alternately, or in addition, one could "justify" elaborating Isa 7–9 by invoking the notion of play, "What happens if . . . "

35. For some contemporary scholarly readings of the difficult Isa 7–8, Andrew H. Bartelt, *The Book Around Immanuel,* 114–31; Hans Wildberger, *Isaiah 1–12,* 279–396; Stuart A. Irvine, *Isaiah, Ahaz;* Ronald E. Clements, *Isaiah 1–39,* 78–106; Otto Kaiser, *Isaiah 1–12,* 86–127.

36. The identities of child and mother have been extensively debated. See Irvine, *Isaiah, Ahaz,* 159–71; his view, represented here, is that the woman is "a wife of Ahaz, whose son (perhaps Hezekiah) would represent the future of the Davidic dynasty" (169; also Wildberger, *Isaiah 1–12,* 306–14). Clements *(Isaiah 1–39,* 85–88) identifies the child as the prophet's son.

37. Scholars have often noted Mosaic-exodus echoes in these opening chapters. See Allison, *New Moses,* 140–65.

38. See for example Jer 4; 6:16–26; 21:1–10; 31: Deut 28:15–68; 29:24–29; 1 Kgs 8:46–53; 2 Kgs 21:10–16; Isa 44:28–45:1. R. W. Klein, *Israel in Exile.*

39. I do not mean from this comment that the audience knows nothing about the rest of the story. In *Matthew: Storyteller,* 55–76, I argue that the audience knows extensive traditions about Jesus. My point here is that in a context of diverse traditions and claims about Jesus, it must read on here to understand or to be reminded of this Gospel's presentation.

40. Davies and Allison, *Matthew,* 1.210; Gundry, *Matthew,* 23–24; Blaine Charette, *Theme of Recompense,* 87.

41. The debate is well rehearsed; see ch. 2 above and the contributions in Balch, *Social History.* Of course certainty is not possible, but Antioch is at least a viable location. If it could somehow be established that Galilee was the location of the Gospel's audience, the proposed reading would stand. See Introduction, and n. 13 above for the relation of the authorial audience to the Gospel's actual first-century audience.

42. In addition to chs. 1–3 above, Klaus Wengst, *Pax Romana,* 1–54; Glanville Downey, *History of Antioch,* 163–210.

43. This perspective of punishment is explicit in 21:41; 22:6–7 concerning the fall of Jerusalem, and in 23:37–39 with its pattern of sin, exile/punishment, and restoration (Graham Stanton, *Gospel,* 247–55). 2 *Bar.* (1:1–4; 13:2–10), 4 *Ezra* (unjustly, 2:7; 3:2, 28–36; 4:23; 5:28–30; 6:18–19; 10:48), *Apocalypse of Abraham* (25–27, 28–32), and Josephus *(J.W.* 6.99–110) also view the fall of Jerusalem as punishment, but not as the removal of Israel from the status of being God's people (so also Isa 7–9 and Matthew). Michael Knowles, *Jeremiah,* 265–311.

44. For comparable analyses of God's control and future victory over Rome, 4 *Ezra* 11:1–12:30, 31–35; 2 *Bar.* 13:4–12; 40:1–4; 72:2–6; *Apoc. Ab.* 31–32.

45. See chs. 6–8; Walter Wink, "Beyond Just War"; Carter, *Matthew and the Margins.*

46. In addition to chs. 1–4 above, see, for example, J. Rufus Fears, "Cult of Jupiter"; Daniel N. Schowalter, *Emperor and the Gods.*

47. Kenneth Scott (*Imperial Cult,* 107) cites a letter from the proconsul of Achaea to the people of Delphi that refers to Domitian as τοῦ Κυρίου ἡμῶν καὶ ἐπιφανεστάτου Αὐτοκράτορος (*tou Kyriou hēmōn kai epiphanestatou Autokratoros*). On ἐπιφάνεια, see Dominique Cuss, *Imperial Cult,* 134–44.

48. Ramsay MacMullen, *Enemies of the Roman Order,* 142–62, for the role of prophecy in resistance and attempts to control it; David Potter, *Prophets and Emperors,* 171–82.

49. Allison, *New Moses,* 140–65; Dorothy Jean Weaver, "Power and Powerlessness," 456–60.

50. For example, Lagrange, *Évangile,* 67–69; Bonnard, *L'Évangile selon Saint Matthieu,* 47–48; Grundmann, *Das Evangelium,* 105–6; Sand, *Das Evangelium,* 75–76; Luck, *Das Evangelium,* 43–44.

51. See n. 21 above.

52. As Deirdre Good notes ("The Verb"), 4:12–17 is an example of a threefold pattern, hostility/withdrawal/prophetic fulfillment. This pattern appears four times (2:14, 22; 4:12–16; 12:15–21), not seven as Good claims (p. 1). It does not fit 2:12–13, 14:13, 15:21, 27:5. See the nuanced discussion by Soares Prabhu, *Formula Quotations,* 123–26.

53. Note that the magi withdraw from Herod's threatening power in 2:12–15, as does Joseph from Archelaus in 2:22–23. Moses withdraws from Pharaoh (Exod 2:15), and Judas Maccabeus from Apollonius (commander of Antiochus Epiphanes, 2 Macc 5:27).

54. On Galilee under Roman rule, see Richard Horsley, *Archaeology, History,* and 112–18 on Capernaum. Also, Horsley, *Galilee: History;* Sean Freyne, *Galilee, Jesus, and The Gospels,* 70–90 for Galilee in Matthew, and 135–218 for social, political, economic, and religious analysis of Galilee. Also Freyne, *Galilee from Alexander the Great.*

55. Amy-Jill Levine, *Social and Ethnic Dimensions,* 99–102.

56. The claims of scriptural support for a Galilean ministry (Richard S. McConnell, "Law and Prophecy," 117–18; Grundmann, *Das Evangelium,* 106; David Hill, *Gospel of Matthew,* 104; Gnilka, *Matthäusevangelium,* 1.95–96; Davies and Allison, *Matthew,* 1.379–80) or of theologically prefiguring Gentile mission (Soares Prabhu, *Formula Quotations,* 134; Gnilka, *Matthäusevangelium,* 1.98; Luz, *Matthew 1–7,* 195; Luck, *Das Evangelium,* 44; Frankemölle, *Matthäus: Kommentar 1,* 191–94) do not go far enough.

57. Lagrange, *Évangile,* 67–69; Bonnard, *L'Évangile selon Saint Matthieu,* 47–48; Gundry, *Use of the Old Testament,* 197; Soares Prabhu, *Formula Quotations,* 133–34.

58. See, for example, Soares Prabhu, *Formula Quotations,* 86–106.

59. Clements (*Isaiah 1–39,* 106) calls the link with Hezekiah a "reasoned conjecture."

60. This is another frequently overlooked dimension of the text.

61. The phrase is a refrain throughout Deuteronomy, Joshua, and Judges. For example Deut 3:20, 25; Josh 1:15; 22:4; 24:8.

62. Horsley, *Archaeology, History;* Freyne, *Galilee from Alexander,* 155–207, esp. 166–68, 180, 193–94.

63. Freyne, *Galilee from Alexander,* 144. C. H. V. Sutherland, "Intelligibility."

64. See Freyne, *Galilee from Alexander,* passim, esp. 138–45.

65. In addition to the context, the genitive of relationship (Γαλιλαία τῶν εθνῶν; *Galilaia tōn ethnōn*) indicates possession. See BDF (F. Blass, A. Debrunner, and R. W. Funk, *A Greek Grammar of the New Testament*) 162.5,7. For parallel constructions, Matt 15:21 (τὰ μέρη Τύρου καὶ Σιδῶνος; *ta merē Tyrou kai Sidōnos;* "the territories controlled/ruled by Tyre and Sidon"), 16:13 (τὰ μέρη Καισαρείας τῆς Φιλίππου; *ta merē Kaisareias tēs Philippou;* "the territories controlled/ruled by/under the control of Caesarea Philippi"), and 22:21 (τὰ Καίσαρος . . . τὰ τοῦ θεοῦ, *ta Kaisaros . . . ta tou theou;* "the things belonging to/under the control of Caesar . . . the things belonging to/under the control of God"). Gentiles have diverse significance in the Gospel. They are included in God's purposes (for instance, the women in 1:1–17 and the magi in ch. 2, though ethnicity is by no means their only importance; 8:5–13; 12:18, 21; 28:19), yet they also display practices and commitments contrary to God's purposes (5:47; 6:7, 32; 10:18; 20:19, 25).

66. Including the hiddenness and majesty of God (Deut 4:11; 5:22; 2 Sam 22:12; Ps 18:11.)

67. Bonnard, *L'Évangile selon Saint Matthieu,* 48; McConnell, "Law and Prophecy," 120; Hill, *Gospel of Matthew,* 104; Davies and Allison, *Matthew,* 1.379–80.

68. Davies and Allison, *Matthew,* 1.210, 380, also 174.

69. Samuel G. F. Brandon, *Jesus and the Zealots;* Ernst Bammel, "The Revolution Theory."

70. Paul Hollenbach, "Jesus, Demoniacs"; John P. Brown, "Techniques of Imperial Control"; Gerd Theissen, *Miracle Stories,* 231–59; John Dominic Crossan, *Historical Jesus,* 313–32.

71. For Moses, see Exod 19:3; 24:12, 13, 18; 34:2, 4; Deut 9:9; 10:1, 3; for Zion traditions, Isa 2:3; Mic 4:2; Ps 23:3; Hag 1:8; 1 Macc 5:54; 7:33. Carter, *Matthew and the Margins,* 129–30.

72. I am not claiming that only Isa 7:14 and 8:23–9:2 do these things. If space allowed, their contribution would need to be assessed, for example, in relation to intratextual features such as the other fulfillment citations, characters and events invoked by the genealogy, the Herod episode, John's ministry, the temptation including the devil's claim to have authority over all the kingdoms/reigns of the world (4:8), various ways of establishing the divine perspective (the baptism), and in a much fuller discussion of the sociohistorical experience of the Gospel's audience.

73. In this chapter I have looked only at the contribution of evoking Isa 7–9 from the two Matthean texts (1:22–23; 4:15–16). A quick survey of the other fulfillment texts suggests that almost all of them also derive from and evoke imperial situations. Isaiah is further quoted in 8:17 (Isa 53:4); 12:17–21 (Isa 42:1–4, 9); and 21:5 (Isa 62:11, in part), employing texts from the context of Babylonian imperialism. If Matt 2:23 cites or alludes to Isa 4:3, that text depicts God's reign restored with

Jerusalem, an imperialist vision. If 2:23 recalls Judg 13, another context of an imperialist struggle is in view (the Philistines). Two of the remaining quotes come from Zech 9–11 (9:9 in Matt 21:5; 11:13 in Matt 27:9–10). This section of Zechariah anticipates the defeat of all of Israel's enemies and the establishment of God's reign or empire. In Matt 2:17–18, Jer 31:5 is cited from Jeremiah's ministry in the light of the Babylonian imperial threat. Hos 11:1, cited in Matt 2:15, recalls the exodus liberation in a context of the Assyrian imperialist threat. Matthew 13:34 cites Ps 78, a psalm that surveys Israel's unfaithfulness and God's faithfulness including deliverance from Egypt. A full-length study would be needed to explore the contribution of evoking these texts. But one of the likely conclusions would be consistent with one of the arguments of this chapter, namely that the intertexts, shaped by contexts of imperial threat, address the Gospel audience's experience of Roman imperialism, contributing insight and encouragement.

7. Take My Yoke Not Rome's: Matthew 11:28–30

1. For discussion of earlier nineteenth and twentieth century scholarship, Hans D. Betz, "Logion of the Easy Yoke"; Graham Stanton, "Salvation Proclaimed," 4–5; reprinted in Stanton, Gospel, 366–69, the version to which I will refer; Frances T. Gench, Wisdom, 1–33.

2. Stanton (Gospel, 371) helpfully identifies these four issues.

3. M. Jack Suggs, Wisdom; also Felix Christ, Jesus-Sophia.

4. Celia Deutsch, Hidden Wisdom; idem, "Wisdom in Matthew," 36–39; idem, Lady Wisdom, 54–60, 117–19. See also Joachim Gnilka, Das Matthäusevangelium, 1.439. For wisdom traditions, Deutsch, Lady Wisdom, 10–41.

5. Marshall Johnson, "Reflections on a Wisdom Approach"; Gench, Wisdom, 91–135.

6. Stanton, Gospel, 370–71. It should be noted that Stanton is responding to Suggs, not Deutsch. Deutsch depends less on particular verbal links and more on motifs and characteristics that the presentations of wisdom and Jesus share.

7. Stanton, Gospel, 369–70.

8. Stanton, Gospel, 371–77.

9. William D. Davies and Dale Allison, Matthew, 2.271–302, esp. 272; Allison, "Two Notes on a Key Text"; idem, A New Moses, 218–33.

10. Davies and Allison, Matthew, 2.297, 288.

11. Davies and Allison, Matthew, 2.289.

12. Blaine Charette, " 'To Proclaim Liberty.' "

13. Russell Pregeant, "Wisdom Passages." An earlier version appeared in the Society of Biblical Literature 1990 Seminar Papers.

14. Pregeant, "Wisdom Passages," 205.

15. Pregeant, "Wisdom Passages," 215.

16. Pregeant, "Wisdom Passages," 225–30, 215–16, 227, 218.

17. Gench, Wisdom, 91–135. Gench protests the discussion of the so-called "wisdom" passages in isolation from their "literary settings" and claims to examine the passages in relation to the Gospel as a whole (Wisdom, 24). But the structure of her book indicates that "relationship to the Gospel as a whole" does not include narrative placement and sequence. She begins her discussion with Matt 23, then moves to 11:25–30, and then discusses 11:2–19.

18. Gench, *Wisdom,* 108–9, 114–17.

19. Deirdre Good, *Jesus the Meek King,* 62–64, 87–88.

20. Charette, " 'To Proclaim Liberty,' " 294.

21. Pregeant is too astute to be unaware of this difficulty. Notice the personal language ("Wisdom Passages," 226) when he recognizes that "alternative readings are possible" but goes on to say that " ... not all readings are equal in the eyes of the implied author. What I would like to offer now is what might be called a 'preferred' reading, the reading *I* believe is most commensurate with the narrator's promptings." Mark Allan Powell ("Expected and Unexpected Readings") uses the language of "expected and unexpected readings" to address this issue, while I have used the notion of "authorial audience"; Warren Carter, *Matthew: Storyteller.*

22. The claimed central role of a Son of God Christology, which both Pregeant and Gench receive from Kingsbury, has been questioned, for example, by David Hill, "Son and Servant," and idem, "Figure of Jesus."

23. Michael Knowles (*Jeremiah in Matthew's Gospel,* 214–17) recognizes the link with Jer 6:16 but does not claim Jesus is a new Jeremiah.

24. As Gench, *Wisdom,* 113–17, for example, argues.

25. Stanton, *Gospel,* 372–75.

26. Seven times in 11:28–30 Jesus refers to himself (I/me), and to his audience. For the latter, he uses the pronoun "you" three times, uses three second-person imperatives, and one second-person verb. In 4:18–20, he refers to himself twice and uses the "you" pronoun twice. The indirect or reported third-person style that typifies 4:20–22 emphasizes personal attachment with the repeated clause "they followed him."

27. This view was common among the early church interpreters. Chrysostom, *Hom. Matt.* 38.3.

28. For example, Deutsch, *Lady Wisdom,* 59; Robert H. Gundry, *Matthew,* 218–19; Donald Hagner, *Matthew 1–3,* 1.323; Wolfgang Wiefel, *Das Evangelium nach Matthäus,* 224; Gnilka, *Das Matthäusevangelium,* 1.439; Daniel J. Harrington, *Matthew,* 167; Craig Keener, *A Commentary,* 384–85.

29. Carter, *Matthew and the Margins,* 262–68.

30. The argument of E. P. Sanders (*Paul and Palestinian Judaism*) that many Jews did not regard the covenantal nomism of first-century Judaism as burdensome or impossible should also be kept in mind. Also Michael Maher, " 'Take My Yoke Upon You,' " 98–102.

31. Gerhard E. Lenski, *Power,* 210; for discussion of "Agrarian Societies," 189–296.

32. Lenski, *Power,* 217–230.

33. Lenski, *Power,* 266.

34. Lenski, *Power,* 267.

35. Klaus Wengst, *Pax Romana,* 26–37, esp. 31–32.

36. Rodney Stark, "Urban Chaos and Crisis." An earlier version exists: idem, "Antioch as the Social Situation."

37. John H. Kautsky, *Politics,* 169–229; Wengst, *Pax Romana,* 40–44.

38. Carter, " 'Solomon in All His Glory'."

39. BAGD 443; Johannes P. Louw and Eugene A. Nida, *Lexicon,* 2.145.

40. Kautsky, *Politics,* 161.

41. Josephus uses the verb ten times, most of which refer to some sort of weariness in battle or conflict situations: *Ant.* 2.320–21 (exodus from Egypt); 7.231 (Absalom's revolt against David); *J.W.* 3.19–20, 316–19; 4.366–67; 6.142–43 (all with Rome).

42. Literally: Ezek 16:33 (its only use in the LXX, for prostitutes "loaded down" with gifts); Acts 21:3 (a ship unloading cargo); Josephus, *Ant* 7.205 (asses loaded with provisions). Metaphorically: Aristobulus and Herod "unload" burdensome followers (Josephus, *J.W.* 1.172, 266); Josephus accuses Apion (using an ass image) of being "overloaded" with lies (*C. Ap.* 2.115); in Luke 11:46 Jesus accuses the Pharisees of "loading" people with burdens hard to bear.

43. Janice C. Anderson, *Matthew's Narrative Web.*

44. Lenski, *Power,* 256–66; Anthony J. Saldarini, *Pharisees,* 35–49. Josephus links "the powerful ones," chief priests, and "leading Pharisees" to respond to the refusal of the lower priests to offer sacrifices for Rome in 66 (*J.W.* 2.411). Notice a similar alliance in *Life,* 20–23.

45. Peter A. Brunt, "Romanization of the Ruling Classes," 161–73; V. Nutton, "Beneficial Ideology"; Martin Goodman, *Ruling Class of Judea.*

46. Clearly I cannot agree with Keener, *Commentary,* 348, who says, "Jesus speaks here of a figurative bondage of unprofitable labor under an inadequate understanding of God's law." Charette, "To Proclaim Liberty," 294, also wants a metaphorical reference.

47. I do not take the future tense as *per se* mandating an eschatological interpretation. It is a logical future dependent on and resulting from coming to Jesus. Whether "rest" has eschatological contours must be determined on other grounds.

48. Alexander Sand, *Evangelium,* 252; Deutsch, *Lady Wisdom,* 59

49. Hagner, *Matthew,* 1.323; Stanton, *Gospel,* 376; Gench, *Wisdom,* 115–16.

50. Charette, "'To Proclaim Liberty,'" 296; Davies and Allison, *Matthew,* 2.288–89.

51. The verb ἀναπαύω occurs elsewhere in Matthew only in 26:45 as a synonym for sleeping. The noun ἀνάπαυσις appears only in 12:43 to designate a resting place. καταπαύω does not appear.

52. E.g., Prov 21:16; Wis 4:7; Sir 30:17; 38:23; 39:11.

53. E.g., Gen 8:9; Esth 9:17; Sir 20:21; 28:16; 31:3–4; 40:5–6.

54. E.g., Exod 16:23; 23:12; 31:5; 35:2; Lev 16:31; 23:3; 25:2, 4–5; Deut 5:14.

55. E.g., Assyria: Isa 7:19; Babylon: Isa 13:20–21; Philistia: Isa 14:30; Damascus: Isa 17:2; Sidon: Isa 23:12.

56. E.g., Babylon: Isa 14:3–4; Jer 42:10; Assyria: Isa 32:16–18; 2 Chr 32:22; all the nations: Isa 25:10; Mic 4:4.

57. E.g., Deutsch, *Lady Wisdom,* 58–59; Donald Senior, *Matthew,* 133–34.

58. Charette, "'To Proclaim Liberty,'" 291–93.

59. Leviticus 19:35, 36; Ps 62:9; Prov 11:1; 16:11; 20:23; Job 6:2; 31:6; Sir 21:25; 28:25; 42:4; Hos 12:7; Amos 8:5; Mic 6:11; Isa 40:12, 15; 46:6; Jer 32:10; Ezek 5:1; 45:10; Dan 5:27 (Theodotian).

60. The terms ζεῦγος and ζεύγη often refer to yoked or saddled animals (oxen, asses, donkeys); see Judg 19:3, 10; 2 Sam 16:1; 1 Kgs 19:19, 21; Job 1:3, 14; 42:12.

61. For those who are counting, one of the sixty-three uses is not discussed. In

Sir 40:1, "yoke" denotes the misery of the human condition marked by hard work and various perplexities and anxieties.

62. On Solomon's harsh rule, Carter, " 'Solomon in All His Glory,' " 16–22.

63. The noun κλοιός, a synonym of ζυγός (see their interchangeable use in Jer 28 [LXX 35]), also designates ruling power; in Deut 28:48, the yoke of serving victorious enemies is the people's punishment for not obeying the covenant; in 1 Kgs 12:4, 9, 10, 11, 14 it denotes Solomon's harsh rule (parallel to ζυγός in 2 Chr 10:4–14); in Jer 27:2 (LXX 34:2) and 28:10, 12, 13 (LXX 35:10, 12, 13), it designates Babylon's punitive imperial rule.

64. On the "kings of the earth," see Carter, "Paying the Tax to Rome," 20–26.

65. The pervasive but misleading translation of "easy" causes great problems. The translation creates a strange paradox (what yoke is easy?) for which commentators have found no satisfactory explanation. Davies and Allison, *Matthew*, 2.291–92, list six possibilities but seem to recognize the problem caused by the translation in urging caution about any claim. The issue is one of translation. The terms "kind, good" are the best way forward.

66. See Pss 100:5 (LXX 99:5); 106:1 (LXX 105:1); 136:1 (LXX 135:1); Jer 33:11 (LXX 40:11); Dan 3:89 (Prayer of Azariah). In the few instances it applies to people, it describes them as kind (1 Macc 6:11), upright (Prov 2:21) or worthy (2 Macc 9:19).

67. The remaining three uses refer to what is good (Lk 5:39; 1 Cor 15:33) and kind (Eph 4:32).

68. The term ἐλαφρόν (*elaphron*) is rare in the Septuagint and New Testament (only 2 Cor 4:17). Exodus 18:26 clearly bears the meaning of "small." In Job 7:6; 9:25; 24:18 it means "swift," somewhat appropriate here given the element of the passing of time.

69. On these alternative households, Carter, *Households and Discipleship*; Stephen C. Barton, *Discipleship and Family Ties*, 125–219.

70. Michael Crosby, *House of Disciples*.

71. Walter Wink, *Engaging the Powers*, 209–29; idem, "Beyond Just War and Pacifism."

72. Ramsay MacMullen, *Roman Social Relations*. On Cicero's contempt for provincials, Brunt, *Roman Imperial Themes*, 316–22.

73. "Lowly" or "humble" is essentially a synonym for "meek." The humble are the righteous lowly who, though oppressed and lacking in resources, anticipate God overthrowing the rich and powerful (Pss 10:17–18; 34:18; Isa 11:4; 49:13; Sir 10:13–17, esp. 11; 12:5; 13:21–22; 29:8).

74. Good, *Jesus the Meek King*, 39–60, 61–93.

75. For discussion, Anthony Marshall, "Governors on the Move"; H. S. Versnel, *Triumphus*: Sabine MacCormack, "Change and Continuity"; Brent Kinman, *Jesus' Entry to Jerusalem*, 25–65; W. Barnes Tatum, "Jesus' So-Called Triumphal Entry"; Carter, *Matthew and the Margins*, 413–18.

76. W. A. Visser 'T Hooft, "Triumphalism in the Gospels," 491; Brunt, "Laus Imperii," 291–93.

8. Paying the Tax to Rome as Subversive Praxis: Matthew 17:24–27

1. On the pre-70 temple economy, K. C. Hanson and Douglas E. Oakman, *Palestine*, 99–159.

2. This polyvalency, or the way in which a passage is read in different ways, is especially evident in the marvelously comprehensive work of David Garland, "Temple Tax in Matthew," and Bruce Chilton, "A Coin of Three Realms (Matthew 17.24–27)."

3. A *theologische Aussage*. Hubert Frankemölle, *Jahwebund*, 176; Georg Strecker, *Der Weg*, 31 n. 1; Rolf Walker, *Die Heilsgeschichte*, 101–3, 134; Alexander Sand, *Das Evangelium nach Matthäus*, 362–63; Garland, "Temple Tax," 204–209; John P. Meier, *Vision of Matthew*, 126; William D. Davies and Dale Allison, *Matthew*, 2.748–49. Ulrich Luz (*Das Evangelium nach Matthäus*, 2.536) cannot discern "a real life setting... in the time after 70 for this text... "("einem aktuellen Sitz im Leben... in der Zeit nach 70 für diesen Text").

4. There are some exceptions: Gunther Bornkamm ("End-Expectation and Church," 19–20) and Reinhart Hummel (*Auseinandersetzung*, 32, 103–6, 159) argue that the pericope instructs Matthew's community, still associated with the synagogue though developing its own life, to pay the temple tax. Also Simon Légasse, "Jésus et l'impôt," 370–72. William G. Thompson (*Matthew's Advice*, 67–68) argues the pericope concerns the *aurum coronarium*, a "legal tax" to support the Jamnia council. But this suggestion fails for lack of primary data as Garland rightly notes ("Temple Tax," 203–4).

5. Davies and Allison, *Matthew*, 2.748.

6. Paul Gaechter, *Das Matthäus Evangelium*, 580–84; Wolfgang Trilling, *The Gospel*, 2.80; Sand, *Das Evangelium*, 363, the freedom of sonship in relation to worldly matters; Garland, "Temple Tax," 206–7.

7. Thompson, *Matthew's Advice*, 62; Richard Bauckham, "Coin," 226–27; Garland, "Temple Tax," 209; Meier, *Vision*, 125–26; Robert H. Gundry, *Matthew*, 356–57; Davies and Allison, *Matthew*, 2.738.

8. Especially Ernst Haenchen, *Der Weg Jesu*, 333–34; Joachim Gnilka, *Das Matthäusevangelium*, 2.116–18; Garland, "Temple Tax," 207–8; Meier, *Vision*, 126; Gundry, *Matthew*, 357 (Gundry dates the Gospel pre-70).

9. Walter Grundmann, *Das Evangelium nach Matthäus*, 409–10; Edward Schweizer, *Good News*, 355–57; Thompson, *Matthew's Advice*, 58–59, 62; Garland, "Temple Tax," 208–9; Donald Hagner, *Matthew 14–28*, 513.

10. Davies and Allison, *Matthew*, 2.748.

11. Gnilka, *Das Matthäusevangelium*, 2.118.

12. Variously, J. Duncan M. Derrett, "Peter's Penny," 261–2; Frankemölle, *Jahwebund*, 357; Garland, "Temple Tax," 204; Meier, *Vision*, 126–27; Daniel Patte, *Gospel According to Matthew*, 244–47; Douglas R. A. Hare, *Matthew*, 205 (Heading), 207; Luck, *Das Evangelium*, 198–99; Davies and Allison, *Matthew*, 2.748–49; Hagner, *Matthew*, 2.512–3; Garland, *Reading Matthew*, 186–87.

13. On the Gospel's "authorial audience," see the Introduction; also Peter J. Rabinowitz, "Whirl without End," 85; idem, *Before Reading*, 15–46; idem, "Truth in Fiction"; Warren Carter, *Matthew: Storyteller*; Carter and John Paul Heil, *Matthew's Parables*, 8–17.

14. Garland, "Temple Tax," 204–5; Meier, *Vision,* 125; Gundry, *Matthew,* 355.

15. Through the use of various interchangeable names and differing groupings, an alliance of religious leaders opposed to Jesus is established. See Sjef van Tilborg, *Jewish Leaders;* Jack Dean Kingsbury, "Developing Conflict"; Carter, *Matthew: Storyteller,* 229–41.

16. Thompson, *Matthew's Advice,* 59–60; Gundry, *Matthew,* 355–57; Davies and Allison, *Matthew* 2.746, 748. Patte (*Matthew,* 247) and Garland ("Temple Tax," 205) observe but underestimate this difficulty. The position assumes that the agents of the religious leaders are the referent for "them."

17. He does so by forgiving sins (9:1–8), eating with tax collectors and sinners (9:10–13), casting out demons (9:32–34; 12:22–32), violating the sabbath (12:1–8, 9–14), not giving signs (12:38–45; 16:1–4), teaching and performing some miracles (13:53–58), and disputes over purity laws (15:1–20).

18. He offends them over matters of marriage and divorce (19:3–12), the temple (21:12–17), his authority (21:23–27), their negative response (21:28–22:14), paying taxes to Caesar (22:15–22), the resurrection (22:23–34), the identity of the Christ (22:41–46). Jesus condemns them because they "know neither the scriptures nor the power of God" (22:29), shames them twice into silence (22:34, 46), and launches a horrific catalogue of woes against them (ch 23).

19. Richard A. Edwards, *Matthew's Story of Jesus,* 64.

20. For the displaying of character through words and deeds, and the consistency between them, Richard A. Burridge, *What Are the Gospels?,* 121, 124, 143–44, 148–49, 175–77, 182–84, 205–6, 208, 211–12. If Jesus does not manifest integrity, he would display hypocrisy, a characteristic of his opponents (6:2, 5, 16; 7:5; 15:7; 22:18; 23:13, 15, 23, 25, 27, 29; 25:51).

21. Rightly Hagner, *Matthew 14–28,* 510, though his suggestion of a chronological link fails for lack of evidence.

22. I will question these identifications shortly.

23. Carter, "Crowds."

24. Meier, "Nations or Gentiles in Matthew 28:19?" *contra* Douglas Hare and Daniel Harrington, " 'Make Disciples of All the Gentiles.' "

25. Amy-Jill Levine (*Social and Ethnic Dimensions,* 165–204) argues ἔθνη (*ethnē*) means "Gentiles" but this command extends, not rescinds, 10:5b–6 (p. 197).

26. Carter, "The Parables in Matthew 21:28–22:14," in Carter and Heil, *Matthew's Parables,* 159–68.

27. Graham Stanton, *Gospel,* 248–50; Carter, *Matthew and the Margins,* 463–65.

28. Chilton, "Coin of Three Realms," 276. If by "historically" Chilton is referring to modern commentators, he is correct. But "historically" a number of commentators in the early church (including Irenaeus, Clement of Alexandria, Origen, Jerome, Ambrose, Augustine, and Gregory Nazianzen) have understood the pericope in relation to imperial demands, the standard reading of the West. For references, William Horbury, "Temple Tax," 265, n. 2–3; Davies and Allison, *Matthew,* 2.740, n. 9; for exegesis in the Greek church fathers, Elno Wilhelms, *Die Tempelsteuerperikope Matthäus 17,24–27.*

29. Chilton ("Coin of Three Realms," 276–78) notes the Gospel's link with a

publican (9:9) and so with the "complex system of taxation." The surprising claim (21:31) that tax collectors and prostitutes precede religious leaders into the reign assumes a common perception that taxes were unjust. Stylistic features connect this incident with another passage concerning taxes and Caesar (22:15–22). He cites the address of Jesus as "teacher" (17:24; 22:16), the question τί σοι δοκεῖ (*ti soi dokei,* what do you think? 17:25; 22:17), and the generalizing of the question to tax and tribute (κῆνσον, *kēnson,* 17:25; 22:17). He also indicates the likely origin of Matthew's Gospel in post-70 Antioch, a "troubled time for Jews in Antioch." See E. Mary Smallwood, *Jews Under Roman Rule,* 358–64; Glanville Downey, *History of Antioch,* 203–11; Wayne A. Meeks and Robert L. Wilken, *Jews and Christians in Antioch,* 4–13.

30. George D. Kilpatrick, *Origins of the Gospel,* 41–43 (though mistaken about Nerva abolishing the tax, corrected by Derrett, "Peter's Penny," 261); Hugh Montefiore, "Jews and the Temple Tax," 63–66; Davies, *Setting,* 389–91 (though not the position taken in Davies and Allison, *Matthew,* 2.737–49); Chilton, "Coin of Three Realms," 275–79; Daniel Harrington, *Gospel of Matthew,* 262; Anthony J. Saldarini, *Matthew's Christian-Jewish Community,* 144–45. Others assert tax paid to Rome without specifying its identity: A. N. Sherwin-White, *Roman Society,* 126; Richard J. Cassidy, "Matthew 17:24–27"; Francis W. Beare, *Gospel According to Matthew,* 371–75; Pierre Bonnard, *L'Évangile,* 264–66; Sand, *Das Evangelium,* 362–63.

31. Garland, "Temple Tax," 199; Sarah Mandell ("Who Paid the Temple Tax?" 223–32) asserts it was levied only on Pharisaic Jews, but Josephus and Suetonius indicate a wider scope. Martin Goodman ("Nerva," 40–41) accounts for these discrepancies more convincingly arguing that Vespasian imposed the tax initially on all Jews assuming that "all ethnic Jews subscribed to the national cult." Domitian reinforced this practice ("that [tax] on the Jews was levied with the utmost rigour, and those were prosecuted who without publicly acknowledging that faith yet lived as Jews, as well as those who concealed their origin and did not pay the tribute levied upon their people" Suetonius, *Dom.* 12.2). However, Nerva came to realize the inadequacy of the equation (ethnic Jews = religiously observant) and released "nonreligious ethnic Jews" from it, so that only Jews who openly professed observance paid it.

32. Garland, "Temple Tax," 201 (my emphasis).

33. Carter, *Matthew: Storyteller,* 77–102.

34. Harrington, *Gospel of Matthew,* 8–22.

35. Saldarini, *Matthew's Christian-Jewish Community,* 124–64; *contra,* for example, Trilling, *Das Wahre Israel,* 95–96, 224. For a more concise statement, Saldarini, "Gospel of Matthew and Jewish-Christian Conflict."

36. Garland, "Temple Tax," 201.

37. For difficulties in getting information, Mireille Corbier, "City, Territory and Taxation," 215–17. Corbier notes a focus in the sources on expenditure not collection and alterations not the "norms." Sources also often confuse taxes for Rome and those for local cities. For additional good discussions, Richard Alston, *Aspects,* 227–45; Peter Garnsey and Richard Saller, *Roman Empire,* 43–103; Fergus Millar, ed., *Roman Empire,* 90–100; Brent D. Shaw, "Roman Taxation."

38. John H. Kautsky, *Politics,* 150; Gerhard E. Lenski, *Power,* 217–19.

39. Lenski, _Power,_ 214.

40. For taxation in Egypt, which in all likelihood resembles Syria, Sherman Wallace, _Taxation in Egypt;_ Colin J. Hemer, "The Edfu _Ostraka._" For analysis of the Roman use of taxes for the elite's benefit, Klaus Wengst, _Pax Romana,_ 26–37.

41. Corbier, "City," 214.

42. On elite values and taxation, Kautsky, _Politics,_ 169–229; Lenski, _Power,_ 250–56.

43. Corbier, "City," 211–39; Millar, _Roman Empire,_ 90–100; Shaw, "Roman Taxation."

44. The translation is from Shaw, "Roman Taxation," 821; see also 810.

45. Lenski, _Power,_ 267; Oakman, _Jesus and the Economic Questions,_ 72; Shaw, "Roman Taxation," 824.

46. This is the argument that Tacitus has the Roman general Cerialis make to the Treviri in Trier (_Hist._ 4.73–74).

47. Five examples: (1) Josephus has Agrippa declare to Jews in revolt against the Roman governor Florus (66 C.E.) that their not paying tribute was an "act of war" (_J.W._ 2.403). Paying the tribute would clear them of the "charge of insurrection" (_J.W._ 2.404). (2) Onias does not pay tribute to King Ptolemy, who responds by threatening war and seizure of land (_Ant._ 12.158–59). (3) The Frisians refuse a tribute of oxhides, attack the supervising Roman soldiers, and overcome the military force sent to subdue and punish them (Tacitus, _Ann._ 4.72–73). (4) Tacitus also notes that discontent with continuous tributes was a factor in a rebellion in Gaul that was put down by military force (_Ann._ 3.40–41). (5) In 36 C.E. Vitellius sends troops from Syria to rectify the Cietae's refusal to pay tribute (Tacitus, _Ann._ 6.41). Ramsay MacMullen, _Enemies of the Roman Order,_ 212–14; Stephen Dyson ("Native Revolts," 254, 267, 269) discusses a further five revolts and military response, noting rebellion against paying taxes and tribute as a factor in three of them.

48. Louw and Nida, _Lexicon,_ 1.578; BAGD, 812; James H. Moulton and George Milligan, _Vocabulary,_ 630–31; Gerhard Delling, τέλος," _Theological Dictionary of the New Testament_ 8 (1972) 51, 52, 57; Cassidy, "Word on Civil Taxes," 572–73. Examples from Josephus include _Ant._ 10.2, tribute of submission to Sennacherib; _Ant_ 12.169, 175, tax-farming rights in submission to King Ptolemy; _Ant._ 17.205 (cf. _J.W._ 2.4) taxes on "public purchases and sales"; _Ant._ 18.90 taxes on agricultural products; _Ant._ 19.25, unspecified taxes; _J.W._ 118, 404, tribute to Rome; Esther 10:1; 1 Macc 10:31; 11:35; Philo, _Migr._ 139, to God.

49. Louw and Nida, _Lexicon,_ 1.578; BAGD, 430; Cassidy, "Civil Taxes," 573.

50. Corbier ("City," 219) notes an example in which _ta telē_ ("the revenues") refers to tax revenues from a territory surrounding a city, but the exact nature of those revenues is vague. They might embrace taxes levied on the population, or on certain activities, or on produce from public rented lands, or to grain production, or to some combination of these possibilities, and might involve some payment to Rome also.

51. Josephus (_J.W._ 7.218) says that "on all Jews wheresoever resident [Vespasian] imposed a poll-tax of two drachma (δύο δραχμάς, _duo drachmas_) to be paid annually into the Capitol as formerly contributed by them to the Temple at Jerusalem." Dio (65.7.2.) comments that after the fall of Jerusalem "from that time forth it

was ordered that the Jews who continued to observe their ancestral customs should pay an annual tribute of two denarii (δίδραχμον, *didrachmon*) to Jupiter Capitolinus." For discussion, see Smallwood, *Jews Under Roman Rule,* 372–76; Goodman, "Nerva."

52. Josephus (*Ant.* 18.312; *J.W.* 7.218) says that the temple tax comprised two drachma or a didrachmon (δίδραχμον). The plural in 17:24 would refer to the collection of numerous didrachma. For discussion, Chilton, "Coin of Three Realms," 271–73; Horbury, "Temple Tax," 277–82; Smallwood, *Jews Under Roman Rule,* 124–26.

53. Josephus, *Ant.* 18.312, Babylon; *J.W.* 7.218 ὁπουδηποτοῦν (*hopoudēpotoun*) "wherever they were living"; Philo, *Spec.* 1.14.78 "in every city." This redefining of the pre-70 temple tax as the post-70 Roman tax enables the narrative, set in the pre-70 context of the life of Jesus, to address its post-70 audience.

54. Smallwood (*Jews Under Roman Rule,* 372–74) summarizes data from Egypt, the Arsinoe papyrus and tax receipts from Apollinopolis Magna (Edfu), which show that the Romans also extended its payees from males over 20 years (Ex 30:13) to male and female over three years old (until age 62 for women) including slaves. Hemer, "Edfu *Ostraka*," 6–12; Goodman, "Nerva," 40.

55. Smallwood, *Jews Under Roman Rule,* 374.

56. Smallwood, *Jews Under Roman Rule,* 300–301; Cecil Roth, "Historical Implications"; Leo Kadman, *Coins of the Jewish War,* 50–71.

57. J. Rufus Fears, "Cult of Jupiter," 71–80.

58. Montefiore ("Jews and the Temple Tax," 65) inaccurately comments that "the tribute money was a secular, not a religious obligation." Thompson (*Matthew's Advice,* 50, 67) also misses this point; Cassidy, "Civil Taxes," 571–80.

59. Notice the same phrase in 9:11 and 23:8; both contexts underline the distinct communal identity of the community of disciples.

60. In confessing Jesus' identity, Peter speaks the confession of all disciples (cf. 16:16 and 14:33); as representative of a community he receives the power of binding and loosing (16:19 and 18:18). Kingsbury, "Figure of Peter," 71.

61. This is underlined by the verb προσῆλθον (*proselthon*), which emphasizes Jesus' authority. Peter is approached as a representative of Jesus in 26:29, 73. Edwards, "Use of προσέρχεσθαι," 68–69.

62. The sense of "paying taxes" is well attested, Rom 13:6–7; Josephus, *Ant.* 12.158; BAGD, 811; Moulton and Milligan, *Vocabulary,* 630. It anticipates the noun τέλη (*telē*) in 17:25. The verb also appears in 7:28; 11:1; 13:53; 19:1; and 26:1 to conclude Jesus' teaching discourses. Its use here invokes that teaching authority.

63. Its previous use by Jesus' opponents, especially by religious leaders (8:19; 9:11; 12:38), suggests a possible alliance in opposition and hostility.

64. Jesus is not called "teacher" by disciples but by both opponents (9:11; 12:38; 22:16) and those interested in discipleship who do not follow him (8:19; 19:16). Jesus (10:24–25; 26:18; 23:8?) refers to himself as "teacher."

65. BDF, 440; David Daube, "Temple Tax," 121.

66. I use praxis to embrace both reflection on the situation of oppression and action toward liberation. So Paula Freire, *Pedagogy of the Oppressed,* 30.

67. While there is ambiguity about who owns houses (9:1–10, 28; 13:1, 36 sug-

gest Jesus does), the location of this house in Capernaum and the prominence of Peter suggest it is his house (8:5, 14; 17:24). Davies and Allison, *Matthew,* 2.99–100.

68. The change from Peter in 17:24 has perplexed interpreters. It may underline 16:17.

69. This example is from Davies and Allison, *Matthew,* 2.744; Garland, "Temple Tax," 193, n.10.

70. Other Psalm usages include LXX Ps 2:2; 75:13 (NRSV 76:12); 88:28 (NRSV 89:27); 101:16 (NRSV 102:16); 137:4 (NRSV 138:4); 148:11 (NRSV 148:11).

71. Carter, " 'Solomon in All His Glory.' "

72. The importance of Ps 2 for Matthew is indicated by its uses in 3:17; 17:5; and 22:41–45.

73. Psalm 75 praises God's power and ultimate control over the destiny of the nations. God terrifies and cuts off the breath of "the kings of the earth" (Ps 75:13 LXX). Psalm 88 celebrates God's power over all creation demonstrated through Israel's king, who is "the highest of the kings of the earth" (LXX 88:28). In distress, Ps 101 looks for God to restore the glory of Jerusalem in such a way that "the nations will fear the name of the Lord, and all the kings of the earth your glory" (LXX 101:16). Both Pss 137 and 148 call "the kings of the earth" to recognize God's name "exalted above everything" (LXX 137:2; 148:11).

74. Similar themes are evident in other uses of the phrase in Josh 12:1 (the kings defeated by Israel in occupying the land according to God's will); Ezra 9:7 (once crushed by the kings of the earth, the people are being restored by God); Lam 4:12 (the kings did not understand God's purposes and plans, even "the impossible" of allowing entry to Jerusalem); Ezek 27:33 (laments that Tyre's wealth and power that enriched kings cannot save the city from God's plans and judgment); 1 Enoch 48:8 (judgment on the oppressive kings and landowners); *4 Ezra* 15:20 (judgment on the kings who have not heeded God's call and ways, and have oppressed God's people); Rev 1:5 (Jesus is ruler of the kings); 6:15 (hiding from the approaching day of wrath).

75. See, for example, the sequence in 1 Macc 8–11. Rome exacts τέλος (*telos,* 1 Macc 8:4, 7) as does the Seleucid Alexander, a burden King Demetrius will lift if the Jews ally with him (1 Macc 10:29–31). Demetrius will exempt the Jews from "payment of tribute and salt tax and crown levies," from levies on the grain (one-third) and fruit (one-half) harvests, and Jerusalem from tax (τὰ τέλη, *ta telē,* 1 Macc 10:29–31). After his death (1 Macc 10:50), Demetrius II tries the same ploy (11:35). And several centuries later, Vespasian levies the δίδραχμον (*didrachmon*) from Jews as tribute (φόρος, Josephus, *J.W.* 7.218).

76. Josephus designates Roman emperors as βασιλεύς (kings) in *J.W.* 3.351; 4.596; 5.563; Titus the βασιλεύς, *J.W.* 5.58.

77. Dorothy Jean Weaver, "Power and Powerlessness," 456–60.

78. Carter, " 'Solomon in All His Glory'."

79. Willoughby C. Allen, *Matthew,* 192; Montefiore, "Jesus," 69.

80. Gundry, *Matthew,* 357; Derrett, "Peter's Penny," 255; David Hill, *Matthew,* 272.

81. Meier, *Matthew,* 197; Bauckham, "Coin," 221–22; Davies and Allison, *Matthew,* 2.744.

82. With Bauckham, "Coin," 221–22; Davies and Allison, *Matthew,* 2.744–45.

That Vespasian could provide successors, unlike Vitellius, was an important gift of the Flavians (Josephus, *J.W.* 4. 592–97; Tacitus, *Hist.* 1.10; 2.77; Suetonius, *Vesp.* 25) and is reflected in the emphasis on Aeternitas on coins (Kenneth Scott, *Imperial Cult*, 42, 95).

83. Schweizer, *Good News*, 356.

84. Davies and Allison, *Matthew*, 2.744–45; M. J. Lagrange, *Évangile selon Saint Matthieu*, 342; Simon Légasse, "Jésus et l'impôt," 369; Thompson, *Matthew's Advice*, 57. The phrase τί σοι δοκεῖ (*ti soi dokei*, 17:25) appears here for the first time in the Gospel. It will be used subsequently to introduce parables in 18:12 and 21:28, and to solicit opinions in 22:17, 42.

85. Allen, *Matthew*, 191–2; Horbury, "Temple Tax," 271; Garland, "Temple Tax," 193, 207; Daube, "Temple Tax," 122.

86. Bauckham ("Coin," 221) names "the implied application of the parable, in relation to God"; Horbury, "Temple Tax," 272, 283.

87. Bauckham, "Coin," 221; Davies and Allison, *Matthew*, 2.745.

88. Garland, "Temple Tax," 200; Hummel, *Auseinandersetzung*, 103–4; Bauckham, "Coin," 219, 221–25; Davies and Allison, *Matthew*, 2.743 n. 26, 745.

89. Christians is the more common claim (so Hagner, *Matthew 14–28*, 512); in favor of Israelites, Horbury, "Temple Tax," 282–84; Bauckham, "Coin," 223; Luz, *Das Evangelium nach Matthäus*, 2.534; Davies and Allison, *Matthew*, 2.745.

90. Davies and Allison, *Matthew*, 2.745; Bauckham, "Coin," 219–25.

91. Davies and Allison, *Matthew*, 2.741, 745; Horbury ("Temple Tax," 271) complains about any obscuring of "the *parallel* between earthly and heavenly kings" (my emphasis). He summarizes the verses (285): "*as* the 'sons' of the kings of the earth are protected from these impositions, *so* Israel should be free from taxation in the name of their God" (my emphasis). So also Allen, *Matthew*, 191; Daube, "Temple Tax," 122; Hill, *Gospel of Matthew*, 272; J. C. Fenton, *Saint Matthew*, 285. Garland ("Temple Tax," 193 n. 10) paraphrases "if this is the case with earthly kings, then *how much more so* with the heavenly king" (my emphasis). But if an *a minore ad maius* argument was intended, surely it would be signaled by πολλῷ μᾶλλον (*pollō mallon*) as in 6:30 or by πόσῳ μᾶλλον (*posō mallon*) as in 7:11 and 10:25.

92. Emphasized by Julius Wellhausen, *Das Evangelium Matthaei*, 85–86; Bauckham, "Coin," 219–25; Hagner, *Matthew 14–28*, 511; Davies and Allison, *Matthew*, 2.741, 743 n. 26.

93. Bauckham, "Coin," 222.

94. Cassidy ("Civil Taxes," 575) calls it "an almost metaphysical-sounding principle." I do not oppose allegory per se (cf. Matt 13:37–43).

95. BDF 439 (1); 444 (2); 451 (2).

96. BAGD 250, citing Josephus, *C. Ap.* 2.134. Note the very political use of various cognates in *J.W.* 2.264, 348–49; 3.480; 5.321; 7.325–26, often in reference to freedom from Rome's rule. Cognate forms (ἐλευθέριος *eleutherios*, liberator) are applied to Augustus (Dominique Cuss, *Imperial Cult*, 138–39), to Nero and Titus as "liberators" on coins and in literature (Scott, *Imperial Rule*, 20–22). Roth ("Jewish Coinage," 41) notes "Freedom of Zion" on some of the Year 2 coins minted in Jerusalem during the 66–70 revolt. Commentators frequently appeal to John 8:31–38 and especially Rom 8, 1 Cor 8–10, and Gal 3:23–5:1 (for example, Sand, *Evangelium nach Matthäus*, 363; Luck, *Das Evangelium*, 199). The Paulinizing link

influences the frequent turn to allegory. It should be noted that the word is a *hapax legomenon* in Matthew.

97. The connective δέ (*de*) at the beginning of 17:27 is translated in the RSV and NRSV as "however" to suggest a contrast with and a concession to the statement that "the sons are free." Commentators assert without support that it indicates a contrast (Thompson, *Matthew's Advice*, 59; Davies and Allison, *Matthew*, 2.746), a claim that reinforces the dominant reading that Jesus is to be included among the free, but he chooses to pay the tax. But while δε with μεν indicates a contrast (BDF 447), δέ on its own more commonly (though not exclusively) indicates a connection as a copulative rather than adversative conjunction (cf. 17:24). So BDF 442–43, which equates δέ with the connective καί and τε. This connective rather than contrastive sense leads to the reading suggested here, which does not place Jesus among the free: "The sons/children are free *and* lest we offend them."

98. The identity of αὐτούς (*autous*, "them") is debated. If one assumes the pre-70 temple tax is in view, the "them" will be the Jewish leaders or their representatives. If I am correct in arguing that the tax concerns that paid to the *fiscus Ioudaicus* post-70, αὐτούς refers to these collectors. This view gains support from observing that the immediate antecedent for αὐτούς is υἱοί, the sons of the kings, at the end of verse 26. The collectors are the agents of the kings and the sons/children collecting the tax from "the others."

99. Davies, *Setting*, 391.

100. Louw and Nida (*Lexicon*, 1.63) identify it as a silver coin worth two didrachma.

101. Allen, *Matthew*, 192; Cassidy, "Matthew 17:24–27," 576; Bauckham, "Coin," 224.

102. Lagrange, *Évangile*, 343; Bonnard, *L'Évangile*, 266; Trilling, *Matthew*, 2.81; Bauckham, "Coin," 224; Patte, *Matthew*, 247; Hagner, *Matthew 14–28*, 512–13; Davies and Allison, *Matthew*, 2.746.

103. Martial indicates that Domitian's numen, not human training, causes eagles and lions to show mercy to their prey (*Epigrams* 1.6; 1.4; 1.22; 1.104); causes leopards, stags, bears, boars, elephants, and bison to perform (*Epigrams* 1.104); enables parrots to greet him (*Epigrams* 14.73; cf. Statius, *Silvae* 2.4.29–30); prompts fish to "know their master and lick his hand" (*Epigrams* 4.30); and a goose to sacrifice itself to provide him a favorable omen in the Sarmatian war (*Epigrams* 9.31). Juvenal, *Fourth Satire*, 1.63–128, esp. 1.69–71, 83–86. Martial in "On the Spectacles" (*Epigrams*, vol. 1) celebrates Titus's power or numen over wild beasts (12), an elephant (20), the sea (28), and hounds (33). Scott, *Imperial Cult*, 116–25.

104. On imperial control of the Galilean fishing economy, see K. C. Hanson, "The Galilean Fishing Economy."

105. Scott (*Imperial Cult*, 52–53) notes that Domitian mints coins that depict dolphins representing and honoring Neptune and Apollo. Andries G. Van Arde ("A Silver Coin," 221–26) points to the discovery of silver Tyrian coins with images of sea monsters, sea horses and dolphins with riders on their backs. While the identity of the riders is unclear in Semitic mythology, they might be Ba'al Shamem, god of the sea, and Poseidon in Greek mythology. The fish under God's control with a stater in its mouth denotes God's sovereignty over all powers. Thompson, "Tyrian Coin."

106. For a similar relativizing and subverting of imperial power through the

characters of Herod, Herod the Tetrarch, and Pilate, see Weaver, "Power and Powerlessness," and ch. 8 below.

107. Though there is no space to pursue it here, 22:15–22 evidences the same relativizing of the act of paying taxes. Nor should it be overlooked that the calling of the tax collector Matthew as a disciple disrupts his occupation (9:9), whether his leaving is understood as a permanent break or as one in which he both follows and continues this task.

108. Walter Wink, "Beyond Just War and Pacifism." Various forms of this article have appeared; for example, Wink, "Neither Passivity Nor Violence," in W. M. Swartley, ed., *The Love of Enemy*, 102–25.

109. For discussion of interpretive options, Carter, "Some Contemporary Scholarship," 198–99.

110. Davies, *Setting*, 391. Patte (*Matthew*, 244–45) notes the link but develops it differently.

9. Pilate and Jesus: Roman Justice All Washed Up (Matt 27:11–26)

1. Pilate is mentioned or appears in 27:1–2, 11–26, 57–65; 28:11–15. I will focus on 27:1–2, 11–26 since this is the crucial confrontation with Jesus, though I will refer to the other scenes as necessary.

2. There is some confusion about Pilate's actual title, whether prefect (ἔπαρχος, *eparchos*) or procurator (ἐπίτροπος, *epitropos*). "Prefect" is, in origin, a military term, while "procurator" is a civilian term that, in origin, denotes fiscal responsibilities. The use, though, of either term for governors did not restrict their responsibilities. The confusion arises in part from the sources. Both Josephus (*J.W.* 2.169) and Philo (*Legat.* 299) use the latter title for Pilate (and Tacitus uses its Latin equivalent, *procurator, Ann.* 15.44). Philo also uses it for the governors of Egypt (*Legat.* 132), Asia (*Legat.* 311) and Syria (*Legat.* 333). But Josephus uses both titles for governors of Judea across the century. So *epitropos* refers to governors who precede Pilate (Coponius in *J.W.* 2.117) and succeed him (Fadus and Tiberius Alexander in *J.W.* 2.220; Felix in *J.W.* 2.247) as does *eparchos* (Gratus in *Ant.* 18.33; Festus in *Ant.* 20.193). Some are identified by both terms (Fadus, *Ant.* 19.363; 20.14). See Jean-Pierre Lémonon, *Pilate*, 45–48. An inscription from Caesarea (for an image, Daniel R. Schwartz, "Pontius Pilate," *ABD* 5.397) confirms Pilate was called prefect, though this title does not restrict his role as governor to military matters. The confusion also arises because under Claudius, the civilian term "procurator" seems to become standard for provincial governors. See Peter A. Brunt, *Roman Imperial Themes*, 163–87.

3. These are the usually ascribed dates based on Josephus's claim that Pilate followed Valerius Gratus who, having been appointed by Tiberius after Augustus's death in 14 C.E., ruled for eleven years (*Ant.* 18.33–35). Consequently Josephus notes that Pilate was ordered by Vitellius, governor of Syria, to return to Rome to explain to the emperor his actions in killing a number of Samaritans. "Pilate, after having spent ten years in Judaea, hurried to Rome in obedience.... But before he reached Rome Tiberias had already passed away" (March 37 C.E.; *Ant.* 18.89). However, Schwartz ("Pontius Pilate," *ABD* 5.396–97) notes some debate about these dates,

and proposes a much earlier starting date of 19 c.e. based on data in Josephus that suggest a much shorter rule for Gratus.

4. Brain C. McGing ("Pontius Pilate," 417) argues that the often-claimed distinction between the sources (Philo and Josephus versus the Gospels) is not sustainable. Helen Bond (*Pontius Pilate*, xvii) also pursues this line.

5. Coins issued by Pilate have also figured in these reconstructions. The key issue concerns Pilate's motivations in issuing coins with conventional imperial symbols on them. Was he influenced by Sejanus, the supposedly anti-Jewish prefect of the Praetorian Guard, to provoke Jewish rebellion (so Ethelbert Stauffer, *Christ*, 119), or were they chosen to emphasize common connections between Judaism and Roman culture in order to integrate the province into the empire (so Bond, "The Coins of Pontius Pilate?" 241–62)?

6. Accounts of his administration highlight insensitivities in trying to set up engraved shields in the temple and using its money for an aqueduct, his commitment to Tiberius, and a readiness to use force to maintain compliance (Josephus, *J.W.* 2.169–77; *Ant.* 18.55–62; Philo, *Flacc.* 299–305).

7. Stauffer, *Christ*, 103, 118–20; Michael Grant, *Jews in the Roman World*, 99–112; M. Stern, "Province of Judea," 1.349–53.

8. McGing, "Pontius Pilate," 438.

9. Lémonon (*Pilate*, 273–79) attributes the trouble to Pilate's personality and authoritarian conception of his role as governor. Bond (*Pontius Pilate*, xvi–xvii) aligns her work with Lémonon and McGing.

10. Schwartz ("Pontius Pilate," *ABD* 5.399) thinks "the grounds for the friction were (not) to be found in the particular characteristics of Pilate's personality, policies or administration. Rather the friction was inherent in the very phenomenon of Roman rule in the land many Jews considered to be God's."

11. Notice Bond's way of proceeding (*Pontius Pilate*, xix–xx, 24–194). In six chapters she examines the literary presentations of Pilate in the six sources, and then attempts to move back through the text to the historical events and person to which they attest, and from which they originated.

12. On characterization by the audience's attention to the traits it notices in the narrative, see Warren Carter, *Matthew: Storyteller*, 189–91, citing Seymour Chatman, *Story and Discourse*, 107–38. For more recent discussions, David Rhoads and Kari Syreeni, eds., *Characterization;* William H. Shepherd, *Narrative Function*, 43–98.

13. For example, Bond (*Pontius Pilate*, 132, 136) says that Pilate is very much in the background, while Craig Keener (*Commentary*, 662) claims that Pilate is its central character and that it is really Pilate who is on trial! Yet both agree that the responsibility for Jesus' death is not, ultimately, Pilate's.

14. This view, in part or in full, is advocated, for instance, by Edward Schweizer, *Good News*, 510; Michael Goldberg, *Jews and Christians*, 188–93; Donald Senior, *Passion of Jesus*, 103–4, 108–22; Alexander Sand, *Das Evangelium*, 550–555; Daniel J. Harrington, *Gospel of Matthew*, 388–93; Douglas R. A. Hare, *Matthew*, 314–18; Donald Hagner, *Matthew 14–28*, 808–28; Craig Keener, *A Commentary*, 662–73.

15. Bond, *Pontius Pilate*, 125–26.

16. Dorothy Jean Weaver, "Power and Powerlessness"; William D. Davies and

Dale Allison (*Matthew* 3.579) indicate that they "are (against many) unpersuaded that the text excuses the Romans." Carter, *Matthew and the Margins,* 523–29.

17. This alliance has often been noted. Sjef van Tilborg, *Jewish Leaders,* 1–6; Jack Dean Kingsbury, "Developing Conflict"; Carter, *Matthew: Storyteller,* 229–31.

18. Jesus predicts this "handing over" in 20:19 as the inevitable fate of those who challenge the imperial order.

19. Gerhard E. Lenski, *Power,* 256–66; John H. Kautsky, *Politics,* 81–83, 161–66; Anthony J. Saldarini, *Pharisees,* 35–49.

20. Brunt, "Social Conflicts," *Roman Imperial Themes,* 282–87.

21. Brunt, "The Romanization of the Local Ruling Classes," *Roman Imperial Themes,* 272; Peter Garnsey, *Social Status,* 77–79.

22. Garnsey, *Social Status,* 65–100, 103–52, 221–80. Klaus Wengst, *Pax Romana,* 37–40. Note Josephus's horror and sense of betrayal at Florus's "cruelty" in doing "that day . . . what none had ever done before, namely, to scourge before his tribunal and nail to the cross men of equestrian rank, men who, if Jews by birth, were at least invested with that Roman dignity" (*J.W.* 2.308). Philo is similarly outraged when the Egyptian governor Flaccus ignores customs about different types of scourges for people of different social standing and treats Alexandrian Jews as being "of the meanest rank" (*Flacc.* 78–80).

23. Garnsey, *Social Status,* 100.

24. Garnsey, *Social Status,* 221–22.

25. BDF, #391. Matthew uses the construction fifteen times.

26. Notice that in 12:14 they "take counsel . . . *how/in what way* to destroy him." That is, the outcome is certain; the only question concerns its means.

27. Often the verb "see" denotes not only physical sight but insight: 13:10–17; 20:29–34; 28:1; see Carter, " 'To See the Tomb.' "

28. For example, Josephus refers to governors of Syria such as Vitellius (*Ant.* 15.405), Titius (*Ant.* 16.270), Saturninus and Volumnius (*Ant.* 16.344), Petronius (*Ant.* 19.301), Marsus (*Ant.* 19.340), Varro (*J.W.* 1.398) and Ummidius Quadratus (*J.W.* 2.239), as well as governors of Judea such as Florus (*Ant.* 18.25) and Pilate (*Ant.* 18:55), as well as Tiberius Alexander, governor of Egypt (*J.W.* 2.492). Lémonon, *Pilate,* 63–71. Philo refers to the Egyptian governor Flaccus by this term (*Flacc.* 31, 163) as well as by ἐπίτροπος (*Flacc.* 43).

29. Brunt, "The Administrators of Roman Egypt," *Roman Imperial Themes,* 215–54.

30. Arnold H. M. Jones, "Procurators and Prefects"; Fergus Millar, ed., *Roman Empire,* 161–69; Brunt, "Administrators of Roman Egypt," *Roman Imperial Themes,* 215; Brunt, "Procuratorial Jurisdiction," *Roman Imperial Themes,* 163–87; G. P. Burton, "Proconsuls, Assizes," 104–5; N. J. Austin and N. Rankov, *Exploratio,* 123–25, 142–84; Lémonon, *Pilate,* 72–98; Richard Alston, *Aspects* 255–59. For the governor's exercise of justice as a delegated representative of, and in consultation with, the emperor, Garnsey, *Social Status,* 72–85.

31. The noun ἡγεμών (*hēgemōn*) appears six times in this narrative at Acts 23:24, 26, 33; 24:1, 10; 26:30.

32. Anthony J. Marshall, "Governors on the Move"; Burton, "Proconsuls."

33. Brent Kinman, "Pilate's Assize."

34. Marshall, "Symbols and Showmanship."

35. Wengst, *Pax Romana*, 35–37.

36. Brunt, "Charges of Provincial Maladministration," *Roman Imperial Themes*, 53–95, 487–506; for *repetundae* trials involving Pliny, Garnsey, *Social Status*, 50–58.

37. Brunt, "Charges of Provincial Maladministration," *Roman Imperial Themes*, 71–95; Garnsey, *Social Status*, 65–85; for the legal privileges of equestrians, 237–42.

38. Garnsey, *Social Status*, 55.

39. Bond, *Pontius Pilate*, 133, 136.

40. A number of scholars connect various diseases and instances of demon possession with circumstances of imperial oppression and class conflict. See Walter Wink, *Unmasking the Powers*, 43–52; Paul Hollenbach, "Jesus, Demoniacs" Gerd Theissen, *Miracle Stories*, 231–64.

41. For texts, Carter, *Matthew and the Margins*, 188–89, 236–37.

42. Davies and Allison, *Matthew* 1.243.

43. Carter, *Matthew and the Margins*, 230–31.

44. Compare Mark 15:1 and Matt 27:1; Mark 15:2 and Matt 27:11 (2*x*); Mark 15:16 and Matt 27:27.

45. Compare Mark 15:9 and Matt 27:17; Mark 15:12 and Matt 27:22.

46. Compare Mark 15:11 and Matt 27:20.

47. A. N. Sherwin-White, *Roman Society*, 25–26. This view does not deny that the presentation may also be influenced by and/or conformed to the suffering servant in Isa 53:7 who also resists imperial power by absorbing its violence for others.

48. Herod was appointed king in 40 B.C.E. by the Roman senate and gained control by 37. Josephus identifies him as "King of the Jews" (*Ant.* 16.311) and has Herod acknowledge Rome as "masters of the world (*Ant.* 15.387).

49. Josephus designates Roman emperors as βασιλεύς (*basileus*, king) in *J.W.* 3.351; 4.596; 5.563; Titus the βασιλεύς, *J.W.* 5.58; see also Appian, *Bell. Civ.* 2.86 (Hadrian).

50. Richard A. Horsley and John S. Hanson, *Bandits, Prophets*, "Royal Pretenders and Popular Messianic Movements," 88–134; also McGing, "Pontius Pilate," 417–24, 435–38.

51. Sherwin-White, *Roman Society*, 24.

52. I find it difficult to agree with Davies and Allison (*Matthew* 3.581–82), who comment, "It is thus odd that, to judge from his response, Pilate does not take the treasonous affirmation to be a threat to Rome. Evidently Pilate views Jesus with incredulous contempt; he is too impotent to be dangerous." Hagner (*Matthew* 2.818) takes a similar line, arguing (correctly) that Pilate finds Jesus guilty of being an insurrectionist, but goes on to claim that Pilate knows from Jesus' silence that he is no threat at all. I am arguing quite the reverse. Pilate does take the affirmation as a threat. That's why he crucifies Jesus. The exchange and actions in 27:15–25 attest not Pilate's doubts about Jesus' innocence but his cunning in apportioning the blame for his execution of a Jewish figure at Passover. One does not crucify someone too impotent to be dangerous.

53. Carter, "'Solomon in all his glory,'" 10–22; Carter, *Matthew and the Margins*, 178.

54. Carter, *Matthew and the Margins*, 413–18, and the literature cited there.

55. Deirdre Good, *Jesus the Meek King*.

56. Bond, *Pontius Pilate*, 128–29.

57. Bond, *Pontius Pilate*, 128.

58. I clearly disagree with Robert H. Gundry (*Matthew*, 561–62) who reads Pilate's words as a confession and argues that Matthew presents him as a convert.

59. See Marinus de Jonge, "Messiah," *ABD* 4.777–88, for an excellent discussion of the texts.

60. Raymond Brown (*Death of the Messiah*, 1.801) distinguishes the two designations as political and religious, but such a division is false to the imperial world in which the two spheres are mixed, as well as to the content of the terms, both of which attest the establishment of God's empire over all, including Rome.

61. I am largely following Weaver, "Power and Powerlessness," 191–92, though I will depart from some of her conclusions.

62. Weaver ("Power and Powerlessness," 193) observes about Jesus: opponents confer against him to put him to death (27:1); bind him and lead him away (27:2); hand him over (27:2, 18, 26); question and speak to him (27:11–13); accuse him (27:12); solicit support for or condemnation of him (27:15–23); dream about him (27:19).

63. Is Barabbas's name "Jesus Barabbas" in 27:16, 17? While the name may have been suppressed subsequently out of reverence, the external support for its inclusion is "relatively slender." See Bruce Metzger, *Textual Commentary*, 67–68.

64. There is no evidence for the custom of releasing a prisoner at Passover. But governors could release prisoners at their own discretion (Albinus, in Josephus, *Ant.* 20.215). Robert L. Merritt ("Jesus, Barabbas," 57–68) argues for an ancient Near Eastern tradition of rulers releasing prisoners at festivals.

65. Weaver, "Power and Powerlessness," 194; Bond (*Pontius Pilate*, 125) also inappropriately highlights Jesus' "innocence," as does Goldberg, *Jews and Christians*, 189–91.

66. Brown (*Death of the Messiah*, 1.802–3) helpfully finds in the word a combination of their envy over Jesus' influence and zealousness to defend their convictions against his attacks on the temple and blasphemous claims to be God's agent in 26:63–65.

67. The strength of the cry, along with the fact that the disciples are in hiding, may account for the lack of action in the narrative against Jesus' followers.

68. The phrase is translated in BAGD, 900, as "he is accomplishing nothing," which I understand to refer not to an attempt to save Jesus, but to his attempts to assess how much support there was for Jesus and so what sort of threat his execution might pose.

69. For discussion of the numerous issues raised by 27:25 (not addressed here), see Carter, *Matthew and the Margins*, 528–29, and the literature cited there.

70. The elite initiate his crucifixion. Various elite factions cooperate to remove this pest (27:1–2). The governor holds a referendum. He indicates he is acting "for them." The religious leaders manipulate the crowd. The crowd says the "right" thing. The prisoner is condemned to die. The governor absolves himself of responsibility and places it on the people. The people accept it.

71. Lenski, *Power*, 50.

72. On 24:27–31, see chapter 5, section 7 above; Carter, *Matthew and the Margins*, 476–79.

73. Carter, *Matthew and the Margins*, 405–7.

Conclusion

1. Warren Carter, *Matthew: Storyteller,* 80–96, and the literature cited there.

2. For these emphases, including a discussion of marginality, Carter, *Matthew and the Margins,* Introduction, 1–14, 43–49.

3. Walter E. Pilgrim, *Uneasy Neighbors,* 202–210.

4. Pilgrim, *Uneasy Neighbors,* 192. Pilgrim goes on to discuss each response and evaluate its appropriateness (192–210). I am reversing the order of Pilgrim/Strieter's paradigm because their third option is closest in my view to Matthew's approach, which has been our focus.

5. Pilgrim, *Uneasy Neighbors,* 193.

6. Pilgrim (*Uneasy Neighbors,* 193) recognizes that some have seen this option to mandate submission and cooperation with a ruling power as God's agent regardless of its policies or actions. I do not think, nor does Pilgrim, that this response mandates such submission.

7. Pilgrim, *Uneasy Neighbors,* 201; for his good discussion of this option, 194–201.

8. Letty Russell, *Household of Freedom,* 83–85; Ada María Isasi-Díaz, "Solidarity," 32, 306 n. 8.

9. The servant image is applied to Jesus at numerous points in the Gospel including by God in the words at the baptism and transfiguration (3:17; 17:5), through the citing of Scriptures in 8:17 and 12:17–21 in a passage that contrasts the ways of the Deutero-Isaiah servant with imperial actions, and by Jesus himself in describing the giving of his life for others (20:25–28).

Bibliography

Note: All citations of ancient writers come from or refer to the Loeb Classical Library editions, with two exceptions. For Aristides, *Roman Oration,* see J. H. Oliver, "The Ruling Power: A Study of the Roman Empire in the Second Century After Christ through the Roman Oration of Aelius Aristides," *Transactions of the American Philosophical Society* 43 (1959): 871–1003. For Malalas, see E. Jeffreys, et al., *The Chronicle of John Malalas: A Translation* (Byzantina Australiensia 4; Melbourne: Australian Association for Byzantine Studies, 1986).

Allen, Willoughby C. 1910. *A Critical and Exegetical Commentary on the Gospel According to S. Matthew.* International Critical Commentary. New York: Charles Scribner's Sons.

Allison, Dale. 1988. "Two Notes on a Key Text: Matthew 11:25–30." *Journal of Theological Studies* 39: 477–85.

————. 1993. *The New Moses: A Matthean Typology.* Minneapolis: Fortress.

Alston, Richard. 1998. *Aspects of Roman History AD 14–117.* London: Routledge.

Anderson, Janice C. 1994. *Matthew's Narrative Web: Over, and Over, and Over Again.* Journal for the Study of the New Testament Supplement Series 91. Sheffield: JSOT Press.

Austin, N. J. and N. Rankov. 1995. *Exploratio: Military and Political Intelligence in the Roman World.* London: Routledge.

Axtell, Harold L. 1907. *The Deification of Abstract Ideas in Roman Literature and Inscriptions.* Chicago: University of Chicago Press.

Bacon, Benjamin W. 1930. *Studies in Matthew.* London: Constable.

Balch, David L., ed. 1991. *Social History of the Matthean Community: Cross-Disciplinary Approaches.* Minneapolis: Fortress.

Bammel, Ernst. 1984. "The Revolution Theory from Reimarus to Brandon." In *Jesus and the Politics of His Day,* 11–68. Edited by E. Bammel and C. F. D. Moule. Cambridge: Cambridge University Press.

Barbalet, J. M. 1985. "Power and Resistance." *British Journal of Sociology* 36: 521–48.

Barclay, John M. G. 1996. *Jews in the Mediterranean Diaspora From Alexander to Trajan (323 B.C.E.–117 C.E.).* Edinburgh: T. & T. Clark.

Bartelt, Andrew H. 1996. *The Book Around Immanuel: Style and Structure in Isaiah 2–12.* Winona Lake, Ind.: Eisenbrauns.

Barth, Gerhard. 1963. "Matthew's Understanding of the Law." In *Tradition and Interpretation in Matthew,* 58–164. Edited by G. Bornkamm et al. London: SCM.

Barton, Stephen C. 1994. *Discipleship and Family Ties in Mark and Matthew.* Society for New Testament Studies Monograph Series, 80. Cambridge: Cambridge University Press.

Bauckham, Richard. 1986. "The Coin in the Fish's Mouth." In *Gospel Perspectives: The Miracles of Jesus,* 219–52. Vol. 6. Edited by D. Wenham and C. Blomberg. Sheffield: JSOT Press.

———. 1993. "The Economic Critique of Rome in Revelation 18." In *The Climax of Prophecy,* 338–83. Edinburgh: T. & T. Clark.

———. 1998. *God Crucified: Monotheism and Christology in the New Testament.* Grand Rapids, Mich.: Eerdmans.

Bauckham, Richard, ed. 1998. *The Gospels for All Christians: Rethinking the Gospel Audiences.* Grand Rapids, Mich.: Eerdmans.

Bauer, David R. 1996. "The Literary and Theological Function of the Genealogy in Matthew's Gospel." In *Treasures Old and New: Recent Contributions to Matthean Studies,* 129–59. Edited by D. R. Bauer and M. A. Powell. Society of Biblical Literature Symposium Series 1. Atlanta: Scholars Press.

Bauer, David, and Mark Allan Powell, eds. 1996. *Treasures New and Old: Contributions to Matthean Studies.* Society of Biblical Literature Symposium Series 1. Atlanta: Scholars Press.

Baumstark, Anton. 1956. "Die Zitate des Mt.-Evangeliums aus dem Zwölfprophetenbuch." *Biblica* 37: 296–313.

Beare, Francis W. 1981. *The Gospel According to Matthew.* San Francisco: Harper & Row.

Beck, Norman A. 1997. *Anti-Roman Cryptograms in the New Testament.* New York: Peter Lang.

Berlin, Andrea M. 2002. "Romanization in Pre-Revolt Galilee" in *The First Jewish Revolt against Rome: Archaeology, History, and Ideology.* Edited by Andrea M. Berlin and J. Andrew Overman. Routledge.

Betz, Hans Dieter. 1967. "The Logion of the Easy Yoke and of Rest (Matt 11:28–30)." *Journal of Biblical Literature* 86: 10–24.

———. 1995. *The Sermon on the Mount: A Commentary on the Sermon on the Mount, including the Sermon on the Plain (Matthew 5:3–7:27 and Luke 6:20–49).* Minneapolis: Augsburg Fortress.

Bilde, P. 1979. "The Causes of the Jewish War According to Josephus." *Journal for the Study of Judaism* 10: 179–202.

Blair, Edward P. 1960. *Jesus in the Gospel of Matthew.* New York: Abingdon.

Bond, Helen. 1996. "The Coins of Pontius Pilate: Part of an Attempt to Provoke the People or to Integrate them into the Empire?" *Journal for the Study of Judaism* 27: 241–62.

———. 1998. *Pontius Pilate in History and Interpretation.* Cambridge: Cambridge University Press.

Bonnard, Pierre. 1982. *L'Évangile selon Saint Matthieu.* Commentaire du Nouveau Testament 1. 2d ed. Geneva: Labor et Fides.

Bornkamm, Gunther. 1963. "End Expectation and Church in Matthew." In *Tradition and Interpretation in Matthew*, 15–51. Edited by G. Bornkamm et al. London: SCM Press.

Bowersock, Glen W. 1973. "Syria under Vespasian." *The Journal of Roman Studies* 63: 133–40.

———. 1986. "The Mechanics of Subversion in the Roman Provinces." In *Opposition et Résistances à l'Empire d'Auguste á Trajan*, 291–320. Edited by A. Giovanni. Entretiens sur L'Antiquité Classique 23. Geneva: Fondation Hardt.

Brandon, Samuel G. F. 1967. *Jesus and the Zealots*. Manchester, U.K.: Manchester University Press.

Branigan, Keith. 1991. "Images—or Mirages—of Empire? An Archaeological Approach to the Problem." In *Images of Empire*, 91–106. Edited by L. Alexander. Journal for the Study of the Old Testament Supplement Series 122. Sheffield: Sheffield Academic Press.

Braund, David. 1993. "Piracy under the Principate and the Ideology of Imperial Eradication." In *War and Society in the Roman World*, 195–212. Edited by J. Rich and G. Shipley. London: Routledge.

Brooke, George J. "The Kittim in the Qumran Pesharim." In *Images of Empire*, 135–59. Edited by L. Alexander. Journal for the Study of the Old Testament Supplement Series 122. Sheffield: Sheffield Academic Press.

Brown, John P. 1983. "Techniques of Imperial Control: The Background of the Gospel Event." In *The Bible and Liberation: Political and Social Hermeneutics*, 357–77. Edited by N. Gottwald. The Bible and Liberation Series. Maryknoll, N.Y.: Orbis Books.

Brown, Raymond. 1993. *The Birth of the Messiah*. New updated edition. New York: Doubleday.

———. 1994. *The Death of the Messiah*. New York: Doubleday.

Broughton, Thomas R. 1975. "Roman Asia Minor." In *An Economic Survey of Ancient Rome*, 4.499–916. Edited by T. Frank. New York: Octagon Books.

Brunt, Peter A. 1990. "Laus Imperii." In *Roman Imperial Themes*, 288–323. Oxford: Clarendon.

———. 1990. "Labor." In *The Roman World*, 2.701–46. Edited by J. Wacher. London: Routledge.

———. 1990. *Roman Imperial Themes*. Oxford: Clarendon.

———. 1990. "The Romanization of the Ruling Classes in the Roman Empire." In *Roman Imperial Themes*, 267–81. Oxford: Clarendon.

Bureth, Paul. 1964. *Les Titulatures impériales dans les papyrus, les ostraca et les inscriptions d'Égypte*. Bruxelles: Fondation Égyptologique Reine Élisabeth.

Burnett, Fred W. 1981. *The Testament of Jesus-Sophia: A Redaction Critical Study of the Eschatological Discourse in Matthew*. Washington, D.C.: University Press of America.

Burridge, Richard A. 1992. *What Are the Gospels? A Comparison with Graeco-Roman Biography*. Society for New Testament Studies Monograph Series 70. Cambridge: Cambridge University Press.

Burton, G. P. 1975. "Proconsuls, Assizes and the Administration of Justice under the Empire." *Journal of Roman Studies* 65: 92–106.

Campbell, J. Brian. 1978. "The Marriage of Soldiers Under the Empire." *Journal of Roman Studies* 68: 153–66.

———. 1993. "War and Diplomacy: Rome and Parthia, 31 BC-AD 235." In *War and Society in the Roman World,* 213–40. Edited by J. Rich and G. Shipley. London: Routledge.

Carney, Thomas F. 1972. *The Shape of the Past: Models and Antiquity.* Lawrence, Kans.: Coronado Press.

Carradice, Ian. 1983. *Coinage and Finances in the Reign of Domitian A.D. 81–96.* British Archaeological Reports, International Series 178. Oxford: B.A.R.

Carter, Warren. 1992. "Kernels and Narrative Blocks: The Structure of Matthew's Gospel." *Catholic Biblical Quarterly* 54: 463–81.

———. 1993. "The Crowds in Matthew's Gospel." *Catholic Biblical Quarterly* 55:54–67.

———. 1994. *Households and Discipleship: A Study of Matthew 19–20.* Journal for the Study of the New Testament Supplement Series 103. Sheffield: JSOT Press.

———. 1995. "Recalling the Lord's Prayer: The Authorial Audience and Matthew's Prayer as Familiar Liturgical Experience." *Catholic Biblical Quarterly* 57: 514–30.

———. 1996. *Matthew: Storyteller, Interpreter, Evangelist.* Peabody, Mass.: Hendrickson.

———. 1996. "Some Contemporary Scholarship on the Sermon on the Mount." *Currents in Research: Biblical Studies* 4: 183–215.

———. 1996. " 'To See the Tomb': A Note on Matthew's Women at the Tomb (Mt 28:1)." *Expository Times* 107: 201–5.

———. 1997. "Matthew 4:18–22 and Matthean Discipleship: An Audience-Oriented Perspective." *Catholic Biblical Quarterly* 59: 58–75.

———. 1997. "Narrative/Literary Approaches to Matthean Theology: The 'Reign of the Heavens' as an Example (Mt 4:17–5:12)." *Journal for the Study of the New Testament* 67: 3–27.

———. 1997. " 'Solomon in all his glory': Intertextuality and Matthew 6:29." *Journal for the Study of the New Testament* 65: 3–25.

———. 1998. "Toward an Imperial-Critical Reading of Matthew's Gospel." *Society of Biblical Literature 1998 Seminar Papers: Part One,* 296–324. Society of Biblical Literature Seminar Papers 37. Atlanta: Scholars Press.

———. 1999. "Contested Claims: Roman Imperial Theology and Matthew's Gospel." *Biblical Theology Bulletin* 29: 56–67.

———. 1999. "Paying the Tax to Rome as Subversive Praxis: Matthew 17:24–27." *Journal for the Study of the New Testament* 76: 3–31.

———. 2000. "Evoking Isaiah: Matthean Soteriology and an Intertextual Reading of Isaiah 7–9 in Matthew 1:23 and 4:15–16." *Journal of Biblical Literature* 119: 503–20.

————. 2000. *Matthew and the Margins: A Sociopolitical and Religious Reading.* The Bible and Liberation Series. Maryknoll, N.Y.: Orbis Books.

————. 2000. " 'To Save His People from Their Sins' (Matt 1:21): Rome's Empire and Matthew's Salvation as Sovereignty." *Society of Biblical Literature 2000 Seminar Papers,* 379–401. Society of Biblical Literature Seminar Papers 39. Atlanta: Scholars Press.

Carter, Warren, and John Paul Heil. 1998. *Matthew's Parables: Audience-Oriented Perspectives.* Catholic Biblical Quarterly Monograph Series 30. Washington: Catholic Biblical Association.

Cassidy, Richard J. 1979. "Matthew 17:24–27—A Word on Civil Taxes." *Catholic Biblical Quarterly* 41: 571–80.

Chandler, Tertius, and Gerald Fox. 1974. *Three Thousand Years of Urban Growth.* New York: Academic Press.

Charette, Blaine. 1992. *The Theme of Recompense in Matthew's Gospel.* Journal for the Study of the New Testament Supplement Series 79. Sheffield: JSOT Press.

————. 1992. " 'To Proclaim Liberty to the Captives': Matthew 11:28–30 in the Light of OT Prophetic Expectation." *New Testament Studies* 38: 290–97.

Charlesworth, James H., ed. 1992. *The Messiah.* Minneapolis: Fortress.

Charlesworth, Martin P. 1925. " 'Deus Noster Caesar.' " *The Classical Review* 39: 113–15.

————. 1939. *Documents Illustrating the Reigns of Claudius and Nero.* Cambridge: Cambridge University Press.

Chatman, Seymour. 1978. *Story and Discourse.* Ithaca, N.Y.: Cornell University Press.

Chilton, Bruce. 1978. "Regnum Dei Deus Est." *Scottish Journal of Theology* 31: 261–70.

————. 1990. "A Coin of Three Realms (Matthew 17.24–27)." In *The Bible in Three Dimensions,* 269–82. Edited by D. J. A. Clines, S. E. Fowl, and S. E. Porter. Journal for the Study of the Old Testament Supplement Series 87. Sheffield: JSOT Press.

Chilton, Bruce, ed. 1984. *The Kingdom of God.* Issues in Religion and Theology 5. Philadelphia: Fortress/SPCK.

Christ, Felix. 1970. *Jesus Sophia: Die Sophia-Christologie bei den Synoptikern.* Abhandlungen zur Theologie des Alten und Neuen Testaments 57. Zürich: Zwingli-Verlag.

Clark, Kenneth W. 1980. "The Meaning of [Kata]kyrieyein." In *The Gentile Bias and Other Essays,* 207–12. Leiden: E. J. Brill.

Clegg, Stewart. 1989. *Frameworks of Power.* London: Sage.

Clements, Ronald E. 1980. *Isaiah 1–39.* New Century Bible Commentary. Grand Rapids, Mich.: Eerdmans.

Cope, Lamar. 1976. *Matthew: A Scribe Trained for the Kingdom of Heaven.* Catholic Biblical Quarterly Monograph Series 5. Washington, D.C.: Catholic Biblical Association of America.

————. 1989. " 'To the Close of the Age': The Role of Apocalyptic Thought in the Gospel of Matthew." In *Apocalyptic in the New Testament: Essays in Honor of*

J. Louis Martyn, 113–24. Edited by J. Marcus and M. Soards. Journal for the Study of the New Testament Supplement Series 24. Sheffield: JSOT Press.

Corbier, Mireille. 1991. "City, Territory and Taxation." In *City and Country in the Ancient World*, 211–39. Edited by J. Rich and A. Wallace-Hadrill. New York: Routledge.

Corley, Kathleen. 1993. *Private Women, Public Meals: Social Conflict in the Synoptic Tradition*. Peabody, Mass.: Hendrickson.

Cornell, Tim. 1993. "The End of Roman Imperial Expansion." In *War and Society in the Roman World*, 139–70. Edited by J. Rich and G. Shipley. London: Routledge.

Cotter, Wendy J. 1996. "The Collegia and Roman Law: State Restrictions on Voluntary Associations 64 BCE–200 CE." In *Voluntary Associations in the Graeco-Roman World*, 74–89. Edited by J. S. Kloppenborg and S. G. Wilson. London: Routledge.

Cramer, Frederick H. 1951. "Expulsion of Astrologers From Ancient Rome." *Classica et Mediaevalia* 12: 9–50.

Crosby, Michael. 1988. *House of Disciples: Church, Economics and Justice in Matthew*. Maryknoll, N.Y.: Orbis Books.

Crossan, John Dominic. 1991. *The Historical Jesus: The Life of a Mediterranean Jewish Peasant*. HarperSanFrancisco.

Cullmann, Oscar. 1963. *The Christology of the New Testament*. Philadelphia: Westminster.

Cuss, Dominique. 1974. *Imperial Cult and Honorary Terms in the New Testament*. Paradosis 23. Fribourg, Switz.: University Press.

Daube, David. 1987. "Temple Tax." In *Jesus, the Gospels, and the Church*, 121–34. Edited by E. P. Sanders. Macon, Ga.: Mercer University Press.

Davies, William D. 1964. *The Setting of the Sermon on the Mount*. Cambridge: Cambridge University Press.

Davies, William D. and Dale Allison. 1988–1997. *A Critical and Exegetical Commentary on the Gospel According to Matthew*. Three volumes. International Critical Commentary. Edinburgh: T. & T. Clark.

de Jonge, Marinus. 1992. "Messiah." In *Anchor Bible Dictionary*, 4.777–88. New York: Doubleday.

de Lange, N. R. M. 1978. "Jewish Attitudes to the Roman Empire." In *Imperialism in the Ancient World*, 255–81. Edited by P. D. A. Garnsey and C. R. Whittaker. Cambridge: Cambridge University Press.

Deissmann, Adolf. 1910. *Light From the Ancient East*. New York: Hodder & Stoughton.

Delling, Gerhard. 1972. "τέλος," *Theological Dictionary of the New Testament* 8: 49–61.

Derrett, J. Duncan M. 1970. "Peter's Penny." In *Law in the New Testament*, 247–65. London: Darton, Longman & Todd.

Deutsch, Celia. 1987. *Hidden Wisdom and the Easy Yoke: Wisdom, Torah, and Discipleship in Matthew 11:25–30*. Journal for the Study of the New Testament Supplement Series 18. Sheffield: Sheffield Academic Press.

————. 1990. "Wisdom in Matthew: Transformation of a Symbol." *Novum Testamentum* 32: 13–47.

————. 1996. *Lady Wisdom, Jesus and the Sages: Metaphor and Social Context in Matthew's Gospel.* Valley Forge, Pa.: Trinity Press International.

Downey, Glanville. 1961. *A History of Antioch in Syria from Seleucus to the Arab Conquest.* Princeton, N.J.: Princeton University Press.

Draisma, Sipke, ed. 1989. *Intertextuality in Biblical Writings: Essays in Honor of Bas van Iersel.* Kampen, Netherlands: Kok.

Dunn, James D. G. 1989. *Christology on the Making: An Investigation into the Origins of the Doctrine of the Incarnation.* 2d ed. Grand Rapids, Mich.: Eerdmans.

————. 1998. *The Theology of Paul the Apostle.* Grand Rapids, Mich.: Eerdmans.

Dyson, Stephen. 1971. "Native Revolts in the Roman Empire." *Historia* 20: 239–74.

Eddy, Samuel K. 1961. *The King is Dead: Studies in the Near Eastern Resistance to Hellenism 334–31 B.C.* Lincoln: University of Nebraska Press.

Edwards, Douglas R. 1992. "Religion, Power and Politics: Jewish Defeats by the Romans in Iconography and Josephus." In *Diaspora Jews and Judaism: Essays in Honor of, and in Dialogue with A. Thomas Kraabel*, 293–310. Edited by J. A. Overman and R. S. MacLennan. South Florida Studies in the History of Judaism 41. Atlanta: Scholars Press.

Edwards, James R. 1987. "The Use of προσέρχεσθαι in the Gospel of Matthew." *Journal of Biblical Literature* 106: 65–74.

Edwards, Richard A. 1985. *Matthew's Story of Jesus.* Philadelphia: Fortress.

Eisenstadt, S. N. 1963. *The Political Systems of Empires.* New York: Macmillan/Free Press.

Esler, Philip F. 1995. "God's Honour and Rome's Triumph: Response to the Fall of Jerusalem in 70 CE in Three Jewish Apocalypses." In *Modeling Early Christianity*, 239–58. Edited by P. Esler. London: Routledge.

Fears, J. Rufus. 1975. "Nero as Vicegerent of the Gods in Seneca's *De Clementia*." *Hermes* 103: 486–96.

————. 1977. *Princeps A Diis Electus. The Divine Election of the Emperor as a Political Concept at Rome.* Papers and Monographs of the American Academy in Rome 26. Rome: American Academy in Rome.

————. 1981a. "The Cult of Jupiter and Roman Imperial Ideology." In *Aufstieg und Niedergang der römischen Welt*, 2.17.1:3–141. Berlin: Walter de Gruyter.

————. 1981b. "The Cult of Virtues and Roman Imperial Ideology." In *Aufstieg und Niedergang der römischen Welt*, 2.17.2:827–948. Berlin: Walter de Gruyter.

————. 1981c. "The Theology of Victory at Rome: Approaches and Problems." In *Aufstieg und Niedergang der römischen Welt*, 2.17.2:736–825. Berlin: Walter de Gruyter.

Fenton, J. C. 1977. *Saint Matthew.* Westminster Pelican Commentaries. Philadelphia: Westminster.

Fewell Dana N., ed. 1992. *Reading between Texts: Intertextuality and the Hebrew Bible.* Literary Currents in Biblical Interpretation. Louisville: Westminster/John Knox.

Foley, John M. 1991. *Immanent Art: From Structure to Meaning in Traditional Oral Epic.* Bloomington, Ind.: Indiana University Press.

France, Richard. 1981. "The Formula-Quotations of Matthew 2 and the Problem of Communication." *New Testament Studies* 27: 233–51.

Frankemölle, Hubert. 1974. *Jahwebund und Kirche Christi.* Neutestamentliche Abhandlungen 10. Munster, Ger.: Aschendorff.

―――. 1994. *Matthäus: Kommentar 1.* Düsseldorf, Ger.: Patmos.

Freire, Paulo. 1993. *Pedagogy of the Oppressed.* Rev. ed. New York: Crossroads.

Freyne, Sean. 1980. *Galilee from Alexander the Great to Hadrian 323 BCE to 135 CE.* Wilmington, Del., and Notre Dame, Ind.: Michael Glazier/University of Notre Dame Press.

―――. 1988. *Galilee, Jesus, and the Gospels: Literary Approaches and Historical Investigations.* Philadelphia: Fortress.

Fuller, Reginald. 1965. *The Foundations of New Testament Christology.* New York: Charles Scribner's Sons.

Gaechter, Paul. 1963. *Das Matthäus Evangelium.* Innsbruck, Aus.: Tyrolia.

Gagé, Jean. 1933. "La théologie de la victoire impériale." *Revue historique* 172: 1–43.

Garland, David. 1987. "The Temple Tax in Matthew." In *Society of Biblical Literature 1987 Seminar Papers,* 190–209. Edited by K. H. Richards. Society of Biblical Literature Seminar Papers 26. Atlanta: Scholars Press.

―――. *Reading Matthew.* New York: Crossroad.

Garnsey, Peter. 1970. *Social Status and Legal Privilege in the Roman Empire.* Oxford: Clarendon.

―――. 1976. "Peasants in Ancient Roman Society." *Journal of Peasant Studies* 3: 221–35.

―――. 1978. "Rome's African Empire Under the Principate." In *Imperialism in the Ancient World,* 223–54. Edited by P. D. A. Garnsey and C. R. Whittaker. Cambridge: Cambridge University Press.

―――. 1988. *Famine and Food Supply in the Graeco-Roman World.* Cambridge: Cambridge University Press.

Garnsey, Peter, and Richard Saller. 1987. *The Roman Empire: Economy, Society and Culture.* Berkeley: University of California Press.

Gench, Frances T. 1997. *Wisdom in the Christology of Matthew.* Lanham, Md.: University Press of America.

Gill, David W. J. 1997. "The Roman Empire as a Context for the New Testament." In *Handbook to Exegesis of the New Testament,* 389–406. Edited by S. E. Porter. Leiden: Brill.

Gnilka, Joachim. 1986, 1988. *Das Matthäusevangelium.* 2 Vols. Herders theologischer Kommentar zum Neuen Testament 1. Freiburg, Ger.: Herder.

Goldberg, Michael. 1985. *Jews and Christians, Getting Our Stories Straight: The Exodus and the Passion-Resurrection.* Nashville: Abingdon.

Good, Deirdre. 1990. "The Verb ΑΝΑΧΩΡΕΩ in Matthew's Gospel." *Novum Testamentum* 32: 1–12.

―――. 1999. *Jesus the Meek King.* Harrisburg, Pa.: Trinity Press International.

Goodman, Martin. 1987. *The Ruling Class of Judaea: The Origins of the Jewish Revolt Against Rome A.D. 66–70*. Cambridge: Cambridge University Press.

———. 1989. "Nerva, the *Fiscus Judaicus* and Jewish Identity." *Journal of Roman Studies* 79: 40–44.

Gottwald, Norman. 1979. *The Tribes of Yahweh: A Sociology of the Religion of Liberated Israel, 1250–1050 BCE*. Maryknoll, N.Y.: Orbis.

Grant, Michael. 1973. *The Jews in the Roman World*. New York: Charles Scribner's Sons.

Grundmann, Walter. 1968. *Das Evangelium nach Matthäus*. Theologischer Handkommentar zum Neuen Testament 1. Berlin: Evangelische Verlagsanstalt.

Gundry, Robert H. 1967. *The Use of the Old Testament in St. Matthew's Gospel with Special Reference to the Messianic Hope*. Novum Testamentum Supplements 18. Leiden: E. J. Brill.

———. 1994. *Matthew: A Commentary on His Handbook for a Mixed Church Under Persecution*. 2d ed. Grand Rapids, Mich.: Eerdmans.

Haenchen, Ernst. 1966. *Der Weg Jesu: Eine Erklärung des Markus-Evangeliums und der kanonischen Parallel*. Berlin: Alfred Töpelmann.

Hagner, Donald. 1993. *Matthew 1–13*. Word Bible Commentary 33A. Dallas: Word.

———. 1994. "Matthew's Eschatology." In *To Tell the Mystery: Essays on New Testament Eschatology in Honor of R. H. Gundry*, 49–71. Edited by T. Schmidt and M. Silva. Journal for the Study of the New Testament Supplement Series 100. Sheffield: Sheffield Academic Press.

———. 1995. *Matthew 14–28*. Word Bible Commentary 33B. Dallas: Word.

Hahn, Ferdinand. 1969. *The Titles of Jesus in Christology*. New York: World.

Hands, A. R. 1968. *Charities and Social Aid in Greece and Rome*. Ithaca, N.Y.: Cornell University Press.

Hanson, K. C. 1997. "The Galilean Fishing Economy and the Jesus Tradition." *Biblical Theology Bulletin* 27: 99–111.

Hanson, K. C., and Douglas E. Oakman. 1998. *Palestine in the Time of Jesus: Social Structures and Social Conflicts*. Minneapolis: Fortress.

Hardie, Alex. 1983. *Statius and the Silvae: Poets, Patrons and Epideixis in the Graeco-Roman World*. ARCA Classical and Medieval Texts, Papers and Monographs 9. Liverpool: Francis Cairns.

Hare, Douglas R. A. 1993. *Matthew*. Interpretation. Louisville: John Knox.

Hare, Douglas, and Daniel Harrington. 1975. " 'Make Disciples of All the Gentiles' (Mt 28:19)." *Catholic Biblical Quarterly* 37: 359–69.

Harrington, Daniel J. 1991. *The Gospel of Matthew*. Sacra Pagina 1. Collegeville, Minn.: Liturgical Press.

Hart, H. St. J. 1952. "Judea and Rome: The Official Commentary," *Journal of Theological Studies* 3: 172–98.

Hartman, Lars. 1972. "Scriptural Exegesis in the Gospel of St. Matthew and the Problem of Communication." In *L'Évangile selon Matthieu: Rédaction et théologie*, 131–52. Edited by M. Didier. Bibliotheca ephemeridum theologicarum lovaniensium 29. Gembloux: J. Duculot.

Hays, Richard. 1989. *Echoes of Scripture in the Letters of Paul.* New Haven: Yale University Press.

Hemer, Colin J. 1973. "The Edfu *Ostraka* and the Jewish Tax." *Palestine Exploration Quarterly* 105: 6–12.

Hengel, Martin. 1972. *Crucifixion.* Philadelphia: Fortress.

Henning, P. 1944. "Murder of the Magi." *Journal of the Royal Asiatic Society* 133–44.

Hill, David. 1972. *The Gospel of Matthew.* Grand Rapids, Mich.: Eerdmans.

———. 1980. "Son and Servant: An Essay on Matthean Christology." *Journal for the Study of the New Testament* 6: 2–16.

———. 1984. "The Figure of Jesus in Matthew's Story: A Response to Professor Kingsbury's Literary-Critical Probe." *Journal for the Study of the New Testament* 21: 37–52.

Hollenbach, Paul. 1981. "Jesus, Demoniacs, and Public Authorities." *Journal of the American Academy of Religion* 49: 567–88.

Hopkins, Keith. 1998. "Christian Number and Its Implication." *Journal of Early Christian Studies* 6:185–226.

Horbury, William. 1984. "The Temple Tax." In *Jesus and the Politics of His Day,* 265–86. Edited by E. Bammel and C. F. D. Moule. Cambridge: Cambridge University Press.

Horsley, Richard A., 1995. *Galilee: History, Politics, People.* Valley Forge, Pa.: Trinity Press International.

———. 1996. *Archaeology, History and Society in Galilee: The Social Context of Jesus and the Rabbis.* Valley Forge, Pa.: Trinity Press International.

Horsley, Richard A., ed. 1997. *Paul and Empire: Religion and Power in Roman Imperial Society.* Harrisburg, Pa.: Trinity Press International.

Horsley, Richard A., and John S. Hanson. 1988. *Bandits, Prophets, and Messiahs: Popular Movements in the Time of Jesus.* San Francisco: Harper & Row.

Howell, David B. 1990. *Matthew's Inclusive Story: A Study in the Narrative Rhetoric of the First Gospel.* Journal for the Study of the New Testament Supplement Series 42. Sheffield: JSOT Press.

Hultgren, Arland J. 1987. *Christ and His Benefits: Christology and Redemption in the New Testament.* Philadelphia: Fortress.

Hummel, Reinhart. 1963. *Die Auseinandersetzung zwischen Kirche und Judentum im Matthäusevangelium.* Beiträge zur evangelischen Theologie 33. Munich: Kaiser.

Hurtado, Larry W. 1988. *One God, One Lord: Early Christian Devotion and Ancient Jewish Monotheism.* Philadelphia: Fortress.

Irvine, Stuart A. 1990. *Isaiah, Ahaz, and the SyroEphraimite Crisis.* Society of Biblical Literature Dissertation Series 123. Atlanta: Scholars Press.

Isaac, Benjamin. 1990. *The Limits of Empire: The Roman Army in the East.* Oxford: Clarendon.

Isasi-Díaz, Ada María. 1990. "Solidarity: Love of Neighbor in the 1980's." In *Lift Every Voice: Constructing Christian Theologies from the Underside,* 31–40,

305–7. Edited by S. B. Thistlethwaite and M. P. Engels. New York: Harper & Row.

Iser, Wolfgang. 1974. *The Implied Reader: Patterns of Communication in Prose Fiction from Bunyan to Beckett.* Baltimore: Johns Hopkins University Press.

———. 1978. *The Act of Reading: A Theory of Aesthetic Response.* Baltimore: Johns Hopkins University Press.

Jauss, Hans R. 1982. *Toward an Aesthetic of Reception.* Theory and History of Literature 2. Minneapolis: University of Minnesota Press.

Jeffreys, Elizabeth, et al., eds. 1990. *Studies in John Malalas.* Byzantina Australiensia 4. Sydney: Australian Association for Byzantine Studies.

Johnson, Luke T. 1999. *The Writings of the New Testament: An Interpretation.* Minneapolis: Fortress Press.

Johnson, Marshall. 1974. "Reflections on a Wisdom Approach to Matthew's Christology." *Catholic Biblical Quarterly* 36: 44–64.

Jones, Arnold H. M. 1960. "Procurators and Prefects in the Early Principate." In *Studies in Roman Government and Law,* 117–25. New York: Praeger.

Jones, Brian W. 1984. *The Emperor Titus.* London: Croom Helm.

———. 1992. *The Emperor Domitian.* London: Routledge.

Kadman, Leo. 1960. *The Coins of the Jewish War of 66–73 CE.* Tel-Aviv, Isr.: Schocken Books.

Kaiser, Otto. 1972. *Isaiah 1–12: A Commentary.* Old Testament Library. Philadelphia: Westminster.

Käsemann, Ernst. 1969. "On the Subject of Primitive Christian Apocalyptic." In *New Testament Questions of Today,* 108–37. Philadelphia: Fortress.

Kautsky, John H. 1982. *The Politics of Aristocratic Empires.* Chapel Hill, N.C.: University of North Carolina Press.

Keck, Leander. 1986. "Toward the Renewal of New Testament Christology." *New Testament Studies* 32: 362–77.

Keener, Craig. 1999. *A Commentary on the Gospel of Matthew.* Grand Rapids, Mich.: Eerdmans.

Kee, Alistair. 1985. "The Imperial Cult: The Unmasking of an Ideology." *Scottish Journal of Religious Studies* 6: 112–28.

Kilpatrick, George D. 1946. *The Origins of the Gospel According to St. Matthew.* Oxford: Clarendon.

Kim, Tae Hun. 1998. "The Anarthrous υἱὸς θεοῦ in Mark 15,39 and the Roman Imperial Cult." *Biblica* 79: 221–41.

Kingsbury, Jack Dean. 1975. *Matthew: Structure, Christology, Kingdom.* Philadelphia: Fortress.

———. 1979. "The Figure of Peter in Matthew's Gospel as a Theological Problem." *Journal of Biblical Literature* 98: 67–83.

———. 1983. "The Theology of St. Matthew's Gospel According to the Griesbach Hypothesis." In *New Synoptic Studies,* 331–61. Edited by W. R. Farmer. Macon, Ga.: Mercer University Press.

———. 1984. "The Figure of Jesus in Matthew's Story: A Literary-Critical Probe," *Journal for the Study of the New Testament* 21: 3–36.

———. 1987. "The Developing Conflict between Jesus and the Jewish Leaders in Matthew's Gospel: A Literary-Critical Study." *Catholic Biblical Quarterly* 49: 57–73.

———. 1988. *Matthew as Story.* 2d ed. Philadelphia: Fortress.

Kinman, Brent. 1991. "Pilate's Assize and the Timing of Jesus' Trial." *Tyndale Bulletin* 42: 282–95.

———. 1995. *Jesus' Entry to Jerusalem.* Leiden: Brill.

Klein, R. W. 1979. *Israel in Exile: A Theological Interpretation.* Overtures to Biblical Theology 6. Philadelphia: Fortress.

Kloppenborg, John, and Stephen G. Wilson, eds. 1996. *Voluntary Associations in the Graeco-Roman World.* London: Routledge.

Knowles, Michael. 1993. *Jeremiah in Matthew's Gospel: The Rejected Profit [Sic!] Motif in Matthaean Redaction.* Journal for the Study of the New Testament Supplement Series 68. Sheffield: Sheffield Academic Press.

Kreitzer, Larry J. 1996. *Striking New Images: Roman Imperial Coinage and the New Testament World.* Journal for the Study of the New Testament Supplement Series 134. Sheffield: Sheffield Academic Press.

Krentz, Edgar. 1964. "The Extent of Matthew's Prologue." *Journal of Biblical Literature* 83: 409–14.

Kupp, David. 1996 *Matthew's Emmanuel: Divine Presence and God's People in the First Gospel.* Society for New Testament Studies Monograph Series 90. Cambridge: Cambridge University Press.

Lagrange, M.-J. 1948. *Évangile selon Saint Matthieu.* 7th ed. Paris: Lecoffre.

Lassus, Jean. 1976. "Antioch on the Orontes." In *The Princeton Encyclopedia of Classical Sites,* 61–63. Edited by R. Stillwell. Princeton, N.J.: Princeton University Press.

Légasse, Simon. 1972. "Jésus et l'impôt du Temple (Matthieu 17, 24–27)." *Science et Esprit* 24: 361–77.

Lémonon, Jean-Pierre. 1981. *Pilate et le Gouvernement de la Judée: Textes et Monuments.* Paris: Gabalda.

Lenski, Gerhard E. 1966. *Power and Privilege. A Theory of Social Stratification.* New York: McGraw-Hill.

Levine, Amy-Jill. 1988. *The Social and Ethnic Dimensions of Matthean Salvation History.* Studies in the Bible and Early Christianity 14. Lewiston, N.Y.: Edwin Mellen.

Lewis, Naphtali. 1968. "Domitian's Order on Requisitioned Transport and Lodgings." *Revue internationale des droits de l'antiquité,"* 15: 135–42.

Lindars, Barnabas. 1961. *New Testament Apologetic. The Doctrinal Significance of the Old Testament Quotations.* Philadelphia: Westminster.

Lohmeyer, Ernst. 1958. *Das Evangelium des Matthäus.* H. A. W. Meyer, Kritisch-exegetischer Kommentar über das Neue Testament. Göttingen, Ger.: Vandenhoeck & Ruprecht.

Louw, Johannes P., and Eugene A. Nida. 1988–89. *Greek-English Lexicon of the New Testament Based on Semantic Domains.* Two vols., 2d ed. New York: United Bible Societies.

Luck, Ulrich. 1993. *Das Evangelium nach Matthäus.* Zürcher Bibelkommentare. Zürich: Theologischer Verlag.

Luomanen, Petri. 1999. *Entering the Kingdom of Heaven: A Study of the Structure of Matthew's View of Salvation.* Wissenschaftliche Untersuchungen zum Neuen Testament 101. Tübingen, Ger.: Mohr Siebeck.

Luttwak, Edward N. 1976. *The Grand Strategy of the Roman Empire.* Baltimore: Johns Hopkins University Press.

Luz, Ulrich, 1989. *Matthew 1–7, A Commentary.* Minneapolis: Augsburg.

———. 1990. *Das Evangelium nach Matthäus.* Vol 2. Evangelisch-katholischer Kommentar zum Neuen Testament. Zurich: Benziger.

———. 1993. *The Theology of the Gospel of Matthew.* Cambridge: Cambridge University Press.

MacCormack, Sabine. 1972. "Change and Continuity in Late Antiquity: The Ceremony of Adventus." *Historia* 21: 721–52.

MacDonald, William L. 1986. *The Architecture of the Roman Empire.* Vol 2. *An Urban Appraisal.* New Haven: Yale University Press.

MacMullen, Ramsay. 1966. *Enemies of the Roman Order: Treason, Unrest, and Alienation in the Empire.* Cambridge: Harvard University Press.

———. 1974. *Roman Social Relations 50 B.C. to A.D. 284.* New Haven, Conn.: Yale University Press.

Maher, Michael. 1975. " 'Take My Yoke Upon You' (Matt 11:29)." *New Testament Studies* 22: 97–103.

Malina, Bruce J. 1987. "Wealth and Property in the New Testament and its World." *Interpretation* 41: 354–67.

Mandell, Sarah. 1984. "Who Paid the Temple Tax When the Jews Were Under Roman Rule?" *Harvard Theological Review* 77: 223–32.

Mann, Michael. 1986. *The Sources of Social Power.* Vol. 1. *A History of Power from the Beginning to A.D. 1760.* Cambridge: Cambridge University Press.

Marcus, Joel. 1988. "The Gates of Hades and the Keys of the Kingdom (Matt 16:18– 19)." *Catholic Biblical Quarterly* 50: 443–55.

Marguerat, Daniel. 1981. *Le Jugement dans l'Évangile de Matthieu.* Le Monde de la Bible. Genève: Labor et Fides.

Marshall, Anthony J. 1966. "Governors on the Move." *Phoenix* 20: 231–46.

———. 1984. "Symbols and Showmanship in Roman Public Life: The Fasces." *Phoenix* 38: 120–141.

Marxsen, Willi. 1993. *New Testament Foundations for Christian Ethics.* Minneapolis: Fortress.

Matera, Frank J. 1996. *New Testament Ethics: The Legacies of Jesus and Paul.* Louisville: Westminster John Knox.

———. 1999. *New Testament Christology.* Louisville: Westminster John Knox.

Mattern, Susan. 1999. *Rome and the Enemy: Imperial Strategy in the Principate.* Berkeley: University of California Press.

McConnell, Richard S. 1969. "Law and Prophecy in Matthew's Gospel: The Authority and Use of the Old Testament in the Gospel of Matthew." Ph.D. diss., University of Basel.

McCrum, Michael, and Arthur G. Woodhead. 1961. *Select Documents of the Principates of the Flavian Emperors*. Cambridge: Cambridge University Press.

McDermott, William C., and Anne Orentzel. 1977. "Silius Italicus and Domitian." *American Journal of Philology* 98: 24–34.

McGing, Brian C. 1991. "Pontius Pilate and his Sources." *Catholic Biblical Quarterly* 53: 416–38.

Meeks, Wayne A. 1983. *The First Urban Christians: The Social World of the Apostle Paul*. New Haven: Yale University Press.

Meeks, Wayne A., and Robert L. Wilken, 1978. *Jews and Christians in Antioch in the First Four Centuries of the Common Era*. Society of Biblical Literature: Sources for Biblical Studies 13. Missoula, Mont.: Scholars Press.

Meier, John P. 1975. "Salvation-History in Matthew: In Search of a Starting Point." *Catholic Biblical Quarterly* 37: 203–15.

———. 1977. "Nations or Gentiles in Matthew 28:19?" *Catholic Biblical Quarterly* 39: 94–102.

———. 1991. *The Vision of Matthew: Christ, Church and Morality in the First Gospel*. New York: Crossroad.

Mellor, Ronald. 1981. "The Goddess Roma." In *Aufstieg und Niedergang der römischen Welt* 2.17.2.950–1030. Berlin: Walter de Gruyter.

Merritt, Robert L. 1985. "Jesus, Barabbas, and the Paschal Pardon." *Journal of Biblical Literature* 104: 57–68.

Metzger, Bruce. 1971. *A Textual Commentary on the Greek New Testament*. London: United Bible Societies.

Millar, Fergus, ed. 1966. *The Roman Empire and Its Neighbours*. New York: Delacorte.

Mitchell, Stephen. 1987. "Imperial Buildings in the Eastern Roman Provinces." *Harvard Studies in Classical Philology* 91: 333–65.

Mohrlang, Roger. 1984. *Matthew and Paul: A Comparison of Ethical Perspectives*. Society for New Testament Studies Monograph Series 48. Cambridge: Cambridge University Press.

Momigliano, Arnaldo. 1986. "Some Preliminary Remarks on the 'Religious Opposition' to the Roman Empire." In *Opposition et Résistances à l'Empire d'Auguste á Trajan*, 103–29. Edited by A. Giovanni. Entretiens sur L'Antiquité Classique 23. Geneva: Fondation Hardt.

Montefiore, Hugh. 1964. "Jews and the Temple Tax." *New Testament Studies* 11: 60–71.

Morawiecki, Leslaw. 1977. "The Symbolism of Minerva on the Coins of Domitianus." *Klio* 59: 185–93.

Mosley, D. J. 1991. "Calgacus: Clash of Roman and Native." In *Images of Empire*, 107–21. Edited by L. Alexander. Journal for the Study of the Old Testament Supplement Series 122. Sheffield: Sheffield Academic Press.

Moulton, James H., and George Milligan. 1959. *The Vocabulary of the Greek New Testament Illustrated from the Papyri and Other Non-Literary Sources*. Grand Rapids, Mich: Eerdmans.

Mowery, Robert L. 1988. "God, Lord and Father: The Theology of the Gospel of Matthew," *Biblical Research* 33: 24–36.

———. 1997. "From Lord to Father in Matthew 1–7," *Catholic Biblical Quarterly* 59: 642–656.

Neusner, Jacob. 1972. "Judaism in a Time of Crisis: Four Responses to the Destruction of the Second Temple," *Judaism* 21: 313–27.

Nutton, V. 1978 "The Beneficial Ideology." In *Imperialism in the Ancient World,* 209–21. Edited by P. D. A. Garnsey and C. R. Whittaker. Cambridge: Cambridge University Press.

Oakman, Douglas E. 1986. *Jesus and the Economic Questions of His Day.* Studies in the Bible and Early Christianity 8. Lewiston, N.Y.: Edwin Mellen.

Oberweis, Michael. 1989. "Beobachtungen zum AT-Gebrauch in der Matthäischen Kindheitsgeschichte," *New Testament Studies* 35: 131–49.

O'Collins, Gerald G. 1992. "Crucifixion." In *Anchor Bible Dictionary,* 1.1207–1210. Edited by D. N. Freedman. New York: Doubleday.

Oepke, Albrecht. 1967. "παρουσία." *Theological Dictionary of the New Testament* 5. 858–71.

Patte, Daniel. 1987. *The Gospel According to Matthew: A Structural Commentary on Matthew's Faith.* Philadelphia: Fortress.

Perrin, Norman. 1976. *Jesus and the Language of the Kingdom.* Philadelphia: Fortress.

Perry, Menakhem. 1979–1980. "Literary Dynamics: How the Order of a Text Creates Its Meaning." *Poetics Today* 1: 35–64, 311–64.

Pesch, Rudolf. 1967. "Der Gottessohn im matthäischen Evangelienprolog (Mt 1–2). Beobachtungen zu den Zitationsformeln der Reflexionszitate." *Biblica* 48: 395–420.

Pilgrim, Walter E. 1999. *Uneasy Neighbors: Church and State in the New Testament.* Overtures to Biblical Theology. Minneapolis: Fortress.

Pippidi, D. M., ed. 1976. *Assimilation et résistance à la culture greco-romaine dans le monde ancien.* Bucharest: Editura Academiei.

Porton, Gary. 1992. "Sadducees." In *Anchor Bible Dictionary,* 5.892–895. Edited by D. N. Freedman. New York: Doubleday.

Potter, David. 1994. *Prophets and Emperors: Human and Divine Authority from Augustus to Theodosius.* Cambridge: Harvard University Press.

Powell, Mark Allan. 1992. "The Plot and Subplots of Matthew's Gospel." *New Testament Studies* 38: 187–204.

———. 1992. "What is 'Literary' About Literary Aspects?" In *Society of Biblical Literature 1992 Seminar Papers,* 40–48. Edited by E. H. Lovering Jr. Society of Biblical Literature Seminar Papers 31. Atlanta: Scholars Press.

———. 1993. "Expected and Unexpected Readings in Matthew: What the Reader Knows." *Asbury Theological Journal* 48: 31–51.

———. 1996. "Matthew's Beatitudes: Reversals and Rewards of the Kingdom." *Catholic Biblical Quarterly* 58: 460–79.

Powell, Marvin A. 1992. "Weights and Measures." In *Anchor Bible Dictionary,* 6.897–908. Edited by D. N. Freedman. New York: Doubleday.

Pregeant, Russell. 1996. "The Wisdom Passages in Matthew's Story." In *Treasures New and Old: Contributions to Matthean Studies*, 197–232. Edited by D. R. Bauer and M. A. Powell. Society of Biblical Literature Symposium Series 1. Atlanta: Scholars Press.

Price, Simon R. 1984. "Gods and Emperors: The Greek Language of the Roman Imperial Power." *Journal of Hellenic Studies* 104: 79–95.

———. 1984. *Rituals and Power: The Roman Imperial Cult in Asia Minor.* Cambridge: Cambridge University Press.

Przybylski, Benno. 1980. *Righteousness in Matthew and His World of Thought.* Society for New Testament Studies Monograph Series 41. Cambridge: Cambridge University Press.

Rabinowitz, Peter J. 1977. "Truth in Fiction: A Reexamination of Audiences." *Critical Inquiry* 4: 121–42.

———. 1987. *Before Reading: Narrative Conventions and the Politics of Interpretation.* Ithaca, N.Y.: Cornell University.

———. 1989. "Whirl without End: Audience-Oriented Criticism." In *Contemporary Literary Theory*, 81–100. Edited by G. D. Atkins and L. Morrow. Amherst, Mass.: University of Massachusetts Press.

Rajak, Tessa. 1991."Friends, Romans, Subjects: Agrippa II's Speech in Josephus' *Jewish War.*" In *Images of Empire*, 122–134. Edited by L. Alexander. Journal for the Study of the Old Testament Supplement Series 122. Sheffield: Sheffield Academic Press.

Ramage, Edwin S. 1983. "Denigration of Predecessor Under Claudius, Galba, and Vespasian." *Historia* 32: 201–14.

Rengstorf, K. H. 1960. "Die Stadt der Mörder (Mt 22:7)." In *Judentum, Urchristentum, Kirche*, 106–29. Edited by W. Eltester. Beihefte zur Zeitschrift für die neutestamentliche Wissenschaft 26. Berlin: Töpelmann.

Rhoads, David, and Kari Syreeni, eds. 1999. *Characterization in the Gospels: Reconceiving Narrative Criticism.* Journal for the Study of the New Testament Supplement Series 184. Sheffield: Sheffield Academic Press.

Rich, John, and Graham Shipley, eds. 1993. *War and Society in the Roman World.* London: Routledge.

Rich, John, and Andrew Wallace-Hadrill, eds. 1991. *City and Country in the Ancient World.* New York: Routledge.

Richardson, J. S. 1991. "*Imperium Romanum*: Empire and the Language of Power." *Journal of Roman Studies* 81: 1–9.

Ringe, Sharon. 1985. *Jesus, Liberation, and the Biblical Jubilee: Images for Ethics and Christology.* Overtures to Biblical Theology 19. Philadelphia: Fortress.

Rohrbaugh, Richard. 1991. "The Pre-industrial City in Luke-Acts: Urban Social Relations." In *The Social World of Luke-Acts: Models for Interpretation*, 125–49. Edited by J. Neyrey. Peabody, Mass.: Hendrickson.

Roth, Cecil. 1962. "The Historical Implications of the Jewish Coinage of the First Revolt." *Israel Exploration Journal* 12: 33–46.

Rothfuchs, Wilhelm. 1969. *Die Erfüllungszitate des Matthäus-Evangeliums: Eine biblisch-theologische Untersuchung.* Beiträge zur Wissenschaft vom Alten und Neuen Testament 88. Stuttgart, Ger.: W. Kohlhammer.

Russell, Donald A., and Nigel G. Wilson. 1981. *Menander Rhetor.* Oxford: Oxford University Press.

Russell, Letty. 1987. *Household of Freedom: Authority in Feminist Theology.* Philadelphia: Westminster.

Said, Edward W. 1994. *Culture and Imperialism.* New York: Vintage Books.

Saldarini, Anthony J. 1988. *Pharisees, Scribes and Sadducees in Palestinian Society.* Wilmington, Del.: Michael Glazier.

———. 1991. "The Gospel of Matthew and Jewish-Christian Conflict." In *Social History of the Matthean Community: Cross-Disciplinary Approaches,* 38–61. Edited by D. Balch. Minneapolis: Fortress.

———. 1994. *Matthew's Christian-Jewish Community.* Chicago: University of Chicago Press.

Saller, Richard P. 1982. *Personal Patronage under the Empire.* New York: Cambridge University Press.

Sand, Alexander. 1974. *Das Gesetz und die Propheten: Untersuchungen zur Theologie des Evangeliums nach Matthäus.* Biblische Untersuchungen 11. Regensburg, Ger.: Friedrich Pustet.

———. 1986. *Das Evangelium nach Matthäus.* Regensburger Neues Testament 1. Regensburg, Ger.: Friedrich Pustet.

Sanders, E. P. 1977. *Paul and Palestinian Judaism.* Philadelphia: Fortress Press.

Schowalter, Daniel N. 1993. *The Emperor and the Gods: Images from the Time of Trajan.* Harvard Dissertations in Religion 28. Minneapolis: Fortress.

Scott, James C. 1985. *Weapons of the Weak: Everyday Forms of Peasant Resistance.* New Haven, Conn.: Yale University Press.

Scott, Kenneth. 1933. "Statius' Adulation of Domitian." *American Journal of Philology* 54: 247–59.

———. 1936. *The Imperial Cult under the Flavians.* Stuttgart-Berlin: W. Kohlhammer.

Schulz, Siegfried. 1967. *Die Stunde der Botschaft. Einfürung in die Theologie der vier Evangelisten.* Hamburg, Ger.: Furche-Verlag.

Schwartz, Daniel R. 1992. "Pontius Pilate." *Anchor Bible Dictionary,* 5.395–401.

Schweizer, Eduard. 1975. *The Good News According to Matthew.* Atlanta: John Knox.

Seeley, David. 1994. *Deconstructing the New Testament.* Biblical Interpretation Series 5. Leiden: E. J. Brill.

Segovia, Fernando. 1994. " 'And they began to speak in other tongues': Competing Modes of Discourse in Contemporary Biblical Criticism." In *Reading from this Place.* I. *Social Location and Biblical Interpretation in the United States,* 1–32. Edited by F. F. Segovia and M. A. Tolbert. Minneapolis: Fortress.

———. 1995. "Cultural Studies and Contemporary Biblical Criticism: Ideological Criticism as Mode of Discourse." In *Reading from this Place.* II. *Social Location and Biblical Interpretation in Global Perspective,* 1–17. Edited by F. F. Segovia and M. A. Tolbert. Minneapolis: Fortress.

Senior, Donald. 1985. *The Passion of Jesus in the Gospel of Matthew.* Collegeville, Minn.: Liturgical Press.

———. 1996. *What Are They Saying About Matthew?* Revised and expanded version. New York: Paulist.

———. 1997. "The Lure of the Formula Quotations: Re-assessing Matthew's Use of the Old Testament with the Passion Narrative as a Test Case." In *The Scriptures in the Gospels,* 89–115. Edited by C. M. Tuckett. Bibliotheca ephemeridum theologicarum lovaniensium 131. Leuven: Leuven University Press.

———. 1998. *Matthew.* Abingdon New Testament Commentaries. Nashville: Abingdon.

Shaw, Brent D. 1984. "Bandits in the Roman Empire." In *Past and Present* 102: 3–52.

———. 1988. "Roman Taxation." In *Civilization of the Ancient Mediterranean: Greece and Rome,* 2.809–27. Edited by M. Grant and R. Kitzinger. New York: Charles Scribner's Sons.

———. 1993. "Tyrants, Bandits and Kings: Personal Power in Josephus." *Journal of Jewish Studies* 44: 176–204.

Shepherd, William H. 1994. *The Narrative Function of the Holy Spirit as a Character in Luke-Acts.* Society of Biblical Literature Dissertation Series 147. Atlanta: Scholars Press.

Sherwin-White, A. N. 1963. *Roman Society and Roman Law in the New Testament.* Oxford: Oxford University Press.

Sidebottom, Harry. 1993. "Philosophers' Attitudes to Warfare under the Principate." In *War and Society in the Roman World,* 241–64. Edited by J. Rich and G. Shipley. London: Routledge.

Sim, David. 1993. "The Meaning of παλιγγενεσία in Matthew 19:28." *Journal for the Study of the New Testament* 59: 3–12.

———. 1996. *Apocalyptic Eschatology in the Gospel of Matthew.* Society for New Testament Studies Monograph Series 88. Cambridge: Cambridge University Press.

Sjoberg, Gideon. 1960. *The Preindustrial City.* New York: Free Press.

Smallwood, E. Mary. 1981. *The Jews Under Roman Rule from Pompey to Diocletian: A Study in Political Relations.* Leiden: E. J. Brill.

Smith, Dennis. 1992. "Meal Customs." *Anchor Bible Dictionary,* 4.650–55. Edited by D. N. Freedman. New York: Doubleday.

Soares Prabhu, George. 1976. *The Formula Quotations in the Infancy Narrative of Matthew.* Rome: Biblical Institute Press.

Stambaugh, John. 1988. *The Ancient Roman City.* Baltimore: Johns Hopkins University Press.

Stanton, Graham. 1982. "Salvation Proclaimed: Matthew 11:28–30: Comfortable Words?" *Expository Times* 94: 3–9.

———. 1992. *A Gospel for a New People: Studies in Matthew.* Edinburgh: T. & T. Clark.

Stark, Rodney. 1996. *The Rise of Christianity.* Princeton, N.J.: Princeton University Press.

——. 1996. "Urban Chaos and Crisis: The Case of Antioch." In *The Rise of Christianity: A Sociologist Reconsiders History,* 147–62. Princeton, N.J.: Princeton University Press.

——. 1991. "Antioch as the Social Situation for Matthew's Gospel." In *Social History of the Matthean Community: Cross-Disciplinary Approaches,* 189–210. Edited by D. Balch. Minneapolis: Fortress.

Stauffer, Ethelbert. 1955. *Christ and the Caesars.* London: SCM.

Stendahl, Krister. 1968. *The School of St. Matthew and Its Use of the Old Testament.* Philadelphia: Fortress.

Stern, M. 1974. "The Province of Judea." In *The Jewish People in the First Century,* 1.308–76. Edited by M. Stern and S. Safrai. Compendia rerum iudaicarum ad novum testamentum. Assen, Neth.: Van Gorcum.

Strecker, Georg. 1962. *Der Weg der Gerechtigkeit.* Forschungen zur Religion und Literatur des Alten und Neuen Testaments, 82. Göttingen, Ger.: Vandenhoeck & Ruprecht.

——. 1983. "The Concept of History in Matthew." In *The Interpretation of Matthew,* 67–84. Edited by G. Stanton. Issues in Religion and Theology 3. Philadelphia: Fortress.

Suggs, M. Jack. 1970. *Wisdom, Christology and Law in Matthew's Gospel.* Cambridge: Harvard University Press.

Suleiman, Susan, and Inge Crosman, eds. 1980. *The Reader in the Text: Essays on Audience and Interpretation.* Princeton: Princeton University Press.

Sullivan, J. P. 1991. *Martial: the Unexpected Classic. A Literary and Historical Study.* Cambridge: Cambridge University Press.

Sutherland, C. H. V. 1959. "The Intelligibility of Roman Imperial Coin Types." *Journal of Roman Studies* 49: 46–55.

Syreeni, Kari. 1987. *The Making of the Sermon on the Mount: A Procedural Analysis of Matthew's Redactoral Activity.* Annales Academiae Scientarum Fennicae 44. Helsinki: Suomalainen Tiedeakatemia.

Taisne, A. M. 1973. "Le thème du triomphe dans le poésie et l'art sous les Flaviens." *Latomus* 32: 485–504.

Talbert, Charles. 1980. "Prophecies of Future Greatness: The Contribution of Greco-Roman Biographies to an Understanding of Luke 1:5–4:15." In *The Divine Helmsman,* 129–41. Edited by J. L. Crenshaw and S. Sandmel. New York: Ktav.

Tatum, W. Barnes. 1998. "Jesus' So-Called Triumphal Entry: On Making an Ass of the Romans." *Forum* 1 ns: 129–43.

Taylor, Lilly R. 1975. *The Divinity of the Roman Emperor.* Philadelphia: Porcupine.

Theissen, Gerd. 1983. *The Miracle Stories in Early Christian Tradition.* Philadelphia: Fortress.

Thompson, Henry O. 1987. "The Tyrian Coin in Jordan," *Biblical Archaeologist* 50: 101–104.

Thompson, William G. 1970. *Matthew's Advice to a Divided Community: Matt 17:22–18:35.* Analecta Biblica 44. Rome: Biblical Institute.

Trible, Phyllis. 1984. *Texts of Terror*. Philadelphia: Fortress.

Trilling, Wolfgang. 1964. *Das Wahre Israel. Studien zur Theologie des Matthäus-evangelium.* Studien zum Alten und Neuen Testament 10. Munich: Kösel.

———. 1969. *The Gospel According to St. Matthew.* 2 vols. New York: Herder & Herder.

van Arde, Andries G. 1994. "A Silver Coin in the Mouth of a Fish [Mt 17:24–27]—A Miracle of Nature, Ecology, Economy and the Politics of Holiness." *Hervormde Teologiese Studies Supplement* 5: 204–228.

———. 1998. "Matthew 27:45–53 and the Turning of the Tide in Israel's History." *Biblical Theology Bulletin* 28: 16–26.

van Berchem, Denis. 1983. "Une inscription flavienne du Musée d'Antioche." *Museum Helveticum* 40: 185–96.

Van Segbroeck, Franz. 1972. "Les citations d'accomplissement dans l'Évangile selon saint Matthieu d'après trois ouvrages recents." In *L'Évangile selon Matthieu: Rédaction et théologie,* 107–30. Edited by M. Didier. Bibliotheca ephemeridum theologicarum lovaniensium 29. Gembloux: J. Duculot.

van Tilborg, Sjef. 1972. *The Jewish Leaders in Matthew.* Leiden: E. J. Brill.

van Unnik, W. C. 1959. " 'Dominus Vobiscum': The Background of a Liturgical Formula." In *New Testament Essays,* 270–305. Edited by A. J. B. Higgins. Manchester, U.K.: Manchester University Press.

Versnel, H. S. 1970. *Triumphus: An Inquiry into the Origin, Development and Meaning of the Roman Triumph.* Leiden: Brill.

Visser 'T Hooft, W. A. 1985. "Triumphalism in the Gospels." *Scottish Journal of Theology* 38: 491–504.

Walker, Rolf. 1967. *Die Heilsgeschichte im ersten Evangelium.* Forschungen zur Religion und Literatur des Alten und Neuen Testaments 91. Göttingen, Ger.: Vandenhoeck & Ruprecht.

Wallace, Sherman. 1938. *Taxation in Egypt from Augustus to Diocletian.* Princeton, N.J.: Princeton University Press.

Weaver, Dorothy Jean. 1992. "Power and Powerlessness: Matthew's Use of Irony in the Portrayal of Political Leaders." In *Society of Biblical Literature 1992 Seminar Papers,* 454–66. Edited by E. H. Lovering. Society of Biblical Literature Seminar Papers 31. Atlanta: Scholars Press.

Weinstock, Stefan. 1960. "Pax and the 'Ara Pacis,' " *Journal of Roman Studies* 50: 44–58.

Wellhausen, Julius. 1914. *Das Evangelium Matthaei.* 2d ed. Berlin: Georg Reimer.

Wengst, Klaus. 1987. *Pax Romana and the Peace of Jesus Christ.* Philadelphia: Fortress.

Weren, Wim. 1997. "Jesus' Entry into Jerusalem: Mt 21:1–17 in the Light of the Hebrew Bible and the Septuagint." In *The Scriptures in the Gospels,* 117–41. Edited by C. M. Tuckett. Bibliotheca ephemeridum theologicarum lovaniensium 131. Leuven: Leuven University Press.

White, John L. 1999. *The Apostle of God: Paul and the Promise of Abraham.* Peabody, Mass.: Hendrickson.

Wiedemann, Thomas. 1981. *Greek and Roman Slavery.* Baltimore: Johns Hopkins University Press.

Wiefel, Wolfgang. 1998. *Das Evangelium nach Matthäus.* Theologischer Handkommentar zum Neuen Testament, 1. Leipzig, Ger.: Evangelische Verlagsanstalt.

Wildberger, Hans. 1991. *Isaiah 1–12: A Commentary.* Minneapolis: Augsburg Fortress.

Wilhelms, Eino. 1980. *Die Tempelsteuerperikope Matthäus 17,24–27 in der Exegese der griechischen Väter der Alten Kirche.* Suomen Eksegeettisan Seuran Julkaisuja 34. Helsinki: Finnische Exegetische Gesellschaft.

Willis, Wendell, ed. 1987. *The Kingdom of God in 20th-Century Interpretation.* Peabody, Mass.: Hendrickson.

Windisch, Hans. 1929. *Der Sinn der Bergpredigt.* Leipzig, Ger.: J. C. Hinrichs.

Wink, Walter. 1986. *Unmasking the Powers: The Invisible Forces That Determine Human Existence.* Philadelphia: Fortress.

———. 1991. "Jesus and the Domination System." In *Society of Biblical Literature 1991 Seminar Papers,* 265–86. Edited by Eugene H. Lovering Jr. Society of Biblical Literature Seminar Papers 30. Atlanta: Scholars Press.

———. 1992. "Beyond Just War and Pacifism: Jesus' Nonviolent Way." *Review and Expositor* 89: 197–214.

———. 1992. *Engaging the Powers: Discernment and Resistance in a World of Domination.* Minneapolis: Fortress.

———. 1992. "Neither Passivity nor Violence: Jesus' Third Way (Matt 5:38–42 par.)." In *The Love of Enemy and Nonretaliation in the New Testament,* 102–25. Edited by W. M. Swartley. Louisville: Westminster John Knox.

Witherup, Ron. 1997. "Jeremiah and the Gospel of Matthew: An Audience-Oriented Perspective." Presented at the Catholic Biblical Association Meeting, Seattle.

Woolf, George. 1993. "Roman Peace." In *War and Society in the Roman World,* 171–194. Edited by J. Rich and G. Shipley. London: Routledge.

Zampaglione, Geraldo. 1973. *The Idea of Peace in Antiquity.* Notre Dame, Ind.: University of Notre Dame Press.

Zanker, P. 1988. *The Power of Images in the Age of Augustus.* Ann Arbor, Mich.: University of Michigan Press.

Ziolkowski, Adam. 1993. "*Urbs direpta* or How the Romans Sacked Cities." In *War and Society in the Roman World,* 69–91. Edited by J. Rich and G. Shipley. London: Routledge.

Selective General Index

Author Index